Why the Magic Matters

Why the Magic Matters

Discovering Disney as a Laboratory for Learning

Edited by
Alexis T. Franzese
Jill Peterfeso

Foreword by Len Testa

BLOOMSBURY ACADEMIC
NEW YORK • LONDON • OXFORD • NEW DELHI • SYDNEY

BLOOMSBURY ACADEMIC

Bloomsbury Publishing Inc, 1359 Broadway, New York, NY 10018, USA
Bloomsbury Publishing Plc, 50 Bedford Square, London, WC1B 3DP, UK
Bloomsbury Publishing Ireland, 29 Earlsfort Terrace, Dublin 2, D02 AY28, Ireland

BLOOMSBURY, BLOOMSBURY ACADEMIC and the Diana logo are trademarks of
Bloomsbury Publishing Plc

First published in the United States of America 2025

Cover design: Kathi Ha
Cover image © Christine Nanji/Moment Unreleased/Getty Images

Library of Congress Control Number: 2025936820

ISBN: HB: 979-8-8818-0265-3
PB: 979-8-8818-0266-0
ePDF: 979-8-7651-5534-9
eBook: 979-8-8818-0267-7

Typeset by Deanta Global Publishing Services, Chennai, India

For product safety related questions contact productsafety@bloomsbury.com.

To find out more about our authors and books visit www.bloomsbury.com and sign up for
our newsletters.

Contents

Foreword

Len Testa

I visited Walt Disney World in the summer of 1995, right before starting a master's program in computer science. After waiting in the Florida sun for two hours for an attraction called the Great Movie Ride, I wondered whether it was possible to write a computer program that would tell you how to see the Disney rides with the shortest possible waits in line.

I proposed this research to my academic advisors that fall. They responded with two questions. First, "Is this problem hard?" (That is, is this problem worthy of a master's thesis?) The answer was yes. It turns out that minimizing your waits in line at Walt Disney World is an example of one of the fundamental problems in math and computer science. It even has its own name: the Traveling Salesperson Problem (TSP). In the TSP, which is a way to define and study a certain class of problems, you are given a list of places to visit and the cost of visiting each place. So the TSP challenge becomes how to "visit places" and do that "as efficiently as possible" while allowing for adaptation; that is, each person can define what "efficiently" means for how they conceptualize the problem. It is common to use a metric such as "miles between point A and point B" to define the cost of visiting point B immediately after point A. Your goal in solving the TSP is to specify the order in which the places should be visited so that your overall cost is as small as possible.

Among its real-world applications, companies such as Amazon, UPS, and FedEx solve TSPs daily as they try to minimize their costs in delivering packages to your door. It is often said that time is money, and the cost that these companies try to minimize is the time it takes to deliver those packages. Part of my master's thesis, in fact, expanded on the PhD dissertation of one of UPS's lead research scientists.

My advisors' second question was this: "Besides you, does anyone care about this?" And the answer again was yes: Disney's domestic theme parks counted over thirty-six million visitors in that year.[1] In fact, Disney's theme parks have become even more popular since then: Disney's domestic parks registered just over seventy-four million visitors in 2023, proving their enduring popularity.[2]

The more field research I did—seeing how thousands of people formed lines that ebbed and flowed from day to day and season to season—the more I realized that visiting and running a place like Disney World is so complicated that it contains examples of almost every academic discipline. Quantitative questions like "What's the cheapest combination of tickets I need to buy to see everything I want?" and "Does purchasing the Disney Dining Plan save me money?" are not only textbook instances of classic operations research (OR) problems, but they are presented in a way that most students can understand and relate to. And engagement is the first step in education.

Disney is also a bottomless mine of qualitative inquiry. You might think of Disney as the company started by kindly Uncle Walt, appearing on TV every Sunday with stories of fantasy and adventure. But the modern Disney company is best viewed as a nation-state that happens to make movies and run theme parks. That's not hyperbole: if Disney were a country, its 2024 revenue of USD 91.4 billion would place it around seventy-first in the world, just above the GDP of Costa Rica and right below Uzbekistan.[3] Disney's financial resources, media reach, and legal and lobbying capabilities might be the envy of national political parties everywhere. (To extend nineteenth-century Prussian general Carl von Clausewitz's observation that war is politics by other means, so too are lawyers and advertising.) Everything Disney makes, from consumer products to music, television, movies, and theme park rides, expresses and advances a particular point of view. It's important to ask whose views those are—and how those views impact consumers.

As an example, the American Adventure stage show in Disney's EPCOT is one of the theme park's two thesis attractions—something that represents the park's central message. When Disney's EPCOT opened in 1982, it had two distinct halves. The front half of the park, known as Future World, represented humankind's use of imagination and technology to improve lives. Future World's thesis attraction—and EPCOT's icon—is Spaceship Earth, presenting the history and future of human communication, all inside one of the world's largest geodesic domes. The other half of EPCOT was and remains World Showcase, designed as a sort of permanent World's Fair and featuring the people, culture, and industry of eleven countries, using rides, movies, and architecture.

Staged in a large, ornate theater, each show scene in the American Adventure covers one important era from US history, using elaborate set decor, film projection, special effects, and lifelike mechanical stand-ins of American icons from Ben Franklin to Rosie the Riveter.

Setting aside its stagecraft, the American Adventure can be analyzed for what it says explicitly and implicitly, and what it does not say at all. The show covers slavery in a more or less straightforward way. What it implies, however, is that the Civil War ended both slavery and racism, avoiding completely any mention of the next hundred-plus years of segregation and Jim Crow. It certainly does not challenge the viewer to ask whether racial disparity still exists, who benefits if it does, or what steps might be taken to fix it. The implication—as with other scenes covering the conservation of natural resources, labor relations, and gender equality—is that these are problems that America has already solved.[4]

What makes *Why the Magic Matters* unique and important is that it brings together educators from a range of disciplines to guide readers in how to do the measured, analytical work of thinking deeply and critically about Disney and its many messages. And, the book provides its authors *and* its readers with frameworks for discussing specific aspects of Disney's influence. Take history as one example:

as contributing author Bethanee Bemis noted in her book *Disney Theme Parks and America's National Narratives*, Disney has been willing to "play fast and loose" in telling the stories of American icons such as Davy Crockett.[5] Similarly, Disney's *National Treasure* weaves together conspiracy theories and actual historical events into a popular and entertaining adventure movie (so entertaining and popular, in fact, that they made two of them and a TV series). It's inevitable that some people will accept Disney's version of history as fact, if only because Disney's is the one they are most familiar with. And outside of historical facts, I note that Disney princesses were exclusively white, cisgender, heterosexual Europeans (and one mermaid) for the fifty-five years after *Snow White and the Seven Dwarfs* was released in 1937.

What happens when many people accept Disney's version of history as true, or accept Disney's portrayal of gender and ethnicity and relationships as "normal?" Are these good things? Bad things? If they are good things, what makes them good and how do we benefit from this positive categorization? And if they're bad things, what's bad about them, who's impacted and how, and what might be done to make it better?

These representation questions are worth answering because excluding some groups directly contradicts Walt Disney's intent for his parks. In his opening day speech in 1955, Walt dedicated Disneyland "to all who come to this happy place." Those exact words would be repeated at the dedications of Walt Disney World's Magic Kingdom (1971), Tokyo Disneyland (1983), Euro Disneyland (1992, now Disneyland Paris), Hong Kong Disneyland (2005), and Shanghai Disneyland (2016) by every Disney CEO at that time. We know those words are more than an ephemeral marketing slogan because they are cast into bronze plaques placed on prominent monuments at each park's entrance. So these subjects and the educators who analyze and discuss them here are the true magic in *Why the Magic Matters*.

We don't expect theme parks to be documentaries, of course, just as we don't expect every book, TV show, or movie to be nonfiction. And that leads to the other major criticism of Disney: that it is not real. Of Disney's theme parks, for example, critics charge that at best they are made-up stories about fake people and pretend places, and at worst, they are substitutes for experiencing real countries and real cultures. The latter is unfairly negative, since Disney does not represent its EPCOT versions of Germany or Norway or China as stand-ins for the actual countries. A more accurate view is to think of those pavilions as inspiration to visit their real-world counterparts.

As to the idea that Disney traffics in made-up stories of fake people and pretend places, I note that the Louvre and the Met are filled with paintings of events that never happened and sculptures of things that never existed. We call that "art," and I'm not sure there's a difference. And if you think that stories are for children and adults should concern themselves only with that which is tangible and real, I say with sincerity: Do you know how money works?

And so, as you embark on the journey of learning that this book promises, the question before us is not whether Disney is a worthwhile field of study. It's "Where do we start?"

.   Notes

1   Gene Sloan, "A Boom Year at the Parks," *The San Bernardino County Sun*, December 31, 1995, 48.
2   "Theme Index Report 2023," AECOM, https://aecom.com/theme-index/ (accessed December 13, 2024).
3   "The Walt Disney Company Reports Fourth Quarter and Full Year Earnings for Fiscal 2024," https://thewaltdisneycompany.com/the-walt-disney-company-reports-fourth -quarter-and-full-year-earnings-for-fiscal-2024/ (accessed December 17, 2024); "GDP (Current US$)," World Bank Group, https://data.worldbank.org/indicator/NY.GDP .MKTP.CD?most_recent_value_desc=true&year_high_desc=true (accessed December 13, 2024)
4   Credit to my friend Kristen Helmstetter who wrote this in her senior thesis at Skidmore College, for sharing the observation. Kristen Helmstetter, "Robotic Presidents: Disney's Representation of America's Past Through the Hall of Presidents and the American Adventure" (American Studies Honors thesis, Skidmore College, 2005).
5   Bethanee Bemis, *Mirror, Mirror, For Us All: Disney Theme Parks and America's National Narratives* (New York: Routledge, 2023), 16.

Introduction

Jill Peterfeso

When one offers Disney courses as part of a regular university teaching load, they invariably receive a comment along the following lines: "College students can take a whole class on Disney!?" When this happens, and the exclaimer is a college student, you can see the wheels turning. "How can I figure out how to get in this class?" or, sometimes, "Should I transfer to *this* professor's college so I can take this course?" Some are so delighted by the idea they ask for details: assignment examples, a list of films watched, and, nearly always, "Do you go to Disney World?" Non-students are often tickled as well. They tell you they would have loved to take such a class in college, how they wanted to work for Disney when they grew up, and how they wish they were still able to take college courses. Sometimes they will ask, "Can I audit?" Other times, they get wide-eyed and state, "I should bring you on our next family Disney trip! I'm sure we'd all learn so much!"

And sometimes, the very same question gets asked, but with a decidedly different tone (and note the telltale punctuation): "College students can take a whole class on Disney??" Here, the professor catches disdain in the word "Disney," the skepticism that college could be a place for such frivolity, the conclusion that nothing "useful" can come of such a thing in a young adult's education. Sometimes, the exchange ends there, with the affronted asker concluding that higher education is at its nadir, and you, the instructor, are single-handedly dragging it there. Other times, however, the single arched eyebrow invites a response, and conversation ensues. The professor patiently explains: Disney is a recognizable cultural powerhouse that ensures student buy-in; Disney provides case studies that can be made relevant to any college-level subject; Disney is fun and can ignite interest in even the most reluctant student. By the end of such an exchange, the instructor just might hear, "Huh. I never thought of it that way. Ok, yeah, that sounds really cool."

Passionate enthusiasm or deep skepticism: this is the duality we face if we teach Disney—and likewise if we create scholarship on Disney. There has long been an expectation, akin to the view that it is contradictory to be scholarly and believe in religious frameworks, that one can't be an academician and "like" Disney.[1] *Why the Magic Matters* refutes that belief, and with gusto. Your editors wish it known that we admire, enjoy, and are inspired by what Disney does. Indeed, we have been teaching Disney classes and taking students to Disney parks for years now, and one does not volunteer for such an undertaking unless there is genuine appreciation for the immersive Disney experience. At the same time, we believe—and instill in our students the idea—that critical lenses must be applied to understanding why Disney does what it does; the social, cultural, psychological, and historical factors that allow Disney to work its "magic"; and the multifold implications of Disney's output.

Allow us to introduce ourselves. The book you are now reading came about when two academics, Alexis and Jill, teaching about 30 miles apart at liberal arts institutions in North Carolina, found in each other kindred Disney spirits who teach Disney courses. I (Jill) heard about Alexis's Disney course while listening to a *Disney Dish with Jim Hill* podcast, hosted by Len Testa. (Len, of course, is both a nationally known Disney expert and the author of this book's Foreword.) I reached out to Alexis, and an energetic discussion ensued.[2]

We come at our Disney research and teaching from different disciplinary perspectives. Alexis is a sociologist and psychologist and brings to this discussion a focus on the ways that Disney shapes and reflects societal and cultural norms, and how Disney offers its guests an invitation to suspend disbelief and engage with a simulated yet surprisingly authentic reality. I am a professor of religious studies, focused on the cultural history of American religions. For me, Disney opens doors to richer questions about human nature, imagination, and the drive to create. Through my humanities lens, Disney exemplifies the power of culture and community through story and shared experience. Our diverse disciplinary starting points, which come with different methodological approaches and often a focus on different sources, helped us see the value in bringing our respective expertise to discovering Disney.

At Elon University, Alexis's course, Happiest Place? The Science of Happiness at Disney involves travel to Disney parks, with itineraries varying to include Walt Disney World (WDW) alone, or WDW and Disneyland in Anaheim, CA, or WDW and other Disney properties like the Disney Vero Beach resort. Alexis's course invites students to unpack commonly held assumptions about Disney and to gain understanding about how and why Disney does what it does and the ways in which that approach contributes to the happiness of guests and cast members. Meanwhile, I started teaching Disney at Guilford College when developing a multidisciplinary first-year seminar. Disney was a wildly successful way to get students thinking and feeling critically about academic questions, as topics around Disney felt immediate and even urgent to students. I want my students to understand Disney as a gateway to the liberal arts and the essential skills developed by the humanities. With Disney as the content, students more easily get excited about texts, written and oral communication, collaboration, and creative problem-solving.

As evidenced by the concept for this book, our enthusiasm for meeting and talking with one another generated a desire to connect with others who personally and professionally (and, in many cases, professorially) hold in tension the celebration and critique of Disney. Living within that dualism—which we will explain is a kind of dialectical imagination—is, for us, the best place to be, vis-a-vis Disney. And we were certain that others who work with Disney as educational material had found their own ways of navigating—and even flourishing within—that dualism.

And so, inspired by the joy of connecting with another Disney professor, and after deciding we wanted to partner on a book, I proposed this volume gather academic authors from a wide array of backgrounds and disciplinary perspectives whose work as educators intersects with Disney. Here, we have chapters that represent a flurry of academic disciplines: art history, curriculum studies, disability studies, English, film and television studies, history, Indigenous studies, management, religious studies, sociology, and statistical sciences. Some of our authors are independent scholars and educators who partner with schools and students. One of our authors is a museum specialist with the Smithsonian. As this breadth of affiliations suggests, there is not a single academic discipline for which experiential learning would not be enhanced through connection to the Disney setting. Education professor Shirley Steinberg wrote, "There is no better topic than Disney to use in the pursuit of our cultural studies."[3] We resoundingly agree. We know Disney is an unparalleled sociocultural force that allows us, our students, and our readers to more clearly see and analyze the "webs of significance" (to give a nod to cultural anthropologist Clifford Geertz) that surround—and even entangle—us.[4]

As editors, we were astonished by how readily our contributors replied with a quick and enthusiastic "yes!" when invited to write for this book. We take that as indicative of many things. First, of course, many academics and educators love Disney and find it a delightful and stimulating place to "hang out," either physically or intellectually. Even though many of us deal with serious and fraught subjects in our professional work and teaching, we still find Disney worth "taking seriously" while providing our students (and ourselves!) with some levity. Second, many educators see Disney as an ideal way to explore material and concepts, often through experiential learning. "Experiential" can and does mean many things for our authors. Several of our contributors have taken students on study-away experiences to Disney parks; one of our contributors, Christopher Tremblay, takes learners on Walt's Pilgrimage, from Chicago through Marceline, Missouri, and Kansas City, and finally to California, for a visit to the Walt Disney Family Museum in San Francisco and ending with a visit to Disneyland in Anaheim. Other contributors do "hands-on" work with Disney materials; Lucy D'Agostino McGowan's students use Disney parks data to analyze datasets, while Smithsonian specialist Bethanee Bemis creates interactive exhibits to engage visitors at the National Museum of American History. Third, we suspect that most of our contributors feel in some ways like their professional identities are connected to this "niche" thing they do with Disney. It reflects something they like about themselves, as creative teachers designing unique pedagogical experiences, even amid possible suspicion and skepticism from students, parents, or colleagues. Whether as Disney fans or as faculty going against the grain of traditional academic subjects—or both—Disney-focused educators know they have homed in on a great gig: teaching Disney is fun, stimulating, and bound to get students engaged. With familiar examples and recognizable characters and a globally recognized brand, Disney facilitates curiosity, discovery, critical thinking, and a greater understanding of the world we inhabit.

The authors within this volume are practiced in using Disney to help students think, see, and imagine more expansively, and now, we want to share all that remarkable fodder for discovery with you, our readers. Just as Walt designed Disneyland for "children of all ages," we imagine this volume for "students of all ages." This book is for anyone with a curiosity about Disney.

Why Think Deeply about Disney?

The Walt Disney Company celebrated its 100th birthday in 2023, and today, the media giant is more relevant than ever. Despite a global pandemic that shut down theme parks and harmed theater attendance, demand for Disney continues to grow, and the company still commands a prime seat at America's cultural table. Disney is everywhere: streaming through Disney+; broadcasting on network television as ABC; hosting the centerpiece of sports viewing on its myriad ESPN channels; serving as the home for IPs (intellectual properties) like Pixar, Star Wars, Marvel, and the Muppets; creating and curating beloved characters and films; and so much more. Over the past decade, Disney fandoms have exploded into online areas, with countless Facebook groups, Instagram accounts, TikTok channels, Disney influencers, and other fan groups expanding access and commitments to Disney narratives and products. Not least of all, Disney is now a hotbed of political friction: there's no surprise to scholars of Disney that the company is at the center of "going woke" attacks from the right and calls to update stories and attractions from the left.[5] That Disney is ubiquitous in American life announces its undeniable cultural power.

Even more fascinating to those of us teaching and researching at the college level, Disney is the ultimate interdisciplinary laboratory: any academic subject can be studied through a Disney lens. Walt Disney himself recognized the educational possibilities in what he was creating. In a 1945 article published in *The Public Opinion Quarterly* and aptly titled "Mickey as Professor," he argued for the value of teaching through animation and film.[6] He would later theorize Disneyland as an educational site, underscoring the differences between his educational-plus-entertaining theme park compared to typical "amusement" parks, and saying, "I want [kids] to learn something about their heritage" in the "exhibits" at his park.[7] We as educators can and should add categories to Walt's examples: we can look at Disney not just through film, animation, and theme parks, but also media and marketing, merchandise, TV shows and streaming channels, and more. Disney has evolved as an American and global entity in the twenty-first century, and there's plenty of room for scholarship to keep pace with evolving trends in Disney studies and to hold up Disney for value outside of entertainment.

This is where this book comes in. As teachers of Disney courses and content at the university level and beyond, we know the value of Disney for twenty-first-century students and intellectually curious audiences. We know that an increasing number of college and university professors have been developing Disney courses and thus centering Disney in realms of critical thinking, scholarship, and self-development.[8] We know that now is the time for this book and its mission: examining Disney within intellectual opportunity and multidisciplinary discovery, and aiming to reach a myriad of audiences, including students, scholars, fellow teachers, and, of course, Disney's global fan base.

Disney, the Teaching Machine

We have written this book with two main audiences in mind: undergraduate students studying Disney and Disney fans of all ages curious to discover connections between

Disney and education. Know that your guides for this journey are educators and professors and Disney-deep-thinkers. We are not Disney-approved authors and historians, who certainly add much to the collective understanding of Disney but are not encouraged to do the critical work that academics must do as part of scholarly pursuit. Though many of us use disciplinary jargon and heady theoretical concepts when we publish in our fields, we've designed this book to be readable, inviting, and—hopefully—engaging for all audiences.

In addition to students and Disney fans, we can imagine other reasons you'd find your way to this volume. Perhaps you are a teacher thinking about ways to bring popular culture into your classes; maybe you're wanting to discover new ways to engage your students and help them grow as active learners. Or you are a parent and want to elevate your family's experience of Disney's philosophies, products, and places. Or you are a Disney fan who reads and devours anything you can about this company and its creations. Or you're just curious (or even skeptical) about this book's premise: that there are innumerable ways Disney can teach us about the world.

Whatever your reason: welcome to *Why the Magic Matters*. Let us give you a quick lay of the land.

First, as surprising as it may sound that there are *college* courses about Disney, it's not so unusual. In fact, one study of Disney courses found that there were nearly eighty such courses, offered in departments ranging from German to integrated studies to recreation education to theater to women's studies, with titles and topics like Math and the Mouse, From Grimm to Disney, and Mickey's American Dream.[9] This volume's own contributors teach or have taught many Disney courses, oftentimes with excursions to Disney parks, through courses with titles like The History of Disneyland (Jeffrey A. Barnes), Religion and Disney (William S. Chavez), Theme Park America (Alex Hofmann), Deconstructing Disney (Gabe Huddleston, with Blake Lentz and Nicole Weinberg), Walt Disney and American Culture (Sarah Nilsen), and Disney and the Wondertale (Bonnie Rudner).

Those of us who teach Disney stand in a lineage of other educators and professors who have engaged with Disney as a site for learning, and even Disney as a teacher. The idea that Disney (its products and places) can be a site for learning is not new; as we noted earlier, this was something Walt Disney himself knew about his films. Over the years, others have also made this very direct claim and have expanded their thinking to include theme parks. Anthropologist Nick Stanley named theme parks' educational value in the context of art education, as he described the efforts of theme park environments to provide a hedonistic experience and theatrically engage both youth and their accompanying adults.[10] Stanley emphasized the value of theme parks within an educational curriculum and even offered initial provocations for teaching through theme parks such as Disneyland. Lots of teachers have discovered that Disney is ripe for critical inquiry, connects to all sorts of academic disciplines, and motivates students to engage the material.[11]

We recognize that some of our readers might be thinking, "Disney as teacher? But Disney doesn't teach me anything. Disney offers escape and entertainment and lightness and fun!" We definitely understand where you're coming from—we have heard this from our students for years. But in fact, there's a lot of scholarship that suggests Disney is not "just" anything: it is a powerful force in creating our understanding of the world and our engagement with it. We know that it can be hard at first to accept that as true and accurate; it's difficult to think about the ways those things we consume—such as Disney movies, merchandise, and theme-park adventures—might be consuming us, acting upon us and our minds, and shaping our values. But that's one premise of Disney scholarship and education: Disney has the power to transform, whether we acknowledge it or not.

In this vein, nearly all scholars and teachers of Disney have to contend with the work of professor and cultural critic Henry A. Giroux, who is one of the earliest and best-known thinkers who juxtaposed Disney with pedagogy. (Pedagogy is the art and practice of teaching.) Giroux's book *The Mouse that Roared: Disney and the End of Innocence* first came out in 1999 and called our collective attention to the enormous power Disney wields to shape ideas, control culture, and even impact democracy. In writing about Disney as a teacher of America's children—and also the world's children, given Disney's global reach—Giroux investigated how Disney was not simply innocent entertainment but something more dangerous. He concluded that Disney's influence *as a corporation aimed at children* gave Disney a democracy-threatening amount of power. Perhaps predictably, Giroux's conclusions aren't always popular with undergraduates and Disney fans, many of whom look to Disney for escapist reminders of childhood innocence and do not like criticisms of Disney. In the preface to *The Mouse that Roared*'s second edition (coauthored with Grace Pollock and published in 2010), Giroux calls Disney "a teaching machine" and avers that "Disney matters to everyone." We concur and, like Giroux, in *Why the Magic Matters*, we recognize Disney's power to instruct. While we do not outright reject his conclusions about Disney and power (or the urgency behind them), we care also about our own power as educators to instruct and shape discourse, and thus to empower students and readers to think critically about Disney—and disarm its potential danger.[12]

Some other books and articles written by professors of education, and published more recently than Giroux's, focus on questions of Disney and curriculum-building. In a 2017 article published in *Review of Education, Pedagogy, and Cultural Studies*, coauthors Jennifer A. Sandlin and Julie C. Garlen wrote that "Disney . . . operates as pedagogy—both inside and outside of schools—that teaches us into particular ways of understanding the world, ourselves, and others." In other words, one need not be sitting in a classroom, learning explicitly about Disney, to be taught and shaped by Disney. Another article, "Discipline and Pleasure: The Pedagogical Work of Disneyland" by Susan L. Aronstein and Laurie A. Finke, focuses on learning via bodily movement through Disney's first theme park in Anaheim, California. These authors invoke Giroux when talking about "Disney's school" and what Disneyland teaches about gender, race, and class. They conclude that the park gives guests constant messages "about production and consumption, docility and domesticity."[13] As you'll see from the chapters within, we also think pedagogically about Disney and believe Disney can facilitate learning and spark interest in subjects and skill sets that extend far beyond Disney itself.

There are a few other important things to note about Disney scholarship. First, most of it tends to focus on films and theme parks,[14] and that is true of the chapters in *Why the Magic Matters* as well. Energies exerted in Disney's parks and time spent with Disney films make the biggest impact on the largest number of people, and that's largely reflected in the examples and conclusions herein. We see this book as talking about "theme parks and beyond": the majority of chapters focus on Disney's theme parks, but we include other forces within the Disney empire, such as films, TV shows, documentary series, video games, and merchandise. Second, when scholars talk about Disney films, they tend to focus on issues of race and ethnicity, gender and sexuality, and class.[15] In contrast, when talking about Disney's parks, there's a tendency to focus on Disney's "Americanness," and the ways capitalism, consumerism, and a distinctly early- to mid-twentieth century ethos permeate the park experience and exemplify a certain, now recognizable, American identity.[16] Such themes and patterns occur in this book as well, yet we also strive to look beyond individual identities (race, ethnicity, gender) in films, and beyond consideration of collective identities (such as nationality) in parks.

Finally, we recognize that some readers may feel resistant to learning about Disney and with Disney in ways that are deep, critical, or unfamiliar. This connects to what English professor Susan Willis described as "the problem with pleasure."[17] Film professor Jason Sperb opens his (revealingly titled) article "How (Not) to Teach Disney" by quoting Willis on this very problem, which Sperb defines as "the difficulty in analyzing something that is intended, or at least seen, as nothing more than innocent and harmless fun."[18] Like Sperb, we know this can be a hurdle; I remember students in my Disney first-year seminar reaching the semester's midpoint only to collectively bemoan, "You're ruining our childhood!" But ruining childhoods is not our intention, nor is removing the pleasure that Disney provides. (And don't worry: my students seem to have largely recovered by semester's end.) Rather, our intention is to deepen your understanding and experience of Disney and its products, productions, and parks by learning about it with the experts who know it better than anyone. Plus, in learning about Disney in this way, you'll learn a lot about learning.

Can anyone really enjoy and analyze Disney simultaneously? Yes, we certainly think so. We who teach, research, and write about Disney enjoy Disney's creations while we critically analyze them. We want our readers to love learning, to discover new things to spark imagination and intellect, and to find reasons to remain open and curious. We want that for our students, and we want that for you, and that is why we've written this book.

A Message for Educators about Disney and Diversity, Privilege, and Opportunity

It's important to note that *Why the Magic Matters* is not a how-to book for educators: while we proudly know this edited volume is full of wonderful concepts and ideas from brilliant educators, we are not aspiring to guide educators on designing the best possible Disney course, nor the best possible course using Disney. We know teachers could pull exciting and innovative ideas from this book for their teaching, and we hope they do. But teaching and learning contexts today are so broad and diverse, and this book does not attend to that deliberately. For instance, we know there's a wealth of new scholarship out there about teaching in a post-pandemic context that takes seriously issues of diversity and inclusion and the challenges around student preparation for college-level learning. Books like *Learning that Matters: A Field Guide to Course Design for Transformative Education* (2021) bring the fields of "education, cognitive science, psychology, and neuroscience" to bear on teaching and learning, and *Inclusive Teaching: Strategies for Promoting Equity in the College Classroom* (2022) guides faculty through addressing privilege and bias.[19] These practical guides, informed by research, do shape our own teaching—but *Why the Magic Matters* is not speaking directly to the science of teaching and learning, even if many of its authors are immersed in it.

As we noted above, many of the chapters here—like many of the best lessons and discussions about Disney in a college classroom—deal with topics of race, ethnicity, gender, heterosexism, and social class. We are sensitive to these issues, as scholars and educators, and we think extensively about what "teaching Disney" means for our students. We know that teaching Disney is not all about joyful childhood nostalgia and engaging students where they are. We know that Disney (especially "classic Disney") tends to showcase traditional gender roles, codify heterosexuality, and reflect racial insensitivities that today's audiences recognize as racist. Thankfully, teachers concerned with Disney and DEI (diversity, equity, and inclusion) in the classroom have at their disposal resources to help with such difficult topics and conversations. *Teaching With Disney*, for instance, is a 2016 edited volume that takes "the study of popular culture [to be] an ethical imperative" and, as such, centers these important topics. The volume is organized into four sections (Teaching Gender, Teaching Race, Teaching Consumers, and Teaching Ourselves) and tackles the thorny issues of approaching Disney in today's sociohistorical context while so many enshrined Disney films and characters are reflective of problematic ideas and stereotypes from the past.[20] Similarly, the 2022 edited volume *Recasting the Disney Princess in an Era of New Media and Social Movements*, which includes a chapter from one of our contributors, Jenny Banh, addresses how the branding of Disney princesses specifically has been shifting from more traditional to awakened representations of women. In short, Disney educators have to think about these topics, and we do, with creativity and sensitivity.

For those of us who teach in contexts where we take students on trips to Disney parks, we must consider what these trips mean about our own academic privilege and the economic surety—or scarcity—of the students we teach. Not every American can afford to go to Disney parks, even when a Disney theme park vacation has long been deemed the ultimate middle-class pilgrimage site and a rite of passage of childhood (and parenthood).[21] These economic limitations extend to our students. Instructors of Disney travel-embedded courses interface with students who worry about showing interest in a Disney course to parents. For those with parents supporting their educational pursuits, students may note strain in convincing their parents to pay for a

"Disney class" and in some cases have (proudly, we've found) announced that they are financing the class on their own. Finally, institutionally, not every college and university can afford to offset the costs of domestic or international study abroad and thereby enable students of limited economic means to participate in such trips. Sometimes, teaching Disney *at* Disney means closing the door to certain student populations.

All of those economic challenges are real, and yet, we'd be remiss if we didn't acknowledge that some vulnerable student populations find the prospect of a course at a Disney park uniquely appealing. First, as expensive as Disney is (and grows more so every year), a college trip to Disney is often (not always, but often) more affordable than trips overseas. Second, a number of students in America's colleges and universities are undocumented and are unable to travel internationally. An intra-national travel experience makes their participation possible. Third, and building on the above, Disney is familiar and feels *safe*. It is the epitome of American values, after all. The food, language, and culture at Disney do not place students in jarringly unfamiliar territory. They are ready to "eat around the world" at EPCOT; they are willing to embark on their first relatively short airplane trip; they are ready to walk miles a day in search of Disney-approved adventure. Those first-generation and low-income students who have limited travel experience tend to view Disney as a place that can escort them out of their comfort zone, gently. Fourth, Disney shows interest in making accommodations for guests with different physical and mental health needs. The most current version of this—DAS, or Disability Access Services—expands accessibility in the parks. Additionally, guests with food allergies may find comfort in Disney Dining's ability to meet their needs. All of this creates an experience that is ultimately far less uncertain than trips abroad, to other countries and continents. In other words, Disney's American parks can offer an excellent "first big trip" for students. And, as those of us who've been fortunate to take students to Disney parks know all too well, there is an incredible amount of learning, personal growth, and community building that can happen there.

Igniting a Love for Learning

Before wrapping up this Introduction, let me share a driving motivation for this book. Whenever I teach, I clearly lay out my course objectives on the syllabus. But I always have "shadow" objectives—goals that are difficult to put in academic terms but are no less important for my students' growth. Sometimes we talk about these openly in class; sometimes students figure them out and name them unprompted.

I will not keep readers of this volume in the shadows: in addition to being a book that allows us as educators and students of Disney to show our love and enthusiasm for Disney—alongside our ability to sight it critically—this book is a love letter to education, and in particular, to a liberal arts education.[22]

We are writing this book during an incredibly fraught time in higher education. We know fewer Americans have confidence in the value of a four-year college degree. We know Covid has aggravated the already difficult "enrollment cliff" that predicted far fewer college-eligible young adults by the mid-2020s. We know the costs of attending college climb higher and higher every year, threatening students with a lifetime of debt and putting increased pressure on young graduates to earn a significant salary. We know scores of small liberal arts colleges have closed and will close. We know stories persist in the media that warn college students and their parents away from certain majors and toward others, all based on (often unsubstantiated) fear around future job prospects. We see firsthand budget challenges (both real and manufactured) that precipitate everything from lost faculty and staff jobs to eliminated departments and programs to closed colleges. We know that education has long been caught in the political crosshairs, and 2020's America is no different. We watch how AI threatens to change the fundamental nature of our work in cultivating students as thinkers and actors in a contentious world. In short, we know that the breadth and depth a liberal arts education promises no longer looks like a sure-fire investment for all college students. Those of us who dedicate our lives to providing a strong, foundational education to students of all backgrounds and identities must be ready to explain why. We cannot take our inherent value for granted as we once did.[23]

Enter *Why the Magic Matters*. As college educators of Disney courses and content, we are used to having to explain the value in what we do: college courses about Disney are not readily accepted as necessary or life-changing educational fare. We have endured the skeptical looks, the arched eyebrows, the occasional eye rolls; we've also had to explain to the occasional student that a class on Disney *does* require their effort and critical engagement. In other words, many of us are adept at explaining not only why Disney's magic matters, but why learning about Disney matters—and by extension, why learning matters. And we want our readers to love the learning offered in this volume as much as they love the Disney that has brought them here.

We could even suggest that, at times, the Walt Disney Company in its 100 years has provided a model of liberal arts' interconnectivity and educational multidisciplinary. Picture the instruments arriving in the opening scene of Disney's 1940 film *Fantasia*, all necessary to make the beautiful music; consider the hands of hundreds of artists bringing life to static images; think about the writers and directors who coordinated the project; imagine the promotional efforts and merchandising tie-ins. Or, take a look at the coffee-table book or Disney+ series titled *One Day at Disney*, which depicts the myriad of skills and talents and personalities required to run Disney parks and businesses around the world, twenty-four hours a day.[24] The book showcases a costumer, machinist, engineer, cruise line captain, pastry chef, fruit and vegetable sculptor, veterinarian, construction manager, performers, animators, managers—and dozens more employees. Disney is not Disney because everyone is the same; Disney functions because it offers innumerable ways for employees and cast members—and guests and consumers—to find their niche. Likewise, at its best, a liberal arts education meets students where they are and guides them toward knowing how to meet the cultural moments and social contexts of our time. What Disney and the liberal arts can do is simultaneously magical and strategic.

Two student testimonies seem important here.

First, a student story from Fall 2016 relayed to me by my two teaching assistants (TAs) from the Fall 2015 iteration of my Discovering Disney first-year seminar. The

TAs ran into a student who had taken the class with them as TAs, a year earlier. As the three were talking, another student came up, enrolled then in my 2016 Disney course. According to my TAs, the first student—himself a sophomore football player who had struck me as confused if not annoyed at times by the course content—said to the first-year, "You're taking the Disney class? I took that." In my TAs' retelling of this exchange, the sophomore speaks with wonder and gravitas. He shakes his head, as if remembering a significant ordeal. "You think that class is about Disney but it's not. It's about *everything else!*"

I couldn't have put it better myself.

Second, and just this Fall of 2024, in another iteration of that Discovering Disney first-year seminar, on the last day of class, I asked students to reflect on what they had learned. One of my most consistently thoughtful students said, with just minutes left in class, "You know. I don't think this class is really just about Disney. I think this is a class about the world." To say I was proud of this young student—and affirmed as a teacher—is an understatement.[25]

Dear reader, this book about Disney is also about *everything else*. And like Aladdin, we authors and educators want to "show you the world." It's shining, shimmering, splendid.

This Introduction ends by invoking Walt Disney, who frequently talked about the relationship between learning and enjoyment: he allegedly said, "I would rather entertain and hope that people learned something than educate people and hope they were entertained."[26] While he saw his work as "edutainment" (education + entertainment), it's lucky for those of us who love Disney's products that Walt stayed focused on what he did best: telling memorable stories through animated shorts, films, live-action series, and theme parks. Lucky for us as educators, Walt is also said to have quipped, "We just make the pictures, and let the professors tell us what they mean."[27] And so, lucky for readers of this volume, we as editors and contributors will stick to what we know best: education. We focus on clear explanations and vivid examples, and we aim to inspire your intellect and perhaps also your imagination. We know you will learn from the expertise and insights herein, and we also know you will be delighted by the journey.

Notes

1   One teacher of Disney, film and media studies professor Jason Sperb, suggests there is no longer the need for this defensiveness. Jason Sperb, "How (Not) to Teach Disney," *Journal of Film and Video* 70, no. 1 (Spring 2018): 47–60.

2   Editors are listed alphabetically on the title page and made equal contributions to this volume. Per credited authorship, each editor solo-authored the introductions to the volume's separate sections, but these introductions do reflect ideas, examples, and feedback we shared with each other. Also, it is academic convention to refer to authors by their last names—and we do so throughout this book when talking about our contributors. But in this Introduction, we follow the example that Walt Disney

set for his cast members: introducing ourselves to you our readers on a first-name basis.

3 Shirley R. Steinberg, "Ruining Disney? A Gentle Point of View," in *Disney, Culture, and Curriculum*, ed. Jennifer A. Sandlin and Julie C. Garlen (New York: Routledge), xiv.

4 Clifford Geertz, *The Interpretation of Cultures* (New York: Basic Books, 1973), 5.

5 For more on Disney's history as a hotbed of political dissent, see Bethanee Bemis, *Mirror, Mirror, For Us All: Disney Theme Parks and America's National Narratives* (New York: Routledge, 2023), 77–88 and 94–107 and Mark I. Pinsky, "Chapter 37: The Baptist Boycott: Culture Clash," in *The Gospel According to Disney: Faith, Trust, and Pixie Dust* (Louisville: Westminster John Knox Press, 2004), 238–61.

6 Walt Disney, "Mickey as Professor," *The Public Opinion Quarterly* 9, no. 2 (1945): 119–25. Credit to Alexis for finding and alerting me to this obscure gem.

7 Karal Ann Marling, "Disneyland, 1955: Just Take the Santa Ana Freeway to the American Dream," *American Art* 5, no. ½ (Winter–Spring 1991): 173, quoted in Bemis, *Mirror, Mirror, For Us All*, 38.

8 Some examples: Johnson Cheu, ed., *Diversity in Disney Films: Critical Essays on Race, Ethnicity, Gender, Sexuality and Disability* (Jefferson: McFarland & Company, 2013); Amy M. Davis, ed., *Discussing Disney* (New Barnet: John Libbey Publishing, 2019); Julie C. Garlen and Jennifer A. Sandlin, eds., *Teaching with Disney* (New York: Peter Lang, 2016); Shearon Roberts, ed., *Recasting the Disney Princess in an Era of New Media and Social Movements* (Lanham: Lexington Books, 2020); Jennifer A. Sandlin and Julie C. Garlen, eds., *Disney, Culture, and Curriculum* (New York: Routledge, 2016).

9 Christopher Tremblay, "Disney in the Academy (and Other Disney Educational Experiences on College Campuses)," *College and University* 92, no. 4 (2017): 49–60, https://static1.squarespace.com/static/5988ab0ecf81e09929049cd5/t/5a28bc0424a 6942a95b51f73/1512619013801/Disney+in+the+Academy.pdf. Tremblay's work was extensive, but even he couldn't capture all the Disney courses out there. My own course(s), for instance, offered annually since 2015, do not appear in the article— almost certainly because there was no way for him to find the course if it wasn't 1. Officially part of the published college catalog, and/or 2. Featured by the school's marketing department. In other words, there are probably many more Disney courses out there than Tremblay found!

10 Nick Stanley, "Out of This World: Theme Parks' Contribution to a Redefined Aesthetics and Educational Practice," *International Journal of Art & Design Education* 21, no. 1 (2002): 24–35.

11 The connection between Disney courses and motivated students has been remarked upon since the following: Margaret J. King, "Instruction and Delight: Theme Parks and Education," in *The Cultures of Celebration*, ed. R. B. Browne and M. T. Marsden (Bowling Green: Bowling Green State University Press, 1994), 105–123.

12 Henry Giroux, *The Mouse that Roared: Disney and the End of Innocence* (New York: Rowman and Littlefield, 1999); Henry Giroux and Grace Pollock, *The Mouse that Roared: Disney and the End of Innocence* (New York: Rowman and Littlefield, 2010), xiv.

13 Jennifer A. Sandlin and Julie C. Garlen, "Magic Everywhere: Mapping the Disney Curriculum," *Review of Education, Pedagogy, and Cultural Studies* 3, no. 2 (2017):

191; Susan L. Aronstein and Laurie A. Finke, "Discipline and Pleasure: The Pedagogical Work of Disneyland," *Educational Philosophy and Theory* 45, no. 6 (2013): 619.

   If you're interested in a deep dive into the kinds of pedagogically focused scholarship we're describing, we suggest you start with Sandlin and Garlen's body of work, including "Magic Everywhere: Mapping the Disney Curriculum"; *Disney, Culture, and Curriculum*, which, through sixteen chapters authored by scholars of Disney across fields, offers readers thoughtful and nuanced analysis regarding how to use Disney to understand cultural phenomena; and *Teaching with Disney*, which aims to "interrogate this notion of Disney as a pedagogical force and to explore what it means to teach, learn, and live in a world where many familiar discourses are dominated by the global media conglomerate" (1).

14   Sandlin and Garlen, "Magic Everywhere: Mapping the Disney Curriculum," 190–219.
15   Two books focusing on these topics include Douglas Brode, *Multiculturalism and the Mouse: Race and Sex in Disney Entertainment* (Austin: University of Texas Press, 2005) and Cheu, ed., *Diversity in Disney Films*. Brode argues that Disney films have consistently and positively depicted various types of diversity, which in turn have moved America in multicultural directions. Cheu's volume also focuses on films but is far more critical in its assessment of Disney vis-a-vis diversity.
16   Two park-focused books that fit this description come from contributors to this volume: Bemis, *Mirror, Mirror, for Us All*; Cher Krause Knight, *Power and Paradise in Walt Disney's World* (Gainesville: University Press of Florida, 2014).
17   Susan Willis, "The Problem with Pleasure," in *Inside the Mouse*, ed. The Project on Disney (Durham: Duke University Press, 1995), 1–11. Here, Willis discusses the patterned responses she often received regarding her critical scholarship on Disney: "Why Are You So Critical? Wasn't Anything Fun?" (1). Her introductory chapter argues for placing pleasure within cultural contexts and alongside consumerist impulses.
18   Sperb, "How (Not) to Teach Disney," 47. Readers interested in Disney, controversy, and race may be interested in Sperb's 2005 piece: "Take a Frown, Turn It Upside Down: Splash Mountain, Walt Disney World, and the Cultural De-rac[e]-ination of Disney's Song of the South (1946)," *Journal of Popular Culture* 38, no. 5 (2005): 924–38.
19   Caralyn Zehnder et al., *Learning that Matters: A Field Guide to Course Design for Transformative Education* (Gorham: Myers Education Press, 2021), 2; Kelly A. Hogan and Viji Sathy, *Inclusive Teaching: Strategies for Promoting Equity in the College Classroom* (Morgantown: West Virginia University Press, 2022).
20   Garlen and Sandlin, eds., *Teaching with Disney*, 2.
21   Cher Krause Knight, "Keeping the Faith: Disney World as a Pilgrimage Center," in *Power and Paradise in Walt Disney's World* (Gainesville: University of Florida Press, 2014), 24–43; Alexander Moore, "Walt Disney World: Bounded Ritual Space and the Playful Pilgrimage Center," *Anthropological Quarterly* 53, no. 4 (October 1980): 207–18. See also Nick Johns and Szilvia Gyimóthy's 2002 article "Mythologies of a Theme Park: An Icon of Modern Family Life," *Journal of Vacation Marketing* 8, no. 4 (2002): 320–31 which addresses visitors' expectations for theme park experiences.
22   We want to resoundingly state that we know the traditional college route is not for everyone, and many vocational and trade programs can and do offer paths to

meaningful lives. But we *do* avow that *learning* is for everyone, and the liberal arts must not be relegated to certain undergraduate curricula only, but rather must better infuse the way all of us make sense of a complicated world.

23   Research and writing about this crisis in higher ed have become ubiquitous, revealing how many college educators and administrators are in an "all hands on deck" phase to solve these mounting problems. To offer just a sampling of sources as a starting point: Jeffrey R. Docking and Carman C. Curton, *Crisis in Higher Education: A Plan to Save Small Liberal Arts Colleges in America* (East Lansing: Michigan State University Press, 2015); Karin Fisher, "The Shrinking of Higher Ed," *The Chronicle of Higher Education*, August 12, 2022, https://www.chronicle.com/article/the-shrinking-of-higher-ed; Jennifer A. Kingson, "Schools Are Bracing for the Looming 'Enrollment Cliff,'" Axios, https://www.axios.com/2024/07/03/education-enrollment-cliff-schools (accessed December 14, 2024); Scott Muir, "Making the Case for Studying the Humanities in a Time of Crisis," National Humanities Alliance, August 25, 2020, https://nhalliance.org/making-the-case-for-studying-the-humanities-in-a-time-of-crisis-a-two-part-webinar/; Inara Scott, "Yes, We Are in a (ChatGPT) Crisis," *Inside Higher Ed*, April 18, 2023, https://www.insidehighered.com/opinion/views/2023/04/18/yes-we-are-chatgpt-crisis.

24   Bruce C. Steele, *One Day at Disney* (Los Angeles: Disney Editions, 2019); Disney Publishing Worldwide, *One Day at Disney Shorts* (2019–20; Disney+), documentary shorts.

25   Credit goes here to Ana Carolina Interlandi for this powerful sentiment. In her writing journal assigned for this day, Ana had expounded on her in-class comments, writing, "To the person I was at the beginning of the Fall 2024 semester I want to tell you this: The Disney seminar is not just about Disney, it's about the world and the people in it. It's about culture and how others perceive the culture we live in. It's also about how people respond to the messages and values Disney teaches us."

26   One can find this quote in many parts of the internet, but finding its source and verifying its authenticity is a different challenge. Walt Disney exists on a spectrum between historical figure and mythic creator, and quotes are attributed to him that he never said. Well-known Disney historian Jim Korkis talked about this particular challenge: Jim Korkis, "Walt Never Said It," *MousePlanet*, https://www.mouseplanet.com/11507/Walt_Never_Said_It (accessed July 15, 2023).

27   This is another quote attributed to Walt Disney whose origins are hard to track down. It has been cited in other academic articles (such as Paula K. McDonald and Keith J. Townsend, "Paid Work in Popular Culture: How Adult Employment is Portrayed in Family-Genre Films," in *Proceedings 15th International Employment Relations Association Conference: Working Lives, Working Choices* (Canterbury, England, 2007), 1–22) but without reference to an original source. It is also worth stating the obvious: just because this quote suggests that Walt imagined himself as an artist and not a meaning-maker doesn't mean he wasn't both. Chapters in this book focus on the many ways Walt's work and Disney's creations can, do, and have done far more than simply "entertain" us.

Disney Dialectic Pairs

Theoretical Framework and Book Structure

The Editors

We are organizing and framing *Why the Magic Matters* around the idea of dialectics. A dialectical method is a particular way of discussing and debating, with the goal of arriving at a clearer, truer understanding of a topic or question. Thinking of things dialectically allows us to put disparate and even contradictory ideas alongside each other to deepen analysis.

A dialectical approach goes back to Greek philosophy, and it is worth offering a quick overview of dialectics and what they have historically meant for robust intellectual discourse. Plato used the dialectical method to imagine debates between his teacher, Socrates, and Socrates' opponents. In going back and forth between two oppositional sides, debaters would come to more reasoned and nuanced understandings. Other uses of dialectics emerged in later centuries: thinkers would stake out an argument and a counterargument (known as the thesis and antithesis), and the juxtaposition of those ideas, challenged by an opponent, would result in greater clarity about the questions at hand. Sometimes, an idea's very premise would be altogether undermined and negated as part of a dialectical process; such are the possibilities of dialectical thinking. Use of dialectics to clarify thought continued for millennia in the Western tradition, and in the nineteenth century, German philosopher G. W. Hegel updated the approach and described the parts of the contradiction as the "thesis" and "antithesis," and the new thing to emerge from it as "synthesis."[1] Other thinkers borrowed and adapted Hegel. The process of developing dialectics has continued to the present.[2]

And so, familiar to many students of philosophy and other fields, and used in a multitude of ways, the impulse behind dialectics is, very simply put, a theory of/ around contradictions. Contradictory ideas exist in relation to one another; in fact, the tension between them often holds the contradictions in place. Furthermore, this contradictory relationship is not an end point but a starting point for new intellectual awareness. Dialectics offer us the idea that contradictions are essential to thought, comprehension, and the generation of new ideas.

As Alexis and Jill were brainstorming ideas for this book, we realized we were both "thinking dialectically," but from our own disciplinary locations. We realized that because dialectical thinking is relevant in the humanities, social sciences, and even clinical psychology, this theoretical framework could help create the interdisciplinarity and multidisciplinarity we strive for in this volume.

Dialectical behavior therapy (DBT) is a psychotherapeutic modality within clinical psychology, and, in fact, Alexis first proposed the framework of dialectics for this book based on her experiences using DBT with her own clients. DBT comes from psychologist Marsha Linehan's efforts to create a both/and approach that holds as fundamental not just the tension between—for example—change and acceptance but also the simultaneous existence and value of both. Linehan was not simply focused on finding a middle ground between contradictory impulses; rather, in the DBT model, change and acceptance are both held as equally critical.[3] Opposite ends of a continuum—the seemingly contradictory ideas—become reconciled. Instead of conflict, both/all are valid, and the individual benefits by holding two things as true.

Jill quickly warmed to a dialectics-focused structure because of her own love for nuancing and both/and'ing ideas and contexts in the classroom, and for the way thinking-about-tensions naturally occurs in her research and teaching.[4] And, because Disney can indeed fit seamlessly into a dialectical analysis. Disney presents and supports seemingly contradictory ideas that seem to be in opposition—ideas that became the foundation for this volume's dialectic pairs.[5] As a result, Disney offers guests and consumers a space and way to hold and understand dialectics. For all the talk of "good versus evil," "hero versus villain," and "virtue versus selfishness," Disney's world is not, in fact, black and white.

Why the Magic Matters is thus organized around four specific dialectic pairs that Alexis proposed and that are evident in Disney products, properties, and experiences: magic and strategy, authenticity and simulation, nostalgia and innovation, and leisure and labor. Disney operates in the liminal space between these seemingly contradictory ideas and is inspired—rather than limited—by these tensions. As you will find when reading, our authors fit their work alongside the dialectic model in a range of ways; some address it overtly, while some nod to it subtly.

In our Magic and Strategy section, we offer chapters that explore and address how Disney has intentionally created its empire while concurrently making their products and experiences feel as if they were effortlessly ("magically") achieved and created. Our second section's dialectic pairing, Authenticity and Simulation, reveals how Disney has managed to create what Alexis calls "the most genuine make-believe imaginable," and these chapters invite readers to explore this tension among the real, the fake, and (what French theorist Jean Baudrillard called) the "hyperreal."[6] The book's third section includes chapters that sit at the heart of the Disney dialectic pairing of Nostalgia and Innovation. Walt Disney saw these two forces as the pillars of his guests' experience and created attractions and themed spaces that wove together a love for the past with an eye toward the future. He allowed nostalgia and innovation to be mutually reinforcing, thus making his life's work so enduring. The volume's final section includes chapters on the dialectic relationship between Leisure and Labor. Disney recruits its consumers as co-creators of the full Disney experience—and that, perhaps surprisingly, often takes a lot of work. Likewise, learning about anything can (and perhaps should!) be laborious, and so the work of learning about the fun of/at Disney adds leisure to educational pursuit.

We, your editors, will offer brief introductions to each of the book's four sections to give you a sense of the topics therein, highlight the implications of each chapter's research, and point out the authors' unique contributions. As you prepare to dive into this book, know that you are invited and even encouraged to jump around. Chapters within the book—and even within each section—can be read in whichever order you choose.

Notes

1 There are many places to learn about Hegel's contributions to dialectics; here's one accessible resource: *Stanford Encyclopedia of Philosophy*, s.v. "Hegel's Dialectics," https://plato.stanford.edu/entries/hegel-dialectics/ (accessed September 30, 2023).

2 We are giving here just a brief overview of thousands of years of complicated and multifaceted philosophy around dialectics. And contemporary scholars still have much to say about dialectics' use today. For more information, we recommend Theodor W. Adorno, *An Introduction to Dialectics*, ed. Christoph Ziermann, trans. Nicholas Walker (Cambridge: Polity Press, 2017); Bertell Ollman and T. Smith, eds., *Dialectics for the New Century* (New York: Palgrave Macmillan, 2008); Karl B. Popper, "What Is Dialectic?" *Mind* 49, no. 196 (1996): 403–26.

3 Marsha Linehan's concept of dialectics is described in her 1987 publication "Dialectical Behavior Therapy for Borderline Personality Disorder: Theory and Method" published within volume 51, issue 3 (261–76), of the *Bulletin of the Menninger Clinic,* and later in her 1993 text *Cognitive-Behavioral Treatment of Borderline Personality Disorder* and the accompanying skills training manual published alongside that text that year.

4 For example, Jill's first book is called *Womanpriest: Tradition and Transgression in the Contemporary Roman Catholic Church* (New York: Fordham University Press, 2020), and though not specifically named as a dialectic pair, the book argues that "tradition" and "transgression" best explain the twenty-first-century Roman Catholic Womenpriests movement. Teaching-wise, Jill's favorite overt use of a dialectical model occurs with C. Eric Lincoln and Lawrence H. Mamiya's "dialectical model of the Black Church." See C. Eric Lincoln and Lawrence H. Mamiya, *The Black Church in the African American Experience* (Durham: Duke University Press, 1990), 11–15.

5 For another book exploring Disney and dialectical analyses, see the work of English scholar Joseph L. Zornado (2017) which also addresses dialectical tensions inherent in Disney, particularly Disney films. Zornado, Joseph L. *Disney and the Dialectic of Desire*. New York: Palgrave Macmillan, 2017.

6 *Stanford Encyclopedia of Philosophy*, s.v. "Jean Baudrillard," https://plato.stanford.edu/entries/baudrillard/(accessed September 30, 2023).

Section I

Magic and Strategy

Section Introduction

Magic and Strategy

Jill Peterfeso

Play word association in the early days of a Disney class—which I have done nearly a dozen times—and "magic" will very likely be one of the top five words students think of when they hear "Disney." Disney—the company, the brand—has built its identity upon successful magic-making and magic-filled storytelling.

From the early decades of cartoon shorts and animated films, Disney stories drew upon folk legends and fairy tales in which magic was interwoven with adventure. Walt Disney's creations became known for the way his studio blended wondrous themes or frightful plot points with cinematic technologies that were themselves magically innovative and unlike anything audiences had seen before. To be sure, *wishing* was more overtly discussed than magic in Disney's first films; think Snow White's "I'm Wishing" song and the "wishing apple" the Queen offers her; think Jiminy Cricket singing the Disney anthem "When You Wish Upon a Star." But although Walt Disney himself talked little of "magic"—and more of "imagination," creative processes, and "doing the impossible"[1]—magic permeated Disney creations. Dumbo held his "magic feather," the Evil Queen intoned to the "Magic Mirror on the wall," and Bambi and his forest friends could talk to one another.

Magical motifs intensified with theme parks. When Disneyland opened in 1955, promotional materials touted it as "Walt Disney's Magic Kingdom."[2] The Walt Disney World (WDW) Resort's first and flagship park is named "Magic Kingdom," and the whole of WDW is called the "Most Magical Place on Earth." Disney ad campaigns invite would-be guests to "stay in the magic," "discover the magic," and—for repeat visitors—"rediscover the magic." Park goers are saturated with reminders that what they experience at Disney parks is "magical." Taking just WDW's Magic Kingdom as an example, guests have experienced parades titled "SpectroMagic" (which ran throughout the 1990s and 2000s), fireworks displays titled "Wishes: A Magical Gathering of Disney Dreams" (which ran from 2003 to 2017), and the Fantasyland 4D film attraction, Mickey's PhilharMagic (open since 2003). Guests visiting the parks can wear MagicBands to facilitate admission and purchasing, and they can have Magic Shots for filters on their in-park PhotoPass pictures. Cast members can "pixie dust" guests with magical and unexpected surprises at parks and resorts, and they cheerfully tell guests to "have a magical day."

Magic extends beyond the parks and films. Of the eight named ships currently part of the Disney Cruise Line fleet, the "Disney Magic" was the first. The Disney Store offers merchandise with "magic" and "magical" names, such as the "Living Magic Sketchbook Ornament" collection (some of which adorn my own holiday tree). Disney Publishing prints books with titles like *Cooking with Magic* and *Magical Worlds* as part of the Disney Princess series. Disney video games like *Disney Magical World* and *Disney Magic Kingdoms* allow gamers to exercise magic with their character avatars. Disney+ subscribers can watch original series with titles like *Magic of Disney's Animal Kingdom*. Magic abounds.

And, nowadays, when critics want to complain that the Disney of today is not the Disney they loved in the past, they often decry Disney's changes with the exclamations "The magic is gone!" or "Disney has lost its magic!"

Indeed, the magic matters.

But while today we think of magic as essential to Disney's identity, the Walt Disney Company's strong emphasis on magic was in fact a strategic move that did not come until the 1980s. As Michael Eisner was settling in as the company's new CEO, Disney's chief strategic officer Larry Murphy conducted extensive market research on the Disney brand. Murphy explained of his survey results: "I've never seen anything like it . . . People loved Disney. It was the most effusive, profound respect and love and appreciation for a brand that you could imagine. Almost every one of them said, in so many words . . . 'magical entertainment. Disney is magic.'"[3] Under Eisner, the company adjusted immediately, and Murphy explained, "We rejiggered every area of the company and expanded [magic] greatly." Decisions like whether to allow chain hotels at the Walt Disney World Resort gave way to magical and uniquely themed Disney resorts, even if the latter were more expensive to design and build. Disney fans had spoken. If magic is what the Disney faithful wanted, if magic is what customers associated with the company, then magic would henceforth be front and center in strategic marketing and branding.

And so, ever since the Walt Disney Company's driving strategy became the question "is this magical or not?," Disney has intentionally paired magic and strategy.[4] But the relationship between these concepts isn't always evident, and even when the "magic" might be obvious, the *strategy* can be easy to overlook.

Uncovering the means to the magic is the learning outcome of one particular Disney class I teach titled How is Magic Made? This undergraduate course focuses on themes of magic, storytelling, and collaboration to help students recognize, dissect, and analyze how Disney makes magic—so that students can start to think about themselves as capable magic makers. Like most Disney consumers, students come into the class able to identify Disney magic in a myriad of ways, thanks to Disney's characters and stories and branding. Students understand Disney magic as something done *for* them, to entertain them. They can think about Disney magic as something *earned* through good behavior, as with the dutiful Cinderella and her fairy godmother or *Encanto's* Casita that protects the generous, intergenerational Madrigal family. Students know magic might be dangerous, like Ursula's witchcraft in *The Little Mermaid* or Elsa's as-yet unmanageable powers in *Frozen*. Students' early definitions are thoughtful yet somewhat simplistic, generally tracking with Americans' cultural idea of magic as "beyond oneself" and "not of this world."

The class seeks to shift that narrative and put magic-making power in students' hands. In other words, students are asked to think strategically about magic. During our WDW trip, each student conducts ethnographic research on a "magical" facet of their choosing. They practice skills like participant observation and informal interviews. They analyze the sensorial extravaganza that is the Disney parks and become attuned to things like the use of color, horticulture and landscaping, food design and presentation, music and sound, and types of animatronics. They take pictures and videos and fill their pocket-sized notebooks with observations and ideas and deeper questions. What students come to realize is that Disney's magic is strategically designed, developed, and deployed. Magic doesn't just happen—it's created through care, camaraderie, and hard work. Imagineers are masters of strategic magic-making; so are cast members. Having started to see "magic" as a manifestation of human imagination and intentionality, students return to magic in Disney animated films, cartoons, merchandise, and branding. They start to see the ways characters make choices that make magic: Dumbo trusts Timothy Q. Mouse and so picks up the magic feather; the Darling children think happy thoughts so that the pixie dust can allow them to fly; Mirabel's love for her family brings magic back to the Casita. Ultimately, I ask students how they plan to "make magic" in their own lives, whether for friends and family or in future jobs and careers. Now, after studying in Disney parks as their laboratory, they have come to see magic differently. Magic doesn't just happen: it takes intent, and making magic beautifully takes strategic planning and care.

The interplay between magic and strategy deserves analysis in the college classroom and in this book. While nearly every chapter in this volume touches on magic in some way (and how could it not, given the way Disney has strategically inserted magic into its very identity at an almost cellular level), the chapters in this section invite readers to see the intentionality behind Disney's magical actions.

The first chapter in this section, titled "Disney's 'Magical' Curriculum: Bibbity, Bobbity, Boo!," analyzes Disney as a teacher that uses both traditional and non-traditional means to educate audiences. It is written by three curriculum theorists whose focus is on how curricula—both inside and outside of educational settings—are shaped by cultural forces and human intent. Using examples from Disney's extensive oeuvre, authors Gabriel Huddleston, Blake Lentz, and Nicole Weinberg introduce readers to two key concepts in curriculum studies: the official curricula (which is the intended learning) and the hidden curricula (which may include values or biases and may also come about unintentionally). The authors then offer a new category, which they devised for this chapter: the magical curricula, which allows us to see how Disney operates as an educating force. Some of Disney's "teaching" is certainly magical, but in these authors' hands, Disney's strategic influence on children and culture shines through, and this chapter empowers readers to see those inner workings clearly.

Art historian Cher Krause Knight is next with "A Private Mouse for Public Art." She talks about Disney as *shared culture*, which takes into account the ways a multitude of audiences—or publics—participate in and thereby create the Disney experience. Using

Disney parks as her locus of study, this chapter shows readers how to hold many dialectic tensions in view: public and private, ideological and logistical, playful and controlled, and, of course, magical and strategic. Rather than either/or, Knight shows us that both/ and is the way to best understand Disney. What if we saw Disney parks not simply as entertainment venues but as public spaces that offer us models for thinking about art, public discourse, and urban planning? By demonstrating that art history is not solely concerned with "high" art, Knight shows readers what discoveries are possible when art historians and their students analyze popular, public powerhouses like Disney parks.

In "To Infinity and Beyond: Understanding Data Science through the Lens of Disney Data," Lucy D'Agostino McGowan demystifies the seeming "magic" of data science and explains how numbers, data sets, and statistical analyses combine to strategically build a better guest experience at Disney parks. Recall that Len Testa's Foreword explained that data science transformed his love for Disney and data into a successful career; here, D'Agostino McGowan—who partners with Testa and Touring Plans on data analysis with her students—walks readers through the moves data scientists make to deliver "real-world" impacts. Doing Disney data science is not only fun and instrumental for D'Agostino McGowan's students: here it shows readers how a Disney park visit is truly surrounded by data points, often hidden in plain sight. This chapter reveals that there are manageable ways to approach and understand all that data, and—like all things Disney—storytelling is at the heart of things.

This section's final chapter comes from Gary Kaskowitz, whose background in teaching business and marketing at a liberal arts university makes him ideally suited to explain "Why and How Walt Disney World Makes You the Star of Its Story." His approach to marketing draws not only on business strategies but also literature, psychology, and religious studies, as he weaves myth and literary archetypes, existential conflicts, and ritual transformation into his analysis. He explains how the Walt Disney Company reaches human hearts and addresses human needs, thereby persuading guests to trust Disney with their family vacations . . . and their hard-earned dollars. Kaskowitz's many examples, all taken from Walt Disney World, reveal deliberate and impactful storytelling at the heart of Disney's marketing successes. This chapter illustrates how the seemingly "magical" branding, emotional appeal, and problem-solving that Disney offers guests is, in fact, "just sound marketing strategy."

As you read these chapters, and as you explore this volume's first dialectical pairing, start to think about ways that magic happens not "magically," but strategically. Notice also how the strategic use of academic disciplines and analyses can yield a richer understanding of how Disney magic works. The magic matters—and so does the way it is intentionally, cleverly, strategically made.

Notes

1   Readers may be surprised to hear that Walt Disney did not constantly invoke "magic" in his public speech. But it's true! Curious readers can consult a myriad of Disney quote books, such as the *Official Walt Disney Quote Book* (Los Angeles: Disney

Editions, 2023), with authorship attributed to Walt Disney and the Staff of the Walt Disney Archives. Count how many times you hear Walt talking about "magic" in these historical sources.

2   Richard Schickel, *The Disney Version: The Life, Times, Art and Commerce of Walt Disney* (Chicago: Ivan R. Dee Inc. Publisher, 1997), 20.

3   Joe Adalian, "Disney Is a TV Company," July 10, 2024, in *Land of the Giants*, produced by Vulture and Vox Media, podcast, 39:16, https://www.vulture.com/article/land -of-the-giants-the-disney-dilemma-podcast.html#ep-1. See also Neil Janowitz, "Rediscovering Its Magic Was Essential to Disney's Success—But TV Was a Close Second," *Vulture*, July 10, 2024, https://www.vulture.com/article/disney-history-saved -magic-television-deal-podcast.html. I owe sincere thanks to Benjamin Wrench for alerting me to this article and podcast series.

4   Ibid.

1

Disney's "Magical" Curriculum

Bibbity, Boppity, Boo!

Gabriel Huddleston, Blake Lentz, Nicole Weinberg

Introduction

The Walt Disney Company has made intentional forays into the world of education, from media, such as Donald Duck in Mathmagic Land and Little Einsteins, to a whole theme park (EPCOT) with the original mission that guests could "learn" while having fun. While these attempts at education are worthy of exploration, in this chapter, we consider how the entire Walt Disney Company, regardless of intentionally trying to educate, might be thought of as a *teacher* whose *curriculum* includes Disney education initiatives but also extends beyond traditional spaces of education. We argue that Disney also *teaches* using the Disney theme parks and the Disney+ entertainment empire as *curriculum*. Through this lens, our purpose is for readers to consider both what they learn from Disney as well as what Disney intends for them to learn, ultimately considering how readers might navigate their engagement with Disney as intentional critical consumers. As such, we make a distinction between the "official" curriculum as that which Disney intends to teach, the "hidden" curriculum as that which is taught without explicit planning from Disney, and the "magical" curriculum as that which is learned and made possible from navigating the former two as a critical consumer of Disney.

A question that we are often asked as academics who write about Disney is, "Why study Disney?" As curriculum studies theorists, we seek to understand what curriculum *is* and how it comes to *be*, rather than how to *develop* curriculum. We believe Disney is worthy of study because it is a cultural monolith that has defined popular culture for generations and has become part of our cultural consciousness. Utilizing a cultural studies framework, we define popular culture as anything that is produced to be consumed by the masses, but also in that consumption is circulated on a large scale.[1] Often creating media, products, and experiences aimed for consumption by children, the Disney company is a form of popular culture that in many ways shapes our formative and ongoing experiences with media and our identity development.

We find that Disney is intrinsically worth studying because—whether we realize it or not—we learn from it and it potentially shapes who we are.

Disney as Curriculum

You might be inclined to ask, "But what does Disney have to do with teaching, learning, and curriculum?" The interdisciplinary field of curriculum studies examines the ways that curriculum interacts with societal structures, particularly in relation to dynamics of power (i.e., the critical perspective).[2] When we apply a curricular lens to larger societal structures, we are able to frame various things outside schools as curriculum. Curriculum theorist W. H. Schubert refers to this curricula removed from school settings as the "big" curriculum, which not only extends far beyond the scope of formal schooling but also includes such things as "corporate and political propaganda" that influence "how identities and overall cultural values are perpetuated."[3]

For readers of this book, we suggest developing a critical perspective for "big" curricula like Disney. Despite common misconceptions, the word "critical" does not refer to criticism in the sense of argumentative or oppositional stances to Disney; rather, we are using the word "critical" to refer to the act of analyzing aspects of the history and culture surrounding Disney in terms of power and oppression. By viewing Disney as a producer of various curricula, we can see that we are learning from Disney, and the company is not just tapping into existing belief structures, but actively creating, sustaining, or—potentially—challenging them.

A useful tool for understanding curriculum in schools is the concept of multiple levels of curriculum.[4] The first is the official curriculum: the intended lessons, akin to the lesson plan or syllabus. The second is the hidden curriculum: the unacknowledged lessons learned outside the official curriculum. These can range from norms and values, such as following rules and interacting with peers, to insidious elements like racism, homophobia, and sexism.[5] We propose a third type of curriculum for this chapter: the magical curriculum. This is where one can understand both the official and hidden curricula at play within the Walt Disney Company. This understanding explores how both curricula interact and contribute to Disney's tremendous societal impact. To become a critical consumer of Disney is not to refrain from experiencing enjoyment of Disney's fantastical world-building, but rather to be able to keep two voices in your head at the same time. In this way, Disney becomes a space in which individuals can learn to walk the line between enjoyment and criticality and perhaps cultivate the skill of critical consumerism. A critical consumer has the potential to examine the ramifications of their economic choices.

The Walt Disney Company has entered the educational sphere both inside and outside of schools. Indeed, Walt Disney himself saw the educational potential of his creations, specifically Mickey Mouse himself.[6] As we detail in this section, inside schools, Disney has developed curriculum to be used in partnership with individual teachers from various disciplinary approaches. Outside of schools, Disney has created educational TV programming for young children (Disney Jr.), developmentally appropriate books rated by age levels, and toys and merchandise labeled as educational.[78] In the parks, Disney incorporates educational aspects through events and exhibits, such as scientific innovation and cultural awareness at EPCOT, as well as environmental conservation at Animal Kingdom.

Disney Education

Bippity: The Official Curriculum

In this section, we focus on two particular curricula, which one of our authors has direct experience teaching to students in K-12 theater education: the Khan Academy Storytelling and Pixar in a Box courses and the Disney Theatrical Licensing JR. and KIDS resources.[9][10] The Khan Academy Storytelling course is split into two units: Imagineering in a Box and Pixar in a Box: the Art of Storytelling.[11] Activities are designed to be completed at an individual pace for online learners or presented in a classroom as individual or group assignments. It emphasizes STEAM education (science, technology, engineering, the arts, and math) and integrates with Google Classroom. Imagineering in a Box is a series of videos and activities that culminates in students designing their own theme park, complete with at least one attraction, characters, and food menu. Pixar in a Box: the Art of Storytelling lets students focus on plot, a bit of animation, and the business of filmmaking. Each lesson consists of a video and an assignment. The videos include direct instruction from employees and experts at the Walt Disney World Company (including legendary Imagineer Joe Rohde), as well as footage of the Disney theme parks and examples from Disney animated movies.

The Disney Theatrical Licensing JR. and KIDS resources are less of an "official" curriculum program than Khan; their primary objective is to manage licensing agreements for theater teachers and theater companies who wish to perform any of the Disney scripts. Disney has produced around a dozen musicals for the Broadway stage, most of which are based on their animated movies, such as *Tarzan* and *Frozen*. Schools and other educational programs that wished to produce these titles had no choice but to use Disney's scripts and music that were intended to be performed by adults. The problem is that these shows are not developmentally appropriate for young actors, since the vocal ranges are often too wide and the complexity of the songs and dances can be difficult for children and less-trained performers. Disney provides a solution by adapting their full-length adult shows into JR. (sixty minutes long) and KIDS (thirty minutes long) versions of the Broadway productions. While the stories remain familiar, the scripts are shortened, some roles are combined or expanded to fit different cast sizes, and vocal parts are adapted to age-appropriate ranges and levels of difficulty. For example, in *Frozen KIDS*, the parts of Young Anna and Young Elsa are expanded to include a new song and more stage time for young actors (a difference from the animated movie), but songs from the Broadway musical designed to showcase vocal and dancing talent like "Monster" and "Hygge" are cut.

When one purchases a theatrical license, most of the time one is purchasing the right to perform the show; however, these JR. and KIDS adaptations are sold as ShowKits to directors and come with resources beyond the text and music. Disney provides a Director's Guide which takes a potential director step-by-step through the process of mounting a show and offers enough resources that even a seasoned director might gain ideas or an easy solution to a problem (through choreography videos or design suggestions). The ShowKit also includes "Curriculum Connections," which tie the elements of producing a show to Common Core State Standards, offering a connection from what students learn through the course of rehearsals and performances to standards in academic classrooms. They sometimes come with suggested lesson plans to incorporate into classroom settings. For example, *The Lion King JR.* includes a lesson plan in which students collaboratively write a story about how Timon and Pumbaa first met. The lesson plan includes guidance for the instructor to tie the activity into the role and responsibilities of a playwright, and the entire lesson meets a few of the core standards for theater and writing classes.

In the above examples, Disney states their official curriculum clearly: Disney wants children to learn about the careers and workplaces that make up Disney parks and theatrical productions, have hands-on experience in creating and telling stories, and learn skills used regularly by Disney employees. It is easy for consumers to see what they are learning and what they are supposed to learn.

Boppity: The Hidden Curriculum

The hidden curriculum lies in how the Walt Disney Company positions itself as an expert in both subject matter and pedagogy. When a teacher chooses to implement either the Khan Academy or the Disney Theatrical Licensing lessons wholesale, without critical analysis or inquiry, they are implicitly accepting that Disney knows best about the standards covered, whether in design, engineering, or performance. Who is actually writing and producing these curriculums? Do they hire expert teachers? Do they consult with students or parents? No individuals are credited in either program; "Disney" is the pedagogical expert and should be trusted.[12]

In this vein, Disney wants its students and teachers to fit a specific mold. While both Khan Academy and Disney Theatrical Licensing encourage creativity and originality, their lessons are prescriptive in a way that ensures students and teachers are reinforcing the branding of the Walt Disney Company. Khan Academy asks you to make a theme park about whatever you want—but you create it their way, with their priorities. In the theater, directors usually are free to interpret a script in whatever manner they "see" it; Disney expects, however, that in using their products, you will follow their design choices and interpretations. This both reinforces Disney-as-expert and ensures that Disney has quality control over how its stories are being told. It is not in their interest for a middle school teacher to present *Moana JR.* as anything but an authentic reflection of the animated movie. Disney wants a consistent, positive experience for people who interact with its brand.

Conversations regarding the ethnic and racial makeup of schools producing shows that have specific geographies and cultures—such as *Moana JR.* or *Aladdin JR./KIDS*—are ongoing in the theater education sphere.[13] While Music Theatre International (who partners with Disney Theatrical Licensing) has language in their contracts forbidding any kind of blackface, decisions regarding "color-blind casting" and who should tell whose stories are left to the discretion of the teacher/director.[14] Many people, including *Moana* composer and lyricist Lin-Manuel Miranda, believe that in the realm of education, it is okay for a predominantly white school to produce plays like *Moana JR.* as long as the representations of the characters are respectful.[15] This is by no means the opinion of everyone; there are many who believe that only actors/directors of an ethnicity should be responsible for representing/telling the stories of that ethnicity.[16] It is worth noting that Disney does not offer any guidance here, either. While they wish to be seen as the experts in theater education, they do not offer any directives in how to handle the intricacies of race and ethnicity in live theater.

Finally, there is an obvious hidden curriculum: any time schools use Disney-produced educational materials, they provide the Walt Disney Company with advertising and promotion. This somewhat obvious Disney agenda might give insight as to why they are silent on the issue of casting and representation regarding the ethnic and racial identities of Disney characters: if mostly white schools are denied access to diverse stories and characters, that means that there will be less engagement by those children—and their parents, siblings, and teachers—with the Disney brand. It is in Disney's interest to not restrict access to their content or engage in political debates but rather to strategically overlook moral issues in service of the carefully crafted "happy endings" characteristic to their stories. This is something Disney excels at: finding ways to balance progressive and conservative values while minimizing the ire of reactionary groups from different sides. As time passes, this balancing act may become more difficult to maintain.

Boo: The Magical Curriculum

"Make it pink! Make it blue!" Aurora's fairy godmothers in Disney's *Sleeping Beauty* can't agree on what color the princess's gown should be. Throughout the movie, they argue back and forth, and the ending moments show Aurora dancing with the prince, oblivious to the fairies continuing to magically change her dress from pink to blue and back again. Just as her dress is two colors at the same time, it is valuable to remember that the official and hidden curriculums of Disney education both exist at the same time. Our magical curriculum is the holding of both of these together in order to decide how to teach and learn. A teacher who invokes the magical curriculum while using Khan Academy might critically examine each lesson or activity and only use that which is useful for their educational goals. A student who invokes the magical curriculum while designing a theme park might remember that Disney does not have a monopoly on themed experiences, and there may be more than one way to create an attraction.

We want to reiterate that the magical curriculum is a call to question and examine what stakes Disney has in entering the educational sphere and how that investment might affect the materials they produce. As stated earlier in this section, one of our authors has taught Khan Academy's Disney units and would do so again (and thinks it is fun!). It is important, however, for a critical consumer to recognize that Disney is serving its own needs. It is important to critically examine what it is that you are learning and teaching and what it is that Disney wants you to learn and teach. It is pink, *and* it is blue.

Theme Parks

Bippity: The Official Curriculum

Although Disney may not be setting out with the explicit intention to educate, consumers are certainly picking up new knowledge and understanding through engagement with their products. Instead of asking "Why do we consume Disney products?" we should ask "What do we learn from them?" In the context of its theme parks, Disney presents an official and hidden curriculum. While the theme parks themselves contain a multitude of curricula from calculating wait times spent in lines for attractions to understanding the differences between a thrill ride and a kiddie ride, in this section, we focus on the curricula specific to planning a Disney vacation.

To get a glimpse into the official Disney vacation planning curriculum, one only needs to watch a commercial or visit the Disneyland or Walt Disney World website, as these show how Disney intends potential guests to envision their vacation experience. The imagery is filled with smiling faces, screams of joy, and expressions of wonder and awe. Words like magic, wonderful, and awesome are frequently used to describe the parks.[17]

Children of all ages feature prominently in most advertisements and images, but they are always accompanied by other family members, ranging from older siblings to grandparents. On the surface, this might appear to be Disney's attempt to persuade potential guests to invest their time and money into a vacation at Walt Disney World, "the Most Magical Place on Earth." This is certainly part of their strategy, but looking at it through the lens of a curriculum, one can discern other underlying messages as well: Disney is subtly educating us on the very concept of vacations.

The official curriculum emphasizes fun as a central "learning objective." Yet if you look closely, you'll see that the guests aren't just having fun—they appear to be having the time of their lives! The imagery portrays individuals at ease as they navigate the park, comfortable and unbothered by crowds. The lesson: not only will you have an exceptional time, but achieving this will be a breeze. One of the most explicit ways that Disney promotes this sense of spontaneity and effortlessness is through the integration of "magic" in its messaging. In the "Stay in the Magic" ad campaign, guests are often depicted interacting with or being guided by animated characters and pixie dust as they effortlessly move through the park.[18] The message is clear: a trip to a Disney theme park isn't just fun; it's magical, and planning is as simple as the flick of a wand.

The final major learning objective of the theme park curriculum is the notion that Disney vacations are primarily geared toward families. While some advertisements feature childless adults, a family unit is nearly always an ad's primary focus, emphasizing parents deriving immense pleasure from their child's joy. Often, grandparents are included in ads, suggesting that a Disney vacation isn't just for the nuclear family, but for the extended one as well.

Boppity: The Hidden Curriculum

There's yet another curriculum at work when it comes to planning a Disney vacation. While the official curriculum aims to teach us that a vacation to a Disney theme park is a joyous, magical experience filled with fun for the whole family, and that spontaneity is the order of the day, the hidden curriculum of trip planning reveals the strategy required to experience the magic. The difference between the official and hidden curriculums of the Disney theme parks can be encapsulated in the distinction between the words "vacation" and "trip." A vacation connotes relaxation, fun, and escape, whereas a trip—although it can include these elements—also implies planning and work. As Huddleston, Sandlin, and Garlen have pointed out, what Disney offers isn't complete spontaneity but rather planned spontaneity in the form of perceived control for the guest and actual control on the part of the theme park. They write,

> By controlling for those fluctuations [such as crowd size and wait times for attractions] through advance planning, attraction reservations, and ongoing digital tracking, Disney's MyMagic+[19] seeks to reassure Walt Disney World guests that their theme park vacation will be predictable, and therefore, more fun. In other words, MyMagic+ expands the controlling reach of Disney while further teaching visitors into a form of leisure that is based on control.[20]

Sure, you can have a blast at a Disney theme park, but you're going to have to put in some effort to make it happen (and give up some privacy as well in the form of your data, constantly being collected as your park experiences and purchases are tracked). The hidden curriculum isn't a prerequisite for a Disney guest to book a Disney vacation, but mastering it is essential for a successful park experience.

One significant aspect of the hidden curriculum is learning how to navigate the heavy crowds. The images on the Walt Disney World website rarely, if ever, show the true extent of just how crowded the parks can be. Disney theme parks are some of the most visited attractions worldwide, which means guests must be prepared to deal with long lines and packed venues. The ability to plan strategically, such as arriving early to avoid the peak crowd times and knowing which attractions have the longest wait times, can drastically improve the overall experience.

Another element of the hidden curriculum is understanding and utilizing Disney's relatively new (and, at the time of this writing, already retired and renamed as

Lightning Lane Multi-Pass) Genie+ system.[21] Introduced in 2021, this service allowed guests to skip the line for a fee. Genie was a two-tiered system, where the free version offered suggestions to the guest on which attractions to visit and in what order, while Genie+ was a paid service offering Lightning Lanes (expedited queue lines that are typically much faster than the traditional standby lines). While Disney mentioned or highlighted the Genie+ system in its advertising, it didn't mention that understanding how to use it effectively requires a grasp of the system's intricacies, such as the timing of making selections and the specific attractions included in the service.

The cost of Genie+ alludes to another significant element of the hidden curriculum: upselling. From dining plans to photo packages to exclusive experiences, Disney offers a multitude of add-ons that can enhance a guest's experience—for a price. Navigating these options requires an understanding of what each offers and determining whether they are worth the cost. The hidden lesson, one that Disney would readily admit to teaching, is that while a Disney vacation has a baseline of a certain amount of magic, one can make it even more magical if you are willing to spend more money!

Securing dining reservations at the theme parks is another crucial part of the hidden curriculum. Disney's dining options range from quick service to fine dining, and many of the most popular restaurants require reservations made well in advance (sixty days prior to reservation date). Understanding how and when to make these reservations, as well as which dining experiences might be worth the effort and expense, is key to maximizing the enjoyment of a Disney trip. This often involves researching restaurant reviews, considering the needs and preferences of each member of the party, and being prepared to log on at the exact time reservations open, months before the trip.

What do all of these lessons in the hidden curriculum have in common? The concept of prosumerism[22] is helpful in understanding exactly what is being taught to theme park visitors. Prosumerism is defined by Ritzer as any consumption of a product in which the consumer is responsible for some amount of labor to produce it. Guests are not merely passive consumers of the Disney experience: their labor is key in delivering the product for which they have paid, and this labor comes as active participation in shaping their experience through planning, strategizing, and purchasing decisions. Disney is producing a hidden curriculum teaching guests that this active engagement, requiring more effort than the official curriculum would have us believe, can result in a more personalized and rewarding experience.

Boo: The Magical Curriculum

The magical curriculum emerges when the learner can make informed decisions based on the understanding of the official and hidden curricula. In the context of Disney vacation planning, the magical curriculum isn't about becoming a master of trip planning by learning the hidden curriculum but rather about understanding how the combination of the official and hidden curricula shapes our perceptions of vacations and influences how we choose to allocate our resources toward them. This understanding allows us to appreciate the complexity of planning a Disney vacation and also helps us assess the value we get for our investment. While the official curriculum presents a carefree vacation, the hidden curriculum exposes the meticulous planning and organization behind it. By acknowledging both aspects, we can make decisions that suit our expectations and budget.

The first step in being a student of the magical curriculum is to recognize that both the official and hidden curriculums exist in an intertwined relationship. This magical curriculum encourages us to view theme parks less as a trip with a "correct" way to plan and experience and more as an experiment in curiosity. One can experience the parks on their own terms, emphasizing vacation aspects that meet their own travel expectations, and not merely what Disney encourages us to anticipate or desire in the "most magical" or "happiest" "place on earth."[23] Learning the magical curriculum offers an opportunity to outright reject both the official and hidden curriculums provided by Disney. It allows us to make informed choices about how we spend our hard-earned money on leisure activities, which might include a trip to a Disney theme park if it aligns with our expectations and time constraints. It also means we don't have to accept a Disney theme park visit as a childhood "must-do" or the best way for family bonding.

Disney and Entertainment

Bippity: The Official Curriculum

The official curriculum, or that which the Disney company hopes for users to learn through their engagement with Disney+, is familiarity with the brand and its content. Not only familiarity, but through the use of specific collections (e.g., Sing-Alongs, Vintage Disney, K-Pop Idols), users of the platform become more engaged in the genre, collection, or series of Disney content of which they are already fans. This engagement with Disney+ media targets engagement with the Disney parks; for example, one collection on Disney+ is entitled "Inspired by Disney Parks" and features options such as documentaries about the history and engineering of Disney Parks, as well as fictional movies inspired by rides, such as *Jungle Cruise* and *Pirates of the Caribbean*. Often, theme parks are thought of as inspired by media content related to the company, with rides or "lands" inspired by the newest feature film. With Disney parks, however, the media is just as influenced by the parks as the parks are influenced by the media, forming a never-ending cycle of content, merchandising, travel, and consumerism.

Boppity: The Hidden Curriculum

Disney+ and the increasing hold that the Walt Disney Company has on the entertainment and media industry speak to the ways in which Disney shapes various sectors of society through a process of "Disneyization." Mike Budd and Max Kirch, coeditors of the 2005 book *Rethinking Disney*,[24] contend that Disneyization differs from Disneyfication; the former is characterized by its broader, power-based nature pertaining to the spread of Disney park elements such as theming and merchandising to non-Disney companies, like the popular chain, Buc-ees. This phenomenon is not necessarily negative; it merely illustrates the pervasive influence of Disney across domains. Disneyfication, in contrast, focuses on the creative processes employed by Disney and involves the transformation of source materials into distinct "Disney" products, often characterized by a mass-produced and somewhat bland flavor. For example, a Mickey ice cream bar purchased in either Florida, California, or a chain grocery store should taste and look uniform to each other because these are mass-produced to create a standardized "Disney" experience. Beyond just seeing Disney as something influenced by culture, or even simply influencing culture, several scholars have compared the influence of the Disney company on American culture to the *Disneyization* of society. Sociologist Alan Bryman defines four mechanisms of the Disneyization of society: theming, merchandising, emotional labor, and dedifferentiation of consumption.[25] Each of these is part of the "hidden" curriculum of Disney+, influencing the ways in which Disney+ relates to and influences the larger entertainment and media industry.

A recent example of Disney+ theming media content was the temporary addition of categories on the platform themed by the "eras" of Taylor Swift's career, which was done as a promotional event for the Disney+ release of *The Eras Tour (Taylor's Version)*. By dividing classic Disney movies into themes based on Taylor Swift's albums—*Cinderella* was put under "Midnights (Disney's Version)" and *Snow White* was put under "Folklore (Disney's Version)"—Disney re-represented the themes from Taylor Swift's Eras Tour with their own content. This type of theming shows the cyclical ways in which Disney influences the theming of society and then taps back into media theming to further promote its own entertainment enterprise.

Disney+ reflects the Disneyization of society by merchandising their content through the Disney+ platform. When users click on their favorite new Disney movie, the phrase "enjoy access to merchandise" pops up, with a button redirecting Disney+ users to shop for clothing, plush toys, and other merchandised items without ever having to leave home or even enter a different application. Links to related Disney park events also make appearances on Disney+ featured media pages. The hidden curriculum of theming and merchandising is, first, that individual expression requires participation in the capitalist market economy. Second is dedifferentiation of consumption, which is the notion that participation in the capitalist market economy via purchasing consumer goods is part of having an enjoyable experience. Finally, the Disneyization of society happens through emotional labor, which Hochschild describes as the self-management of one's own emotional states in order to meet the emotional demands of the job.[26] For Disney+, the emotional labor is embedded in language on the platform that appeals to emotions, with phrases such as "where great stories live forever."[27] Disney+ not only gives sole access to Disney content but actually redefines what a streaming platform is and how consumers relate to, and spend money on, it.

Boo: The Magical Curriculum

Noticing the Disneyization of society, particularly in relation to media, is an essential part of being a critical consumer of Disney. Feeling a strong personal affinity for a specific Disney princess is not inherently a harmful thing, but by noticing how Disney engages in processes of theming, merchandising, emotional labor, and dedifferentiation of consumption to sell you *things* and *experiences* related to the princess, you might be able to see both the pink and blue. You might be able to both enjoy the experience of affiliating with a specific princess, if it pleases you to do so, as well as notice the ways in which Disney+ and its related media enterprises are *teaching* you that enjoyment of your affiliation with a princess requires handing over money to the corporation through meeting the princess at the Magic Kingdom, buying a dress of that princess for your child, or purchasing a limited-edition designer bag with that princess's iconography on it. Then, as a critical consumer of Disney, you become empowered to select the degree in which you are able to *choose* your involvement with the company and their stories, navigating through their intricate commercial strategies and recognizing the cultural implications.

Conclusion

Understanding Disney's influence in society requires us to recognize the official, hidden, and magical curricula that pervade its products, from its intentional creation of curriculum in school settings to theme park vacations to online media content. The official curriculum presents the intended learning outcomes, such as the joy of a Disney vacation or the family-friendly content on Disney+. The hidden curriculum reveals the complexities and consumeristic tendencies necessary to achieve the magical experience promoted officially. The magical curriculum emerges when we grasp both the official and hidden curricula, allowing us to make informed decisions and understand the broader implications of Disney's influence.

Disney isn't just a provider of entertainment: it's a teacher that subtly instructs us on various aspects of societal norms, expectations, and behaviors. The company's reach affects our perceptions of education, vacations, family bonding, and how we consume media. As consumers, we are active participants in shaping our Disney experiences, be it planning a trip to a theme park or navigating content on Disney+. Disney provides a framework of inquiry to similar companies that seek our attention as a means to become ingrained in our lives, fostering a deep sense of brand loyalty that ultimately translates to dollars in their pockets.

By recognizing Disney curricula, we can critically engage with its products and services, understanding the value and implications of our choices. We argue that this understanding doesn't diminish our enjoyment of Disney; instead, it empowers us to consciously decide how we interact with the company and its offerings.

Notes

1   John Fiske, *Reading the Popular* (London: Routledge, 2017).
2   William Pinar, *What Is Curriculum Theory?*, 2nd ed. (London: Routledge, 2012).

3   W. H. Schubert, "Focus on the Big Curriculum," *Journal of Curriculum and Pedagogy* 3, no. 1 (2006): 100.

4   Pamela Bolotin Joseph, *Cultures of Curriculum* (New York: Routledge, 2011).

5   The question of whether Disney intentionally embeds its products with these insidious elements is difficult to answer. Disney is good at reading potential audiences and delivering what they will buy. It would follow that they would create products that would reflect all cultural elements, from the good to the bad. In other words, the material (ideas, thoughts, beliefs, norms, etc.) that Disney uses to construct its products is cultural itself. This doesn't mean we can't hold them accountable for what they produce, but it also means we have to realize that we are all implicated in those products.

6   Walt Disney, "Mickey as Professor," *Public Opinion Quarterly* 9, no. 2 (1945): 119–25.

7   Disney Books, https://books.disney.com/teachers-librarians/ (accessed June 26, 2024).

8   See this section of Amazon Toys, https://www.amazon.com/stores/page/B3E41676 -DB73-4056-8911-7A899E437EDF (accessed June 26, 2024).

9   "Storytelling," Khan Academy, https://www.khanacademy.org/humanities/hass -storytelling (accessed May 7, 2024).

10 Disney Theatrical Licensing, https://disneytheatricallicensing.com/ (accessed May 7, 2024).

11 "Storytelling."

12 It is worth noting that this idea of company over individuals began with Walt Disney, as documented by Neal Gabler in Walt Disney's biography. Walt refrained from giving animators and artists attention or accolades, sweeping everyone's work under the umbrella of the company name—which, of course, was his own.

13 A. Netsky, "Race & Theatre: Some Questions," *OnStage Blog*, November 3, 2016, https://www.onstageblog.com/columns/2016/11/3/race-theatre-some-questions.

14 Music Theatre International, https://www.mtishows.com/ (accessed May 7, 2024).

15 H. Sherman, "What Does 'Hamilton' Tell Us about Race in Casting?," Howard Sherman, December 3, 2015, https://hesherman.com/2015/12/03/what-does -hamilton-tell-us-about-race-in-casting/.

16 C. Peterson, "Schools Can Whitewash 'In the Heights' But I Really Hope They Don't," *OnStage Blog*, March 3, 2020, https://www.onstageblog.com/editorials/2020/3/3/ schools-can-whitewash-in-the-heights-but-i-really-hope-they-dont.

17 The Walt Disney Company, "This Is Magic | Feel It at Walt Disney World Resort-the Most Magical Place on Earth," YouTube, July 2, 2024, https://www.youtube.com/ watch?v=uZb0_GWWG8I; The Walt Disney Company, "Walt Disney World Resort 50th Anniversary | Stay in the Magic Disney Resort Hotel Commercial (2021)," December 27, 2021, https://www.youtube.com/watch?v=8Ml9U4kXCOk; The Walt Disney Company, "Four Amazing Theme Parks at Walt Disney World," Disneyworld .disney.go.com, https://disneyworld.disney.go.com/destinations/all-parks/ (accessed July 2, 2024).

18 The Walt Disney Company, "Walt Disney World Resort 50th Anniversary | Stay in the Magic Disney Resort Hotel Commercial (2021)."

19 MyMagic+ was the precursor to the current Genie+ trip planning system.

20 Gabriel S. Huddleston, Jennifer A. Sandlin, and Julie C. Garlen, "A New Dimension of Disney Magic: MyMagic+ and Controlled Leisure," in *Disney, Culture, and*

Curriculum, ed. Jennifer A. Sandlin and Julie C. Garlen (New York: Routledge, 2016), 226.

21 These services are in a constant state of revision, it seems. At the time of this writing, Disney is revamping their Genie system (Eve Chen, "Goodbye Genie+? Big Changes Are Coming to Disney World's Ride Reservation System," *USA Today*, June 26, 2024, https://www.usatoday.com/story/travel/experience/theme-parks/2024/06/25/disney -genie-lighting-lane-changes/74207057007/).

22 George Ritzer, "Prosumption: Evolution, Revolution, or Eternal Return of the Same?," *Journal of Consumer Culture* 14, no. 1 (2014): 3–24

23 The nickname of Walt Disney World is "The Most Magical Place on Earth." The nickname of Disneyland is "The Happiest Place on Earth."

24 Mike Budd, "Introduction," in *Rethinking Disney: Private Control, Public Dimensions*, ed. Mike Budd and Max H. Kirsch (Middletown: Wesleyan University Press, 2005), 7.

25 A. Bryman, "The Disneyization of Society," *The Sociological Review* 47, no. 1one (1999): 25–47.

26 Arlie Russell Hochschild, "The Managed Heart," in *Working in America* (New York: Routledge, 2022), 40–8.

27 Disney+ (@disneyplus), "Where Great Stories Live Forever," February 11, 2024, https://www.instagram.com/p/C3Oz1SOCt1h/.

2

A Private Mouse for Public Art

Cher Krause Knight

Disney theme parks are public phenomena. They are wildly popular destinations, promoted through the Walt Disney Company's synergistic marketing and a global social media presence. Disney theme parks are also private places. They are business enterprises run by a multinational conglomerate, and only paying customers gain entrance to their gated wonders. In truth, the theme parks are public *and* private, neither one nor the other but of necessity both. Yet the public and private are often conceived as resolutely opposite spheres of activity with competing agendas and stakeholders. Discussions of Disney and its theme parks frequently segregate into two camps: one celebrating all things Disney without hesitation, particularly through the company's own efforts; and the other condemning Disney, often without firsthand knowledge of it. But I wish to speak to both readerships, and those in between, hopefully bringing new perspectives to a subject some already know well, while asking skeptics to remain open-minded. This chapter endeavors to follow a productive path, circumventing common assumptions about Disney without dampening fascinations (including my own) with its theme parks. It becomes too easy to divide issues into ideological or logistical, public and private, black and white. Sometimes the most enlightening, radical position is in the gray, for which I aimed in my book *Power and Paradise in Walt Disney's World*. Now we will see how purportedly divergent concerns are brought together, making meaningful connections between theory and practice (aligned respectively with "magic" and "strategy," as per *Why the Magic Matters*'s organization). Disney's lessons are not just conceptual but have tangible applications relevant to our past, present, and future. Here we will consider how audience response impacts placemaking, public art, and the built environment—bridging the practical and aspirational—by examining the centering of visitor experiences in Disney park design.

Over the years, I have encountered opposite reactions when people find out about my Disney studies: those familiar with the theme parks often love them and excitedly share their knowledge; those who easily dismiss the parks, even if they have not visited any, see little merit in my endeavors. As an art historian specialized in public art, I think it unwise to ignore Disney's theme parks and what can be learned from them. My approach (as educator, writer, scholar, consultant) always combines research with fieldwork. I communicate with students, and other teachers, authors, and public art professionals, but also with wider audiences who might often go neglected. Thus, I developed the term "shared culture," an alternative to "popular culture," to convey my methodology and mindset; rather than segregating those studying from those participating in a given culture, I emphasize how those studying also help make and take part in it. This concept of *shared culture* is well suited to Disney parks, where boundaries between the supposedly "high" and "low" get muddled, and audience engagement is foregrounded. While writing *Power and Paradise*, I considered how Disney parks are related to places such as pilgrimage centers and fairgrounds, identifying three consistent imperatives in their design: fostering community, intensifying experience through sensory immersion, and enhancing existence beyond the everyday. I believed then, as I do now, that the Disney parks are essential to our cultural history, not exceptions to it.

Disney and Evolutionary Design

Disney's entwined design philosophy and practice garner attention from professionals in numerous fields including art and architectural history, urban planning and design, and visual and popular culture (by no means an exhaustive list), alongside many fans and general enthusiasts. Regardless of one's interests, anyone who wants to learn about Disney design must understand that Walt Disney never wanted to build an *amusement* park; to him, these were dirty, unimaginative places, poorly managed and maintained. He envisioned a *theme* park to narratively frame and shape experiences within it. Today there is an extensive range of Disney theme parks. Those in the United States came first. Disneyland in Anaheim was the original (1955), with its companion park, California Adventure, opening about a half-century later (2001). Disney World Resort in Orlando, Florida, came after Disneyland, with four parks in total: Magic Kingdom (1971); EPCOT Center (1982); Disney's Hollywood Studios (formerly Disney-MGM Studios, 1989); and Animal Kingdom (1998). Tokyo Disneyland (1983) in Japan was joined by Tokyo DisneySea (2001). In France, the Disneyland Resort Paris (previously Euro Disney, 1992) was followed by Walt Disney Studios Park Paris (2002). Next came Disneyland Hong Kong (2005) and Shanghai Disney Resort (2016), though there will certainly be park enhancements and expansions in the future. Yet Disneyland was the paradigm, offering a template for Disney World and the international parks.[1] As described by J. Philip Gruen, professor of architectural history and theory, Disneyland's impact was physical, cultural, and nearly instantaneous, with implications exceeding its own borders, "a model environment that Disney hoped would reform the vagaries of the outside world."[2]

Disney World may have never been built had Walt been happy with Disneyland; he was dissatisfied with the California park almost immediately upon its completion. Having not secured enough property to insulate Disneyland from encroachments that soon sprung up, Walt was dismayed by how quickly "low brow" businesses (cheap motels, parking lots, souvenir stands) surrounded his park. Without a buffer, he could not stop their siphoning off profits or tarnishing his pristine park through proximity to it. But likely most frustrating was that the limited acreage (initially 180) did not allow him to tinker with Disneyland as much as he wanted. Disney World offered a chance to correct what went wrong in California, an opportunity Walt embraced even as his health declined. Creating a place that would never be finished, however, required plentiful land. He found such—temperate and cheap—in central Florida, acquiring 27,443 acres (nearly 43 contiguous square miles). Fearing price gouging if identified as the buyer, Disney secretly acquired the swampland; over eighteen months, Walt's compatriots purchased the property through forty-seven different transactions and five dummy corporations. (Windows on Magic Kingdom's Main Street read "M.T. Lott," punning on the enormous parcel). In Florida, Walt expelled Los Angeles' "automobility, suburban sameness, and the lack of a memorable civic center" while intensifying its fantastical architecture, period styles, and manicured landscaping.[3]

Today, Disney World is a massive resort, with more people, traffic, hotels, and restaurants than many cities. It is the largest single-site employer in the United States, operating every day of the year. With an average annual attendance of over fifty-eight million, Disney World is the most visited resort globally. In addition to its theme parks, there are also golf courses, spas, convention facilities, lodging, time-share properties, a sports complex, a wedding pavilion, mixed-use shopping/dining/entertainment sectors, transportation systems, and a vast roadway network. There is so much to see and do that many visitors never leave Disney World's property during their entire vacations,[4] which is exactly what the company intends.

To best understand Disney World and the other parks, it is important to consider their origins in California. Disneyland's planners conducted extensive research, making detailed studies of famous sites, including Fifth Avenue in New York, The Mall in Washington, D.C., and the French Quarter in New Orleans. Cultural institutions were visited and their novel features adapted, as was the moving sidewalk from Chicago's Museum of Science and Industry. The planners also consulted with amusement operators who recommended practical tweaks such as widening attraction openings to accommodate crowds. Meanwhile, consumers were primed beforehand through a bravado approach to branding and placemaking. To help fund and advertise the park, Disney struck a deal with the ABC network to air the *Disneyland* television series starting in 1954. By the time the park opened in 1955, viewers were transformed into visitors already acquainted with its layout. The footprint of Disneyland (and many of the other parks that followed) is heart-shaped with a single entry at the point, and a central hub providing visual and physical access to themed zones. Clear "environmental cues" were embedded in this plan such as marking the hub with a "wienie"—a tall landmark orienting pedestrians. Art historian Karal Ann Marling describes Disneyland's Sleeping Beauty Castle as "magical," "the ultimate wienie, so crucial to the meaning of the place and to its spatial comprehension, so distinctively present to the viewer at every turn in the path, that it became, first, the trademark for the park, and finally, the logo for the films from which the park had fitfully evolved." These films, she reminds us, provide unique themes only Disney parks can offer. "Lands" radiate outward from the hub, each with its own gate as orienting signage to maintain theming; within the park, people ride vehicles or move through attractions at fixed rates of speed.[5] All this results in such highly organized spaces that we do not worry about their functionality.

Walt's approach to urban planning was *evolutionary* rather than revolutionary, drawing upon "preexisting forms, theories, and techniques." The layout and philosophy of Disney's parks are directly indebted to historical prototypes for ideal cities. In particular, planner Ebenezer Howard, who "sought to resolve the garden and the city as a single entity," inspired Walt. Howard conceived a sanitary, lively place that would exist as "a physical manifestation of mental well-being." The radial plan for his Garden City (1902) isolated urbanism's best features within a greenbelt to manage size and growth, in terms of both land and population. Yet Howard's plan had its limitations, relegating it to a satellite city. Le Corbusier's *Plan Voisin* for The Radiant City (1925) was another model for Disney, especially in its separation of pedestrians from vehicles. *The Heart of Our Cities* (1964), by architect and urban planner Victor Gruen, was also an important source. Walt personally owned multiple copies of Gruen's book, detailing possible solutions to urban woes—banishing disorganization through public amenities, coherent radial planning, and placemaking design—and restoring a sense of community. In fact, Gruen cited Disneyland as a planning exemplar and shared Walt's admiration for Howard. At the time of Disney's death, both Howard's *Garden Cities of To-Morrow* (1902, reissued 1965) and Gruen's *Heart of Our Cities* were in his office. The influence of such city planning is most keenly felt in Walt's original concept for EPCOT (Experimental Prototype Community of Tomorrow). A deep dive into EPCOT is beyond our scope here (as is the planned community of Celebration, originally founded by the Walt Disney Company in 1994), but we must underscore that he envisioned it as an operational city. Disney's EPCOT would be an antidote to crime, pollution, and poverty, adapting much of Gruen's approach by prioritizing pedestrianism and clustering mixed-use "cells." Yet Walt's plan for EPCOT was carefully edited—emphasizing picturesque and practical aspects while ignoring political ones, including socioeconomic inequities and racism. Disney died before his city could be realized and would have been disappointed by its manifestation as a theme park. Yet while the model city of EPCOT remains unbuilt, Disney World is, in effect, a working city with comprehensive planning and a massive, if temporary, population.[6] Given these factors, it is not coincidental that World's Fairs profoundly impacted Walt, who even developed attractions (later adapted for his own parks) for New York City's 1964–1965 World's Fair.

It is fitting that EPCOT's two sectors, devoted to technology and world cultures, are descended from the Fairs. Of special significance is the City Beautiful movement—balancing formal order with aesthetic delight—inspired in the United States by Chicago's World Columbian Exposition of 1893. City Beautiful planners utilized wide boulevards, clustered buildings by function, and punctuated their designs with water features and enclosed public spaces, all aspects that eventually found their way into "city plans throughout the country and at the Disney parks." As I observed previously, such planning was intended to project national pride, economic confidence, and sociopolitical well-being: "In the wake of industrialism, the fair seemed to prove that cities could be rehabilitated through good design, spotless maintenance, and tight security." But, of course, these images of civic perfection were not benign; the labor to produce them went largely unseen, and the classism and racism embedded within were rarely acknowledged. Cultural historian Neil Harris asserts the "quest for sanitized decency that Walt Disney adopted had a lengthy American pedigree," most especially the World's Fairs, which "had a special gift for looking backward and forward simultaneously." At the Fairs, amusements, good-natured crowds, and lush settings coalesced into holistic environments, "enveloping in their scale, their novelty, their string of surprises." Walt also looked to European pleasure gardens as theme park prototypes, studying how they built community and promoted civility within healthful, uncongested settings. For Disney, these amalgams of function and fantasy, along with higher expectations for public space, made a heady mix. Harris contends Walt came to see such places as archetypes of "spectacle management," correctives for urbanity's shortcomings with the added benefit of moral uplift. Amid life's uncertainties, their efficient facilities and impeccable maintenance conveyed optimism.[7] Ultimately these sources translated into Disney's "visionary capitalism," endeavoring to enlighten and entertain visitors at once. EPCOT as city rather than theme park, however, would have been difficult to actualize given Walt's stringent social planning. While he focused upon entrepreneurialism and new technology, he did not pay enough attention to the diversity upon which cities thrive; his narrow-minded reformism would have made EPCOT a hard sell for residents. Here he differed from Howard, who advocated for a municipality to nurture equity. Walt, unable to cede that much control, would not give residents voting rights; thus, his EPCOT could have only had temporary ones. But for today's designers, planners, and artists, it is instructive to study the user-friendly infrastructure of Disney's EPCOT: service roads underground, reliable public transportation, managed crowd flow, and prime pedestrian space—a welcoming brand of urbanism from which to borrow.[8]

Public Art and Audience

Walt was, in many ways, a public artist. As Marling affirms, he made "mass art" appealing to "tastes and preferences of a vast multiregional, multigenerational, and multinational audience," conceiving theme parks to "soothe and reassure . . . to give pleasure." While many academics continue to dismiss Disney's parks, architects, planners, and artists have long apprehended how these relate to their own practices. As an art historian, I do much the same in my public art classes, using the theme parks not only as logistical models but also as symbolic ones that can create transformative experiences. Disney's parks address wide-ranging social issues: the environment, politics, economics, and identity. And they prompt us to ponder how conceptions of space, time, and community are established, maintained, and changed. Distinctions between what is private and public have also evolved. Evermore frequently, designing public-minded spaces involves private entities. Here, Disney provides a platform to explore frictions between the public and private, which illuminate public art's processes of commission, creation, patronage, and placement. Public art's earliest roots were cultivated through privatized agendas spurred, I wrote, by "human desire to translate ideas into tangible forms and share these with an audience larger than one's own immediate circle, with the hopes of satisfying aesthetic needs, instilling morals, teaching lessons, codifying history, swaying opinions or securing allegiance." As public art's context shifted, increased focus was not on patrons but audience members—their interests and responses.[9] Art historian Miwon Kwon offers three useful models based upon approaches to site.[10] The first, *art-in-public-places*, values a particular artist or work more than any given location. The second, *art-as-public-spaces*, elevates a site's function and meaning, frequently coupling physical amenities with aesthetic sensibilities. Disney parks are most obviously related to this second model, though a respective park generally imbues the designated location with its sense of place, not the other way around.

The third model, *art-in-the-public-interest*, is clearly derived from "new genre public art," a term coined in the mid 1990s by artist Suzanne Lacy. As Lacy clarifies, this art breaks down traditional boundaries between media, while its artists employ new forms with "a developed sensibility about audience" and "social strategy." New genre public art is overtly sociopolitical, often radically so; Disney avoids political alignments, appealing to widely constituted, international audiences. Yet Lacy's description of new genre public art bears similarities to Disney's design approach, despite the theme parks' functioning as commercial ventures. This comparison becomes especially engaging as Lacy probes the nature of publicness: "Is 'public' a qualifying description of place, ownership, or access? Is it a subject, or a characteristic of the particular audience? Does it explain the intentions of the artist or the interests of the audience? The inclusion of the public connects theories of art to the broader population." New genre art, she explains, forges profound relationships between artist and audience in which notions of the public are not "singular" but "complex and multiple." I would add, hopefully, these audiences become increasingly inclusive as social justice initiatives work to dismantle systemic discriminations. Lacy also warns that public art's "visionary potential" and "ability to generate social meaning" can get lost in "the bureaucratic and structural."[11] Disney often circumvents "design by committee" outside the orbit of its own Imagineering efforts (see below), which can be troubling given the company's considerable reach and power. It can also be instructive, and even inspiring.

Critic Patricia Phillips shares concerns about public art being "predetermined by its own bureaucracies, dulling legislation, and compromising requirements. While these mandates often support public art, they invariably thwart challenging ideas." In contrast, Disney has far fewer dictates, beyond its own, with which to contend. This situation privileges Disney in sidestepping processes to which others must adhere, but it also enables the company to fast-track projects otherwise mired by oversight and red tape. And Disney's centering of audience response aligns with Phillips's assertion that "the issue of its reception" is at the heart of public art: "The formation of audience is the method and objective, the generative intention and the final outcome." As she asserts, the goal "is not just to produce another thing for people to admire, but to create an opportunity—a situation—that enables viewers to look back at the world with renewed perspectives."[12] Curator Mary Jane Jacob, renowned for exhibitions built upon social engagement, complains that public art focused upon audience response is frequently viewed as "necessarily unsophisticated," with the "audience's involvement in and comprehension of the work" seen as "a limitation of the artwork's status."[13] Although Jacob was referring to new genre art, her explication of how accessibility is interpreted as a lack of seriousness and depth of meaning is apt and relevant to how many critics treat Disney. Reviling artworks and places because they are too relatable, to too many people, is exclusionary, inaccurate, and near-sighted.

Increases in private-public partnerships highlight economic challenges but also possibilities for public art. In an arts funding essay, I asserted that bringing together "the shared interests of public and private sectors to jointly support art is not only crucial, but also perhaps inevitable," and growing in urgency. Combining public and private resources can realize ambitious projects more effectively and quickly, and make them available to diverse audiences. Such hybridity helps collapse "the distance between public place and private enclave," advocate for collaboration, and "(re) invigorate both well-known and overlooked places." That being said, I cautioned, "we must remain wary of the compromises and trade-offs . . . if we are to protect the public from being in servitude to the private,"[14] a common concern whenever the Mouse is involved. Disney parks are, albeit, private places, though aimed at broad audiences and better maintained than most public spaces. A sense of specialness is conferred within their inscribed borders, marking liminal transitions from daily life. An invaluable resource for public artists, urban planners, and general interest readers is *Designing Disney's Theme Parks: The Architecture of Reassurance*, accompanying the first major show of concept renderings, architectural models, and design resources (1997–1999), curated by Marling. Although "unprecedented access to the Imagineering collections" likely made authors "inclined to cast favorable eyes on Disney," this exhibition catalog imparts many valuable lessons. Early on, this private corporation assumed exceptional levels of social and ecological responsibility. For example, with environmentalists hired as development consultants, conservation zones and water recirculation systems were established and cleaner vehicles adopted at Disney World. Disney's parks are models for sustainable planning, utilizing novel construction materials and practices. The company's green efforts, recognized by an Urban Land Institute Award for Excellence (1981), continue to this day. Perhaps Disney's most curious innovation is its "utilidors," utility corridors underneath the Magic Kingdom—a theme park basement tucking workaday realities out of sight. Designed by Admiral Joe Fowler to emulate a submarine, the utilidors extend over a mile and cover more than 9 acres. Along with their functionality comes magic: while reducing eyesores and maximizing efficiency, the color-coded utilidors also reinforce narrative coherence so employees do not traipse above ground in costumes discordant with respective themes.[15]

Disney's fanatical maintenance standards would be impossible for many places. Faded blooms are removed, trampled plants replaced in the evening. Trash is collected continuously, and all employees work "custodial." Garbage cans are no more than twenty-six paces apart (determined by studying how far people carried rubbish). The first automated AVAC system in the United States whisks away tens of thousands of pounds of trash at 60 miles an hour. But protests that the Disney parks are "too sterile" have not deterred prominent artists, architects, and planners from admiring them. At a 1963 conference, James Rouse claimed Disneyland was "the greatest piece of urban design in the United States today."[16] More than thirty years later, Curator Nicholas Olsberg professed: "Disney's approaches to designing recreational space, to the representation of historic architecture, and to the shaping of an urban narrative have had a massive impact," combining "fun fair and civic center."[17] Admittedly theme parks differ vastly from cities, but Disney's design tenets can help make our built environment less banal, more beautiful.

Imagineering and Immersion

Disney's parks are criticized for an alleged "lack of aesthetic virtue and intellectual rigor," yet they create meaningful, "popular, social spaces" that attract repeat visitors "through their efforts at community building and social engineering." Urban planners and public artists who conceive places to congregate and interact can learn much from Disney's "Imagineering" (Walt's mashup of "imagination" with "engineering"). Founded in December 1952, Imagineering brought together members of "Walt's creative think tank" and those with "the technical know-how to pull off Disney's fantastical schemes."[18] To this day, its employees, the Imagineers, determine every creative direction and plan for, and design and build every attraction within, Disney's parks. As described by the Imagineers themselves, latitude to think broadly and boldly comes with their role, as does working collectively and calculated risk-taking. Tackling unforeseen issues in the built environment, Imagineers must use critical thinking and novel problem-solving while sustaining enthusiasm, all instructive for designing public spaces outside of Disney's realm. Imagineers find effective ways to communicate with visitors, telling resonant stories without dumbing these down. They must also anticipate "technological and cultural changes, without losing sight of the core concept of family-friendly fun," grappling with budgets and schedules to keep "a dream alive in a world of concrete and steel, exit signs, politics, gravity and physics."[19] Also key to Imagineering's formula is a productive sort of dissatisfaction. Orrin Shively, previously executive director of Imagineering research, explained: "There is always room for improvement. . . . We are never completely satisfied with our results, whether it's our first solution or the last."[20]

The parks rely upon self-proclaimed cornerstones of Disney's business: 1. Safety; 2. Courtesy; 3. Show; 4. Efficiency. (Please note: these are the original four cornerstones established as per Walt's direct influence; a vital fifth cornerstone, Inclusion, was finally added in 2020. For inclusivity and Disney, please see below.) We can surely understand why Safety is essential to operating theme parks. Courtesy underscores the emphasis upon consumer satisfaction in Disney's employee training, studied by other organizations trying to raise the bar on their own customer service. Efficiency is interrelated with Courtesy; doing things well positively impacts visitor perceptions. But it is the third cornerstone, Show, that we turn to here. Show is the narrative consistency of Disney's experiences, evident throughout all aspects of the parks. For example, to maintain immersion in these themed environments, Disney Speak is used—

every employee is a cast member and each visitor a guest. As Tim Delaney, a prior Imagineering executive indicated, each detail contributes to sensory—not just visual— immersion, building "emotional connection."[21] The company's roots in theatrical productions merge experiences of their parks with movie watching. Imagineers adopt filmic "structure and content," relying upon visitors navigating "massive stage sets, taking in highly composed scenes leading one from the next," with all attractions and lands "mapped out as an edited progression of long shots and close-ups."[22] J. P. Gruen likens Disneyland's "entry sequence" to a utopian vision, bringing guests through Main Street, U.S.A., a nostalgic promenade "emblematic of Disney's values." Main Street was significantly modeled after Marceline, Missouri, a town Walt lived in during boyhood, idealized by his Imagineers. On Main Street, American urbanism and small-town values sat side-by-side, an ageless place devoid of sociopolitical strife. From here, guests proceeded to themed "lands" (originally Adventureland, Fantasyland, Frontierland, and Tomorrowland), "each of which endeavored to further remove tourists from the ordinary."[23]

Immersion requires "plussing," an Imagineering technique enhancing Disney's parks through precise details to create coherent focus. As John Hench, a longtime Disney employee and leading Imagineer, summarized: "Most urban environments are basically chaotic places, as architectural and graphic information scream at the citizen for attention. This competition results in disharmonies and contradictions that . . . cancel each other [out]."[24] Gruen interprets Disneyland as Walt's reaction to social and political turmoil, bolstering faith in technology and "American abundance" while coping with "Cold War anxieties and fears of the unknown." Disney looked to themed prototypes such as World's Fairs, which utilized "architecture and planning as instruments of social change," immersing guests "in an idyllic dream world that provided a glimpse of what the world *could* be—not just what it was."[25]

Play and Choice

Walt's attempts to tightly control his parks while fixing our interpretations of them produced spaces of physical and conceptual clarity, despite their complexity. And since he could never control audiences anyway, the competing ideas and agendas coalescing at them ensure the parks remain dynamic places. Likewise, Imagineers do not represent a monolithic view. Their collaborations exist across widely ranging disciplines, life experiences, and perspectives, with purposeful efforts to include lesser heard voices.[26] As Anne Tryba, former manager of Imagineering's graphic design, observed, "over the years it has become clear that the most diverse teams—rather than the most homogenous groups—are often the most effective in seeing various aspects and multiple solutions."[27] This fostering of inclusivity is reflected in how the Imagineers encourage self-selected play, much like prominent public art professionals who value investigative play. Phillips advocates for public art that is "about the free field—the play—of creative vision." Curator and administrator Penny Balkin Bach agrees. Considering private funding for public art, Bach envisioned "laborator[ies] for artistic experimentation" that prioritize "opportunities for creative expression," while providing "technical expertise and a support structure" for "artist-driven concepts and responses to contemporary civic life." Such projects, she notes, even offer the public celebratory or contemplative breaks from daily existence.[28]

Perhaps the most important aspect of Disney's philosophy is empowering visitors through design that is more adaptable than it seems. Disney cannot mandate but only invite us to play; each guest chooses whether or not to do so. Joe Garlington, previously from Imagineering's creative development team, highlighted audience engagement through interactive play and storytelling: "Though you do need a vision . . . you can't dictate to them how they're going to read your design." Embracing guests' diversity and imagination, he advised, "let the guest fill in the specifics of their own story as they play. And you'll discover . . . the more flexible your world is, the more ways in which it can be interpreted." To this end, Harris accentuates how Disney's understanding of "feelings of self-directed movement, control, and choice stimulated public patronage."[29] Park goers are participants making their own discoveries, though without fear of being lost or disoriented; at Disney, some chance is welcome, chaos is not. An apt example of empowering guests is evidenced through forced perspective, the scaling down of structures to provide physical and contextual cues throughout the parks. Main Street, characterized by Marling as "a strip mall . . . in a scintillating Victorian costume," demonstrates forced perspective. Walt described Main Street as a "scale model"; at street level, things are nearly life-size, but diminish increasingly going upward. This technique, influenced by movie set design, uses proportional relationships to evoke an "aura of well-being, fantasy, and delight." Akin to children playing with dollhouses or train sets, learning is heightened by feeling command over the toys. Marling perceives such "architecture of reassurance" as a barometer of how "profoundly disquieting" the issues raised by Disney's parks actually were, and how much Walt wanted to escape these.[30]

Critiques of Walt's Westernized privilege and fixation upon American culture, including jingoistic impulses to whitewash history, are not wrong.[31] Yet complaints about the parks as wholly artificial and predictable are off the mark. Scott Bukatman, a cultural theorist specializing in media studies, analyzed how Disney parks "intricately combine" real and simulated motion so "the actual position of the observer's body becomes a means of support for illusionistic position."[32] Thus sensory experiences within the theme parks sophisticatedly mix our corporeal and intellectual faculties. In this way, the parks build confidence as guests switch codes within them, playing in spaces made for us that enfold "our awareness of the constructed quality of the Disney phenomenon into our experience of it." These are real places, as I attest, where "commercialism and fantasy are so inextricably and clearly linked" that "most visitors can readily discern, and accept or reject, the consumptive overtures and Disney's particular brand of fun." "To assume otherwise disrespects Disney's public, and discounts the running critiques to be heard between visitors . . . on any given day." No matter how clever and enveloping the Imagineers' work, the parks depend upon people, guests and cast members alike, to activate what would otherwise be dormant places: in short, both cohorts are "savvy consumers" of Disney. My most recent visits to

Disneyland and Disney World (2023) confirmed this, and that the parks are now more welcoming of personal identity expressions from workers and visitors than Walt would have likely ever tolerated. Several years ago, I took a behind-the-scenes Disneyland tour, which ended with a visit inside Walt's apartment overlooking Main Street. Here, a by-then-reclusive man heated up Hormel chili, keeping vigilant watch over his precious park from this private perch.[33] The theme parks have grown through him, but have grown beyond him, too. Over twenty years ago, Susan Davis, a professor of communication, stated the twenty-first century's challenge would be weaving together the collective and private spheres.[34] Disney the man is long gone, but his company remains and is adept at doing just that.

Notes

1   Cher Krause Knight, *Power and Paradise in Walt Disney's World* (Gainsville: University Press of Florida, 2014); Cher Krause Knight, "From Land to World: Disney's Theme Parks," *Faculty Fellow Talk*, Emerson College Los Angeles, October 10, 2023.
2   J. Philip Gruen, "Disneyland, Anaheim, California," in *American Tourism: Constructing a National Tradition*, ed. J. Mark Souther and Nicholas Dagen Bloom (Chicago: Center for American Places at Columbia College, 2012), 69.
3   Karal Ann Marling, "Imagineering the Disney Theme Parks," in *Designing Disney's Theme Parks: The Architecture of Reassurance*, ed. Karal Ann Marling (Montreal/ Paris: Canadian Centre for Architecture/Flammarion, 1997), 169–70.
4   Knight, *Power and Paradise*, 166; Knight, "From Land to World."
5   Marling, "Imagineering," 29–30, 63–4, 66, 68, 70, 73–4, 85; Knight, *Power and Paradise*, 15.
6   Marling, "Imagineering," 146–8; Knight, *Power and Paradise*, 15, 55–7, 112–14; Knight, "From Land to World."
7   Neil Harris, "Expository Expositions: Preparing for the Theme Parks," in *Designing Disney's Theme Parks*, 19–22, 24, 26–7.
8   Knight, *Power and Paradise*, 10–11, 55–7, 106, 113–16; Knight, "From Land to World"; Nicholas Olsberg, "Foreword," in *Designing Disney's Theme Parks*, 10.
9   Marling, "Imagineering," 83; Cher Krause Knight, "Public Art," in *Oxford Encyclopedia of Aesthetics*, ed. Michael Kelly, 2nd ed. (Oxford and New York: Oxford University Press, 2014), 312.
10 Miwon Kwon, *One Place After Another: Site-Specific Art and Locational Identity* (Cambridge, MA: MIT Press, 2004).
11 Knight, "Public Art," 314; Suzanne Lacy, "Introduction: Cultural Pilgrimages and Metaphoric Journeys," in *Mapping the Terrain: New Genre Public Art*, ed. Suzanne Lacy (Seattle: Bay Press, 1995), 19–20, 33–8, 46.
12 Patricia C. Phillips, "Public Constructions," in *Mapping the Terrain*, 65, 67, 70.
13 Mary Jane Jacob, "An Unfashionable Audience," in *Mapping the Terrain*, 58–9.
14 Cher Krause Knight, "The Public More Private, the Private More Public," *Art Journal Open*, Launched October 25, 2018. http://artjournal.collegeart.org/?page_id =10384.

15 Cher Krause Knight, *Public Art: Theory, Practice and Populism* (Malden: Blackwell Publishing, 2008), 90; Knight, *Power and Paradise*, 14, 61–2, 164, 167–8.

16 James Rouse quoted in Marling, "Imagineering," 170; Knight, *Power and Paradise*, 62.

17 Olsberg, "Foreword," 9.

18 Knight, *Public Art*, 104; Knight, *Power and Paradise*, 13.

19 Imagineers, *The Imagineering Way*, ed. Jody Revenson (New York: Disney Editions, 2003), 12–14, 75.

20 Orrin Shively, "A Question of Time and Money," in *Imagineering Way*, 97.

21 Tim Delaney, "Creating Visions," in *Imagineering Way*, 72–3.

22 Knight, *Power and Paradise*, 10, 17.

23 Gruen, "Disneyland," 70–4.

24 John Hench quoted in Marling, "Imagineering," 81.

25 Gruen, "Disneyland," 70–3.

26 Knight, "From Land to World"; Knight, *Power and Paradise*, 152; Imagineers, *Imagineering Way*, 12–14, 75.

27 Anne Tryba, "Never Underestimate the Power of a Team!," in *Imagineering Way*, 90–1.

28 Phillips, "Public Constructions," 65, 67, 70; Penny Balkin Bach, "Private Support for Public Art: Three Model Organizations," in *Public Art by the Book*, ed. Barbara Goldstein (Seattle: University of Washington Press/Americans for the Arts, 2005), 52–5.

29 Joe Garlington, "Designing Interactive Worlds," in *Imagineering Way*, 136–7; Harris, Expository Expositions," 27.

30 Marling, "Imagineering," 35, 79, 81, 169.

31 Knight, *Power and Paradise*, 58, 74–5; Gruen, "Disneyland," 72–6.

32 Scott Bukatman, "The Artificial Infinite: On Special Effects and the Sublime," in *Visual Display: Culture Beyond Appearances*, ed. Lynne Cooke and Peter Wollen (Seattle: Bay Press/Dia Center for the Arts, 1995), 260.

33 Knight, *Power and Paradise*, 10–11, 76, 100–1, 152; Knight, *Public Art*, 92; Knight, "From Land to World."

34 Susan G. Davis, "Space Jam: Media Conglomerates Build the Entertainment City," in *Gender, Race, and Class in Media: A Text Reader*, ed. Gail Dines and Jean M. Humez, 2nd ed. (Thousand Oaks: Sage, 2003), 160.

3

To Infinity and Beyond

Understanding Data Science through the Lens of Disney Data

Lucy D'Agostino McGowan

In our increasingly data-driven world, an ability to understand data is not only an academic pursuit confined to the classroom but a fundamental skill, one that informs decisions in medicine, science, industry, policy, and daily life. Developing a strong foundation in data science and statistics is crucial, not just for folks tasked with completing data analyses but for all of us as *consumers* of information extracted from data. Honing this skill helps us understand *how* the world works and allows us to contribute to informed decision-making.

Everything magical at Disney is strategically and statistically calculated. As a statistics professor at Wake Forest University, I find fun data sources to inspire my students' data science journey, from the introductory level all the way through capstone and graduate-level statistics courses—and Disney is a data treasure trove. Consider park attendance, food and merchandise sales, guest demographics, and attraction wait times to start.[1] The Walt Disney Company undoubtedly uses data science and data analytics at every level of park operations: to optimize operations, enhance guest experiences, drive business decisions, and, ultimately, make "magic" through data strategies. What we can do—as academics, students of data science, and Disney fans—is think about the ways Disney parkgoers and travel planning apps like TouringPlans collect, analyze, and utilize Disney data for a maximized, more "magical" visit to the parks. Indeed, guests visiting EPCOT (which will be the focus for this chapter) will marvel at the way things fall into place: wait times are published on screens and in the My Disney Experience app; lines move smoothly as cast members load and unload guests from ride vehicles; and parkgoers are directed to different parts of the park by the Genie+ tip board. That which seems magical is, in fact, informed by data science strategies. In this chapter, I'm going to help you think like a data scientist, analyzing examples of Disney data and therefore seeing practical applications for statistical methods—and perhaps finding the study of statistics engaging, relevant, and even *magical*.[2]

Disney, Data, and Decision-Making

For a Disney park goer, whether you realize it or not, you are immersed in a world meticulously designed with data analytics.[3] Disney uses data to shape nearly every part of the guest experience—and you can too.

For example, in 2020, Disney temporarily implemented a reservation system to manage park capacity due to Covid-19, relying on data to balance guest experience with safety.[4] Or, consider Disney's Lightning Lane service, launched to help visitors minimize waits for a fee: the cost is variable based on several factors; Disney likely uses predictive data models to suggest optimal fees.[5]

It's not just Disney that collects and utilizes data about their parks: other companies have emerged that do this as well. For example, TouringPlans is a popular third-party service that emerged to help guests navigate the parks with less wait time, giving them more time to enjoy all that Disney has to offer. Founded by Disney enthusiasts and data scientists, TouringPlans provides many data-driven services. One such tool is a park tour optimizer, where custom plans are provided based on guests' interests and the predicted ride wait times for a particular Disney park on a particular date. TouringPlans relies on volunteer data submissions to make its crowd predictions and wait-time forecasts more accurate. Guests can report attraction wait times through an application designed by TouringPlans called *Lines* by simply tapping a stopwatch icon as they join a queue and tapping it again when they board the ride, providing a real-time database of wait times. TouringPlans also dispatches employees to collect data directly, bolstering its predictions and helping guests craft optimized Disney days.

Both Disney and its consumers can use data strategically, to make experiences more manageable, predictable, and enjoyable.

Beginning to Analyze: Description, Prediction, and Explanation

Recognizing the value of data for decision-making, there are many applications of real Disney data and aspects of data analysis that we can explore. Awareness of these topics helps us understand quantitative information and ultimately think about decision-making and how and where we want to spend our resources (time, money, and others). Data scientists often use data to achieve one of the following three goals: description, prediction, or explanation.[6] These objectives form the backbone of data analyses, with each serving a distinct purpose. Description is the process of summarizing the current state of data to understand what is happening. It involves collecting and presenting data in forms such as averages, variances, and frequencies, to paint a clear picture of existing patterns, without attempting to infer future events or underlying causes.

For example, describing the average wait times for rides at Disney World on a typical Saturday offers a snapshot of guest experiences, highlighting the most and least popular attractions at that time. Prediction goes a step further by using existing data to *forecast* future occurrences. This is where a data scientist may employ statistical models such as machine learning algorithms to make educated guesses about what will happen next, based on patterns observed in the past. Thinking about Disney parks, prediction could be used to forecast future guest attendance or ride wait times, based on factors like seasonality, holiday periods, and special events, thereby aiding in planning and operational efficiency. Explanation, sometimes known as *causal inference*, seeks to uncover *why* certain patterns or trends are observed in the data. It aims to identify the underlying causes and effects, distinguishing correlation from causation. For instance, explanation can help determine why certain marketing strategies increase park attendance or why some rides have longer wait times than others, by isolating and analyzing the factors that directly influence these outcomes.

These three goals—description, prediction, and explanation—though distinct, are interconnected. Description provides the foundation, offering a clear understanding of the snapshot of data at hand. Prediction builds on this knowledge, extending it to anticipate future trends. Explanation goes deeper, striving to understand the mechanisms behind observed data patterns. Let's see some real examples of Disney data applied to each of these contexts. Along the way, we will learn some key points to look out for when consuming quantitative information.

Description

Descriptive statistics are the cornerstone of data analysis, providing a straightforward summary of data sets through measures of central tendency (mean, median, mode) and dispersion (range, variance, standard deviation). These statistics offer a glimpse into the data's overall shape, often serving as a preliminary step before delving into more complex analyses.

Understanding Basic Descriptive Statistics

Descriptive statistics offer a concise overview of data distributions, enabling data scientists to grasp the essence of their datasets. For example, in assessing the average wait times across various attractions at Disney parks, measures of central tendency can highlight the most and least time-consuming lines for rides, while measures of dispersion provide a sense of variability and predictability in guest experiences.

Let's look at a concrete example.

At Walt Disney World in Orlando, the EPCOT park has a dark ride called Spaceship Earth, which allows guests to "travel through time and explore the remarkable history of human communication from the Stone Age to the computer age."[7] Here, I have pulled wait time data for Spaceship Earth in 2018, as collected by TouringPlans.[8] Let's just look between the hours of 10 a.m. and 11 a.m.—Figure 3.1 will give us a sense of

Spaceship Earth Wait Time Distribution

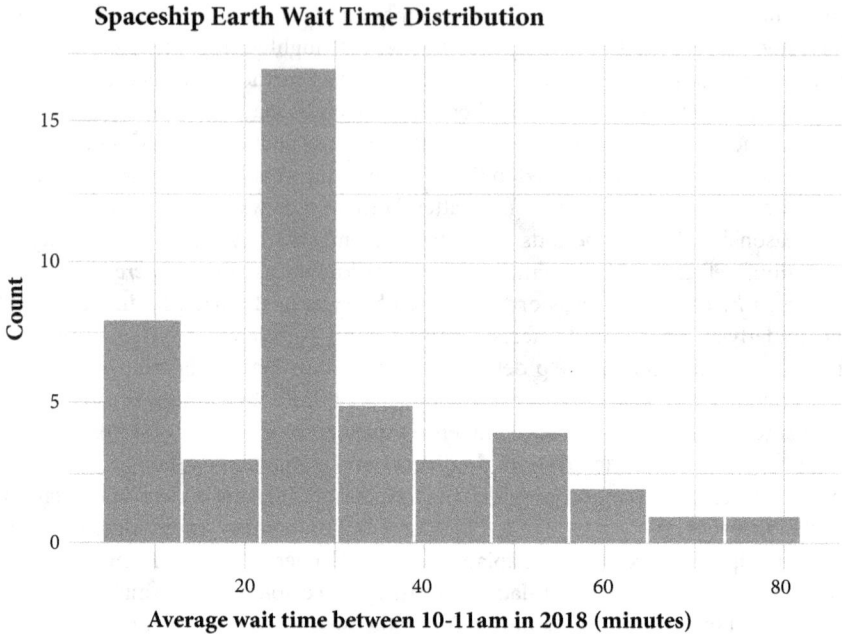

Average wait time between 10-11am in 2018 (minutes)

from Disney World Ride Wait Time Datasets, Touring Plans.com, Accessed 28 August 2023

Figure 3.1 Average wait time for Spaceship Earth between 10 a.m. and 11 a.m. in 2018. Disney World Wait Times. Available for Data Science and Machine Learning, TouringPlans.com.

what we can expect to see on average during this time in our snapshot of data. Each observation in these data represents one day at EPCOT in 2018; in our case, we have data on forty-four days. (Why not 365? These data consist of dates when someone manually recorded a wait time and submitted it to TouringPlans between 10 a.m. and 11 a.m. in 2018, and there are simply many days when this did not happen.) For each of these days, we capture what the average wait time was between 10 a.m. and 11 a.m.

Figure 3.1 is called a *histogram*—it shows us lots of things about this dataset, including information about the central tendency, the dispersion, and the shape of the underlying data. Let's start by talking about *central tendency:* measures that represent the center or typical value of a dataset. Two measurements we use to capture this are the mean and the median. In what follows, we will look at each of these measures in the context of Figure 3.1, Spaceship Earth's wait times between 10 a.m. and 11 a.m. in 2018.

The mean, or average wait time, is calculated by summing all of the average posted wait times and dividing by the number of observations. Recall here that each observation represents a day at EPCOT in 2018. In this dataset, the mean is thirty-one minutes. The *mean* provides a general idea of the wait time that a guest might expect if they were to have approached the attraction in 2018 between 10 a.m. and 11 a.m. Notice we are not making any claims *yet* about what a guest may expect now, as we are still just in the description phase, describing what the data looked like in 2018, not *predicting* what we might expect tomorrow. One fact about the mean is that it can be influenced by exceptionally long or short wait times; for example, if there was an usually long wait one day, it could make the overall mean look larger than you might expect on a typical day. Not all measures of central tendency are sensitive to unusual observations like this. For instance, the median, which we will describe next, is not as influenced by extreme values.

The median represents the middle value when all the average wait times are arranged in order. This measure is less sensitive to outliers and can often give a better sense of a "typical" wait time experience than the mean. In this dataset, the median average wait time between 10 a.m. and 11 a.m. for Spaceship Earth is twenty-eight minutes.

Now that we've discussed the *central tendency* of wait times for Spaceship Earth at EPCOT, we can talk about measures of *dispersion*. These statistics help us understand the variability, or spread, of the average wait times, giving us a fuller picture of guest experiences during the 10 a.m. to 11 a.m. window. Measures of dispersion include the range, variance, standard deviation, and interquartile range (IQR).

Range captures the difference between the maximum and minimum wait times, offering a quick glimpse into the overall variability of guest experiences in our dataset.

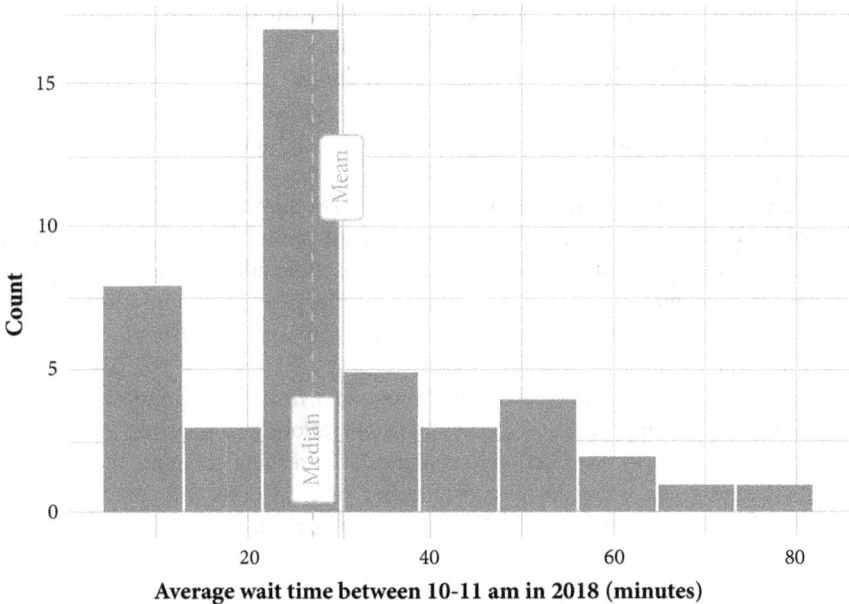

Spaceship Earth Wait Time Distribution

from Disney World Ride Wait Time Datasets, Touring Plans.com, Accessed 28 August 2023

Figure 3.2 Average wait time for Spaceship Earth between 10 a.m. and 11 a.m. in 2018; annotated with measures of central tendency, the mean (solid) and the median (dashed). Disney World Wait Times Available for Data Science and Machine Learning, TouringPlans.com.

A large range suggests a wide disparity in wait times, indicating periods of both walk-ons and potential long waits. For these data, the range is sixty-nine minutes, from a minimum posted wait time of six to a maximum of seventy-five minutes.

Variance and its square root, the standard deviation, quantify the spread of wait times around the mean. A high variance or standard deviation indicates that wait times vary significantly from the average, suggesting that guests might experience highly unpredictable wait times. Conversely, a low value points to more consistent wait times, with most data clustering around the mean. In these data, the variance is 288 minutes.

The IQR, calculated as the seventy-fifth percentile and the twenty-fifth percentile of the data, focuses on the middle 50 percent of posted wait times. In these data, the twenty-fifth percentile is twenty-two minutes and the seventy-fifth percentile is thirty-seven minutes.

Common Pitfalls

Two critical validity concerns in descriptive analyses are measurement and sampling errors. In the context of Disney parks, this could manifest, for example, as inaccurately reported wait times due to system glitches or systematic differences in the days that have recorded wait times by TouringPlans versus those that do not.

Measurement error occurs when there is a discrepancy between the actual data value and the value recorded by the researcher. The severity of measurement error's impact on the analysis depends on its magnitude and the specific research question at hand. The data we analyzed were collected by TouringPlans, either by their employees or by volunteers who timed their waits. If the people who submitted these times do so inaccurately (such as forgetting to "end" their stopwatch at the front of the line), this could impact results, making waits appear longer than they actually were.

Sampling error arises from differences between the sample population and the overall population one aims to describe. In this example, if days when TouringPlans employees or volunteers collected wait time data differ in a meaningful way from days when they do not, this could make our data not represent the entire set of potential wait times.

Descriptive analysis serves as a critical first step in data exploration, offering a window into the complexities of Disney park operations and guest experiences. By mastering the nuances of descriptive statistics and keeping in mind the common pitfalls, analysts can pave the way for deeper investigations into prediction and explanation, grounded in a solid understanding of their datasets.

Prediction

Prediction helps us forecast future events and trends based on historical data. In the Disney parks, where thousands of variables intersect to influence guests' experiences, the ability to predict outcomes is invaluable—and can be a bit like magic. Leveraging statistical techniques to build accurate prediction models can be useful for a range of Disney enthusiasts, from park goers to travel agents to Disney data analysts. For example, data-savvy park goers and travel agents can enhance their strategic planning; likewise, Disney can use prediction models to improve guest satisfaction or optimize operational efficiency. This could involve using statistical models and machine learning algorithms to anticipate changes in park attendance, ride wait times, or guest behavior. These predictions can help address several practical challenges, such as resource allocation, staffing requirements, and maintenance scheduling. For instance, predicting high attendance days allows park management to adjust staffing levels and entertainment offerings to better accommodate increased guest numbers. Similarly, forecasting ride wait times can help guests plan their days or could be used to smooth out the distribution of crowds across different attractions.

This section will demonstrate how Disney data can be used for building a prediction model. We will discuss how data collected from the past can inform models that predict what may happen in the future, along with common pitfalls when building predictive models.

Understanding Prediction Models

Let's suppose we are going to the EPCOT park at Disney World and want to approximate how long the wait time will be for Spaceship Earth; if it is less than ten minutes, we will go straight there, otherwise we will go on another attraction first instead. Previously, we looked at a *descriptive* analysis of the actual wait time for Spaceship Earth recorded in 2018 between 10 a.m. and 11 a.m., and now we want to perform a *predictive* analysis of the wait time. While some of the statistical tools may be the same, the assumptions are different. For the descriptive analysis, we basically just had to assume that the data were measured accurately. Now, we need to assume that the data we have from the past will accurately represent what we expect to see in the future. Concretely, let's think about this particular data set. We have data from 2017 to 2018—are the dynamics from EPCOT in this range the same as they are today? Likewise, we have to assume that we have sufficient information from the past to accurately predict what will happen in the future. What factors influence the wait time for Spaceship Earth? Have we measured enough of these to be able to make an accurate prediction?

Let's suppose we used a predictive model known as a decision tree to predict whether the wait for Spaceship Earth would be less than ten minutes. Figure 3.3 shows the output from this model. This model was fit using 945 recorded wait times between 2017 and 2018. The model takes into account four factors: the posted wait time, the time of day, the day of the week, and the ticket season (i.e., how expensive the ticket was for that date relative to other dates in the year, binned into three categories: value, regular, or peak).

There are a couple of things we can learn from this model. First, we can build a *prediction* for a given future moment. For example, suppose today I am heading into EPCOT; it is a *value ticket* day, meaning it is among the least expensive days to purchase a ticket at Disney World, and it is 2 p.m. I checked the My Disney Experience app, and the posted wait time for Spaceship Earth is fifteen minutes. Let's

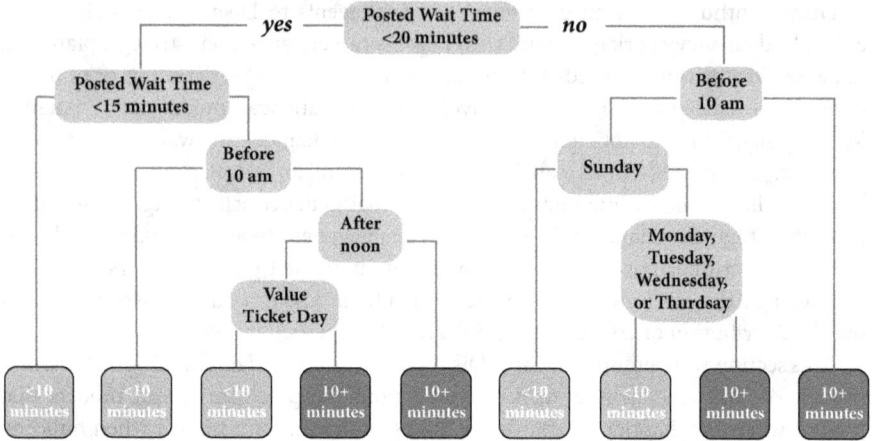

Figure 3.3 Decision tree: Will Spaceship Earth have a < ten-minute wait? Disney World Wait Times. Available for Data Science and Machine Learning, TouringPlans.com.

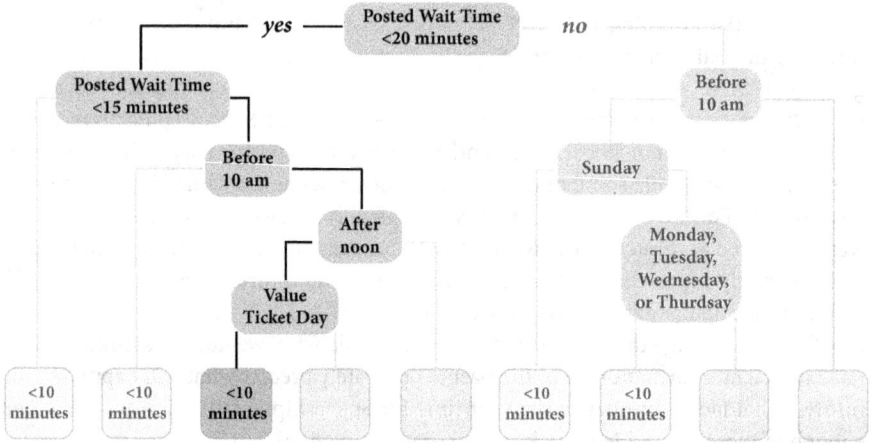

Figure 3.4 Decision tree: Will Spaceship Earth have a < ten-minute wait today (it is 2 p.m. on a "value ticket" day and the posted wait time is fifteen minutes)? Disney World Wait Times. Available for Data Science and Machine Learning, TouringPlans.com.

check out our prediction model to see whether we would predict the wait time to be less than ten minutes; Figure 3.4 shows the decision tree highlighted to reflect our reality.

Of course, this is just a model; we may want to understand how *accurate* it is. Often, when fitting prediction models, data scientists trade off *parsimony* (how easy the model is to understand) with *accuracy*—decision trees like the one we fit here are typically very easy to understand (especially if they do not include many factors) but sometimes are not as accurate as more complex prediction models. We can look at two measures of accuracy: in-sample accuracy and out-of-sample accuracy.

In-sample accuracy captures how well the model performs on the 945 recorded wait times between 2017 and 2018 we used to create it (our *training* data). In our case, this is 0.78, meaning that 78 percent, or 737 of the 945 recorded wait times, were correctly classified by our decision tree prediction model.

Out-of-sample accuracy captures how well the model performs on *other* days that we did not use to create the model. This can give us a more realistic sense of how the model might do at guessing whether the wait time will be less than ten minutes *today* (since we did not have information about today when we originally created our tree). We could, for example, use 2019 data as our *testing* sample. We have 418 observations from 2019. Running these through our model, our out-of-sample accuracy is 0.75, meaning that 75 percent or 314 of the 418 recorded wait times were correctly classified by our decision tree prediction model. This is pretty good! Not quite as good as our in-sample accuracy when calculated using our *training* data, but that is to be expected.

Common Pitfalls

We often determine the validity of a prediction model by calculating how *accurate* it is, as we did above with the *in-sample* and *out-of-sample* accuracy. A key concern here is overfitting; that is, we could build a model that has perfect in-sample accuracy but performs very poorly in a new sample—this would not be useful at all for a main reason people use prediction models: to predict what will happen next. In the context of Disney, imagine you built a prediction model to estimate how long the wait time would be for Spaceship Earth using just ten observed wait times. If we know ten different factors about each of these ten observations, we could probably *perfectly* predict whether the wait was more than ten minutes or not using those factors. However, this model would likely perform poorly when applied to new data, as it may have simply memorized patterns specific to those ten observations rather than generalizing to broader patterns in wait times. This phenomenon underscores the importance of validating models on out-of-sample data to ensure they are robust and genuinely predictive, rather than merely fitting the noise or specific quirks of the initial dataset.

With prediction models, we are also still concerned with measurement error, as we were with descriptive analyses above. If our data are not measured accurately, our predictions will also likely be inaccurate.

To mitigate overfitting, data scientists will often examine both *in-sample* and *out-of-sample* accuracy to make sure that the models not only perform well on the data they were trained on but also on new data sets. Similar to descriptive analyses, carefully collecting and understanding the data that goes into the prediction models can help mitigate measurement error.

Explanation

The final pillar of data science, after description and prediction, is *explanation*, or causal inference. This process seeks to uncover the underlying causes of observed phenomena, providing answers to the "why" behind the patterns and trends detected in data. In the context of Disney parks, folks may be interested in understanding the "why" so they could intervene to improve guest satisfaction and business outcomes.

Explanation goes beyond merely describing what happens or predicting what will happen next. It involves delving into the relationships between variables to determine which factors *cause* outcomes. For instance, knowing that attendance spikes during certain times of the year is useful; understanding what drives these spikes—be it school holidays, special events, or seasonal promotions—allows park managers to plan more effectively and allocate resources more efficiently. Explanation helps people distinguish the difference between mere correlations and genuine causative links.

Understanding Causal Models

Thinking More about "Value Ticket" Dates

Maybe you are wondering why "value ticket" dates have lower wait times—it could be natural to expect that on days where you can go to Disney for less that more people would purchase tickets and therefore the waits would be longer. The phenomenon that we are seeing is likely driven by Disney's own look at the data—ideally, they could spread guests across the whole year, without having any exceptionally busy times—this is likely what they are trying to do by setting ticket prices as they do. Looking at Table 3.1, for example, we see that there are never any "value ticket" dates in June, July, or December. For many families with school-aged children going to Disney, these are going to be the easiest times to take the vacation, since most schools are out during this time. While these families would likely prefer to travel during dates that would allow them to purchase a less expensive ticket, they are trading off this expense for the convenience of not having to pull their children out of school during the academic year. Thinking through these mechanisms is exactly what data scientists interested in estimating causal effects do every day (and now you are doing it too!).

Let's suppose Disney parks managers are interested in changing how long the line is for Spaceship Earth—they want to see if they can intervene to make the wait time to be more likely to be less than ten minutes on certain days. In order to build this intervention, they need to understand *why* Spaceship Earth's wait time is less than ten minutes at certain times on certain days. Looking at the variables from our prediction model, one that Disney has control over is whether it is a "value ticket" day. According to the decision tree prediction model in Figure 3.3, even if it is the afternoon and the posted wait time is fifteen minutes, if it is a value ticket day, the predicted wait time is *less than ten minutes*, suggesting this is an important factor for determining wait time. Is this factor *causally* related to the wait time, or is this just a correlation?

Let's first try to quantify this supposed effect. Among our 945 recorded wait times between 2017 and 2018, the average recorded wait time on "value ticket" days is four minutes less than those on other days, with a 95 percent uncertainty interval from six to three minutes, suggesting that there is at least a correlation between these factors. (To understand the direction of this effect, check out the above Text Box "Thinking More about 'Value Ticket' Dates.")

A first step when trying to build a causal model is to draw our assumptions of the causal relationships between our variable of interest (in this case, whether it is a "value ticket" day) and our outcome of interest. Data scientists often do this by drawing a picture with factors they think may influence these variables linked by arrows (Figure 3.5). For example, what *caused* a day in our data set to be a "value ticket" day? Some ideas could be the *month* of the year—perhaps Disney selected dates to discount based on when crowds are more likely to be in Orlando due to things like weather or

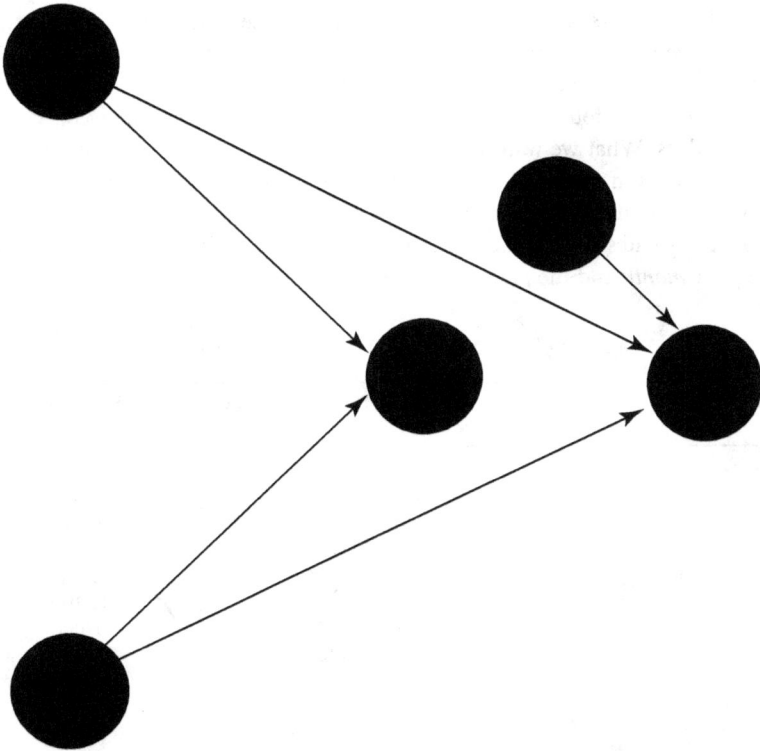

Figure 3.5 Causal relationships for whether it is a "value ticket" date and Spaceship Earth's wait time: Disney World Wait Times. Available for Data Science and Machine Learning, TouringPlans.com.

holidays. Another factor could be the *percent of schools in session* in the United States—perhaps Disney discounts days where more schools are in session to leave common school breaks at regular or peak pricing. Now we can think about factors that cause our outcome of interest, the wait time at Spaceship Earth. The month of the year and percent of schools in session likely also impact wait time, as they would impact the crowd levels. Another factor may be the weather on a given day (if it's rainy, perhaps fewer people want to queue in the outdoor line); while this could potentially impact the wait time, it likely did not impact whether Disney set this as a "value ticket" day, since they would not have known what the precipitation would be on that date far in advance when the price was set (and thus we only see an arrow from this factor to the outcome in Figure 3.5).

Assuming our diagram is true (i.e., these are the *only* factors that influence our variable of interest), we can try to estimate whether there is a *causal* relationship between whether it is a value ticket day and Spaceship Earth's wait time. The main factors we will need to take into account are the *month* and the *percent of schools in session*. In simple terms, we need to adjust for factors that affect both the cause of interest (whether it is a value ticket day) and the outcome (the wait time for Spaceship Earth). These factors are known as confounders; they are the main reason why sometimes we observe *correlations* that are not actually *causal*. Why? Well, if these factors are imbalanced across "value ticket" days, that imbalance could be driving the observed effect, the four-minute average difference in wait time between value and non-value days. What we want to do is construct *counterfactuals*—what would have happened to a given observation if the variable of interest was flipped? In other words, what would have happened on days that were classified as "peak" or "regular ticket" dates if Disney had switched these to "value ticket" dates? Let's look at some *descriptive statistics* for *month* and the *percent of US schools in session* by whether it was a "value

Table 3.1 Table Examining Balance between Value and Non-Value Dates

Characteristic	Regular or Peak Ticket Date, N = 726	Value Ticket Date, N = 219
Month		
January	53 (7.3%)	44 (20%)
February	40 (5.5%)	33 (15%)
March	54 (7.4%)	20 (9.1%)
April	67 (9.2%)	5 (2.3%)
May	74 (10%)	5 (2.3%)
June	91 (13%)	0 (0%)
July	63 (8.7%)	0 (0%)
August	52 (7.2%)	30 (14%)
September	41 (5.6%)	40 (18%)
October	72 (9.9%)	16 (7.3%)
November	67 (9.2%)	26 (12%)
December	52 (7.2%)	0 (0%)
Percent of US schools in session	78 (34, 93)	93 (92, 95)

Source: Disney World Wait Times Available for Data Science and Machine Learning, TouringPlans.com.

ticket" date (Table 3.1) to get a sense of the potential imbalance. Looking at this table, we can definitely detect some imbalance between the two groups. For example, the median percent of schools in session on "value ticket" days is 93 percent, whereas the median on "peak" or "regular ticket" days is only 78 percent. January and February were much more likely to be "value ticket" days than not, whereas April and May were more likely to be "peak" or "regular ticket" days. Likewise, we have several months (June, July, and December) that *never* had "value ticket" days. This means we cannot say anything causal with our data about these months, as we do not have a data-driven way to construct a counterfactual. We will exclude these three months from the rest of our analyses.

There are many ways to create these counterfactuals. One easy way is to use matching. In other words, we can find observations that look like each other based on these imbalanced factors (month and percent of schools in session) but that are in opposite groups in terms of our causal factor of interest (whether it is a value ticket day or not). We can build a model to help us match based on these factors. After matching, we end up with a more balanced dataset (Table 3.2). Notice now our two groups ("value ticket" days and non-value days) are more comparable.

After matching, among our 224 recorded wait times between 2017 and 2018, the average recorded wait time on "value ticket" days is less than a minute different from other days (0.96 minutes, with a 95 percent uncertainty interval from −2 to 4 minutes). This suggests that the bigger difference we originally saw is likely just due to the imbalance in these factors rather than due to whether it is a "value ticket" day (in other words, here the correlation we saw is likely *not* causation). This suggests that if Disney just switched all the days to "value ticket" days, they

Table 3.2 Matched Table Examining Balance between Value and Non-Value Dates

Characteristic	Regular or Peak Ticket Date, N = 112	Value Ticket Date, N = 112
Month		
January	17 (15%)	25 (22%)
February	12 (11%)	20 (18%)
March	6 (5.4%)	5 (4.5%)
April	6 (5.4%)	5 (4.5%)
May	5 (4.5%)	5 (4.5%)
June	0 (0%)	0 (0%)
July	0 (0%)	0 (0%)
August	9 (8.0%)	11 (9.8%)
September	23 (21%)	13 (12%)
October	13 (12%)	16 (14%)
November	21 (19%)	12 (11%)
December	0 (0%)	0 (0%)
Percent of US schools in session	93 (92, 95)	93 (92, 94)

Source: Disney World Wait Times Available for Data Science and Machine Learning, TouringPlans.com.

likely would not see a four-minute decrease in wait times for Spaceship Earth as was originally estimated.

Common Pitfalls

Building valid models for *explanation*, or *causal inference*, require several assumptions. Two key ones are (1) we have to have measured and accounted for all of the potential factors that could introduce confounding into our model, and (2) all observations need to have a non-zero chance of being classified into any category of the cause of interest (sometimes this is called overlap). This pitfall highlights a broader challenge for Disney data enthusiasts of trying to identify the *cause* of some outcome of interest. For example, if Disney thought they could manipulate crowd levels by changing whether a specific date was labeled as a "value ticket" day, when in fact the crowd levels are more likely determined by the seasonality and number of US schools in session, they might misjudge the resources needed on those days, resulting in either overcrowding or underutilized attractions.

In our example, in order for our matched model to be valid, the two factors we accounted for (month and the percent of US schools in session) need to account for all of the potential confounding between whether it was a "value ticket" date and the wait time for Spaceship Earth. We also saw an example of the overlap assumption being violated, since we did not have *any* observations in June, July, or December that were "value ticket" days. This means we cannot say anything conclusive about what would happen during these months if Disney decided to make a day a "value ticket" day in terms of the impact on Spaceship Earth wait time.

Wrap Up

From basic descriptions of data that offer a snapshot of the current state to advanced predictive and explanatory analyses that venture into the realms of forecasting and causal inference, our exploration in this chapter has demonstrated how data science is a technical skill *and* a vehicle for understanding and improving our interactions with complex systems—like those found at Disney.

What then can we conclude about the interplay of Disney and data science? It is clear that data science is a powerful tool—not just for data scientists but for anyone interested in making informed decisions based on evidence. Whether planning a visit to Disney parks or allowing parkgoers to pull back the curtain and consider how data science is impacting park operations and experiences, the principles and methods discussed here provide a solid foundation for engaging with the complexities of a data-driven world.

What might feel like "magic" at Disney parks, such as accurate posted wait times or just the right number of cast members at each attraction, stems from Disney's strategic use of data science and analysis. Similarly, platforms like TouringPlans use data science to deliver seemingly magical insights to guests, leveraging several data sources, such as historical wait times, crowd patterns, and seasonal attendance trends, to help visitors plan their trips or perfectly optimize their park itineraries.

The true power of data science lies in its ability to take seemingly ordinary data points and weave them into a meaningful story, giving both consumers and organizations actionable insights. In the unique, immersive world of Disney, data science translates countless interactions and details into a seamless guest experience, while enabling families to craft their own "magical" adventures in the parks. Ultimately, data analysis is about relationships, storytelling, and context, and in the Disney parks, it can help guests create magical vacation experiences of their own.

Notes

1 Lauren E. Luechtefeld, "The Expanding Role of Analytics in Operations" (Undergraduate honors thesis, University of Dayton, 2021), https://ecommons.udayton .edu/cgi/viewcontent.cgi?article=1324&context=uhp_theses/; Dayanira Mendoza, Wenbo Wu, and Mark Leung, "Predicting the Expected Waiting Time of Popular Attractions in Walt Disney World," *Journal of Undergraduate Research & Scholarly Work* 6 (2019), https://hdl.handle.net/20.500.12588/99.
2 Concetta A. DePaolo and Aimee Jacobs, "Analyzing Disney World Wait Time Data: A Lesson in Visualization Using Tableau," *Journal of Information Systems Education* 29, no. 4 (2021): 249–52.
3 Madeline Rose Sanfilippo and Yan Shvartzshnaider, "Data and Privacy in a Quasi-Public Space: Disney World as a Smart City," in *Diversity, Divergence, Dialogue,* ed. Katharina Toeppe, Hui Yan, and Samuel Kai Wai Chu, conference proceedings at *iConference 2021*, vol. 12646 (Cham: Springer, 2021), https://doi.org/10.1007/978-3 -030-71305-8_19.
4 Brooks Barnes, "Disney World Draws Excitement and Incredulity as Reopening Nears," *New York Times,* July 8, 2020, https://www.nytimes.com/2020/07/08/business/ coronavirus-disney-world-reopening.html.
5 Katie, Rice, "Disney World Replaces Fastpass System with Paid Reservation Service," *Orlando Sentinel,* August 18, 2021, https://www.orlandosentinel.com/2021/08/18/ disney-world-replaces-free-fastpass-system-with-paid-reservation-service/; Nora Walsh, "Visiting a Disney Park? Here's How to Spend Less Time in Line," *New York Times,* October 2, 2024, https://www.nytimes.com/2024/10/02/travel/disney-world -disneyland-lines.html.
6 Malcolm Barrett, Lucy D'Agostino McGowan, and Travis Gerke, "Causal Inference in R," October 23, 2024, https://www.r-causal.org.
7 "Spaceship Earth," Disney World, https://disneyworld.disney.go.com/attractions/epcot/ spaceship-earth/ (accessed May 30, 2024).
8 "Disney World Wait Times Available for Data Science and Machine Learning," TouringPlans, https://touringplans.com/blog/disney-world-wait-times-available-for -data-science-and-machine-learning/ (accessed August 28, 2023).

4

Why and How Walt Disney World Makes You the Star of Its Story

Gary Kaskowitz

If you travel to Walt Disney World (WDW) in central Florida, you join the approximately fifty-eight million other people who will make this journey in any given year. And how much is everybody spending, you might ask? In 2024, if you are frugal, two adults can visit Walt Disney World for a week for about $4,000 (not including your transportation). If these same two people want to have a somewhat more luxurious experience, then about $10,000 for the week should do the trick. Oh, and let us not forget our souvenirs and miscellaneous experiences, which add another $200 to $900 for our couple. Bringing your children will add about 50 percent to this number, assuming you share a room. Realizing that approximately 70 percent of your fellow guests are repeat visitors, and this "once-in-a-lifetime" vacation is an annual trip for many, you have now contributed to Disney's 2024 revenue to the tune of almost $33 billion a year. And of course, by the time you read this, these numbers are sure to have gone up![1]

As a marketing professor, I am often asked how Disney has become such a successful brand and created such deep loyalty among its customers such that people are willing to pay large sums of money for the experience, and repeatedly. To answer this question, we need to understand the power of experiential business models as well as some storytelling, psychology, sociology, and philosophy.

While many successful businesses understand the power of using story to create a strong brand, fewer do this intentionally, and fewer still incorporate story through physical space and experience. Disney World is one of the few places on earth that masterfully blends story, experiences, and physical structure into deep emotional loyalty and branding. In thinking about why and how WDW makes you the star of its story, I focus on storytelling, mythic structure, and archetypes; navigating conflict and solving philosophical problems; putting guests in Disney's story; and transformative rituals and strategic perception. I showcase how product solutions that seem magical to us are just sound marketing strategy.[2]

My research primarily focuses on WDW and not Disneyland because the real success of Walt Disney World is based on the lessons learned from Disneyland. While Disneyland is a stunning success, it never quite achieved the level of mythic structure that Walt Disney World has achieved. It was incredibly successful, but Walt himself felt that it was crowded and did not fully live up to his expectations. Walt Disney and his Imagineers envisioned building a utopian destination for families to play and bond, but the logistics of Disneyland did not allow for Walt's vision to be fully achieved. From these early lessons, Disney hoped to combine entertainment, education, escapism, and aesthetic reward into a single space, resulting in the birth of Walt Disney World.[3]

Storytelling, Mythic Structure, and Archetypes

Walt Disney and the Disney corporation built their empire on storytelling techniques. Walt Disney thought of himself as a storyteller first and a businessman second. He recognized that to truly connect with your audience, you need to tap into timeless principles of appealing to your audience's inner fantasies and desires. Walt Disney was able to apply classic mythic structure and archetypes to create these common fantasies among his audiences in his films. Likewise, modern-day marketers rely upon classic storytelling principles to form deep emotional connections with their audiences. Showcasing consumers' internal frustrations through characters in a story allows the consumer to relate to the problem and solution more completely, while bypassing our natural desire to raise objections. This is a result of our "suspension of disbelief" that we, as consumers, have, making us more likely to receive the message put forth by the marketer and develop a stronger relationship with the product being sold. The Disney corporation then applied these same structures and other marketing principles to the Walt Disney World Resort.[4]

At their heart, mythic structure and archetypes allow a common and appealing method to tell a story. Groups create stories to share their "truths" and desired manners of behavior. Adroit storytellers identify universal characters that all of us relate to and populate their stories with these familiar characters, such as "the best friend" or "mentor." They also typically follow classic plot development (situation, complication, resolution), which has been honed over thousands of years of storytelling with different genres (e.g., romantic comedy, coming-of-age story). Because common plots and story threads have existed for as long as humans have told stories, the best business storytellers understand and use these plots repeatedly, merely changing the window dressing to conform to the story's context. Brands that create deep emotional connections with their audiences often do this by using the power of story and universal archetypes to build these brand connections, whereby marketers showcase people in their pre-solution state (the ordinary world), point out their problem and incite them to action (refusal of the call), and show them what their world could look like if they purchase the product (the sacred world).[5]

Archetypes are another aspect of storytelling and mythic structure. In marketing terms, WDW is positioning itself as a "magician" archetype that allows a working parent to transform from an overworked parent to one who deeply bonds with their family. In the case of other family members and guests, WDW is also taking advantage of the "innocent" archetype who can bring happiness and calm to otherwise hectic lives.[6]

Because the Walt Disney Company began its life in movie-making, it implemented classic storytelling structures in their products beyond the cinema. Disneyland and then Walt Disney World were designed as applied movie sets following cinematic storytelling principles. This story structure is so ingrained in our lives and thoughts that when we are involved with a good story, we suspend all disbelief and form a deep emotional connection to what is transpiring in the story. In essence, we become part of the story and see ourselves and our lives through the story being told.[7]

Navigating Conflict and Solving Philosophical Problems

What makes for a good story then? In a word, conflict! The bigger the conflict, the more powerful the story. In life, these conflicts present as problems—and good marketers are adept at understanding and identifying problems and their solutions. In consumer behavior, a problem is defined as the difference or discrepancy between where you are and where you would like to be. Small problems are often ignored, while larger ones typically capture our attention and demand that we resolve them. There is a paradox here, though, because if the problem is seen as too large, then we likely ignore it because we have no idea how to proceed on our own and require a trusted brand to help us.

Problems can range from low-level external problems to mid-level internal problems, to the highest level of philosophical problems. This high-level problem is where Walt Disney World truly shines. Such problems arise when our frustrations and fears lead us to question our very sense of self-worth. According to Maslow's hierarchy of needs, these situations would be considered "self-actualization" needs. In marketing terms, we would classify this as self-image and identity. Existential problems are so large that consumers will do almost anything to resolve them. While we truly want to resolve these problems, they are so deep and large that we often do not know where to begin. Usually, we cannot even express what the problem is that needs to be solved; we just know that something must happen. This is where a marketer (Walt Disney World in this case) steps in and shows you your problem and how to resolve it. When a brand properly positions itself to the consumer, it is seen as the ONLY logical choice to purchase. No other brand will do![8]

I often ask my students what problem Walt Disney World is resolving. The answer typically comes back as the need for "fun" or "entertainment." More enlightened students will often tell me that Disney offers "exceptional service" or "bonding" experiences to create memories. While these are all true, in and of themselves they are not enough to drive the type of business and loyalty that Disney commands. The best way to understand the problem Walt Disney World is resolving is to understand their primary market. While Walt Disney World does everything in its power to be family friendly and cater to children, children are not Disney's primary customers. After all, it is the parents that have the money to spend. What can induce the parent to spend $6,000 or more for this family trip? The best trip of all . . . the guilt trip!

Walt Disney World takes advantage of the natural guilt parents feel and then presents itself as a solution. The ideal market for Walt Disney World is a working parent. Working parents deal with many conflicts in their day-to-day lives with respect to their families. Many parents can certainly relate to the age-old conundrum with their internal dialogue.

> I need to work to provide for my family. While I am working to provide for my family, I am not as available to my family, and I am missing soccer games and dance recitals. If I work less to attend more to my family, then I will not make as much money to take care of them. If all I do is work to take care of my family, then one day I may be seen as having been an absentee parent and my children won't have time for me in the future. If all I do is attend to my children, then I may not be able to provide for them and they will suffer and possibly blame me for that as well. I believe I am a good parent, yet I don't feel like it. What am I to do?!

While Walt Disney World did not create this inner monologue in parents' heads, it knows this monologue indeed takes place and has directed much of its advertising to this. As any true friend would, Disney shows these parents how a trip to Walt Disney World can resolve this philosophical problem. Disney promises,

> Because Walt Disney World is such a magical and transformative place, when you take your family and/or friends here you and your group will create memories that last a lifetime and beyond. The experiences you will share are so profound that a mere $6000 is nothing. You will instead be remembered forever by your family as having shared this experience that you created together!

Putting Guests in Disney's Story

Now that Walt Disney World has identified this philosophical problem, the one so large that your expenditures seem insignificant in comparison, they deliver on this promise. Let us not ever forget one simple business fact: Walt Disney World's goal is to separate you from your money. It is a profit-maximizing operation. The way it does this, however, is to provide you with such value for your money that you feel like the winner several times over.

Walt Disney World succeeds in building this value by designing its entire resort as a magical, immersive experience where you and your fellow travelers create your own stories in the form of meaningful experiences leading to lasting memories. At Walt Disney World, the stories you create for yourselves help create and/or reinforce a sense of self-identity. These memories will be shared and re-lived and the happy times will be fondly remembered.[9]

All successful stories have four core elements—(1) the characters, (2) the message, (3) the plot, and (4) the aesthetics—and each element plays a part in creating an immersive guest experience.

When using story structure in marketing, the key is to have your audience identify with one or more of the characters in your story. The characters of any given story are the various roles that are fulfilled throughout the story. Common character types include the protagonist, antagonist, mentors, guides, allies, and obstacles. These various character types ultimately connect to what we will call relatability. You do not need to identify with the character demographically in any way. The relatability comes from whether you identify with the character's desires and yearnings. Walt Disney World provides its guests with multiple opportunities to encounter and identify with its characters. Most of these characters are iconic figures that guests know and love. We feel like they are our friends, and we understand them. We know that Mickey Mouse is playful and that Goofy is silly. We know that Tinker Bell is a little jealous and Gaston is a blowhard. These and other characters can be our allies and mentors as we make our way through the parks, helping provide us with reference points for how we can and should behave. We are "guests" in their home. Most importantly, however, are the real stars of the story: us! When we encounter a land or an attraction, such as Fantasyland or Haunted Mansion, we can relate to the characters there and see ourselves as part of their story. We are in the movie with them!

The message of Walt Disney World—or the central point that its story conveys—is simple: you and your party will create your own story and be transformed by this experience. Walt Disney World gives us the building blocks of good stories by diligently removing distractions (e.g., no trash on the ground), thus allowing us to focus on the time and memories we are creating with our companions.

The plot of a story can be thought of as the flow of events from beginning to end. Walt Disney World's Imagineers (the designers of the park and attractions) have created an environment where you create your own story through the park's established structure. Strategic use of space and "wienies" (those attractions that capture our attention and focus, such as Cinderella Castle, thereby drawing us along) let the guests choose their own path and create the story that is most meaningful to them. The design of Walt Disney World parks creates a sense of flow where we make our own stories within these (usually non-perceived) boundaries. Attractions are story-driven and designed to make full use of our imaginations and emotions.[10]

The aesthetics of the Walt Disney World story include the use of atmospherics and servicescape. Atmospherics and servicescape are the physical and service representation of an establishment. Atmospherics are how the business's physical structure is laid out, and servicescape is how you are treated by the staff. For example, note the sidewalks in Liberty Square and pay attention to the brown paths in the middle. Our ancestors did not have the advantage of modern plumbing and sewage, and these paths are designed to symbolize a river of waste! While you are there, ride the Haunted Mansion and note the design of the queue (atmospherics) and how the cast members are dressed and talk to you (servicescape). Note that the cast members inside the attraction will not smile at you and will act a little creepy.[11]

Walt Disney World brings the story to life through its use of atmospherics and servicescape (the aesthetics of storytelling). Whether it is using music to evoke childhood memories and nostalgia on Main Street, U.S.A. or using play and learning to create a space with which all guests can identify, Walt Disney World is built to draw its guests into, so that they may truly experience, the story that is being told. By shaping the experiences that guests encounter, Walt Disney World relates guest experiences to the common story structure (situation, complication, resolution) that we already know.[12]

Transformative Rituals and Strategic Perception

This applied story structure employed at Walt Disney World creates a strong emotional bond between WDW and its guests. The reason this seems so magical to us is because we feel that WDW truly understands us and our needs (relationship marketing), and it can deliver on its brand promise (creating memories that last a lifetime through a shared experience), which resolves a philosophical problem we have and maybe could not quite identify (I now feel closer to my family/group). Namely, WDW gets us and has now become a trusted friend. If this isn't magic, then what is? Disney strategically cultivates this certain perspective within its guests through ritualized experiences.

When guests at WDW venture through the parks (thereby writing their personal plot), they are being led through an applied ritual. Marketing rituals are incredibly powerful, emotionally bonding techniques. Strategic marketers take full advantage of this. Rituals are an applied way for a group to help transform its members from one psychological state to another. Rituals show the importance of group beliefs and norms and have the appropriate buy-in from the participants. Disney applies the belief of family bonding through the family's physical and emotional interaction with its parks.[13]

The goal of a ritual is to transport the person undergoing the ritual from an existing emotional or psychological state to a new state. For example, in a wedding ritual, two people enter as individuals and become "joined" in matrimony. The two people are not physically different after the ceremony, but socially and psychologically, things are not the same. When you graduated high school, you were probably no different than you were before the ceremony, but in your and others' minds, you were. To perform a marketing ritual, three things are necessary: (1) an audience; (2) a prescribed sequence of events (the plot); (3) symbolic tools.[14]

How does Disney apply this? You will notice that at Walt Disney World, most people explore the parks in pairs or groups. Being with others (the audience) is critical to having and sharing the experience of Walt Disney World. And, if you do happen to find yourself alone in the single-rider line, you are not truly alone: chances are you are surrounded by fellow like-minded individual riders. Walt Disney World is a collective experience where you and your fellow guests are interacting, whether you realize it or not. At a minimum, there are always cast members around as both your fellow characters and audience (yes indeed, Walt Disney World is always watching).

Okay, we have an audience, check. What about that prescribed sequence of events? One of the characteristics that makes Walt Disney World such a magical experience is its use of space to drive narrative. While guests are free to wander throughout the parks at their own pace, the parks' design draws our attention to elements that carry us along the story (the wienies mentioned earlier). This sense of self-discovery within bounded limits allows guests to make stories unique to themselves within the parameters that WDW has set.[15]

The tools used in the Disney bonding ritual are the physical attractions and park layout, as well as the cast members themselves. Disney has everything in its place from the attraction queues to the gift shops after. It is near impossible to find a Disney cast member who is "on stage" and yet out of costume or character. All is by design.

The Walt Disney World transformation ritual is thus: you and your family or other party members will have a shared experience that will move you from your ordinary lives to the world of bonding and lifelong memories. You create your own story through Disney's carefully curated and designed setting. While your experience will be unique to you, it is programmed into Disney's design so that you can take WDW's components and build your own Disney story. The use of these techniques (characters, plot, message, and aesthetics) combines with prescribed experiences to create consumers' perceptions of Walt Disney World that distinguish it from its competition.

Putting the Story's Pieces Together

Let's use the Magic Kingdom as an example. Imagine the following scenario: harried parents finally arrive at the parking lot after a long drive or flight. The kids are cranky from the trip and super excited to be going to Disney. The parents are somewhat excited, but the thought of leaving work behind weighs heavily. Now they are entering the vast parking lot in the parking center outside the Magic Kingdom, along with several thousand others. At last, they see it! A parking space. The space is a good distance from the Magic Kingdom's entrance, and the parents are not looking forward to taking the kids on an extended hike to the gate. Suddenly, a tram appears! This tram stops at a designated spot near where the parents have parked. The family shuffles on board, thankful that they do not have to walk to the gate after all. The family is dropped off at the ticket counter to purchase their tickets or Magic Bands. The kids are now really squirming because they can finally see Cinderella Castle in the distance (the wienie)!

At most theme parks and other places of business, you would enter the establishment immediately upon purchasing your admission. At this point though, the family members (especially the parents) are probably not in the best frame of mind. They are truly still in their world of worry and hassle. Instead of just entering the park, Magic Kingdom has one last hurdle. The family now needs to get on a monorail or a boat and cross Seven Seas Lagoon, which separates the TTC (Transportation and Ticket Center) from the Magic Kingdom. While many businesses would deem this last step to be unnecessary and counterproductive, Imagineers understand differently. This leisurely boat or monorail ride serves two purposes: (1) it allows the Magic Kingdom to grow ever closer, thereby heightening the anticipation and (2) it allows the family time to mentally and physically leave their "ordinary" world behind.

Why not just put the family on another parking shuttle? While this method might allow the family time to decompress, it is nowhere near as powerful as the way the Magic Kingdom transports its guests. Disney not only physically transports guests from the ordinary world of parking lots and jobs to the sacred world of story and fantasy, but it also transports them symbolically and emotionally through its use of atmospherics.

Once guests get off the boat or monorail, they can enter the Magic Kingdom itself. Newly arrived guests now find themselves as central characters in the Walt Disney World story. There is not a speck of trash to be seen. Colors, music, and smells are purposely chosen and placed to evoke mood. Looking up, you can now see, in all its glory, Cinderella Castle. Main Street, U.S.A. is designed to lead guests to the various parts of the park, while conjuring images of an idealized American life. All cast members are in character and costume, and all appear to be happy. Throughout its parks, everywhere one turns, aesthetics and authenticity rule the day.[16]

As our family continues, they find that the entire theme park is a giant story brought to life. Through experiences and symbolism, the family is magically transformed, and they comprehend their relationship with Disney and each other differently than they did before. This experience also creates new memories that will be shared and relied upon to draw the family back to WDW in the future, either together or alone. Walt Disney World has done its job. It has successfully separated guests from their money, and the guests are not only happy about the exchange, but they are also looking forward to doing it again in the future.

When you visit the Magic Kingdom at Walt Disney World, you will find a statue of Walt Disney and Mickey Mouse in front of Cinderella Castle. This statue, named "Partners," has a dedication plaque which reads: "We believe in our idea: a family park where parents and children could have fun—together."

Walt Disney World fulfills its promise through the effective use of experiential marketing and storytelling to create deep and lasting loyalty from its guests. When we visit the parks, we create shared experiences with those closest to us and create memories that are recalled years into the future and passed down through generations. Long after we have paid off the credit card, we fondly remember these experiences and cannot wait to go again.

Through the strategic use of experiential marketing and effective storytelling techniques, Walt Disney World elicits deep emotional bonds with its guests, thereby elevating itself to a specialty brand whereby consumers are willing to pay high prices for the opportunity to interact with the brand. Marketers who wish to create stronger loyalty and charge higher prices can follow these same principles in their own organizations. These ideas of using story and experience to create strong buying behavior can also be used by individuals looking to position themselves for career advancement or other roles they seek. If you or your business solves the external problem of your consumer, the strategic use of these sound marketing principles will help elevate your brand above others—as if by magic.

Notes

1 "Investor Relations," https://thewaltdisneycompany.com/investor-relations/#reports (accessed July 1, 2024).

2 B. Joseph Pine and James H. Gilmore, *The Experience Economy: Work Is Theatre & Every Business a Stage* (Boston: Harvard Business Press, 1999).

3 Sam Gennawey, Bob McLain, and Werner Weiss, *Walt Disney and the Promise of Progress City* (Self-published: Ayefour Publishing, 2014).

4 Christopher Vogler, *The Writer's Journey—25th Anniversary Edition: Mythic Structure for Writers* (Studio City: Michael Wiese Productions, 2020).

5 James Bonnet, *Stealing Fire From the Gods: The Complete Guide to Story for Writers and Filmmakers* (Studio City: Michael Wiese Productions, 2006).

6 Margaret Mark and Carol S. Pearson, *The Hero and the Outlaw: Building Extraordinary Brands Through the Power of Archetypes* (New York: McGraw Hill Professional, 2001).

7 The imagineers, *Walt Disney Imagineering: A Behind the Dreams Look at Making More Magic Real* (New York: Disney Editions, 2010).

8 Abraham Maslow, "A Theory of Human Motivation," https://psychclassics.yorku.ca/Maslow/motivation.htm (accessed August 1, 2024).

9 Pine and Gilmore, *The Experience Economy: Work Is Theatre & Every Business a Stage*.

10 M. Sklar, *One Little Spark!: Mickey's Ten Commandments and the Road to Imagineering* (New York: Disney Editions, 2015).

11 J. Chytry, "Disney's Design: Imagineering Main Street," *Boom: A Journal of California* 2, no. 1 (2012): 33–44.

12 C. Carson, "'Whole New Worlds': Music and the Disney Theme Park Experience," *Ethnomusicology Forum* 13, no. 2 (2004): 228–235.

13 F. Amati and F. Pestana, "Consumption Rituals: A Strategic Marketing Framework," *Economic Studies* 2, no. 1 (2015): 229–246.

14 M. W. Liu, Q Zhu, and X Wang, "Building Consumer Connection With New Brands Through Rituals: The Role of Mindfulness," *Marketing Letters* 33, no. 2 (2022).

15 G. Dehrer, "Imagineers in Search of the Future," *The Futurist* 45, no. 2 (2011): 36.

16 H. R. Houston and L. A. Meamber, "Consuming the 'World': Reflexivity, Aesthetics, and Authenticity at Disney World's Epcot Center," *Consumption Markets & Culture* (2011), doi: 10.1080/10253866.2011.562019.

Section II

Authenticity and Simulation

Section Introduction

Authenticity and Simulation

Alexis T. Franzese

Disney's unofficial anthem, "When You Wish Upon a Star," tells us that when we wish, it "makes no difference who you are. Anything your heart desires, can come to you." It is unsurprising that these lyrics have become so central to Disney's operations. They tell us that our background, our past, our status at present are irrelevant to the likelihood that we will be able to attain what we most desire in the future. (Oh, what a fantasy!) Our wishes, our longings can come to pass, what we desire can become reality, and this manifestation makes simulation become authentic. Thus, our second dialectical pairing, that of authenticity and simulation, reveals how Disney has managed to create the most genuine make-believe imaginable. Guests of Disney properties find themselves questioning what is real and what is unreal; indeed, this can be part of the fun. Viewers of Disney films—from the animated and fantastical to even documentaries—are asked to trust that what Disney presents is "real." If Disney consumers can suspend disbelief, they can fully embrace and be embraced by environments that never were but that they wish could be.[1] How nice it would be if every town had a clean, safe, lovely Main Street, U.S.A.! The fact that simulation exists alongside authenticity reveals Disney magic and strategy at work.

The term "authenticity" has roots in philosophy and was picked up by psychology and sociology in the 1900s.[2] It was traditionally used to refer to individual behavior and interactions; in recent decades, scholars have additionally considered the authenticity of places and experiences. Potential travelers looking to book travel online can merely search the phrase "authentic travel experiences" and be overwhelmed with companies that are similarly named and/or feature such getaways.[3]

The concept of simulation, like authenticity, spans disciplinary boundaries and offers a perspective for understanding Disney products and operations. Simulation can be conceived as the re-creation of something real, or as the creation of the *quality* of realness rather than something that *is* real. Much credit here is owed to French scholar Jean Baudrillard, who worked at the intersections of sociology and philosophy and brought attention to these topics in 1981 with *Simulation and Simulacra*, which offered a framework for considering how the suspension of reality through simulation can result in a new condition, which Baudrillard called simulacra.[4] Simulacra is not reality but in fact replaces it. Baudrillard did not celebrate this cultural development; his writings on simulation were deeply dystopian and were, in many ways, a warning.

Today's technologies allow for almost endless simulacra, and the lines between the real and the manufactured can be almost imperceptibly blurred. Animation techniques like CGI (computer-generated imagery), for example, both represent an effort by creators to recreate the actual and result in the creation of something that gives the quality of realness. The motivation for these efforts likely includes both a desire to see what is possible with new innovations and technologies as well as a drive to earn money for Disney and its shareholders, as both innovation and monetization are longstanding forces within Disney operations.

Disney's animation, films, parks, merchandising, and corporate culture blend authenticity with simulation.[5] Animation lies at the heart of authenticity and simulation, and this has been part of Disney's oeuvre for 100 years.[6] Animated films are not composed of "real" people—and yet, in some ways, those characters are fully authentic in their human experiences; after all, the term "animate" comes from the Latin verb *animare*, which means "to instill with life" or "to make alive."[7] This ability to bring "life" to millions of hand-drawn images is how Disney has amassed a catalog of literally thousands of beloved animated characters. And Disney specifically discusses simulation when talking about its animation processes. For instance, on a Walt Disney Animation Studios webpage titled "Simulation," readers learn about "a suite of advanced physically-based simulation systems" that help bring characters like Moana and Raya to life.[8] Walt Disney Animation Studios likewise explains its "novel snow simulation method" to depict the complicated phenomena of snow's movement.[9] Disney appears to be indicating that "simulation" is tied to a form of next-generation animation endeavors, and that the future will represent what can be done—that is, what can be simulated—with advanced technology and software.

Disney films include examples of the tension between authenticity and simulation. Disney's protagonists are known for struggling to find themselves and gain acceptance for who they truly are. This is particularly true of characters from the Disney Renaissance onward; think of Ariel, Aladdin, Moana, Mulan, Hercules, and Mirabel, to name but a few. These characters' identity quests parallel the emotional milieu of the time the films were released and mirror changing understandings about self that have been felt society-wide. Characters struggle with who they think they should be as opposed to who they really are. In displaying that struggle, viewers are able to entertain the possibility that what happened just might be authentic, and thus possible.

Disney draws on and fulfills the personal fantasy (wish, need) that we can improve ourselves, be who we really are meant to be, and attain perfect happiness (all within ninety minutes!). In presenting narratives that capture common sentiments and feelings, Disney films have an air of authenticity through the act of simulation. The degree to which certain princesses or villains resonate with people is testament to their success in this regard. So many of us can relate to Ariel's feeling of wanting something more, Peter Pan's refusal to grow up, Mulan's desire to be accepted for who she is rather than who others want her to be. Disney's themes are grounded in reality, even if the artistry that brings the films to life is grounded in simulation. The tension between authenticity and simulation is by design within Disney films. In fact, we might go as far as to say that Disney makes a genre promise or contract with its consumers: viewers are willing to suspend disbelief in exchange for the ability to indulge in the belief or comfort that, at the end of the day, everything works out.[10]

The type of simulation technology available provides interesting opportunities for the evaluation of authenticity in the films. The live-animation versions of films, using real actors, may serve to make the simulation feel more real and, as such, may be even more effective at fulfilling the wish or need. For others, the live-animation versions of films are too authentic and thus inadvertently alienate viewers who rely on the nostalgia of the original films to achieve a sense of authentic wish fulfillment.[11] Consider the conditions that make it easier to suspend disbelief and engage with the simulated as authentic. For example, is it easier to suspend disbelief if characters are animated and not flesh and blood? Readers are invited to consider, too, how Disney films originally had more of a self-proclaimed focus on the educational and how authenticity and simulation have been enacted differently across the development of Disney films, from the educational to the fantastical.[12]

Disney parks also recreate the real, by constructing replicas of places and presenting educational exhibitions, and create a feeling of realness in language, interactions, and settings that make it easy to imagine that the fabricated is reality.[13] The examples of this within the parks are endless—from exquisitely crafted structures made with great attention to detail, to themed dining with foods that align with the setting, to interactions and exchanges with cast members that are central to the authenticity of the experience for guests. Within the park setting, Walt Disney's use of animatronics introduced characters that move and sound believable—and seem real.[14] Consider, further, EPCOT's World Showcase, a simulation of places from around the world that has been designed to feel as authentic as possible. Imagineering strategically creates a feeling that what guests are experiencing is like the real, yet better. ("Better" in that the setting is reliably clean, safe, has bathrooms just a short walk away, and requires no lengthy or expensive international flights). Yet, World Showcase's countries cannot actually be authentic, because Disney representations are composites of places.[15] Various regions of EPCOT's countries are placed side-by-side yet maintain a feeling of "authenticity" as a whole through sightlines that blend scenes and maintain a cohesive aesthetic. Some visitors can be so compelled by the efficacy of the simulation that they lose the desire to see the authentic. As marketing scholars H. Rika Houston and Laurie A. Meamber write:

> Some nearby guests declared that by "traveling around the world" at EPCOT's World Showcase, it would no longer be necessary to actually travel around the (real) world. The perceived cultural authenticity of the pavilions at EPCOT World Showcase, it seems, was not only embraced without question, but also acknowledged as an adequate cultural proxy for visiting the selected countries. We [as Disney scholars] were dismayed by the audacity of this possibility.[16]

Architects have been encouraged to visit Disney parks for inspiration alongside European (authentic) monuments.[17] Within the Magic Kingdom, Main Street, U.S.A. is a version of Marceline, Missouri, that never actually existed but that Walt wished had: "sanitized memories of an America that never was but that many wish would be again."[18] The simulated inspires the real as city planners reference Main Street, U.S.A. as the exemplary Main Street, ideas at the heart of Bethanee Bemis's chapter in this section.[19]

The lands themselves connect to our authentic wishes and need to understand our past, present, and future. Frontierland, Main Street, U.S.A., Adventureland, and Liberty Square (at Walt Disney World) can be interpreted as offering connections to what was, Tomorrowland to what could be, and Fantasyland to what we wish was. In fact, all of these lands are simulations of "what we wish was." Guests expect Disney parks to simulate places where nothing can go wrong and that uphold the authentic need of guests (I might argue *adult* guests) for the Disney way to be true. The inability to deliver on this longing was tragically revealed in a 2015 incident at the Grand Floridian, when a child playing at the edge of Seven Seas Lagoon was attacked and killed by an alligator. Disney was under scrutiny for the fact that the incident occurred on Disney property, the implication being that Disney should have had the ability to control nature.[20] Disney is expected to offer a safe environment, and visitors have agreed to engage in the suspension of disbelief until they leave. The alligator incident breached the contract Disney purports to give to its visitors and audiences. That seismic event shifted the idea that nothing bad can happen at Disney. Likewise, there is lore that nobody dies at Disney—which of course is inaccurate in a place of that size where injuries and fatalities are inevitable amid the heat and thrills of the attractions.[21] The Disney "bubble" feels like a place of perfection where it is easy for parkgoers to ignore reality, including the realities of the surrounding area and the impact of the parks on the broader community.[22]

Disney understands and delivers on authentic wishes and needs held by children and adults alike. Disney is curated as the go-to destination for the pursuit of joy, a testament to its fulfilling of an authentic longing. Perhaps unsurprisingly, a visit to a theme park is the most popular request of children participating in the Make-A-Wish Foundation program, made by more than 40 percent of those children.[23] Adults have been inundated with the idea that Disney is not only the place parents should take their children, but the place adults should want to go. ("I'm going to Disney World!" proclaimed with [simulated] enthusiasm after Super Bowl victories is one example.[24]) Disney has been constructed and sold to children and adults as the penultimate example of celebration. So for those of us who wish to experience celebration (or even perform or simulate celebration), Disney is the place to go.

Disney's allure connects to the authentic wish, longing, and perhaps even need for an easier time and way. Social media has helped popularize the idea of Disney as a place for when you are done "adulting." Walking around Disney's American parks, you will likely see many adults donning garments that indicate that they have shunned the responsibilities of adulthood. This reflects an authentic and very real desire for a simplicity of sorts, and Disney's efforts at the intersection of authenticity and simulation speak to this human urge to imagine an easier reality. Disney's corporate efforts have leaned into this longing with products and experiences targeting such sentiment.[25]

Within its merchandising and corporate culture, too, we can see the intersections of authenticity and simulation.[26] In merchandise and games, Disney helps to generate authentic experiences, even amid simulated stories. Take costuming as one strong example: princess dresses, shoes, and tiaras allow wearers to pretend to be something they are not. The costumes, offered at various price points of course, allow wearers to see themselves as royalty. And there is something for everyone, children and adults alike. The ears worn by parkgoers have expanded well beyond the basic Mickey ears of the Mickey Mouse Club, with Minnie Mouse headbands ubiquitous and available in almost every possible character style. Disney fans can engage in games and quests that deepen their sense of belonging with Disney.

For Disney employees, the interplay of authenticity and simulation is evident in the fact that the operations of Disney (its films, its parks, its corporate activities) may be made to feel like a simulation of labor (through labels like "imagineer" and "cast member"), but require authentic labor.[27] Corporate expectations for employees require an upholding of the Disney brand and ways. Cast members within Disney parks and resorts are tasked with laboring to make the simulation feel authentic for guests. Cast members achieve this through language and interaction styles that align with the setting. Even in less themed areas, cast members make the simulation more authentic for guests by interacting in ways that match the suspension of disbelief, or the feeling of the place. A cast member witnessing a fallen ice cream will rush over to replace it: nothing bad happens here.

To understand the interplay between Disney's use of authenticity and simulation, one need only consider the Disney enterprise in the absence of each aspect of the dialectical pairing. In terms of films, it seems less important that films be authentic in terms of matching reality, but more important that they be authentic to the Disney construct. A film more representative of human experience—with characters who do not recover from major loss or find a way out of their struggles—would be off-brand.[28] Take, for example, the pushback to Bing Bong dying in the Disney film *Inside Out*. Bing Bong's death violates the Disney narrative that everyone's dreams can come true.[29] Yet, if Disney did just simulation, if Disney didn't reflect any of the messiness of reality, consumers would likewise be dissatisfied.

Looking at Disney's physical spaces, Disney parks in the absence of simulation would be more like a museum (even though museums are, of course, curated).[30] Visitors expect museums to be as factual as possible, and while they can rely on stories, they are expected to not indulge fantasy or simulation, which is at the heart of Disney. Yet, Disney parks that were simulation only, that didn't pull on the heartstrings, the possibility of "what if this is real," would be significantly less compelling (and, in fact, would have lost the essence of what distinguishes Disney from other theme parks). The magic is truly in the mix of groundedness and fantasy that extends not only to Disney's films and parks, but even it seems to its corporate operations.

In teaching my course, Happiest Place: The Science of Happiness at Disney, I unpack the ways that Disney creates, curates, and sells happiness while inviting students to suspend disbelief and critical analysis and appreciate the world that Disney offers. There is a degree of self-deception in this practice of suspending disbelief. Critics of

Disney might say, "It's so fake!" Yet what this criticism fails to take into account is that *constructed* or *curated* is different from being fake, and that built environments like those created at/by Disney contain, by design, enormous amounts of authenticity, even amid the technical savvy that purports to bring visitors to new worlds (Pandora, Batuu, even the American Frontier).[31] The application of new technologies will continue to shape the story of how Disney toggles between authenticity and simulation.

Our contributors can help us think more deeply about this dialectical pairing. To begin, we have public historian Bethanee Bemis's chapter, "From Magic to Memory: How the Physical Experiences of the Disney Parks Contribute to Historical Memory and Learning What It Means to Be an American." Here, by focusing primarily on Magic Kingdom's Main Street, U.S.A., Bemis invites the reader to consider how Disney creates and conveys a historical memory through its parks. Bemis highlights the ways in which the actual design and physical structure of the parks contributes to this memory. In this way, Disney is using a simulation of the real as a way to create narrative.

Walt Disney attempted not only to entertain but to educate, and he sought to transmit meaningful and important information about the real and inarguably authentic, including nature. Sarah Nilsen, a scholar of film and television studies, describes this history in "True-Life Adventures: Walt Disney and the Modern Environmental Movement." Nilsen places Disney's *True-Life Adventures* documentary series within the twentieth-century environmental movement, thereby revealing Walt Disney to be a conservationist. He did not work solely in the fantasy realm, but found his love for animals motivating him to use authentic footage for the documentary films. In so doing, he shaped generations of Americans' values toward the natural world.

Lucy Buck comes next with "Urban NDNs and the House of Mouse: A Journey of Education and Self-Discovery." Buck comes to this material as a recent college graduate who is rethinking Disney, self, and American culture as a result of his education.[32] Buck reveals how his Indigenous identity has forced him to exist within this tension between authenticity and simulation—and how Disney has exacerbated that tension. Examining his Indigeneity through both his education and his life experiences, Buck shares, with deep personal reflection, discomfort in supporting a company "that barely cares about [his] story" while also recognizing some of Disney's positive efforts. Certainly Buck's analysis can extend to other underrepresented groups who experience real and lived consequences of Disney's misrepresentation and failure to achieve authenticity.

In the final chapter of this section, Jenny Banh, a scholar of Asian American studies and anthropology, presents "Asian Disneyland, Local Community Reactions, and the Role of Cultural Spaces." The reader is taken out of the American context and into the three Asian Disney parks: Tokyo Disney Resort, Hong Kong Disneyland, and Shanghai Disneyland. Banh briefly traces the history and development of each park, then takes readers on a journey to explore and understand the non-Disney Asian parks. How do these parks compare to their American versions, and what can we learn about authenticity and simulation when looking at the social, cultural, and historical underpinnings of the Asian parks? Readers may find themselves asking, Are Asian parks a simulation of American parks, and what makes for an "authentically Asian" park?

When we walk down Main Street, U.S.A. and long for that place, or watch a film in which everything ends favorably, or dream about (inaccurately) what it is like to be an "Imagineer," many of us experience longing. Those ideals are simulations, even though the emotional appeal of them is not. Disney taps into feelings that are authentic, that resonate as aspiration. Disney connects to our authentic longing for a past that may or may not have occurred and a future that may or may not be possible. Through its strategically designed and implemented actions, Disney creates magic through its authenticity and its simulation. The interplay between authenticity and simulation is central to Disney's success and to the story Disney is telling: no matter who you are, your dreams can come true. As Disney embarks on the future—a technologically advanced future in which the ability to simulate authenticity will only expand—we are left with a question: How does Disney artistically create connection and believability for its consumers with the technical tools available? The means have changed and will continue to change, but I expect that the simulated authenticity Disney offers will continue to be central to its operations and its appeal.

Notes

1 "Suspension of disbelief," a phrase coined in 1817 by English poet and philosopher Samuel Taylor Coleridge, captures the idea of willingness to disregard logic and reason and just surrender oneself to believing something that is otherwise implausible. While I am unaware of any writings that link Coleridge to Walt Disney or Disney functioning, it seems to me the most apt description for what Disney requires that we do in order to have the full Disney experience.

2 For a review of authenticity research, see Phillip Vannini and Alexis T. Franzese, "The Authenticity of Self: Conceptualization, Personal Experience, and Practice," *Sociology Compass* 2 (2008): 1621–37 and Alexis T. Franzese, "Authenticity: Perspectives and Experiences," in *Authenticity in Culture, Self and Society*, ed. P. Vannini and J. P. Williams (London: Ashgate, 2009), 87–101.

3 Studies of authenticity in tourism are plentiful. See Ning, "Rethinking Authenticity in Tourism Experience," in Annals of Tourism Research 26, no. 2 (1999) and John P. Taylor, "Authenticity and Sincerity in Tourism," *Annals of Tourism Research* 28, no. 1 (2001): 7–26.

4 While the text was first published in 1981, I rely on a 1994 translation of the text of Jean Baudrillard. *Simulacra and Simulation*, trans. Sheila Glaser (Ann Arbor: University of Michigan Press). See also Alexander Hoffman's Chapter 11 in this volume for more on Baudrillard.

5 See Dean MacCannell, "Staged Authenticity: Arrangements of Social Space in Tourist Settings," *American Journal of Sociology* 79, no. 3 (1973): 589–603. While Disney is not the focus of the article, Disneyland is indeed named and I consider this article the first to address the topic of authenticity at Disney. Stephen F. Mills' "Disney and the Promotions of Synthetic Worlds," *American Studies International* 28, no. 2 (1990): 66–79, is a critical publication in this area of study. A more recent take on staged authenticity is Deepak Chhabra, Robin Healy, and Erin Sills, "Staged

Authenticity and Heritage Tourism," *Annals of Tourism Research* 30, no. 3 (2003): 702–19.

6 Interested readers may enjoy Frank Thomas and Ollie Johnson, *The Illusion of Life: Disney Animation* (New York: Hyperion, 1997). Note, too, that akin to more recent criticisms of Disney products, accusations of inauthenticity did plague Walt Disney's early work with animation. Specifically, critics doubted Walt's desire to make full-length animated films, and people doubted the medium he used to tell stories for children and adults alike.

7 Merriam-Webster s.v "animate," https://www.merriam-webster.com/dictionary/animate.

8 Walt Disney Animation Studios, "Filmmaking Process: Simulation," November 1, 2024, https://disneyanimation.com/process/simulation/.

9 See Walt Disney Animation Studios, "Tech Project: Matterhorn," November 1, 2024, https://www.disneyanimation.com/publications/a-material-point-method-for-snow-simulation/ and https://disneyanimation.com/technology/matterhorn/.

10 The comfort and reassurance offered by the park design has been discussed within Karal Ann Marling, ed., *Designing Disney's Theme Parks: The Architecture of Reassurance* (Paris: Flammarion, 1997).

11 See, for example, Bonnie Rudner's discussion of *The Little Mermaid* in Chapter 9.

12 Walt Disney, "Mickey as Professor," *The Public Opinion Quarterly* 9, no. 2 (1945): 119–25.

13 Amanda Koontz, "Constructing Authenticity: A Review of Trends and Influences in the Process of Authentication in Consumption," *Sociology Compass* 4 (2010): 977–88. According to Koontz people have metrics for evaluating authenticity. For example, "consumers judge marketers' attempts to construct a nostalgic sense of the past in comparison to their own preconceptions," 985.

14 Described in the section opening for "Nostalgia and Innovation" in this volume.

15 An enlightening conversation with my university colleague Dr. Scott Windham, Associate Professor of German in the Department of World Languages and Cultures at Elon University, revealed this clearly as Dr. Windham named the actual spatial distances of the regions/areas depicted in the Germany pavilion of EPCOT's World Showcase.

16 Pp. 181–2 in H. Rika Houston and Laurie A. Meamber, "Consuming the 'World'": Reflexivity, Aesthetics, and Authenticity at Disney World's EPCOT Center," *Consumption Markets and Culture* 14, no. 2 (2011): 177–91.

17 See this suggestion described in Margaret J. King, "Disneyland and Walt Disney World: Traditional Values in Futuristic Form," *The Journal of Popular Culture* 15, no. 1 (1981): 116–40.

18 Virginia A. Salamone and Frank A. Salamone, "Images of Main Street: Disney World and the American Adventure," *Journal of American Culture*, 22, no. 1 (1999): 85–92.

19 Margaret J. King, "The Theme Park: Aspects of Experience in a Four-Dimensional Landscape," *Material Culture* 34, no. 2 (2002): 1–15. Also cited within King (2002) is Richard F. Snow, "Disney: Coast to Coast," *American Heritage* 38, no. 2 (1987): 22–4.

20 The idea that Disney should be able to control nature is put forth by Chris Wright, "Natural and Social Order at Walt Disney World: The Functions and Contradictions of Civilising Nature," *Sociological Review* 54, no. 2 (2006): 303–17.

21   The motivations for ensuring that death does not occur at Disney may be in part to avoid bad publicity, but I believe also reflect a desire on Disney's part to allow parkgoers to fully engage in fantasy and suspend disbelief, reinforcing the view that Disney is essentially too happy a place for death.

22   See Kevin Archer, "The Limits to the Imagineered City: Sociospatial Polarization in Orlando," *Economic Geography* 73, no. 3 (1997): 322–36.

23   Make-a-Wish Foundation USA 2019 fact sheet, https://wish.org/sites/default/files /2019-08/2019%20Fact%20Sheet.pdf.

24   This campaign was launched by Michael Eisner (with his wife credited for the idea) and involves winners of the Super Bowl, often the quarterback or star player, declaring that they are "going to Disney World," as Phil Simms first announced in 1987 (and again in 1991). This continued with Tom Brady and Rob Gronkowski proclaiming they were "going to Disney World" in 2021. Many of these videos can be viewed on the YouTube platform, accessed with a simple search of "Going to Disney Super Bowl video."

25   See, for example, Disney travel advertising that boasts of "special magic created just for adults" (https://www.disneyholidays.co.uk/walt-disney-world/cruise-and-stay/just -for-adults).

26   See Chavez (Chapter 12) for more on Disney merchandising and gamification.

27   See the section introduction for "Leisure and Labor," which appears later in this volume.

28   While outside the scope of this section introduction, this tension between authenticity and simulation undoubtedly relates to the strong societal response to the idea of Disney "going woke," as such actions may be considered a deviation from the Disney way.

29   Online discussion boards and articles in a variety of sources address this topic. See, for example, Nina Terrero, "'Inside Out': Bing Bong Scene Was Supposed to Be Even Sadder," *Entertainment Weekly* online, November 3, 2015.

30   See Jan Penrose, "Authenticity, Authentication and Experiential Authenticity: Telling Stories in Museums," *Social and Cultural Geography* 21, no. 9 (2018): 1245–67.

31   Author Josef Chytry offers consideration of such built environments in two 2012 publications: "Walt Disney and the Creation of Emotional Environments: Interpreting Walt Disney's Oeuvre from the Disney Studios to Disneyland, CalArts, and the Experimental Prototype Community of Tomorrow (EPCOT)," *Rethinking History* 16, no. 2 (2012): 259–78, and "Disney's Design," *Boom: A Journal of California* 2, no. 1 (2012): 33–44.

32   Buck's chapter is a unique one in this volume and emerged serendipitously (and with a good amount of pixie dust) when we learned that the planned chapter on related topics would not be completed.

5

From Magic to Memory

How the Physical Experiences of the Disney Parks Contribute to Historical Memory and Learning What It Means to Be an American

Bethanee Bemis

There is no cultural memory without individual memory. There is no individual memory without the senses, as senses mediate our experience of the physical world.[1] In my work as a museum specialist, I strive to engage the senses in museum exhibits and experiences because I know that makes what one learns through them more memorable. Museum educators know from visitor testing, for instance, that offering a tactile model of an object guests can feel will be more of an impactful experience than simply viewing that object in the case. But beyond places created explicitly for learning, such as museums, few spaces cater so carefully to ensuring that their guests have a multi-sensory experience than the Disney theme parks. The attention to detail Imagineers (those who conceive and build the Disney parks) exert is second to none, and you can be sure that whatever you are touching, tasting, smelling, hearing, or seeing at a Disney theme park has been carefully thought about and deliberately chosen to simulate authenticity. This is one of the founding principles of Disney parks. As Imagineer John Hench said, "Walt [Disney] knew that if details are missing or incorrect, you won't believe in the story. If one detail contradicts another, guests will feel let down or even deceived."[2] Yet the details of one's sensory experiences at Disney parks have less to do with historical fact than with creating the experience of an ideal: an ideal America as understood by Disney. The things that you feel, eat, smell, and hear on your Disney trip are crafted in such a way that they don't just create a pleasant experience but lasting memories of certain American ideas and ideals that inform how you think about America today.

While Walt mandated that what you saw, smelled, heard, felt, and even tasted must all contribute to the immersive environment without removing you from "the story," he didn't mandate that every sense experience be historically accurate. While it was important to Walt, for instance, that the vehicles going up and down Main Street, U.S.A. be as historically accurate in their visual details as possible, it was also important to Walt that the manure that was a natural fact of life for the horses pulling the Main Street trolley not be seen nor smelled. It is here where the sense memories—that is, how we "remember" a space feeling, tasting, smelling, or sounding—of a turn-of-the-century American small town differ from that experienced in Walt's Magic Kingdom. Yet in part because of the meticulous attention given to other sensory details on Main Street (Walt insisting that the houses on Main Street have real wrought iron railings at their uppermost levels rather than the more cost-effective plastic, for instance), and in part because of the lasting power of these sense-based memories, it is Disney's version of Main Street that looms large in the American imagination today.[3] This chapter explores the impact of sense memory at Disney theme parks on Americans' historical memory.

The ways in which the Disney parks engage our senses is key to how they create such long-lasting and impactful individual memories that, in turn, become shared memories across time and space. Yet the types of sense memories we experience at Disney can also influence how we remember certain historical events or time periods that Disney parks have been inspired by or recreate. Having a multisensory "experience" of a turn-of-the-century American small town is much more memorable than reading about it in a textbook—even if the textbook is more historically accurate. The built environment's sensory engagement allows the visitor to establish a sense of their own self in a place, both physically and temporally, by creating what memory researchers call "secondary memory," or what the layman often calls "long-term memory."[4] Primary or short-term memory comes from anything actively under consideration, but it can be fleeting.[5] Think of all the times you crammed for a test in school. How much of that information can you recall now? You may have aced your test, but the majority of the information wasn't inscribed in the part of your brain that carries that information throughout your life. You may, however, remember the anxiety you felt leading up to tests, or the taste of the gum you always chewed while studying. That background information remains with you.

Let's choose a Disney Parks example to use throughout this chapter. Specifically, let's take a walk down Main Street, U.S.A. A balloon vendor comes into view, and your child immediately asks for one. Your brain begins running through all the factors that will help you make the decision to say yes or no: what does the balloon cost? How will we carry it? Can I take it on the plane home? What are the chances it pops, leaving me with a devastated child? These questions, under active consideration, will for a short time be top of mind when you look at the balloon after you inevitably purchase it. "That balloon costs $15," you think. "Make sure it's tied on tight, so we don't lose it." Meanwhile, as the active part of your brain helped you to make the decision of whether to purchase the balloon, your senses were taking in information from the cues around you that you might not have noticed at the time: a secondary memory of the experience. Rusiko Bourtchouladze, a pioneer of behavioral genetic research, calls this "the knowledge of an event, or fact, of which we have not been thinking," or "memory without remembering."[6] What is learned during these moments, without a conscious effort of doing so, is remembered long after the experience itself.

While you were consciously deliberating about your balloon purchase, your senses were still unconsciously taking in information about the space around you, mediating the experience for your memory. Everything you are touching is helping you to establish a "sentient border with the world."[7] The feet take in the ground on which one stands. On Main Street, this could be the tarmac of the road surface, the concrete sidewalk, or perhaps most memorably, the tracks for the trolley car that runs up and down the street (which in my experience have taken down many an unsuspecting guest). You might be touching a family member, a stroller handle, or your phone. Your skin registers the weather, either that of Southern California for Disneyland guests or Florida for those at Walt Disney World. In your peripheral vision, people dash by, hurriedly on their way to nowhere in particular. You hear their conversations, and perhaps too the whistle of the train and the clanging of the trolley car making its way past. You might even smell the scent of baked goods and sugar wafting from the confectionary, or coffee from the nearby Starbucks, smells you associate with the taste of those foods and beverages. Handing the balloon to your child, your whole body registers their pure joy, and indeed it is the emotion present in that moment that is ultimately associated with all these sense memories that seals the moment in your synapses. The brain links emotion and memory strongly, transferring sometimes "meaningless stimuli" into "meaningful cues," binding them "into one meaningful context"—in this case, a memory of Disney's Main Street, U.S.A.[8]

Because this is the only experiential referent you have of this "time" and place (or one of perhaps a few, if you frequent historically themed spaces), these physical memories you've developed of Main Street now make up the strongest association in your brain with a turn-of-the-century American small town. Professor of Anthropology C. Nadia Seremetakis calls sense memory "a culturally mediated material practice" that becomes "a temporal conduit."[9] In the case of a visit to the Disney Parks, your memories are not just a temporal conduit to your vacation but to the time and place depicted in the themed space as mediated for you by Disney and the dominant cultural understandings of the time in which the spaces were built. Walt Disney and his Imagineers, probably unconsciously, were (and are) shaping park guests' memories of a version of an American Main Street that never really existed, but in which they deeply believed.

Social and economic turmoil in the times spanning First and Second World Wars led to a romanticizing of the American small town in the national consciousness as an ideal time, when the town was "a refuge of community, a place where people who knew each other live[d] in a localized, entrepreneurial, organic society" that was essentially the opposite of modern urban life.[10] The Midwestern small town in particular took on meaning as being *the* American heartland; it "became metropolitan America's hometown" as Americans increasingly moved to urban centers in search of economic opportunities (and indeed, 1920 was the first year in which more Americans lived in cities than in rural areas).[11] Katherine Fry, a professor of media studies, describes the Midwest in American imagination as a "vernacular" space, with no "'clearly marked political' boundary," the perfect canvas on which to ascribe values that the creator might assume to be, or wish are, universal rather than the purview of one particular political party.[12] In tying even urban citizens back to this imaginary small town, Americans pointed to it as the place that established what it meant to be an American, making the idealized touchstone of the small town incredibly important in American identity. The foundation of Main Street, U.S.A. therefore, isn't really in historical main streets at all, but in the ways in which Americans of later time periods wanted to remember early main streets.

Walt Disney himself could legitimately tie his personal narrative back to a small, Midwestern town: that of Marceline, Missouri, where he spent several years in his youth (though not, it should be noted, where he was born or even spent the majority of his childhood). This small-town nostalgia became a strong piece of his public identity. Disenchanted with urban life and yet inextricably tied to it, he often referenced his small-town roots in ways designed to connect himself to the American values of optimism, free enterprise, and community that dominated popular conception of the turn-of-the-century Main Street during Walt's lifetime. Walt spoke of Marceline as his hometown all his life, famously writing, "to tell the truth, more things of importance happened to me in Marceline than have happened since—or are likely to in the future . . . I'm glad I'm a small town boy."[13] He described Main Street, U.S.A. in terms that connected it both to himself and a larger American community:

> Many of us fondly remember our "small home town" and its friendly way of life at the turn of the century. To me, this era represents an important part of our heritage, and thus we have endeavored to recapture those years on Main Street U.S.A. at Disneyland. Here is the America of 1890-1910, at the cross-roads of an era . . . Main Street represents the typical small town in the early 1900s-the heartline of America.[14]

Walt only tended to recall the pleasant memories of his time in Marceline—his first circus parade, arriving on the train and riding to his home "just outside the city limits," the farmyard animals being "a big thrill." His recreated Main Street, keeping with the dominant culture of the 1950s in which it was built that seemed, in the words of Mike Wallace, "determined to come up with a happy past to match its contented present," only recreated the most pleasant experiences associated with the now distant reality.[15]

Cities, even small ones, are generally places filled with what architect Robert Venturi dubbed "messy vitality," a cacophony of sensory cues that are sometimes at odds with one another but which add up to what we could term a vibrant yet "messy reality."[16] Because Walt's "meticulous attention to period detail did not extend to the unpleasant," he sought to leave in the past some of the sensory experiences from Main Street, U.S.A. that might have clashed with the storyline and overall pleasant feeling of his imaginary town.

Disney wasn't the first to romanticize Main Street; Americans had already been doing that for years. What Disney did was attach that romanticized ideal to a physical place filled with sense memories. Disney visits have shaped how we as a culture reproduce the idea of any nineteenth-century American Main Street. A comparative walk down Disney's Main Street alongside some historical realities of the real small towns that inspired it will illuminate some of the differences in the sense memories generated by those places. These differences show us what Disney is communicating about American values through mediated experiences. Let's take a look at some of those differences on an imaginary walk right down the middle of Main Street, U.S.A.

All visits to Walt Disney World's Magic Kingdom or Disneyland Park begin with a walk up to and under the train station for Main Street, U.S.A. The train station not only provides a practical way to funnel guests out of "today" and into "yesterday" by forming a berm through which guests must pass to enter, but it also sets the stage for the primary message of Main Street: Americans thrive on free enterprise. The railroad isn't just an entrance into a Disney fantasy: it stands as a symbol of economic growth and possibility for turn-of-the-century small-town Main Streets.[17]

What the guest sees on entering Disney's Main Street is Victorian-inspired architecture, where buildings' fanciful facades are designed to be in perfect harmony. At the terminus of the street as one enters is the town center, evoking a ceremonial gathering space with a flagpole, benches, and greenery. To one side of the entrance is the town hall and fire house; on the other, an opera house. Walking along the street, one passes a cinema, a penny arcade, a general store/emporium, a clothier, a bakery, and a soda shop. While today every shop along Main Street on both coasts sells Disney merchandise, consumables, or Starbucks coffee, when Disneyland first opened, many of the stores were individually leased to vendors whose wares themselves evoked the needs of small-town life: a bank, a tobacco shop, a "dry goods" store, a pharmacy, a candle store, a jellies and jams store, an intimate apparel store, and a china and glass shop. At the far end of the street rises a castle (Cinderella's or Sleeping Beauty's, depending on the location) directly behind what is known as the "hub," another ceremonial center offering communal space. The overall sense is one of a prosperous community engaged happily in capitalism, an idea that Walt Disney was happy to promote, having greatly benefited from American capitalism himself.

The smells and tastes associated with Main Street can best be summed up as "sweet." While there are restaurants that offer savory fare, the majority of the food for sale in this land is sugar-based: confectionary, bakery goods, and ice cream top the billing, though buttered popcorn is also high on the list of both scents and desired snacks. The scent of Main Street consists mostly of sugar, vanilla, and cinnamon. These aromas don't come solely from the bakery on the street; they are enhanced by scent machines the Disney community has dubbed "smellitzers." Certain desired smells are pushed into the environment on Main Street and beyond via pressurized air. Disney has even patented what they call "scent-blending," which is a way to strategically release scents so that they are timed with other sense cues to create a maximum congruity of experience.[18]

The sounds of Main Street both create and elicit fond memories in the unique setting of Disney. Beyond the general ruckus of families and the shouts of children, background music loops play in every Disney land. The musical selections, like the scents, are made to enhance the immersive environment and result in the formation of an associative memory. Main Street's music consists of ragtime and swing, along with versions of classic, well-known Disney tunes arranged in turn-of-the-century musical styles. Main Street also plays the most frequent host to live music of any land in the Magic Kingdom, with groups such as the Dapper Dans (a barbershop quartet) singing "Yankee Doodle Dandy," the Main Street Philharmonic (a marching band) proudly playing "Take Me Out to the Ball Game," and a ragtime pianist at Casey's Corner restaurant banging out "Maple Leaf Rag." High school marching bands from small and not-so-small towns across the United States can frequently be found giving a performance. For many guests, this music may only be experienced on Main Street, U.S.A. as it isn't prevalent in current American culture unless actively sought out (when is the last time you heard "In the Good Old Summertime" playing in a public space?). Guests may or may not enter Main Street already knowing that this music represents American popular culture of the early 1900s, but they will leave Main Street with a secondary memory associating it with Disney's version of America in the early 1900s. Other sounds worth noting amid the unique Main Street soundscape are the train whistle and the playing of the "Star-Spangled Banner" and "Retreat" at the daily lowering of the American flag in the center square.

The tactile experiences on Main Street vary widely. There is, of course, the exchange of goods for currency, as in our earlier balloon scenario. The literal and metaphorical rubbing of shoulders with a diverse array of other guests. The hot sidewalk and tarmac where guests sit and wait for a parade or fireworks. Along the street, visitors can converse with the costumed "Citizens of Main Street." The Citizens include a group of suffragists, a journalist, the mayor, a fire chief, and more, who function to make guests feel as if they are a member of the small turn-of-the-century town community themselves, lending a sense of authenticity to the "town." This sense of belonging and physical inclusion is not only important for immersion but also for the way it evokes the sense of the small-town population as "average citizens"—not elite politicians, wealthy bankers, or academics in ivory towers, but the "common man" so often vaunted by Walt Disney and others as the backbone of the nation.

Taken as a whole, the sensory experiences of Main Street, U.S.A. represent what has come to be known as the "Gay Nineties," a term for the idealized vision of the 1890s Americans began referring back to in the 1920s. They are not experiences and memories of an authentic 1890s Main Street, but rather representations of what Americans wanted to think America had been when Disney's experiences were conceived and created in the 1940s and 50s. The experiences instead represent a time in American idealized memory before the First World War, where towns were small enough to engender strong bonds of community, where patriotism went unquestioned, and where technology promised an ever-easier life. It was these ideals that Walt wanted to evoke with his Main Street.

In reality, in the words of architect and architectural historian Fred Koetter and Colin Rowe, "Main Street was never very pretty nor, probably, even very prosperous."[19] While Main Street, U.S.A. has its roots in turn-of-the-century American Midwestern towns, it isn't (as most of us know on an intellectual level) an exact replica of historical reality. Disney's Main Street is full of promises of prosperity: the train has just arrived, and the business owners on Main Street are excited to welcome new customers and, in turn, their own economic successes. The storefronts are shiny, new, and in tune with one another. In truth, lack of town regulations often meant the visual experience of Main Street was a hodgepodge of signage, telephone/telegraph wiring and buildings of different types all vying for your attention at once.[20] In "real" Main Street, U.S.A., some sensory experiences were physically unpleasant and were often associated with feelings of anxiety or loss—very different from the pleasant feelings engendered by Disney's Main Street.

The cheery whistle of the train, which at first brought excitement, eventually brought chain stores that drove the mom-and-pop shops out of business. "The Wells Fargo Wagon" (the delivery vehicle that would deliver a variety of goodies to one's home long before the Amazon truck) brings more joy as a song played on Main Street, U.S.A. today than what it actually represented for local shops in the past. The trains also brought immigrants from other towns and countries whose different backgrounds threatened the degree of social control that the predominantly American-born white middle class who built Main Street depended on to make sense of their own identities.[21] The central street that Disney keeps neat and tidy (and paved) would more likely have been made of dust or mud, depending on the weather, and, due to heavy reliance on horses and other livestock to move people and goods, resembled nothing so much as an "equine latrine," the scent of which I will leave to your imagination.[22]

Notably lacking on Disney's Main Street are two staples of historical community life: the church and the local bar. Given how ubiquitous these institutions were, it is clearly a deliberate choice on Disney's part not to have them represented. Walt Disney didn't want alcohol anywhere in his park because he felt it would lead to undesirable behaviors. He didn't put a church anywhere on Main Street because he didn't want to be seen as favoring any one denomination or religion, as this would emphasize division rather than harmony.[23] In each case, Walt sacrificed authenticity in favor of the ideals he was promoting.

Koetter and Roe note that the jumbled, incongruous realities of many historical main streets reflect an "almost frenzied effort . . . to provide stability to an unstable scene, to convert frontier flux into established community."[24] Historian Richard Francaviglia contends that the "true" Main Street experience required a large "expenditure of mental energy" between the place and the people experiencing it, to see optimism and hope amid disarray and dung. The true emotions evoked by Main Streets of the past would not have been as pleasant as those we feel on Main Street, U.S.A., but more akin to a feeling of "optimistic desperation."[25] This is precisely why the memory of Disney's pleasant Main Street sticks in our collective consciousness far beyond those that might be more factual. The sights, sounds, smells, tastes, and tactile experiences of Main Street have all been carefully selected to offer the guest a predictable, pleasant environment that allows them to expend minimal mental energy, to switch off the parts of their brain that are normally making sense of the details the senses are constantly taking in, flooding the brain with good feelings. Because the brain associates these cues with good feelings, they stick with us as secondary memories, and ultimately become the only memories we have of these historical representations.

Themed designer and former Disney Imagineer Joe Rohde describes the work of designing a space such as Main Street, U.S.A. as doing the work of putting the environment in tidy order for the visitor in a way that aligns not necessarily with fact, but with "narrative intention," what the creator wants the visitor to feel throughout the experience, both physically and emotionally.[26] On Main Street, Walt Disney wanted to evoke an American ideal of community, happiness, and prosperity through free enterprise. A street in which one sees, smells, and perhaps unfortunately feels, fetid horse feces evokes a much different association and accompanying emotion (not to mention very real health risks), and so Disney did not include those details. When visiting Disney parks, our brain doesn't need to do the work of reconciling a "good feeling" with a bad scent. On Main Street, free enterprise equals prosperity equals American small town equals the wafting scent of baked goods equals happiness.

According to Rohde, a space that successfully achieves that feeling of "structured complexity" toward a specific narrative fools the guest's brain into thinking it has done the work of making meaning of the signals it receives and rewards itself with a flood of good feelings.[27] As we saw at the beginning of this chapter, that flood of good feelings marks the experience in the brain as important and enhances our ability to remember it.[28] Main Street is the idealized version of our collective past on which we build our current identity precisely because it has engineered out unpleasant sense experiences. Through its harmonious sensory experiences, it becomes implanted in our individual and then collective consciousness, becoming the archetype for "the American Main Street." In the present day, Americans are most likely to recognize a place as a "Main Street" "by its ambience and the feeling it generates" much more than by any physical markers. That's the power of Disney's Main Street sense memories on our collective consciousness.[29]

We have seen how the sense memories of Main Street, U.S.A. create collective memories of a nonexistent past. A look at some of the ways those cues have changed over time will give insight into what purpose the space truly serves in the American experience.

In 2021, an update at Walt Disney World's Main Street confectionary added decorative panels and theming describing a fictitious "Sweetest Spoon Showcase" baking competition. The bakers that appear in signage around the shop are a diverse group, including the first (and as of early 2024, only) openly LGBTQ+ characters to appear at a Disney theme park: Saul Fitz and his partner, Gary Henderson; Dr. Alsoomse Tabor of the Blackfeet Nation; and Toshi Hayakawa, a firefighter who is known for his mochi.[30] This means that the sense memories of the confectionary, a place filled with colorful candies and treats, that smells like sugar and engenders feelings of anticipation, are associated not only with the images of the turn-of-the-century architecture but with a diverse group of people as well. A few months before the debut of the Sweetest Spoon bakers, Disney also updated its Main Street announcements, changing the beginning of the announcement from "Ladies and Gentlemen, Boys and Girls" to "Good evening, Dreamers of all ages" to promote gender inclusivity.[31] This alters the sense memory of the sounds of Main Street. Historically authentic songs now mingle in our memory with inclusive language. The additions of these images, stories, and sounds give the Disney visitor a broader image of peoples with which to populate their "memories" of American history than they may have held before, which in turn affects how they understand the America of today and tomorrow.

From a historical perspective, these changes would be inaccurate. Minorities in an American 1900s small town would not have had the resources to bake for fun nor would they have been allowed to compete in national competitions. Saul and Gary, while they may have been together at the turn of the century, would not be public about their relationship. While American Indians had long played a role in "unofficial" paleontology in the United States, it is highly unlikely Dr. Alsoomse Tabor would have been allowed to be both a university graduate and a leader in fieldwork.[32] Being both a woman and a person of Indigenous descent would have been a double barrier for Tabor: systemic bias and poverty, as well as cultural isolation, have led to American Indians making up less than one percent of all PhD recipients even in the last few years.[33] Asian Americans were largely seen as a threat to Western values at the turn of the century and relegated to their own communities on the outskirts of town, not welcomed to into the local fire hall.

Just as the Main Street of Walt's day was idealized and edited to speak to his current time, these edits bring Main Street's expression of ideals more in line with those of the present. These changes came right after the announcement of the addition of the "Inclusion Key" to Disney's "Four Keys" (now Five) list of guiding principles.[34] These principles (Inclusion, Safety, Courtesy, Show, and Efficiency) are what Imagineers consider in building Disney's themed worlds. "Historical accuracy" is not one of them. This means that while the cumulative effect of our sense memories of Disney's Main Street U.S.A. might be a collective memory of America's turn-of-the-century small towns, what Disney is showing us is actually much more reflective of what the company—compounded by the culture it operates in—values at the time the themed space is built. The Sweetest Spoon Showcase isn't teaching us about the history of American small towns, nor is it trying to. Rather, it's making a statement about who Disney and their consumers are including as part of their American identity *today*. The sense memories and experiences created on Main Street have *always* been crafted to express who America is (and who the creators hope it will be) than who it was. Because the physical experience created in the park has such deep and lasting power in our individual and collective memory, understanding its intended meaning is incredibly important. This is what Disney guests who wish to have an informed experience need to remember. Disney experiences are key to American identity—making not because they accurately show us who we *were*, but because they show us, and shape us into, who we *are*.

Your experience of Disney's turn-of-the-century town is not, clearly, the same experience someone had living in an actual American turn-of-the-century town. But that doesn't mean that it isn't valuable. Your memory, and the collective memory you share with others today of that past time, is reflective of what Walt Disney believed was the very best of the American spirit. Your memories are not factually accurate historically speaking, but they are no less important for what they communicate to you about American identity today. If we as consumers understand that (1) Disney visits hold immense power in our memories because of their curated, multisensory components working in tandem to bind positive emotion to our experience, and (2) those memories must be understood separately from actual historical events for what they are, not as facts of the past but as mediators of current values, we will be well-positioned to both enjoy our time at the Disney parks without fretting about what is "incorrect" and study what the Disney parks truly mean in American culture.

Notes

1   Public historians have been particularly keen to explore this idea in relation to historic sites and recreated sites, noting, according to historian Amy Levin, that at such physical locations "public history may be transformed into collective memory as visitors come to remember the experience of visiting the site rather than 'pure history.'" Media professor Scott Bukatman has written on how the physical movement within the space of a site, particularly Disney, transforms into "a simulated temporal trajectory," that is, a real sense of movement within time, a memory of an event that didn't exactly happen. Amy Levin, ed., *Defining Memory: Local Museums and the Construction of History in America's Changing Communities* (Lanham: AltaMira Press, 2007), 45 and Scott Bukatman, "There's Always Tomorrowland: Disney and the Hypercinematic Experience," *October* 57 (Summer 1991): 75–7. See also Richard Handler and Eric Gable, *The New History in an Old Museum: Creating the Past at Colonial Williamsburg* (Durham: Duke University Press, 1997).

2   Quoted in Chris Nichols, *Walt Disney's Disneyland* (Cologne: Taschen, 2020), 72.

3   Ibid., 58 and Bethanee Bemis, "How Disney Came to Define What Constitutes the American Experience," *Smithsonian Magazine*, January 3, 2017, https://www.smithsonianmag.com/history/how-disney-came-define-what-constitutes-american-experience-180961632/.

4   Nancy Brennan, "Interpretation in the Built Environment: New Opportunities for Museum Education," *Roundtable Reports* 4, no. 1 (1979): 12–15, 12. https://www.jstor.org/stable/40479476.

5   Rusiko Bourtchouladze, *Memories Are Made of This: How Memory Works in Humans and Animals* (New York: Columbia University Press, 2002), 14–15.

6   Ibid., 14–15, 37.

7   Elizabeth Harvey, "The Portal of Touch," *The American Historical Review* 116, no. 2 (April 2011): 385–400, 386, https://www.jstor.org/stable/23307702.

8   Bourtchouladze, *Memories*, 77.

9   Anna Harris, "Eliciting Sound Memories," *The Public Historian* 37, no. 4 (November 2015): 14–21, 19, https://www.jstor.org/stable/10.1525/tph.2015.37.4.14.

10   Timothy R. Mahoney, "The Small City in American History," *Indiana Magazine of History* 99, no. 4 (December 2003): 311–30, 313.

11   Ibid., 317.

12   Sheila Webb, "A Pictorial Myth in the Pages of 'Life': Small-Town America as the Ideal Place," *Studies in Popular Culture* 28, no. 3 (April 2006): 35–58, 44, https://www.jstor.org/stable/23416170.

13   Walt Disney, "The Marceline I Knew," *The Marceline News and the Bucklin Herald*, September 2, 1938.

14   Walt Disney quoted in Steven Watts, *The Magic Kingdom: Walt Disney and the American Way of Life* (Columbia: University of Missouri Press, 1997), 22.

15 Disney, "The Marceline," and Mike Wallace, *Mickey Mouse History and Other Essays on American Memory* (Philadelphia: Temple University Press, 1996), 137.

16 Nichols, *Walt Disney's*, 63.

17 There are, of course, many, many sense experiences to be had at any given place and time in a Disney Park. I have selected only a few of those that are most relevant here for brevity. Much of this sensory walk-through is adapted from Bethanee Bemis, *Disney Theme Parks and America's National Narratives: Mirror, Mirror for Us All* (New York: Routledge, 2023), 40–3.

18 Rose Schnabel, "Disney Demystified: The Science of Magic," *SciIU*, November 13, 2021, https://blogs.iu.edu/sciu/2021/11/13/disney-demystified/.

19 Richard Francaviglia, "Main Street, U.S.A.: A Comparison/Contrast of Streetscapes in Disneyland and Walt Disney World," *The Journal of Popular Culture* 15, Issue 1 (Summer 1981): 141–56, 145.

20 Ibid., 144.

21 Mahoney, "The Small City," 316.

22 Francaviglia, "Main Street," 144.

23 Mark Pinsky, "In Walt's World, No Churches on Main Street or on Screen," *Orlando Sentinel*, July 16, 1995.

24 Francaviglia, "Main Street," 145.

25 Ibid.

26 Joe Rhode, Personal communication, April 25, 2024.

27 Or, in scientific terms, with the chemicals dopamine and/or norepinephrine.

28 If you really want to get into the science of this, I suggest Hauser, Tobias with Eran Eldar, Nina Purg, Michael Moutoussis, and Raymond Doland. "Distinct Roles of Dopamine and Noradrenaline in Incidental Memory," *Journal of Neuroscience* 39 (September 25, 2019): 7715–21, https://www.jneurosci.org/content/39/39/7715.

29 Francaviglia, "Main Street," 147.

30 Mike, "LGBTQ, Native American, and More Characters among Diverse Lineup of NEW Characters at Magic Kingdom," *BlogMickey*, https://www.chicagomanu alofstyle.org/tools_citationguide/citation-guide-1.html#cg-website (accessed April 18, 2024).

31 Greg Gately, "Disneyland Removes 'Boys and Girls' from Fireworks Announcement to Promote Gender Inclusivity," *Chip and Co.*, July 4, 2021, https://chipandco.com /disneyland-removes-boys-and-girls-from-fireworks-announcement-to-promote -gender-inclusivity-436321/.

32 One of the first women in the United States to earn a PhD in paleontology, Carlotta Joaquina Maury didn't complete hers until 1902. "$10,000 Bequest To Cornell Woman From Mrs. Draper," *The Ithaca Journal*, December 21, 1914.

33 Vimal Patel, "Why So Few American Indians Earn Ph.D.'s, and What Colleges Can Do about It," *The Chronicle of Higher Education,* May 27, 2014, https://www .purdue.edu/naecc/documents/2014%205-27%20Why%20So%20Few%20American %20Indians%20Earn%20Ph.D.pdf and "Who Earns a U.S. Doctorate?" *National Science Foundation*, https://www.nsf.gov/statistics/2018/nsf18304/report/who-earns -a-us-doctorate/race-and-ethnicity.cfm#:~:text=As%20a%20result%2C%20the %20proportion,1%25%20from%202006%20to%202016 (accessed April 18, 2024).

34 Josh D'Amaro, "A Place Where Everyone Is Welcome," *DisneyParksBlog*, April 13, 2021, https://disneyparks.disney.go.com/blog/2021/04/a-place-where-everyone-is -welcome/.

6

True-Life Adventures

Walt Disney and the Modern Environmental Movement

Sarah Nilsen

Over twenty million people across America turned out for the first Earth Day in April 1970 to celebrate the natural world and to advocate for the creation of laws to protect the environment. This mass movement for the environment was unprecedented and prompted the administration of Republican president Richard Nixon to implement many of the most important and enduring environmental policies in American history, including the signing of the National Environmental Policy Act, the creation of the Environmental Protection Agency (EPA) and the National Oceanic and Atmospheric Administration (NOAA), and the signing of the Clean Air Act, the Clean Water Act, the Endangered Species Act, and the Marine Mammal Protection Act.

What many Americans do not realize is that the values necessary to mobilize an entire nation to act in a pro-environmental way grew, in part, from generations of children learning about the importance of the biospheric values espoused in Walt Disney's animated films, nature documentaries, cartoons, television shows, theme parks, and publications. Children who develop strong biospheric values that reflect a concern for the quality of nature and the environment for its own sake are more likely to manifest a lifelong engagement with pro-environmental behaviors. As we now face a global environmental crisis, with catastrophic climate change, the collapse of biodiversity, and a large percentage of Americans questioning the existence of human-caused global warming, it is crucial to understand how Disney was able to use his entertainment studio to unify the nation in supporting the creation of the modern environmental movement.

As a Disney historian who regularly teaches undergraduate courses on Walt Disney and American Culture and has appeared in multiple national documentaries about Walt Disney, I am regularly asked about the source of Disney's magic. Disney's interviews, his writings, and his lifetime of creative work reveal Disney's love of animals and nature and his ability to share this love with millions of viewers around the world. Even though the vast majority of Disney's creative work is populated with animals and nature, many Disney fans and students in my Walt Disney and American

Culture classes are surprised to learn that Walt Disney was a dedicated and vocal lover of animals and a major conservationist who advocated for wildlife and habitat conservation and preservation throughout his lifetime.

In the last decades of his life, Disney, the founder of one of the most successful media companies in the world, became a nationally recognized spokesperson for the modern American environmental movement. Already a universally recognized public figure due to his weekly appearances as the host of the *Disneyland* television series, Disney became a spokesperson for the National Wildlife Federation, one of the country's largest non-profit conservation organizations. Between 1956 and 1966, Disney, as honorary chairman for the NWF's National Wildlife Week, appeared regularly in public service announcements on millions of television sets advocating for the conservation of wildlife on public lands. Disney received national recognition from the most important conservation organizations and federal agencies in the country, including the Sierra Club, the Audubon Society, the Wilderness Society, the National Organization for Conservation Education and Publicity, the National Geographic Society, the American Forestry Association, and the US Department of the Interior, for his work advocating for the protection of the environment. As the head of a vast media company, he was able to communicate to a national audience the urgent need for individuals to adopt pro-environmental behaviors by consciously seeking to minimize the negative impact of each individual's actions on the natural world and its inhabitants.[1]

Early Years in Marceline

Research has documented that spending time outdoors as a child is formative in developing biospheric values. Disney himself frequently described the importance of the five years he spent on a small rural farm in the Midwestern prairie town of Marceline, Missouri. From the age of four until ten, Disney freely roamed and explored the natural world around him. Disney vividly recalled his years on the farm and surrounding land as the source for his lifetime love of animals and his view of nature as a source of wonder. Like much of the undeveloped Midwestern prairie at the time, wildlife was plentiful. Migrating birds would layover at the farm's pasture pond, and though the farm was only 45 acres, there were orchards, grapevines, and berry plants along with willows, mock orange trees, silver maples, cedars, lilacs, and dogwoods. Disney recalled that his time on the farm "imbued him with a special feeling toward animals that he would never lose."[2] Years later, when discussing the mood he wanted to capture in animating the "Pastorale" section of *Fantasia*, Disney expressed his emotional memory of his time living in a rural setting. "That's what it is—a feeling of freedom with the animals and characters that live out there. That is what you experience when you go into the country. You escape the everyday world—the strife and the struggle. You get out where everything is free and beautiful."[3]

A considerable amount of research has highlighted the role that childhood nature experiences have on the development of adult connections to nature and the development of biospheric values that lead to pro-environmental behaviors. "Ordinary" nature experiences in childhood, such as hiking, camping, gardening, or spending time outdoors, have been correlated to positive attitudes and behaviors toward the environment during adulthood.[4] These values develop in early life and tend to remain stable over time, providing a guide to direct a person's behavior.[5] Direct experiences with nature contribute to an emotional bond with nature, and frequent ordinary nature occurrences allow a deeper development of psychological sensitivity and connection to the natural environment.

Disney's early years exploring the nature surrounding his family farm in Marceline provided the ordinary experiences of nature that would impact his later pro-environmental advocacy. Being very young, Disney was not expected to work on the farm, so he was able to spend much of his days immersed in nature, studying the lives of the animals. His careful and close observation of the natural world led to his initial forays at a very early age in capturing the essence of the natural environment through drawings and sketches. Scribbling with a crayon on a piece of packing paper, Disney's first sketches were of the wild rabbits around the farm, whose natural behaviors thrilled and excited him.[6] These early sketches motivated him to study and draw more of the animals on the farm and the surrounding wild areas. By carefully observing these animals and forming close emotional ties with them, Disney used his creativity to capture their distinct individual personalities. Disney reported that these early explorations of drawing were motivated by his symbiotic relationship with animals, in which he learned about them, felt that he could communicate with them, and in the process they grew to understand each other.[7]

These symbiotic relationships would be the wellspring from which he developed many of his most memorable and moving characters and stories. Disney became particularly attached to one of the family's sows, Porker, whom he called a "close friend." Disney recalled, "I used to horse around with her a lot. I guess I really loved that pig. She had an acute sense of fun and mischief."[8] Disney's strong empathetic identification with these animals led him at an early age to grant them sentience and subjectivity, making them into emotionally rich characters in his early attempts at storytelling. Porker became a model for Disney's Academy Award-winning Silly Symphony, *The Three Little Pigs* (1934). According to Disney, "I did the preliminary sketch from remembering Porker, and I was practically weeping with nostalgia by the time I had finished."[9] Disney's early emotional attachment to the farm animals and the wildlife in Marceline was formative for the development of his strong biospheric values, and these relationships impacted his creation of animal characters. Indeed, Disney's animal characters became international stars because of the strong personal emotions and attachments he shared with these animals and nature throughout his life.

Research has shown that past experiences with nature are an important source of biospheric values, especially if those experiences are shared with the family and important others.[10] Another key component of Disney's strong connection with nature was his formative and close relationship with his father's brother, Uncle Ed, who had a cognitive disability and traveled freely by train between family members. From his Uncle Ed, Disney learned about and shared with a close family member the awe, wonder, and beauty of the natural world. According to Disney, his Uncle Ed was so much at home in the fields that all the "birds, animals, and insects seemed to know instinctively that he would never harm them. . . . Field mice thrilled to creep up his arm and snuggle in his pockets, where he always kept bits of cheese. He could do uncanny imitations of birds, which came down, flew around his head, and perched on his shoulder."[11] With Uncle Ed, Disney saw wildlife and animals as not separate from humans and not as utilitarian objects to use, discard, and ignore at will; nature was a place of wonder where human and animal relations could be developed that respected the life of all beings. Disney was able in his creative work to bring to life these powerful feelings, creating a sense of love, emotional connectedness, and interconnectedness with nature, which led his audiences to share in his care, responsibility, and commitment to protecting nature.[12]

Against the backdrop of Disney's bucolic vision of nature was the harsh reality of rural and farm life. In the rural Midwest during this time, animals were defined by their use value and not their intrinsic value as living beings. Human-animal relations in Marceline entailed the regular killing of both wildlife and domesticated animals for human consumption and enjoyment. The Marceline community would come together for an annual hog slaughter, where many of Disney's close pig friends would be slaughtered, boiled, and processed at the farm. While Disney immersed himself in the teeming biodiversity of the Midwestern prairie, his regular exposure to the killing of animals was also central to the development of his own love for animals and his personal deep connection with them. Soon after the family moved to the farm, Disney's older brother Roy was given an air rifle to "keep down those thieving grackles[13] you're going to find around the farm."[14] Disney recalled many years later that Roy took the rifle and shot a large rabbit that they had been joyfully watching together as it ran around the fields. When the brothers ran over to the rabbit, Disney discovered that it was "alive and squirming," and he "burst into tears as his older brother casually broke its neck." Disney refused to eat the rabbit stew that was made that night and was "appalled at the idea of harming such delightful creatures."[15] While Disney's interactions with animals were typical for rural Missouri, his own emotional response and interpretation of these events were different. The cognitive dissonance caused by witnessing his closest friend and brother casually kill another living creature was particularly traumatic and discomforting. Disney would share with the rest of the world the emotional toll of these experiences in his production of the most important anti-hunting film ever produced, *Bambi*. Disney's norm-breaking aversion toward the killing of animals impacted the creative output of the entire studio and created a workplace that mandated the recognition and practice of biospheric values. At the time, there was a "written code around the Disney studio," Janet Martin reported in *Nature Magazine* in 1942 during the making of *Bambi*, "that no bird or animal must ever be hurt or abused in a Disney film."[16]

While "ordinary" nature experiences are central to the development of a love of nature, "extraordinary" nature experiences, which are characterized by a strong emotional response—including environmental epiphanies and moments of intense clarity in one's perception of the relationship with nature—are also meaningful.[17] Extraordinary childhood nature experiences are found to be significantly related to biospheric values.[18] One incident in Disney's childhood that was particularly significant for him concerned his own killing of an animal. Disney would often recall this experience as one that evinced a deep interest and wonder in nature and a realization that animal lives had intrinsic value. When he was eight years old, Disney encountered a spectacular large owl roosting in a tree and excitedly approached it. When he reached out to touch the owl, Disney recalled that it clawed at him. In response, he threw it to the ground and stomped on it, killing it. In an interview recorded over fifty years after the event, Disney retold the story with considerable shame, revealing that he had recurring nightmares about the incident and even retelling the story made him "shudder," signaling the emotional impact of the experience.[19] Unlike the majority of rural Americans at the time who had been taught at an early age that killing animals was not only necessary but also an enjoyable pastime, Disney would frequently report in interviews that he never killed another animal after this incident. Disney's extraordinary attachment to animals and nature did not represent the dominant social practices of the time, and yet these early nature experiences developed into the strong biospheric values that moved millions of spectators to recognize the intrinsic value of all life.[20]

Building the Studio

One of Disney's most famous quotes, stated in a 1954 television interview, is, "I only hope that we never lose sight of one thing . . . that it was all started by a mouse." Disney's earliest nature experiences involved his emotional connection with and love of animals. According to his daughter, Diane, "I've gone into this next trait before, but it's impossible to overemphasize it. Father's love for animals is deep and sincere."[21] Disney's wife, Lillian, in the same interview, discusses his ability to see individual personalities in animals that they are like people to him and that they have human characteristics. The mouse that created the Walt Disney Company was based on Disney's field mouse companions from his childhood, a friendship that continued at the start of his animation career in Kansas City. Disney would feed the mice that lived in the studio where he worked, and one of them became so tame that it ran across the top of Disney's drawing board. When Disney moved to Los Angeles to pursue his animation career, his final farewell act was to release the mouse he had befriended into the field behind the animation studio.

For Disney, mice and animals were part of his community. His original motivations for creative expression, like for many young children, grew out of his curiosity and attachment to the animals that inhabited his world. This emotional connection led to his rendering of those animals in a wide variety of aesthetic forms, as he sought ways to express through art what those animals meant to him emotionally. Disney's first popular animated character, Oswald the Lucky Rabbit, was based on his years of enjoyment watching and drawing wild rabbits in the fields around Marceline. Mickey Mouse was a character created from Disney's beloved field mice that he had learned to engage with through Uncle Ed. In a 1953 article, "What I Learned From Animals," Disney states that

> the most fascinating people I've ever met are animals. For some 25 years, I have been creating cartoon animal characters . . . I've studied real animals as models for Mickey Mouse, Donald Duck, Pluto the dog, Bambi the deer, Dumbo the elephant, and all the others. . . . But the more I looked at the world of bird, beast, fish, and insect the more I realized that actual living animals are more strange and wonderful and entertaining than anything it's possible to conjure up out of the imagination.[22]

Cartooning provided Disney with a template to express the liveliness and flourishing of the animals around him, and he would continue throughout his career to seek out the most effective ways artistically to express his connection with animals and nature.

The remarkable success of the early Oswald the Lucky Rabbit and Mickey Mouse shorts is often attributed to the personality animation developed at the Disney studio. These cartoon characters had complex and individual personalities for which audiences feel an emotional attachment. Disney's earliest experiences in Marceline, where he sketched to capture the wonder and connection he felt to nature, led him to create distinctive personalities that expressed the biospheric values that these diverse and unique animals elicited. It seems obvious to note—though often underappreciated— that the most beloved and well known of Disney's cartoon characters are all animals. Mickey Mouse, Donald Duck, Goofy, Pluto, Bambi, and Dumbo are all examples of Disney's mastery of personality animation. The famous Disney animators, Frank Thomas and Ollie Johnston, explain in their foundational book, *Disney Animation: The Illusion of Life*, that it is so powerful and emotive because of the "love we feel for characters so heroic, so tender and funny and exciting—all of them entertaining, yet each different, each thinking his own thoughts, and experiencing his own emotions. That is what makes them so real, and that is what makes them so memorable. It is also what gives them the astounding illusion of life."[23] By the time the studio began production on *Bambi*, it was a "well-known fact at the Disney studio that a man has to love an animal thoroughly before he can draw it well."[24] In preparation for the making of *Bambi*, Disney cartoonists spent two years studying live models and movies of the animals their characters were based on. They additionally visited zoos and national parks, making hundreds of sketches and taking thousands of photos of the animals in their natural habitats before they were ready to "turn to the personality studies" of the *Bambi* characters.

> From thorough study of live animals, from talks with . . . Walt himself, and from looking at the thousands of character models and mood sketches created by others . . . the animators found their minds crystallizing the individualities of the *Bambi* characters. They came to know Bambi, Faline, Thumper, Old Friend Owl, Flower the Skunk and all the rest as well as they knew their next-door neighbors.[25]

Just as was true when Walt grew up on the Marceline farm, Disney's early love of animals and the natural world was far from American social norms of that time, which tended to view wild animals as having mostly instrumental value as a tool to be used for human needs. Biospheric values are linked to pro-environmental behaviors because they encourage people to consider the interests of the group and community when making choices about the environment. This would include showing respect for the earth, unity with nature, and protecting the environment. Disney's experiences of the widespread killing of animals during his time in Marceline embodied the common American perception of wildlife as either prey that was meant to be eaten or predators that were a threat that needed to be eradicated. Nature was seen as meant for human use, and when animals interfered with human interests, many conservationists advocated and initiated their eradication.[26] Throughout this period, organizations like the Audubon Society advocated for the killing of all raptors, including hawks and owls, because they were "predators." The widespread extermination of wildlife occurred under the guidance and actions of the federal government. While Disney was creating his first Mickey Mouse shorts in Los Angeles, in the Buena Vista[27] lakebed outside of the city, millions of mice exploded across the fields of southern California, intentionally killed by an oil company. Los Angeles newspapers covered the mouse massacre, describing highways "plastered with dead mice, and millions of them alive chasing across the highways; it's sickening . . . The Honolulu [oil] Company killed four tons of mice."[28] The cause for the explosion of mice resulted from an intensive poisoning campaign waged by the federal government for the benefit of local farmers, yet causing the extermination of all wildlife within the vicinity.[29] As Mickey Mouse became an international star, the vast majority of Americans viewed mice and wildlife as vermin and pests to be eradicated and killed. In 1915, Congress funded the creation of the Bureau of Biological Survey (BBS) of the USDA. During the time that the Disney studio was producing its lovingly drawn, personality-driven animal characters for its immensely popular Mickey Mouse and Silly Symphonies shorts and its animated feature films, BBS tax-funded employees shot, trapped, poisoned, or set afire nearly two million coyotes. By 1929, so few wolves remained in the wild that they were rarely mentioned in federal reports. Other species suffered a similar fate as agents killed 7,000 to 10,000 bobcats, 100 to 200 mountain lions and 300 to 600 bears each year from 1937 to 1945. The National Park Service also participated in the program, killing thousands of predators within the National Park System.[30]

While the widespread slaughter of wildlife occurred across the country, Disney explored new mediums in which to share with his audiences his deeply held biospheric values. His use of living wildlife models during the production of *Bambi* piqued his interest in combining authentic footage of real animals for a new type of storytelling. In 1944, Disney set up a meeting with an official of the New York Zoological Society with a plan to "make films on animals, bird life, fish life, and any other type of living creature around which there is a real story to tell."[31] After producing training documentaries for the US military during the Second World War, Disney was convinced that live-action nature documentaries could successfully tell stories about the fascinating lives of animals with their own distinct and individual personalities. Nature documentaries up to this point were hunting and safari films, or natural history films. No one had considered films that showcased the lives of wildlife without human interference to be commercially viable. For historians of nature documentaries, Disney's decision to move into the production of nature films seems quixotic, but this decision needs to be viewed as a continuation of his childhood fascination with the natural world and his love of animals.

In 1945, Disney pursued his nature documentary idea by having Alfred and Elma Milotte, a husband-and-wife photography team in Alaska, shoot over 100,000 feet of film of the state. When Disney viewed their footage, which included people cutting timber, catching salmon, building railroads, climbing Mount McKinley, and hunting game, his immediate response was "More Animals." The Milottes suggested seals, and Disney's only communication back was "More Seals." The final film, *Seal Island*, took three years to complete and contained no human characters. Disney's distributor, RKO, refused to distribute it because they could not conceptualize the idea that animals could be the subject of any film, and no other distributors would touch it. According to Roy, the distributors' response to the film was to ask who wants "to watch seals playing house on a bare rock?"[32] Disney ended up screening the film at the Crown Theater in Pasadena in December 1948 to a transfixed audience, which qualified the film for the Academy Awards, and *Seal Island* won the Oscar for Documentary Short Subject a few months later. Thus began Disney's unprecedented success in the production of nature documentaries starring animal subjects.

Although wildlife policy and practice in the United States focused on the use value of wildlife, the immense popularity of Disney's animated films starring animals with distinctive personalities testified to how receptive audiences were to Disney's vision of nature and his biospheric values. These audiences, raised on Disney's animated shorts and features, became enamored of the animal characters that populated the Disney screen and were nudged toward seeing them as worthy of concern and interest. These young baby boomers were a ready-made audience for the *True-Life Adventures* nature documentaries. Developing characters with personalities that audiences could identify with, Disney viewed the live-action animals that appeared in his documentaries as individual personalities beyond species categories. For Disney, "every living thing has a personality of its own. . . . Individual animals are distinct and different as the personalities we find in our human friends."[33]

Following the immense popular success of *Seal Island*, over the next twelve years, the Walt Disney Studio released twelve more *True-Life Adventures* films. For three decades spanning the 1950s to the 1970s, *True-Life Adventures* media, including film, television, books, and comic strips, became woven into America's education about the natural world. These productions ascribed human traits to animals and "encouraged viewers to empathize with creatures in the natural world, nurturing a belief that animals deserved respect" and even admiration.[34]

Critics have long attacked Disney for his anthropomorphism or "Disneyfication" of nature. But in the context of this study of Disney's relationship with animals, it should instead be clear that anthropomorphism and "Disneyfication" are in fact aesthetic expressions of Disney's biospheric values. Recent research has shown that "anthropomorphism is a basic human attitude that . . . persists throughout life, and that one of the most effective ways to increase support for conservation is to 'personalize' nature."[35] Scholars trying to encourage conservation have recognized the need to employ "biocentric anthropomorphism," that is, using human terms to explain animal emotions or feelings to make animals' worlds more accessible. The purpose of anthropomorphism within conservation is to create empathy toward animals and their ecosystem by emphasizing their human characteristics, an aesthetic technique mastered by Disney throughout his career.[36] Researchers have found that animals placed in a visual context associated with human representation "increased viewers' feelings of kinship with animals and the perceptions of animals as individuals with personality."[37] In his animated productions, Disney made it clear that he anthropomorphized animals to create sympathetic identification with them. "In approaching the problem of storytelling," he explained, "once we ha[d] the basic [live-action] footage, we use[d] the same technique to be found in the Disney cartoons. We look[ed] for personality, and we d[id] this for a reason. If audiences can identify themselves with the seeming personality of an animal, they can sympathize with it and understand its problems better."[38] As with his animated renderings of animals, Disney was adamant that nature and animals be treated with respect in the nature documentaries. As a commentator at the time noted, Disney was "bent on demonstrating the human aspects of animal life. Animals, he says, have tender feelings, intelligence, and even a sense of humor."[39] The *True-Life Adventures* series director James Algar recalled how Disney admonished that "no condescending attitude was to be taken about nature. Creatures were to be viewed not as 'dumb animals' but as 'our friends, the wise animals.'"[40]

Theme Park Development and Expansion into Television Production

As Disney was producing his *True-Life Adventures* films, he was also developing the company's theme park and its expansion into television production. Both projects, directly linked to the *True-Life Adventures* nature documentaries, would transform the Walt Disney Studios into one of the most powerful media companies in the world— and would also be instrumental in the rise of the modern environmental movement. When Disney needed to raise the funds required to build his long-planned amusement park, Disneyland, he turned to the newest entertainment medium: television. Disney's interest in television began in the 1930s, but as television ownership boomed in the postwar period, Disney was the first major studio head to embrace it. By 1953, two-thirds of American families owned television sets, and Disney began negotiating with the major television networks to get them to agree to purchase his television programming along with an ownership stake in the Disneyland theme park. ABC and Walt Disney Productions announced a joint agreement on April 2, 1954, with ABC funding the *Disneyland* television show along with purchasing a 34.48 percent interest in Disneyland Park. The Disneyland television show premiered on October 27, 1954, and with the financial backing of ABC, the Disneyland Park opened on July 17, 1955. Both were unmitigated successes that established Walt Disney as a national American hero and brand. During the *Disneyland* television show's first season, it attracted over 50 percent of the audience in its time slot, and its audience and ratings kept growing.[41] With much of the early network television programming coming out of radio, the Disney Studios' original proposal for their first television shows included a one-hour series that incorporated material from Disney movies, promotions for new Disney films, and an ongoing progress report on Disneyland. The proposal also suggested a five-day-a-week fifteen-minute program called *The Mickey Mouse Club* to air live from Disneyland and a weekly half-hour True-Life program taken from the studio's nature footage.[42] When putting together the format for their primetime *Disneyland* series, Disney knew the program "had to be synergistic; it had to promote both Disney films and Disneyland." He suggested that they set up "four production units—one for each 'land' in the Disneyland Park. Disney envisioned "a program on how the *True-Life Adventures* were shot [that] would promote the latest *True-Life Adventures* in Africa."[43] Eventually, the *Disneyland* series and *The Mickey Mouse Club* would regularly broadcast material from the *True-Life Adventures* films.

The Disneyland theme park was designed to include the *True-Life Adventures* as the source of one of the main four lands that structured the park. Originally designated True-Life Adventureland, it was meant to bring to life in three-dimensionality Disney's beloved wildlife and nature. Before park guests arrived at what would become Adventureland, they first walked down Main Street, U.S.A. modeled on Marceline, the turn-of-the-century town that had so inspired Disney's imagination. Guests would then enter Adventureland, whose main attraction was the immensely popular Jungle Cruise, based on the recently released *True-Life Adventures* film, *The African Lion* (1955). The original plans for the Jungle Cruise included the use of authentic, living animals, but this decision was dropped because of concerns about their care. Another of the earliest attractions was a simulated recreation of the landscapes and wildlife in the immensely popular, Academy Award-winning *True-Life Adventures* film, *The Living Desert* (1953). Guests embarked on a narrated train ride through a simulated Western desert that recreated scenes from the documentary. Striving for greater authenticity in his reconstruction of nature and wildlife, soon after Disneyland's opening, Disney invested millions of dollars into upgrading the attraction with heavy investment in creating over two hundred lifelike, audio-animatronic animals. In June of 1960, the newly renamed Mine Train Through Nature's Wonderland added a "sense of realism heretofore unseen at Disneyland."[44] Millions of Disneyland Park guests from around the world experienced Disney's *True-Life Adventures* and the wildlife personalities that starred in these films in a simulated, three-dimensional model of the nature captured in the original documentaries. Disney's dream of using authentic, live animals in his theme parks finally came true in 1998 with the opening of the Animal Kingdom in Walt Disney World.

Disney projected his biospheric values onto America's film and television screens and into Disneyland, thereby changing forever the way that Americans understood animals and nature. Between 1940 and 1965, the US population between the ages five and thirteen almost doubled, resulting in one-third of Americans being under the age of fourteen. The *True-Life Adventures* were one of the most widely accessible sources about the natural world available to these seventy-eight million baby boomers.[45] These programs introduced nature and wildlife to millions of suburban children who were growing up removed from wildlife and wilderness. The *True-Life Adventures* nature documentaries gave them an immediate experience of nature that was exciting, authentic, and readily available, and these animal films prepared Americans to appreciate and advocate for the protection of nature in new and effective ways.[46] Animals and plants were shown living together in complex ecosystems that necessarily included keystone species, including predators like wolves and coyotes that had long been maligned and killed. As the public had "less and less opportunity to see animals, they provided a form of vicarious experience that shaped a generation's picture of the world around them."[47] The author and scholar Dan Flores describes in his histories of US wildlife policy how Walt Disney had made him and millions of other baby boomers into conservationists. Flores recalls growing up an "undying disciple" of Disney, who developed the biospheric values that shaped his life after watching the anti-hunting film *Bambi*, the anti-kill shelter film *Lady and the Tramp*, and the pro-coyote conservation film *The Coyote's Lament*. But it was the *True-Life Adventures* films that showed young Americans "that a fascination with the country's wild birds and animals and their stories was in fact apolitical and paved the way for even more nature programming." Flores and millions like him were the first generation in American history to have their pro-environmental sensibilities shaped directly by the media—and Disney played a huge part in that.[48]

By the late 1960s, many people who had grown up watching Disney's programming viewed nature as a complex, fragile web, of which animals—all animals—were integral parts. These baby boomers believed humans could destroy nature through uncontrolled industrial development. They demonstrated their commitment in votes, rallies, and petitions, and they demanded government action to protect the environment and preserve ecosystems.[49] Protecting nature and wildlife became a popular crusade with many millions of middle-class, average Americans who had grown up experiencing Disney's biospheric values through his films, television shows, and Disneyland theme park. In a decade-long burst of enthusiasm spanning 1964 to 1974, Americans wrote their biospheric values into the first major wildlife and nature conservation laws in the country, leading to the first nationwide Earth Day celebration in 1970. Disney had inspired both conservatives and liberals to unite in a coalition to clean up the nation's air and water—and save its wildlife and wilderness.[50] As our world currently faces an unprecedented collapse of biodiversity due to human-caused habitat destruction, hunting, and climate change,[51] it is more important than ever to recognize and celebrate how Walt Disney was able to use his creative genius to instill in multiple generations of Americans biospheric values that allowed the modern environmental movement to come into existence.

Much of the academic writing on Disney tends to be critical and negative. Relying heavily on media literacy methodologies, the over hundred-year history of the Walt Disney Company is often framed by and analyzed through the lens of contemporary understandings of the issues of race and gender. This analysis lacks a historical dimension that reveals how Walt Disney is embedded within specific cultural, social, and political contexts. Because of this, you might be surprised to learn that Disney's films are overwhelmingly pro-social and encourage people to work together as a group for the betterment of all. Why, then, are so few people aware of Disney's biospheric values and his significant involvement in the development of the modern environmental movement?

Notes

1   A. Kollmuss and J. Agyeman, "Mind the Gap: Why Do People Act Environmentally and What Are the Barriers to Pro-environmental Behavior?" *Environmental Education Research* 8, no. 3 (2002): 240.

2   Neal Gabler, *Walt Disney: The Triumph of the American Imagination* (New York: Vintage Books, 2007), 11.

3   Ibid., 18.

4   Stanley T. Asah et al., "Mechanisms of Children's Exposure to Nature: Predicting Adulthood Environmental Citizenship and Commitment to Nature-Based Activities," *Environment and Behavior* 50, no. 7 (2018): 808.

5   Paul C. Stern, Thomas Dietz, and Gregory A. Guagnano, "The New Ecological Paradigm in Social-Psychological Context," *Environment and Behavior* 27, no. 6 (1995): 727.

6   Leonard Mosley, *Disney's World: A Biography* (New York: Stein and Day, 1985), 28.

7   Ibid., 30.

8   Ibid.

9   Ibid.

10 Erica Molinario et al., "From Childhood Nature Experiences to Adult Pro-Environmental Behaviors: An Explanatory Model of Sustainable Food Consumption," *Environmental Education Research* 26, no. 8 (2020): 1150.

11 Mosley, *Disney's World*, 31.

12 Helen E. Perkins, "Measuring Love and Care for Nature," *Journal of Experimental Psychology* 30, no. 4 (2010): 456.

13 Grackles are gregarious passerine birds native to North and South America.

14 Mosley, *Disney's World*, 28.

15 Ibid.

16 Janet Martin, "Bringing Bambi to the Screen," *Nature Magazine* 35, no. 7 (1942): 352.

17 A. Vining and M. Merrick, "Environmental Epiphanies: Theoretical Foundations and Practical Applications," in *The Oxford Handbook of Environmental and Conservation Psychology*, ed. S. D. Clayton (New York: Oxford University Press, 2012), 499.

18 Molinario et al., "From Childhood Nature Experiences to Adult Pro-Environmental Behaviors," 1139.

19 Martin, "Bringing Bambi to the Screen," 352.

20 Walt Disney still holds the record for the most Academy Awards won, and the most wins and nominations for an individual in history.

21 Diane Disney Miller and Pete Martin, *The Story of Walt Disney*, 1st ed. (New York: Henry Holt & Company, 1957), 214.

22 Walt Disney, "What I've Learned about Animals," *American Magazine* 155 (February 1953): 23.
23 Frank Thomas and Ollie Johnston, *Disney Animation: The Illusion of Life* (New York: Abbeville Press, 1981), 357.
24 Martin, "Bringing Bambi to the Screen," 352.
25 Ibid.
26 Lisa Mighetto, "Wild Animals in American Thought and Culture, 1870s–1930s" (PhD diss., University of Washington, 1986), 108.
27 Buena Vista is the name Disney would later select for the distribution company he created to distribute his True-Life Adventure nature documentaries.
28 E. Raymond Hall, "An Outbreak of House Mice in Kern County, California," *University of California Publications in Zoology* 30, no. 7 (1927): 189.
29 Ibid., 201.
30 Mighetto, "Wild Animals in American Thought and Culture, 1870s–1930s," 109.
31 Gabler, *Walt Disney*, 445.
32 Ibid., 446.
33 Disney, "What I've Learned about Animals," 108.
34 Charles Dorn, "I Never Saw as Good a Nature Show Before: Walt Disney, Environmental Education, and the True-Life Adventures," *History of Education Quarterly* 63, no. 2 (2023): 245.
35 Cameron Thomas Whitley, Linda Kalof, and Tim Flach, "Using Animal Portraiture to Activate Emotional Affect," *Environment and Behavior* 53, no. 8 (2021): 841.
36 Ibid., 842.
37 Ibid.
38 The Walt Disney Studios, *The Story of Walt Disney's True-Life Adventure Series* (Burbank: Walt Disney Productions, 1952), 178.
39 Louis Berg, "Disney's Greatest Gamble," *Los Angeles Times*, March 15, 1953, H36.
40 Dorn, "I Never Saw as Good a Nature Show Before," 246.
41 Gabler, *Walt Disney*, 512.
42 Ibid., 506.
43 Ibid., 510.
44 Pete Docter and Christopher Merritt, *Marc Davis in His Own Words: Imagineering the Disney Theme Parks* (New York: Disney Edition, 2019), 26.
45 Dorn, "I Never Saw as Good a Nature Show Before," 269.
46 Mighetto, "Wild Animals in American Thought and Culture, 1870–1930s," 102.
47 Ibid., 103.
48 Dan Flores, *Coyote America: A Natural and Supernatural History* (New York: Basic Books, 2016), 152.
49 Thomas R. Dunlap, *Saving America's Wildlife* (Princeton: Princeton University Press, 1988), 98.
50 Mighetto, "Wild Animals in American Thought and Culture, 1870s–1930s," 152.
51 Pedro Jaureguiberry et al., "The Direct Drivers of Recent Global Anthropogenic Biodiversity Loss," *Science Advances* 8, no. 45 (2022). DOI:10.1126/sciadv.abm9982.

7

Urban NDNs and the House of Mouse

A Journey of Education and Self-Discovery

Lucy Buck

¹Yá'át'ééh, shik'éí dóó shidine'é. Shí éí Luciano Buck yinishyé. Bilagáana nishłi. Kinyaa'áanii báshishchíín. T'áá Bilagáana dashicheii. Tłizi'łani éí dashináli. Kót'éego Diné nishłi.

Welcome my friends and family to this chapter of *Why the Magic Matters*. Many Americans would call me an Indian; I prefer NDN, which sounds like "Indian" when said out loud, but it is more than that. NDN is a misspelling popularized through the internet that is jestering at the mistaken identity bestowed on Native people when first "discovered" by Christopher Columbus.² But mostly, I refer to myself as an "urban Native." I am called Lucy. My mother is white clan and born for the Towering House clan.³ My maternal grandfather is white clan. My paternal grandfather is Many Goats. This is how I am Diné.

I grew up in Pomona, California, living just a twenty- to thirty-minute drive to the Happiest Place on Earth and a television set away from films and TV shows created by the Walt Disney Company. I was ten years old the first time I entered Disneyland with my aunt and my cousin. As a young urban Native, the idea of living near Disneyland never felt like a big deal or had any significance, but as I have grown older, it has become apparent the influence Disney has had on my self-understanding and identity. The journey that I am following within higher education leads me to understand how academia can help someone to recognize one's own self.

Disney can be more than just a theme park and movie studio. It can be our classroom as we learn about Disney's history and the role Disney plays in influencing our day-to-day lives. As a young person, I never thought for a second that Disney could be more than the fantastic park designed by Disney's Imagineers. Like so many American youth, I loved Disneyland automatically because it was introduced to me as an impressionable child, and Disney offered ways for me to find meaning in something bigger than myself. But my affection for Disney was not straightforward. While my days visiting Disneyland could not seem any better—walking down Main Street, U.S.A. laughing and creating beloved memories—I still felt like I did not belong in the Happiest Place on Earth. Disney parks display an overwhelming amount of

Western culture, and I could not understand what my place was within that realm. This unease extended to movies as well. Children who are influenced easily like I was can automatically interpret Disney's creations that are relevant and familiar as acceptable and appropriate. Take, for example, *Pocahontas*, a 1995 Disney film that was first introduced to me by my maternal grandmother as an example of a "positive" portrayal of Native communities. But, in fact, the film is an inaccurate story told to whitewash a real-life tragedy.[4] "Pocahontas's" given name was Amonute, and the real story is a tragedy in which a fourteen-year-old girl was forcibly removed from her traditional lands, made to move to England, raped, and then died before returning home. There was no happy conclusion as Disney made it out to be. So, what scholars call "Disney-fying" can mean to censor a story to make Western colonizers look a particular way.[5] Of course, there are many factors to enjoy about Disney, but how can we learn what we do not know?

This chapter chronicles my intellectual journey and explores how the lives of urban Natives like me are shaped by places such as Disneyland and popular films like Disney's *Peter Pan*, *Pocahontas*, and *Moana*. In doing this analysis, I use my identity and my education to dive into the magic that Disneyland and Walt Disney Animation Studios create for their guests and audiences. Doing so allows me to produce a critical view into the current state of representation of Natives in Disney films and theme parks. Specifically, I investigate how Disney's portrayal of Indigenous people impacts urban Natives' identity and why and how this matters. And I reflect on how Disney combined with education have impacted my own self-understanding.

My work here is informed by interdisciplinary research, which is a way of combining two or more disciplines to create a new outlook on a particular issue. Using an interdisciplinary approach offers scholars an ever-evolving academic journey with limitless solutions, and what we know today can and will change tomorrow.[6] Specifically, this chapter explores those academic fields that shaped my intellectual development in college, namely Applied Indigenous Studies (AIS) and ethnomusicology.

Grappling with Representation: A Sense of Belonging in Academia and America

Despite living near the magical place of Disneyland, growing up in Pomona was difficult because mass media (including Disney) provided only a limited perspective of Indigenous communities. That sort of portrayal shaped the community I grew up in and how non-Natives viewed me, often as a "savage" or even an "Indian." This in turn influenced my identity, whether I knew it or not; I barely understood who I was. I remember the first time I watched *Pocahontas*: I was about four or five years old, and because I was trying to identify with characters in films, I thought that Pocahontas and I were related because she was also Native. Little did I know this was far from being true. As I grew older, I made the same mistake, assuming every Native person I met was related to me. My grandfather would correct me on this all the time.

As a Dinè hosteen (Navajo grown man), where I grew up made a significant difference in shaping my own positionality and understanding of my intersectional identity. Among Native communities, I am considered a city Native or urban Native. This term refers to someone of Native ancestry who lives and grew up away from their traditional homelands. This division is intentional and ties into a history of US policies toward Natives. The United States created the relocation program to displace Natives and assimilate them into mainstream society.[7] Had it not been for my few summers on shí ma saní (my grandmother's) land in Teec Nos Pos, Diné Bikéyah (Navajo Nation), I would not have had the experiences of my cultural heritage within my community. My upbringing in an urban setting heavily influenced the popular culture I digested, and I did not yet have a critical outlook to use when watching things like the mass media produced by Disney.

I would only overcome this ignorance through learning that my life experiences were part of being an urban Native. Someone who grew up on a reservation would not have thought about Disney's *Pocahontas* as I did, because where one grows up defines their own connections to who they are and how their identity connects them to their own people. Moreover, a Native who grew up on the reservation (rez) is affected differently than urban Natives by places like Disneyland or movies like *Peter Pan* (1953). When I have conversations with friends or family who grew up on the rez, the mention of Disney is usually met with disdain or negative feedback. Unlike me, who grew up exposed to Disney, my family (cousins) on the rez were not allowed to watch Disney films with Indigenous characters because of the stereotypes inherent in those depictions.

This ties into the idea of representation. Today, in academic circles, cultural representation has become more expansive, focusing on stories and historical figures that reflect lived experiences. But as so many of us know all too well, past portrayals of people of color on television, radio, or in movies were often stereotypical and limited in perspective, offering only a narrow glimpse into lives that Western society labeled as "too odd" or not reflective of its dominant culture. This does not just apply to Native cultures; Disney has stereotyped Black people with animated films like *Dumbo* and *Song of the South* and with rides like Splash Mountain.[8] *Pocahontas*, I came to understand, was an example of cultural *mis*representation. When cultural misrepresentation happens, audiences' perspectives are misguided, and it becomes easy to misunderstand the individuals and cultures that the films and stories and rides reflect.

Though we are discussing representation and misrepresentation, there is a third type of representation, and that is *no* representation. To understand this, let me use the example of the cigar store Indians at Disneyland. There are two in the park, one on Main Street, U.S.A. and one in Frontierland. They are nearly identical painted wood statues, about five feet tall each, depicting a male Plains Native wearing a headdress, holding a gun, and carrying a medicine pouch. Victoria Lantz, a performance artist and scholar of culture and representation, uses tribal critical race theory (TribCrit) to break down how misrepresentation and absence of representation are presented through Disneyland theme parks: "TribCrit tells us that passively walking by the statues or making a point to interact with them *both* indicate the normativity of indulging in stereotyped nativeness."[9] To expand on what Lantz states, it is critical to understand that representation matters but, based on the example of the cigar store Indians, Disney sidesteps meaningful engagement with Native representation whether guests ignore *or* interact with the figures. Perhaps the cigar store Indians exemplify Disney's effort to make their parks inclusive to everyone, but this effort falls flat. Disney does not teach or show guests how to interpret and interact with these figures. It feels like an ever-lasting battle when it comes to the inclusion of Native voices because even when Native voices are included, they are poorly engaged.

Some might say that being included is better than being omitted. Being included may have its perks, but what I take away from this is that it takes small strides to create social justice for underrepresented communities like Natives. In recent years, we have seen many positive firsts for not just Native people but Native nations as well. For instance, the "land back" movement is a process by which Native nations are reclaiming stolen lands. Other examples from pop culture include representation in major motion pictures like 2023's Oscar-nominated *Killers of the Flower Moon*; in other areas, Native artists are being recognized for their work, such as textile artist and designer Naiomi Glasses. As scholars, we can historically track when representation began, what it looked like, and even where it is heading. These shifts allow young people a thrilling moment of recognition: seeing someone who resembles you achieve something remarkable can inspire the belief that you too can carry out remarkable things.

Though I grew up knowing the magical lands of Disney were mere miles from my home, it was not until I was in college and encountered academic writings by Indigenous scholars that I began to see the many mistakes around representation, about my people, made by Walt Disney Animation Studios. When exposed to more literature and research related to Disney's representation of Natives, my perspective started to shift. I could no longer overlook Disneyland's history and physical location. Before Disneyland existed, before the city of Anaheim was built, and underneath the path that takes you down Main Street, U.S.A. are the stolen lands of the Acjachemen Peoples.[10] Though Disneyland has now existed for seventyyears, the lands that it occupies existed long before. The structural rise of Disneyland perpetuates the Western ideology of colonialism through the process of urbanization. The creation of the park whitewashes the long history of ancestral lands stolen from the Acjachemen People. I could now see what scholars had been saying: the physical existence of Disneyland excludes, masks, and whitewashes the acts of colonialism designed to erase the California Natives that once called the lands home.[11]

Ethnomusicology: Culture and Colonialism

Disney truly shaped my identity and self-understanding through my passion for music. In high school, I performed at Disneyland two different times with my high school band and two other times with the local community concert band. These invited performances took place at Carnation Plaza Garden just west of Sleeping

Beauty Castle and at the Hollywood Backlot Stage. That first performance gave me the confidence in what I believed would make me feel validated and academically equipped to succeed. I was overwhelmed with excitement and joy because I had earned my place to perform. In the music world, talented young people usually take one of two paths, instrumentalist or vocalist; I myself am an instrumentalist, and my primary instrument was the trombone. Months before the performance, our music director required every student who wanted to perform at Disneyland to learn to play all twelve major scales. Though it was difficult, my desire to go and play at the Happiest Place on Earth motivated me to practice hard. And I succeeded. Through many years of dedication, I had worked my way up to where I found my place within music. My dream was coming true.

As a result of endless hours of practicing and rewarding performances, I followed my passion for music toward the study of trombone performance in college, and later I would discover my new interest in ethnomusicology. Ethnomusicology is a combination of cultural studies and musicology. What I learned is that, primarily in the nineteenth century, wealthy white men would travel the world and brag to fellow enthusiasts about the "new" or "odd" musical skills they acquired. More often than not, they considered these new techniques, instruments, and stylings inferior to those from Western culture.[12] These cultural comparisons primarily began in social clubs and birthed ethnomusicology as an area of study within musicology.

As I learned more about my discipline, I became unhappy and unfulfilled. My ideas were not going to be able to flourish through my choice of discipline. Ethnomusicology tends to rely on a Eurocentric vision of non-Western cultures, and Western music is always the standard bearer. I was not the first to critique ethnomusicology for these issues; Constantin Brăiloiu, a Romanian ethnomusicologist, said something similar in the 1940s.[13] But as an urban Native, I felt pained by the cultural severance I was creating by participating in a discipline so rooted in the Western academic system not created for individuals like me. This is a problem because, for many cultures— including many Indigenous cultures—the word "music" does not even exist within the language. As a discipline, ethnomusicology is unable to allow cultures like mine to define music for themselves or to accept the "music" that comes from generations of cultural embeddedness in non-Western contexts.

When it came to practicing music in college, nearly all of it was either Western or conformed to fit within Western standards. Students in my classes were taught to call this "Westernizing," a process that removes cultural significance from those of non-Western backgrounds. Even though ethnomusicology is inherently interdisciplinary, researchers tend to enforce Western ideologies in order to grasp what they are studying, which in turn leaves out the people being researched.

I came to realize this "Westernizing" problem went deeper than ethnomusicology research. Western education limits how students can study music and that limitation leads to policies that create education standards. This problem does not start in college but impacts some young people in K-12 education. For instance, because I went to a Title I school, the curriculum I was allowed to learn was determined by budgets set by local governments; the communities surrounding Title I schools are considered low income, and this results in lower tax revenue for those schools. Because of economic challenges combined with Western cultural biases, students like me (who were low income) did not get to study music theory, did not have access to private instructors, and could not travel to compete in state-wide competitions (like the regional and state SCSBOA Solo/Ensemble Festival). We learned exclusively a set of genres connected to Western composers or American composers; for the trombone, this meant Johann Sebastian Bach and Joseph Alessi. By not updating the curriculum and including non-Western cultures, students are not exposed to the cultural creations of underrepresented communities. In addition, many Title I students are not encouraged to pursue careers because of passion (as higher-income students in wealthier school districts are) and instead are only presented opportunities that emphasize career paths for monetary gain.[14]

As I reflected on my past educational experiences, I realized that I had internalized the idea that I needed to choose a career path that gave me material gain—but given my passion for music and awareness of my indigeneity, I knew I had to pursue a career that gave me *cultural* gain as well. I had also problematically learned that I had to categorize parts of Indigenous culture separately—into pieces like art, music, and literature. That's what Western music theory and approaches taught me to do; Western thought puts culture into separate boxes. But I eventually learned through my coursework that categorizing like that would not work for Indigenous cultures, and that ethnomusicology does not have to revolve solely around Western ideologies and methodologies. The scholarship of Dylan Robinson helped me understand this. Robinson, a scholar and Indigenous ethnomusicologist, shows the way that educational institutions are Westernizing Indigenous cultures to fit them into Western boxes.[15] I taught myself to understand this complicated idea in this way: in Western thought, pieces of culture are added: $1 + 1 = 2$. But in Indigenous culture, the arts are *not* additive: $1 + 1 = 1$. This is because the arts (and music and literature) are simply part of the oneness of the culture; they are not separate. It may seem paradoxical, but it all connects back to Indigenous values of self, the nature surrounding us, and the universe.

Robinson says that we can unify ideas to create something more than what we currently have in ethnomusicology specifically and music education generally. This approach would create a different solution to how we learn music. To obtain and sustain cultural integrity, Robinson states that Western music theory and Indigenous music theory "may demonstrate a sharing of space—a visual and kinetic intermingling of bodies on stage, an acoustic blending of musics, or a mixed use of languages—but this integration often remains premised on finding a way to 'fit' Indigenous musicians into western paradigms of performance."[16] Robinson deconstructs and re-materializes the integration of two ideas, but instead of conceptualizing it as two adding to one (or Western + Indigenous = ethnomusicology), we can think of them as equal to each other in value (or Western = Indigenous), even though the culture underneath them is so vastly different. Doing so allows Indigenous culture to weigh as heavily in ethnomusicology as Western culture currently does. The paradox continues.

Disney had fueled my passion for music, and that led me to believe I could reach my goal of being a professional musician. So I pursued the study of music in college. But in time, I realized that I was not finding what I needed even within music anymore; ethnomusicology was too rooted in colonialism to help me explore and understand my own culture as a Diné hosteen.

I had to look elsewhere.

Self-Discovery through Applied Indigenous Studies

After I left ethnomusicology, my focus began shifting toward Indigenous research, which meant a huge change in how I conducted my studies. When it comes to studying Indigenous cultures, curious students can pursue either Indigenous Studies or Applied Indigenous Studies. Indigenous Studies looks at histories, cultures, languages, and stories of Indigenous people all around the world; it also looks at the causes and effects of settler colonialism. AIS involves conducting holistic research that prepares students to contribute to Native nation-building, with careers in Native communities or for organizations that serve Native populations.[17] I became an AIS student, and I learned how I could contribute to processes of reclamation and reconciliation in Native communities and counter the impacts of settler colonialism.

To better understand AIS and its impact on urban Native students like me, we can look to scholar Margaret Kovach, who developed the methodological framework for Indigenous research and, in turn, created ethical research that expands Indigenous ways of living and thinking. Through this, we can see the critical and analytical thinking skills that are overall embedded within the culture and way of life of Indigenous peoples.[18] Kovach writes, "For a methodology to be correctly identified as an Indigenous methodology, it must be anchored in Indigenous epistemology, ethics, story, and community."[19] She continues,

> When we consider Indigenous scholarship and community knowledge, there are at least four core foundations in an Indigenous conceptual framework: Indigenous epistemology, Indigenous ethics, Indigenous community, and the self. These four core foundations, as embedded in Indigenous thought, experience, and context, define an Indigenous conceptual framework and make Indigenous methodologies distinctive from other qualitative approaches.[20]

Research such as Kovach's helps set the framework that is best for working with Indigenous communities in order to create the best outcomes for both the researcher and the lives being studied. In short, Indigenous research is not only about the study being done; it is about how as scientists we are hearing and seeing the people being studied and meeting their concerns. The research should not only change the lives of the communities and people being researched but the researcher as well.

As a college student, I learned to use an Indigenous methodology by including self-experience alongside academic insight. This is in contrast to a Western methodological approach where the researcher is typically detached from who and what they are researching. I was also taught to discern the different cultural frameworks of the people being researched versus the researcher. I learned to think academically about my own frameworks and experiencing self. Disney became part of this exploration. I thought about how, as a child, consuming Disney as popular culture helped me connect with my peers and even attain popularity and comfort in social settings. Though I knew I was not fully fitting in, having something in common with other kids made it easier to have friends. But sometimes the Native stereotypes would surface in my encounters with friends, and I would wonder if they intended to be harmful or were just unaware. I think usually they were unaware of how the misrepresentations not only made me feel misunderstood but also alone. I started to realize how the poor representation of Natives within the Disney movies and theme parks is far more problematic than I previously thought. The absence of authentic Indigenous cultures and voices is both notable and concerning and can ultimately shape urban Native youths' identity and self-understanding—as it did for me.[21]

This brings us back to the issue of representation and the way mass media shapes perceptions of underrepresented communities. The media gives consumers messages that do not honestly depict these communities, and the media can also alter minorities' perceptions of themselves. Media can shape someone's idea of what success looks like for them and whether success is even possible.[22] So when Disney inaccurately represents Indigenous communities in its films and parks and merchandise, consumers begin to view Indigenous lives in that incorrect way. And when urban Natives who have consumed this media connect back to their Indigenous communities, they bring those misrepresentations along with them. The misrepresentation breeds more misrepresentation.

When one grows up with a limited idea of who they can become, their voice is also limited. Even when included, Indigenous voices can be misunderstood. To move forward, we must decolonize our way of thinking and continue our best efforts to bring equal and accessible opportunities for underserved and underrepresented communities. My personal journey as an urban Native and as a college student shows this. Once I began my journey learning and conducting research in AIS, I saw how even Indigenous scholarship has traces of Western ideologies.[23] And I realized that I did not know how much of a privileged life I had had until I started at Northern Arizona University, especially in how I had been given opportunities to study music.

Colonization through Visualization and Sound

In 2020, Disney added a content warning to certain films streamed on Disney+. Here is what Disney+ provides for its users to warn of racist depictions used throughout movies such as *The Aristocats* (1970), *Dumbo* (1941), *The Jungle Book* (1967), and *Peter Pan* (1953):

This program includes negative depictions and/or mistreatment of people or cultures. These stereotypes were wrong then and are wrong now. Rather than remove this content, we want to acknowledge its harmful impact, learn from it, and spark conversation to create a more inclusive future together. Disney is committed to creating stories with inspirational and aspirational themes that reflect the rich diversity of the human experience around the globe.[24]

Though Disney as a company is making efforts to correct themselves, the correction is insufficient in that these films allowed stereotyping to be carried off of movie screens and TV screens into the "real" world.

I have shown above the ways representation can shape consumers' ideas of how people from underrepresented communities talk and behave, and we shall now analyze how Disney films have depicted Natives. *Peter Pan* is the first Native representation within a Disney film. Premiering in 1953, Disney's portrayal of Natives reflected how the world was viewing Natives at this time. The film stereotypes Native people by making no distinctions about which Native nations or First Nation the Indigenous characters belong to.[25] When differentiating First Nations representation from Native American representation, how it is executed matters even more than the idea of inclusion. Members of Native nations know who their people are and can recognize themselves through the art and cultural styles used in a film; Disney's *Peter Pan* paid no attention to these distinctions. The first time Natives are introduced in *Peter Pan*, Captain Hook is looking at a map for places to search for Peter, and he notes the "Indian Territory" and refers to the people there as "redskins." "What Makes the Red Man Red?" is the song the Lost Boys sing as they march through the woods, on their way to hunt the NDNs. No doubt the film influenced audiences and likely established a standard for how Hollywood would portray Natives.

Not until more than forty years after *Peter Pan* did audiences get the 1995 movie *Pocahontas*, the first animated Disney movie featuring Natives as main characters. As I explained in this chapter's opening, Disney's version is historically inaccurate and takes liberties with the historical figure Pocahontas is modeled upon. Amonute was her real name; Pocahontas was her nickname, meaning "playful one." Disney romanticizes what was in fact a tragedy for the Powhatan people.[26] In the Disney film, audiences follow a love story between a European settler and a Native woman. Though audiences want to believe the story Disney tells, it is the only version with a happy conclusion for the young Powhatan woman. The real story ends with the death of Pocahontas after she was assimilated to domesticity within the Western world. As scholar Sophie Mayer argued, Disney's movie made Native women vulnerable by justifying colonial representations of Native women and depicting them as sexual objects in need of assimilation.[27] Mayer also points out that Pocahontas's story parallels William Shakespeare's *Romeo and Juliet*, thereby adding romance that is familiar to non-Native audiences. What also makes the story as told by Disney so problematic is that the narrative is told largely from the perspective of John Smith, a European settler. These elements of *Pocahontas* bring us back to the misrepresentation of Indigenous peoples through Disney's storytelling.

Fast forward to 2016 when Walt Disney Animation Studios presented *Moana*. *Moana* was the second time Disney depicted Pacific cultures; the first was 2002's *Lilo and Stitch*, an animated film that represented the Native Hawaiian population.[28] Audiences can recognize a significant improvement in how Disney aimed to more authentically represent and reflect Pacific Indigeneity. Unfortunately, the film *Moana* still falls short because of cultural appropriation and Westernization of the Pacific culture itself. For example, my main note would be that the music scored for the film still undercuts the Pacific Indigeneity cultural integrity by hybridizing the Indigenous music with Western culture. The music in *Moana* exemplifies the problem of what Robin Armstrong calls "musical colonization." This term refers to the ways Western instruments, rhythms, and styles are inserted into non-Western cultures, thereby changing them to a hybridized version.[29] *Moana's* opening musical number, "Tulou Tagaloa," written by Opetaia Foa'i, creates a disillusion that viewers are being immersed in Moana's Pacific Islander culture and gaining new knowledge about Moana's people. The third musical number, "Where You Are" by Foa'i, Mark Mancina, and Lin-Manuel Miranda, opens with a blending of two non-Western languages, Samoan and Tokelauan.

As I think about *Moana*, my training in AIS and ethnomusicology forces me to ask some questions about this film, specifically with hybridization and representation. The songs use a Western chordal structure, even though Pacific cultures do not recognize sounds or music in the form of chords. As a result, the music immediately becomes hybridized, removing its Pacific cultural integrity.

Moreover, does Disney's combining of Polynesian dialects bring proper representation to the communities they are meant to depict? Is Disney suggesting that these cultures are interchangeable? Because of colonization and assimilation, we are unable to remember a time when Indigenous communities were united. Disney's representation and use of hybridization in *Moana* can be seen as erasing the Indigenous struggles that colonization has wrought, which separated communities and pitted communities' own people against each other.

As progressive as the Pacific communities had hoped the movie would be, what made it more disappointing was the performative preparation that Disney storytellers allegedly took to capture the "true essence" of Moana's Pacific culture. In the extras of the movie (available for viewing through Disney+), there is a twelve-minute short titled *They Know the Way: Making the Music*, which features *Moana's* composers giving audiences a behind-the-scenes look at the music-making process. Miranda and Mancina are two non-Indigenous composers working alongside Foa'i, a Samoan composer. As I watched this extra, I got hopeful that what the composers considered would show up on the big screen. But when the film premiered, Pacific communities were disappointed because the film was not executed as they expected.[30] Disney had given these cooperative Indigenous communities false hope that their cultures and struggles would be displayed with true authenticity, but the final product did not deliver. Language, music, clothing—in short, the cultural elements, combined with the story itself—were all Westernized.[31] This illustrates the idea of hybridization of Western with Indigenous, which took away from the film's hoped-for cultural integrity. To return to Robinson's theories from above, Disney's *Moana* did not present Pacific culture as $1 + 1 = 1$, but rather, $1 + 1 = 2$ (or, Westernized Disney + Pacific = hybridized *Moana*).

The *Moana* example shows that there is a monetizing motivation for Disney to bring more representation through Pacific cultures, but by undercutting their promises, we can see that Disney's values are more about audience than accuracy. I understand budgets do exist so not everything will be included, but Westernizing Indigenous cultures (such as music) is still a form of settler colonialism. This will lead Indigenous audiences to believe that to be represented on the big screen, they must compromise who they are and where they come from to fit into the entertainment industry.

While much work remains, progress toward a more inclusive future continues.

Conclusion

When I watch Disney now, I have mixed emotions. I feel guilty that I am supporting this conglomerate of a company that barely cares about my story. But at the same time, Disney is demonstrating that they are putting in the effort. With new shows, shorts, and movies being produced, the stories being told now are beginning to feel more authentic not only in the manner of being told but in who is telling the story. In the beginning of 2024, Disney+ premiered a new Marvel hero show *Echo*, where we know our hero Maya Lopez has roots in the Choctaw Nation. Or, the Native story I connect to the most is Disney's 2023 short *The Roof*, which shares the journey of a young man being taught his cultural ties as a Two-Spirit individual from his grandfather. These two productions bring Indigenous representation that had not been up to par earlier in Disney's 100 years of existence. When I see that type of storytelling, I see it as Disney demonstrating they are listening to their Indigenous audience. Those changes are what mark the beginning of actual change, rather than promised change.

Changes, in my view, are important because they can lead to the inspiration for the next Walt Disney. We are already seeing Indigenous animators and Indigenous storytellers, and the future is waiting for the next great visionary. The inclusion and authenticity of Indigenous voices allow us to remain resilient in order to sustain the cultural integrity of individual voices with struggles known all too well. Audiences get to see a different side of Indigenous people—different from what is typically told through American history, world history, pop culture, and mass media like Disney's popular films. Inclusion and authenticity will change how future Native generations are represented in mass media and how they are looked at in their surrounding communities. And it changes their way of education. They will be learning who they are differently from the way I learned. We will close generational gaps that separate urban NDNs and reservation NDNs. There will be fewer stereotypes that follow urban Natives and reservation Natives. These groups will not hold anything against each other; a change in cultural representation can lead to healing between urban and reservation Natives.

As time has progressed, representation has evolved and must continue to evolve. Disney has attempted to do this by including Indigenous voices, and we can mark this as a positive change in how these communities are being included in Disney's magic. But we must recognize that simply including Indigenous voices is the beginning step. Next steps include listening to and understanding Indigenous communities as they are, instead of making their stories "digestible" for a Western consuming audience.

When I began my studies in ethnomusicology, I could not study who I wanted to study (Indigenous communities) because the Western research methods do not use a holistic approach and felt inhumane to me. I know that making these kinds of changes requires a systematic approach when it comes to research. By not allowing myself to follow my passion for music, I took the academic journey of going into AIS, and by changing my path, I was able to gain a new way of approaching research into Indigenous communities, especially through music. This path still allowed me to learn my own values that I adhere to—values that allow me to connect myself to who I believe I am but also who I am trying to be. Doing so has allowed me to connect to a part of myself I did not grow up with.

Indigenous stories—our stories—are complex and should be understood as such. They deserve authentic representation. And I know it will take more than magic to make these dreams come true.

Notes

1　I would like to acknowledge my writing coach Jill Peterfeso. Thank you for making the process enjoyable through this challenge.

2　The title of this chapter was suggested by a fellow Native scholar, Koi /Kaɪ/ Begay.

3　In a traditional Diné introduction, one would introduce themselves by stating their clans, beginning with who their mother's clan "is" and then who they are "born for" through their father's clan. It is a rough translation into English, but in Diné bizaad (Navajo Language), the significance it holds plays a key role in how you connect yourself through clanship. For a scholarly account of kinship and clanship connections, see Raymond D. Austin, *Navajo Courts and Navajo Common Law: A Tradition of Tribal Self Governance* (Minneapolis: University of Minnesota, 2009), 87.

4　Whitewashing is a harmful misdirection of stories told by the oppressors who create them. Historical and fictional stories that are whitewashed have been altered by people telling the story, making events seem less harmful than what really took place. See Claire Gillespie, "What Is Whitewashing, and Why Is It Harmful?," May 26, 2023, https://www.health.com/mind-body/health-diversity-inclusion/whitewashing.

5　For some treatments of "Disneyfy," see Mike Budd, "Introduction: Private Disney, Public Disney," in *Rethinking Disney: Private Control, Public Dimensions*, ed. Mike Budd and Max H. Kirsch (Middletown: Wesleyan University Press, 2005), 7; *Merriam-Webster s.v* "Disneyfication," https://www.merriam-webster.com/dictionary/Disneyfication.

6　Allen F. Repko and Rick Szostak, "Chapter 1: Introducing Interdisciplinary Studies," in *Interdisciplinary Research: Process and Theory* (Thousand Oaks: Sage Publishing, 2021), 6.

7 The Indian Relocation Act, also known as Public Law 959, was put into action in 1956 to encourage Native adults to move off the reservation to assimilate within Western society.

8 Jason Sperb, "'Take a Frown, Turn It Upside Down': Splash Mountain, Walt Disney World, and the Cultural De-rac[e]-ination of Disney's Song of the South (1946)," *Journal of Popular Culture* 38, no. 5 (2005): 924–38.

9 Victoria Pettersen Lantz, "What's Missing in Frontierland? American Indian Culture and Indexical Absence at Walt Disney World," in *Performance and the Disney Theme Park Experience: The Tourist as Actor,* ed. Jennifer A. Kokai and Tom Robson (Cham, Switzerland: Palgrave Macmillan, 2019), 47.

10 See "Maps," Native Land Digital, https://native-land.com/ (accessed October 27, 2024). Native Land Digital's mission is to map Indigenous lands to change and challenge colonialism.

11 Pierre Bélanger, Ghazal Jafari, Pablo Escudero, Hernán Bianchi-Benguria, Tiffany Kaewen, and Alexander S. Arroyo, "No Design on Stolen Land: Dismantling Design's Dehumanising White Supremacy," in *The Landscapists: Architectural Design* (Hoboken: Wiley, 2020). The article can be found on this website: https://issuu.com /o-p-e-n-s-y-s-t-e-m-s/docs/2020-ndsl_ad90.

12 Constantin Brăiloiu, *Problems of Ethnomusicology,* trans. A. L. Lloyd (Cambridge: Cambridge University Press, 2009).

13 Ibid.

14 For more on this debate about passion versus monetary gain for under-resourced students, see the California State University, "Jeffrey Duncan-Andrade, Ph.D.," https://www.calstate.edu/impact-of-the-csu/student-success/Profiles/Pages/Dr-Jeffrey -Duncan-Andrade.aspx (accessed September 8, 2024).

15 Dylan Robinson, "Chapter 1: Hungry Listening," in *Hungry Listening: Resonant Theory for Indigenous Sound Studies* (Minneapolis: University of Minnesota Press, 2020).

16 Dylan Robinson, "Introduction," in *Hungry Listening: Resonant Theory for Indigenous Sound Studies* (Minneapolis: University of Minnesota Press, 2020), 9.

17 "Applied Indigenous Studies, Bachelor of Science," Northern Arizona University, https://nau.edu/ais/bs/ (accessed September 3, 2024).

18 Margaret Kovach, *Indigenous Methodologies: Characteristics, Conversations and Contexts* (Toronto: University of Toronto Press, 2009).

19 Ibid., 42.

20 Ibid., 46.

21 Peter A. Leavitt, Rebecca Covarrubias, Yvonne A. Perez, and Stephanie A. Fryberg, "'Frozen in Time': The Impact of Native American Media Representations on Identity and Self-Understanding," *Journal of Social Issues* 71, no. 1 (2015): 39–53, https://doi.org/10.1111/josi.12095.

22 Ibid.

23 One might assume we can solve this problem by simply separating Western and Indigenous methodologies altogether. This is not the case, however. Margaret Kovach would argue that because Indigenous research methods would not exist without the existence of their polar opposite because of how much they borrow from each other when it comes down to research and conceptual frameworks. Within my insight, I believe Indigenous research uses its counter to provide a variant of results that Western methods cannot provide. To explore more, see Kovach, "Chapter 2: Creating

Indigenous Research Frameworks," in *Indigenous Methodologies: Characteristics, Conversations and Contexts* (Toronto: University of Toronto Press, 2009). Kovach, *Indigenous Methodologies,* Chapter 2 Indigenous Conceptual Framing in Indigenous Methodologies.

24 *Peter Pan,* directed by Hamilton Luske, Clyde Geronimi, and Wilfred Jackson (1953; Walt Disney Productions), Disney+. The warning is a content warning for Disney's streaming service.

25 When I distinguish Native nations from First Nations, I am talking about Natives in the United States and Natives in Canada, respectively. When I say Native American here, I mean Natives from the United States.

26 "Pocahontas: Her Life and Legend," National Parks Service, https://www.nps.gov/jame/learn/historyculture/pocahontas-her-life-and-legend.htm (accessed October 7, 2024).

27 Sophie Mayer, "Pocahontas No More: Indigenous Women Standing Up for Each Other in Twenty-first Century Cinema," *Alphaville: Journal of Film and Screen Media*, no. 10 (December 16, 2015): 113–28, https://doi.org/10.33178/alpha.10.07.

28 Pacific identity is also known as Pacific Islander. As time has progressed, so has the political identity that some Indigenous communities are recreating for themselves. Roger M. Keesing, "Creating the Past: Custom and Identity in the Contemporary Pacific," *The Contemporary Pacific* 1, no. 1/2 (1989): 19–42.

29 Robin Armstrong, "Time to Face the Music: Musical Colonization and Appropriation in Disney's Moana," *Social Sciences* 7, no. 7 (2018): 113, https://doi.org/10.3390/socsci7070113.

30 Michelle Anya Anjirbag, "Mulan and Moana: Embedded Coloniality and the Search for Authenticity in Disney Animated Film," *Social Sciences* 7, no. 11 (2018): 230, https://doi.org/10.3390/socsci7110230.

31 Ibid.

8

Asian Disneyland, Local Community Reactions, and the Role of Cultural Spaces

Jenny Banh

For over fifteen years, as an anthropology and Asian American studies professor, I have used examples of Disney's Asian theme parks as an educational tool to illustrate to my Anthropology of Asia college students the concepts of globalization. By using Disney-informed pedagogy, my students are able to identify concepts of space, labor, and consumption in an Asian context. My new book, *Fantasies of Hong Kong Disney*, explores the internationalization practices of a single Asian Disney park. The scope of the book, however, leaves little room for analysis of the local non-Disney theme parks that compete fiercely with Disney parks in Asia.[1] This comparative transnational study of globalization examines how the establishment of Disney theme parks in three Asian cities, namely Tokyo Disneyland (TDL), Hong Kong Disneyland (HKDL), and Shanghai Disneyland (SDL), elicited different reactions from local communities and businesses, particularly existing theme parks. For example, local communities viewed TDL as a complement to their existing theme parks. In contrast, imperial control prevailed over how HKDL entered the market and did business.

Consistent with previous research, a process of "glocalization" occurred within TDL, which helped to minimize competition and facilitate its profitable coexistence with local theme parks. However, in other cultural and socioeconomic contexts (i.e., Hong Kong and Shanghai), local communities viewed Asian Disney parks as competitors to existing theme parks, despite the glocalization that favored Asian Disney parks. I argue that different local communities perceive Asian Disney parks as either complements or competitors to their local theme parks depending on their unique social, cultural, and economic contexts. The success of Disney parks in Asia turns on their adaptability to local cultures and their local theme park competitors. By examining how Asian Disney parks have been received in Tokyo, Hong Kong, and Shanghai, this chapter contributes to our understanding of how the byproducts of globalization shape and are shaped by local cultural spaces.

There are currently three Asian Disney parks: SDL, HKDL, and TDL. Disneyland's local competitors in Asia and community responses are important because of the direct impact of the large American multinational corporation on local Asian communities' social, cultural, and economic development. This article is a corrective addition to my 2025 book that illustrates the importance of Asian Disney parks' local Asian competitors for seeing the wider East Asian regional impact. Many academic disciplines can benefit from the insights I offer here, particularly business, tourism, and anthropological studies. I argue that Asian Disneylands, originating in the United States, act as a driver, co-facilitator, and challenger for local theme parks and cultural spaces in Asia.

This chapter does something that is probably unfamiliar to most readers: it shifts our gaze away from the Western-centric Walt Disney Company behemoth and toward Disney's Asian parks and their Asian regional competitors. There are currently twelve Disney theme parks and six Disney resorts worldwide. It is important to contextualize and analyze Disneyland's competitors in Asia because they are economically and culturally affected by American Disney theme parks and each other. The Walt Disney Company is one of the largest transnational corporations in the world that has expanded and affected other countries. Local Asian theme parks do not enjoy the political, social, and economic power held by the transnational Disney corporation. Disney owns movies, TV shows, theme parks, and a plethora of intellectual property. When the Walt Disney Company enters a new country, its voice plays an important economic, cultural, and political role. Regional theme parks in Asia are majority-owned by their respective Asian governments and, not surprisingly, are economically affected by Disney's arrival into their countries.

The three Asian Disney parks have different ownership models. TDL is 100 percent owned by Japan's Oriental Land Company (OLC), which manages and oversees the park. This is important in that TDL is fully owned by Japan, which has full management of the park. OLC only pays the Disney corporation a franchise fee. HKDL is jointly owned by Disney (48 percent) and Hong Kong International Theme Parks Limited (52 percent) with US management. HKDL does not have independent management authority and must obtain permission from the US leadership team. SDL is jointly owned by the Walt Disney Company (43 percent) and Shendi (57 percent),[2] so there is a mix of management between the Chinese and US executive teams.

Most importantly, however, there is a dearth of information about Asian Disney parks and their competitors, which this chapter seeks to address.

Local Competitors of Asian Disney Parks

How do we define the "competitors" of Asian Disney parks? Here, the term "competitors" refers to Asian theme parks and regional cultural sites. Therefore, I connect their experiences of being East Asian, even though they are located in different countries. In China, this can refer to cultural and heritage sites such as the Great Wall. In Japan, regional competitors might be a Japanese theme park. In Hong Kong, a local competitor is Ocean Park (OP) Marine theme park. There are many competitors as well as diverse consumers who want different venues and activities.

Different age groups have different consumption patterns and needs. Children or young adults are generally the main consumers of theme parks. Families are also more frequent park visitors than single individuals, although interestingly, TDL is visited by a large number of young Japanese women.[3] These women go to TDL in groups, finding the park's atmosphere to be fantastic and fun. Middle-aged tourists may prefer a child-free environment, while seniors may prefer heritage sites. Another consideration is foreign versus local tourists as these have different desires. Foreign tourists may want to visit traditional Asian cultural sites such as the Great Wall of China, Mount Fuji, or the Golden Buddha. Tourists' timing for travel adds another important factor; for example, when neighboring Asian countries celebrate Lunar New Year, Asian tourists may visit these countries during that period. Interregional Asian tourism is also a factor, which includes travel to relatively close Southeast Asian countries.

Tokyo Disneyland

Social: History of Opening

When the first Disney theme park opened, Walt Disney said,

> To all who come to this happy place: Welcome. Disneyland is your land. Here age relives fond memories of the past—and here youth may savor the challenge and promise of the future. Disneyland is dedicated to the ideals, the dreams and the hard facts that have created America—with the hope that it will be a source of joy and inspiration to all the world.[4]

This statement—from a man who dared to dream—set the world on fire.

The idea for Disneyland was born when Walt Disney took his daughters on outings to local amusement parks. Eventually, after many years of hard work, tenacity, and dreaming, his wish to open a family-friendly amusement park came true. The first California theme park, Disneyland, opened on July 17, 1955, in Anaheim, California. It was immediately successful, both locally and nationally. More importantly, people outside the United States recognized Disneyland as a vacation destination. This spectacular success led Japan, France, the Hong Kong Special Administrative Region, and mainland China to want to open their own Disneyland-type theme park or to import the Disney theme park into their countries.

Japanese executives approached the Disney corporation to establish a Disneyland in the late 1950s. Japanese businessman Kunizo Matsuo asked the multimedia American corporation to create a Disneyland in Nara, Japan. In 1961, the Walt Disney Company built a Disneyland-type theme park in Nara, but a licensing dispute arose and the deal fell apart. This theme park was called Nara Dreamland and had no official Disney ties.[5] Disneyland's influence in Nara Dreamland is seen in some similar architecture that resembles Main Street, U.S.A. and Sleeping Beauty Castle, plus in having a Matterhorn-like mountain and a train depot at the park entrance.

Nara Dreamland showed that Japanese guests would visit a Western-style park, which helped plant the seeds for a full Disney park with Disney characters. In 1974, eight years after Walt Disney's death, a Japanese company, Oriental Land Company (OLC), invited Disney executives to visit Japan. The company's president, Chiharu Kawasaki, proposed to bring the Disney theme park with its characters to Japan. Kawasaki was successful in his aspirations, and TDL opened its doors on April 15, 1983, in Urayasu, Chiba, Japan. Under the terms of OLC's contract with Disney, Japan fully owns TDL and pays a franchise fee to Disney.[6] According to Raz, "OLC, which owns and operates TDL, is a partnership between companies: Mitsui Real Estate Development (Mitsui Fudosan) and Keisei Electric Railway (Keisei Dentetsu). Mitsui owns 48% of OLC and Keisei 52%."[7] This was the Disney corporation's first official theme park partnership outside the United States.

In *Riding the Black Ship* (1999), sociologist Aviad Raz documented the globalization practices that TDL offers to its Japanese "guests." He concluded that employees, management, and visitors experience *glocalization*, which he defined as "local adaptation to global culture."[8] One example of glocalization includes the fact that TDL does not have a Main Street, U.S.A. Instead, it has a World's Bazaar, which is a more globalized marketplace than Main Street, U.S.A. which is themed as an early twentieth-century Midwestern American town. Also notable is that vending machines, while focal to Japanese culture and ubiquitous all over Japan, are specifically excluded in the park; this gives Japanese visitors the feeling that they are no longer in Japan. TDL also serves food that is a mix of Japanese, Western, and other Asian cuisines. Raz argued that TDL markets itself as American but essentially follows many Japanese labor structures designed for Japanese consumers. Japanese visitors make TDL their own by incorporating their own cultural norms of having a fusion of Western and Japanese items.

Cultural: Success due to Japanese Preexisting Kawaii Culture

TDL is one of the most successful Disney parks because Japanese people have always loved *Kawaii* (meaning "cute") cultural items, such as Pokémon, Hello Kitty, and Sailor Moon.[9] Toyoda argued that TDL is successful because it offers the Japanese a world that is unfamiliar to them. This means that TDL is not a typically modern Japanese robotics space or a traditional Japanese heritage area hundreds of years old. TDL was so successful and popular with locals that it was expanded in 2001, resulting in the creation of an adjacent park, Tokyo DisneySea, featuring characters from *Finding Nemo* (2003) and *The Little Mermaid* (1989). TDL is successful because of the synergy of two cultures that have some overlap in terms of cuteness.[10]

Japanese women who visit the park also dress up, showing their love of *Kawaii* culture that overlaps with Disney culture. Toyoda revealed that "In terms of demographics, over 70% of [Japanese] visitors are women, more than half of TDR visitors are between the ages of 18–39, and visitors aged 40 or over account for 18%."[11] Some young Japanese female Disney fans who live near TDL have visited the park more than 100 times. They love TDL for several reasons, mainly that it is a safe and fantastic place to dress up and visit with a group of girlfriends. This is similar to US park visitors who dress up in Mickey hats, Minnie ears, and Disney t-shirts, although there are some differences. For example, some women wear British maid outfits inspired by Alice in Wonderland. Other women wear Sailor Moon and other Japanese school uniform outfits. There are also women who wear anime-inspired outfits that are very elaborate. Some female visitors wear outfits that are Disney-themed and also incorporate their own Japanese culture, such as a Disney-themed kimino.[12] Finally, some women wear traditional Japanese kimonos, but the fabric features different Disney characters.

There are many overlapping Disneyland and *Kawaii* cultural elements, but some are more Japanese, like Duffy the Disney Bear, who is Mickey Mouse's personal teddy bear. Disney created new dolls marketed exclusively for TDL because these resonated more with the Japanese *Kawaii* taste. Mickey Mouse has obvious roots in the United States whereas these new characters have roots in Japanese culture. As a result, these new consumer products are more accessible and relevant to Asians.

Duffy and his fellow stuffed animals are a prominent point of merchandise in Asian Disney parks but are sold in smaller and more limited quantities in the United States. One can easily see this in Asian Disney parks where almost all the guests wear some type of Duffy and Friends headgear and clothing. In fact, I would argue that Duffy is more popular than Mickey Mouse in East Asia. Thousands of male and female Asian tourists can be seen buying merchandise featuring Duffy and his friends, such as LinaBell, StellaLou, 'Oul Mel, Gelatoni, ShellieMay, and CookieAnn. Duffy the Disney Bear is a small brown bear in a sailor outfit featured prominently in Asian stores. LinaBell is a light pastel pink fox with a flower who loves nature and mysteries. StellaLou is a lilac bunny who is a ballet dancer. 'Olu Mel is a turtle and Aulani representative who is a musician and singer. Gelatoni is a green cat who loves to paint and draw. ShellieMay is a brown bear wearing a bow on her head. CookieAnn, the newest Duffy friend, is a small yellow dog from HKDL; she loves to bake and is a chef. Once Tokyo built its own Disneyland park, TDL created new plush characters that now, in Asia, exceed the popularity of Mickey Mouse.

Economic: Asian Competitors Are Complementary

TDL's regional competitors (see Table 8.1), such as Hanayashiki, Yomiuriland, Sanrio Puroland, and Fuji Q, are complements to the park. Table 8.1 shows the locations and years that the TDL competitors opened. They do not compete directly with TDL nor do they offer something different; they are quite similar in several respects. Some Japanese parks have an intense *Kawaii* culture, such as Sanrio Puroland, while other parks pay special attention to garden landscaping.

Asakusa Hanayashiki (浅草花やしき) is Japan's oldest amusement park, which opened in 1853. The entrance fee is very low, and the park has a garden theme. This is ideal for older Japanese visitors who deeply revere gardens. This park offers its visitors a bit of sentimentality in the form of older rides. It also features traditional Japanese gardens and food.

Table 8.1 TDL Competitors, Locations, and Opening Dates

Local Asian Competitors	Location	Opening Date
Hello Kitty land or Sanrio Puroland (サンリオピューロランド)	1 Chome-31 Ochiai, Tama, Tokyo 206-8588, Japan	December 7, 1990
Fuji-Q Highland (FQH) (富士急ハイランド)	5 Chome-6-1 Shinnishihara, Fujiyoshida, Yamanashi 403-0017, Japan	March 2, 1968
Asakusa Hanayashiki (浅草花やしき)	2 Chome-28-1 Asakusa, Taito City, Tokyo 111-0032, Japan	1853
Yomiuriland (よみうりランド)	4015-1 Yanokuchi, Inagi, Tokyo 206-8725, Japan	1964

Source: https://en.puroland.jp/language/, https://www.fujiq.jp/en/index.html, https://www.hanayashiki.net/english/, https://www.yomiuriland.com/en/

Yomiuriland (よみうりランド) is another older theme park that opened in 1964. Located in Tokyo, it is home to the famous (in Japan) Yomiuri Giants Stadium, where the Yomiuri Giants baseball team trains. At this amusement park, visitors can learn about mechanical manufacturing processes via workshops. This is similar to the steampunk aesthetic in the United States. This park appeals to *Otaku*, a derogatory term for Japanese youth obsessed with trains, anime, and computers (similar to the American term "geeks").

FQH is located at the foot of the majestic Mount Fuji. Mount Fuji (富士山) is sacred to Japanese people who make pilgrimages there. There are many shops and religious shrines in the area. FQH is well known for its three roller coasters: Fujiyama, Takabisha, and Eejanaika. FQH differs from TDL in that entry is free and people only pay for individual rides.[13]

Sanrio Puroland (サンリオピューーロランド) opened on December 7, 1990, and features the globally iconic Hello Kitty. In *Pink Globalization: Hello Kitty's Trek across the Pacific* (2013), Yano argued that Hello Kitty is a perfect example of Japanese cute culture. This local competitor to TDL is perfectly suited to Japanese tastes.

Looking at these Japanese theme park competitors, one can conclude that there is no direct competitor to TDL as they all offer slightly different things. The creation of TDL is part of Japan's strong economic growth and boom, which frees up the population for more leisure activities. TDL fits perfectly into Japan's *Kawaii* culture and is very profitable. It is important to remember that TDL's profits go directly to a Japanese company, OCL, wholly owned by the Japanese government, and benefit Japanese people economically, culturally, and politically.

Because TDL is wholly owned by Japan, all losses and gains are borne by the Japanese government. TDL is one of the most profitable theme parks in the world, so it can be considered culturally complementary to other Japanese theme parks. This contrasts with HKDL, which is not wholly owned by HK Special Administrative Region, and to which we now turn.

Hong Kong Disneyland

Social: History of Opening

The origin of HKDL (香港迪士尼樂園) is linked to the British colonial history of HK SAR, China (1841–1997). The British distributed opium to China, which Chinese authorities opposed when they saw the harmful effects of opium on individuals and society. This led to the First Opium War (September 4, 1839–August 29, 1842) and the Second Opium War (October 8, 1856–October 18, 1860), which China lost, resulting in the cession of both Macau and HK to Britain. These humiliating territorial losses are collectively referred to in China as the Unequal Treaties.[14] With the Japanese occupation during the Second World War (December 8, 1941–August 15, 1945), HK was a British colony for 156 years.[15]

During the over one century of colonization, HK rose in economic and cultural status over mainland China. The HK people could speak English and had freedom of expression, yet were still treated unequally by the British. During colonization, HK quickly rose to become business-friendly as a global trading hub. Many in HK wanted to keep up this elevated social and economic status. HK, along with Singapore, South Korea, and Taiwan, are known as having tiger economies, which means they have a highly industrialized, globalized economy focused on exports.

Cultural: Capitalistic Culture, Bird Flu, Asian Financial Crisis, Social Unrest

During the period leading up to decolonization in 1997, and because HK citizens did not want to be under mainland China's rule, there was a massive migration of HK people to other countries such as Australia, the United States, and Canada. In addition, in 1997, both the Asian Financial Crisis and the Avian influenza (N5N1) outbreak occurred, leading to many deaths. It was during this bleak time for HK that Disney entered into talks with the Walt Disney Company about developing a Disneyland. The HK government wanted HK to become a premier Asian regional family destination; HKDL was part of the plans to accomplish this.

When the original contract terms between HK and the Walt Disney Company were disclosed, there was a lot of bad publicity of the unequal nature of the contract between the HK government and the Walt Disney Company. Specifically, the HK SAR government paid 90 percent of the building costs and held a 57 percent stake, while the Walt Disney Company had a 43 percent stake and only paid 10 percent of the original costs.[16] Even to date, HKDL must pay the Walt Disney Company fees even when they are losing money. "This means the Lantau-based park could have paid between HK$1.68 and HK$3.37 billion to the California-based conglomerate since it started releasing financial figures in 2009, the *Post* has calculated—despite recording losses in eight of its 11 years."[17] Critics call the Disney deal the "unfair treaty," which is reminiscent of the colonialism in which HK was taken from mainland China. This information was made public, and public criticism arose, leading to bad publicity when the park first opened on September 12, 2005. To date, HKDL has lost money every year since its opening, with few exceptions.[18]

HKDL is located on Lantau Island, HK, and has some Chinese cultural elements. HK is only a short flight away from Japan, so it is easy for HK people to travel to Japan. The original architecture of HKDL when it first opened was a carbon copy of the original Disneyland in Anaheim, California, which can be seen in elements such as Main Street, U.S.A. and some of the themed lands. However, HKDL implemented some principles of Chinese feng shui, which is an Asian geomancy location system.[19] These feng shui features include the positioning of buildings at certain angles and the specific arrangement of natural elements throughout the park. Another example is the tilt of the HKDL entrance gate, which is tilted according to the lucky angle of feng shui.

Arguably, there could be more HK culture and historical elements displayed in the park. For example, they could have a themed HK Film land. HK is globally famous for many of its actors, such as Jackie Chan and Bruce Lee. It is also known for its internationally popular Kung Fu movies. They could also include an historical HK fishing village to highlight prominent HK culture.

HKDL continues to be criticized for its lack of profits, poor working conditions, cultural imperialism, and tax burden on HK taxpayers. HKDL has not made a profit for almost all the years it has operated, and as a result, HK taxpayers are supporting the park. HKDL workers have been in the media complaining about being mistreated by the company, with no given break time and becoming overheated in the hot, humid HK weather. The HKDL employee union, which is not directly associated with the Disney Company, alleged that not all HKDL workers were treated the same. There were also local community complaints that the park was too small when it opened.[20]

These local community grievances sparked discussions about local Hong Kong competitor offerings being a better economic deal and more culturally appropriate. The local HK community members noted that the following HKDL competitors even made a profit. Ocean Park was talked about as a larger venue and was cheaper. The Hong Kong Museum was seen as culturally competent in that it fully highlighted Hong Kong's history, culture, and global film contributions. Hong Kong's gigantic bronze Golden Buddha is visited by lay tourists as well as Buddhists from all over the world. Table 8.2 shows the address and location of these important tourist sites. It also shows the opening dates, which predate HKDL by many years. These are nostalgic places for the local community who have familial memories of these places. Hong Kong people are very cost conscious and efficient with their spending. All three sites are beloved by global and local tourists.

Economic: Asian Competitors Innovated

There are many local Asian competitors to HKDL (see Table 8.2). The main local competitor of HKDL is Ocean Park (OP: 香港海洋公園). OP was developed for the

Table 8.2HKDL Competitors Names, Locations, and Opening Dates

Local Asian Competitors	Location	Opening Date
Ocean Park Hong Kong 香港海洋公園	180 Wong Chuk Hang Road, Aberdeen, Hong Kong Island	1977
Hong Kong History Museum 香港歷史博物館	100 Chatham Rd S, Tsim Sha Tsui, Hong Kong	1975
Golden Buddha (statue) 天壇大佛	Lantau Island, Hong Kong	1993

Source: https://www.oceanpark.com.hk/en, https://hk.history.museum/en/web/mh/index.html, https://plm.org.hk/eng/buddha.php

local community and is owned by the island government. It was donated to the HK Jockey Club, a horse racing club that donates part of its revenue to local residents. It opened on January 10, 1977, and is located on the main part of HK Island. Set against the backdrop of the beautiful South China Seas, the park offers dozens of marine species and mammals as well as roller coasters and rides for adults. People have to be a certain height to ride the roller coasters, which excludes children. OP is nicknamed the "HK People's Theme Park." It is popular with local residents, although it is not always profitable. With the creation of HKDL, Ocean Park was rumored to be closing, but it was redeveloped with a HK$1 billion redevelopment.

The arrival of HKDL boosted the city's growth, innovation, and local pride in its cultural resources. For many Hong Kongers, OP was their first real experience with a theme park. OP made people feel appreciated as they would receive a free ticket on their birthday, creating many positive associations and memories. Although the park was older and some might say run down, the arrival of HKDL transformed OP into a world-class theme park by igniting renovations. In 2005, in response to the arrival of HKDL, OP unveiled a multimillion-dollar redevelopment plan to compete against Disneyland.

Similarly, in *Golden Arches East* (1998), anthropologist James Watson discussed how the initial opening of McDonald's restaurants in East Asia transformed the region in terms of changing spatial locales, consumption patterns, and labor practices. For example, in HK there was no queuing culture: Chinese people were not accustomed to standing in line and instead jostled in a crowd to move to the front of the line. McDonald's introduced Western queuing norms on the island, which was transformative and affected the overall culture.[21] The fast-food chain had Hong Kong people stand in line. Additionally, McDonald's reputation for cleanliness and decor inspired Asian fast-food restaurants to do the same. The arrival of HKDL to the city had a parallel effect of upgrading and transforming the old marine theme park. OP was slated to be closed but instead transformed itself to meet Disney park standards.

The newly renovated marine theme park now features two world-class hotels, rides, and new exhibit updates. In 2019, OP opened a luxury Marriott hotel with 395 rooms. OP is also home to two rare Chinese giant pandas, orcas, and dolphins. It is home to one of the largest Asian Halloween theme events in the world. There is also a themed area based on the city's past. OP has surpassed HKDL in attendance for many years and is one of the most visited theme parks in the world.[22]

Outside of OP, there are other iconic HK tourist attractions and locally important sites. There is the world-famous giant Golden Buddha statue, which is a true World Heritage wonder and is synonymous with Hong Kong. In the past, this religious statue was only accessible by a long bus ride, but now there is a superb cable car ride. The Golden Buddha is both locally and internationally significant.

Another competitor of HKDL, the Hong Kong Museum, allows visitors to understand the archaeological and historical history of the city. This is the perfect place to learn more about the local people. It primarily attracts tourists visiting museums and school-age students.

Overall, these competitors are complements to HKDL. However, in the case of Ocean Park, local people prefer it to HKDL because of the unfair initial deal and the continued bad publicity associated with HKDL. HKDL is still a work in progress and loses millions of dollars each year.

Shanghai Disneyland

Social: History of Opening

In the 1990s, the Disney corporation was in talks with Shanghai Shendi Group to develop SDL (上海迪士尼乐园), but negotiations fell through when Disney produced the film *Kundun* (1997). Matt Glasby's article, "How Disney got kicked out of China over Martin Scorsese's *Kundun*, a 1997 movie that ripped a hole in US-China relations," details how Shanghai was the ideal original site for China's first Disneyland.[23] Contract discussions fell through because Disney would not pull the film *Kundun*, which showed the early life of the Dalai Lama. China felt that the movie would be Sinophobic. "[O]n November 1, 1997, China's Ministry of Radio, Film and Television sent a memo to the Motion Picture Association of America blacklisting Disney, Columbia TriStar (regarding *Seven Years in Tibet*) and MGM/United Artists (regarding *Red Corner*) for making films that 'viciously attack China.'"[24] All Chinese business activities with these three companies temporarily ceased without exception, including of course business with Disney. Therefore, Hong Kong was selected as the site for China's first Disneyland, which opened in 2005.

Over the years, Disney continued to court mainland China, sending former secretary of state Henry Kissinger to smooth relations, and Michael Eisner apologized to Chinese Prime Minister Zhu Rongji in 1998.[25] In 2009, Bob Iger, then CEO of the Walt Disney Company, signed an agreement with the Chinese government and Shanghai Shendi Group to open SDL (上海迪士尼乐园) on June 16, 2016. SDL is the most technically advanced Disneyland in the world, using extended reality technology including augmented, virtual, and mixed reality.

Culture: "Authentically Disney and Distinctly Chinese"

Disney had to adapt to the Chinese government's demands, which wanted the park to feature Chinese elements that Disney chairman Bob Iger called "authentically Disney and distinctly Chinese." *The Glocalization of Shanghai Disneyland*, written by Ni-Chen Sung, argues that SDL is not cultural imperialism but glocalization.[26] SDL exceeded first-year expectations for attendance with over fourteen million visitors.

Economic: Asian Competitors

Disneyland represents the West, and there have been different periods in Chinese history where China was subjected to humiliating defeats and colonization by the West. Some Chinese feel like they have been victims of Western aggression throughout the centuries.[27] All the more important, then, to look at the parks that Chinese companies build—parks that compete with Asian Disneylands.

Disneyland has many competitors throughout China, including national heritage sites like the Great Wall of China, the Terracotta Army, and high-tech Chinese cities. There are also technologically advanced tourist areas, such as a cyberpunk city named Chongqing, where it is not uncommon to have touchless food delivery. Some local Chinese like to travel internally thanks to low-cost flight tickets and bullet train travel. Guilin, Shanghai, and Beijing are popular destinations within China. In short, China—the most populated country in the world—boasts many relatively inexpensive travel options.

In Hangzhou, China, there is the Hangzhou Paradise theme park (杭州乐园) which has many thrill rides, musical entertainments, and a Ferris wheel. In Beijing, there is the Beijing Shaijigshan Amusement Park (北京石景山游乐园), one of the oldest amusement parks, with many roller coasters. Wanda Group at one time owned

Table 8.3SDL Competitors Names, Locations, and Opening Dates

Local Asian Competitors	Location	Opening Date
Wanda Nanchang Outdoor Theme Park (Wanda Group)	MV42+H5P, Ganjiang S Blvd, Xinjian District, Nanchang, Jiangxi, China, 330038	2016
Wanda Nanjing Theme Park (Wanda Group)	China, Jiangsu, Nanjing, Qixia District, Xigang Neighborhood, 181, Xianlin Blvd, 181号4幢 邮政编码: 210033	2018
Wanda Movie Park (Wanda Group)	9 Yanxia Rd, Wuchang District, Wuhan, Hubei, China, 430062	2014
The Great Wall of China 長城	Built along the northern border and expanded under different dynasties	7th century BC

Source: https://forrec.com/projects/wanda-nanchang-outdoor-theme-park/, https://kcc.be/portfolio-item/nanjing-indoor-theme-park/, https://www.archdaily.com/581056/wanda-movie-park-stufish-entertainment-architects, https://www.mutianyugreatwall.com/

thirteen theme parks and had some pointed words about the arrival of the USA Disney theme park coming to China (see Table 8.3). Wanda Group is owned by one of China's richest billionaires, Wang Jianlin, who had pointed words about Disney's arrival: "Disney didn't believe that China has Wanda," Wang said in a CCTV interview. "They shouldn't have entered China. We have a [saying]: one tiger is no match for a pack of wolves. Shanghai has one Disney, while Wanda, across the nation, will open 15 to 20."[28] Wang seemed to imply that the Disney corporation was not taking mainland Chinese theme park competitors seriously enough. Wang further stated that Disney copies previous intellectual property products, is not cost-effective, and does not bring any innovation. Wang said that his theme parks would compete with Disney and make SDL unprofitable within the next ten to twenty years. Wang stated, "By the end of 2020, Wanda says its goal is to amass 200 million tourist visits and $15.5 billion in tourism revenue."[29] Wang's nationalistic comments indicate his intention to be a major competitor to SDL. One could argue that Wanda Group is against SDL because of capitalist and cultural rivalry. This competition is a common business motivation. If the mainland Chinese patron goes to Shanghai Disneyland, then they might not go as often to the local Chinese theme parks.

Conclusion

Asia is booming, and its population represents 60 percent of the world population. The three Asian Disney parks and their local competitors are therefore significant areas of study. HKDL, SDL, and TDL act as drivers, economic co-facilitators, and challengers for local theme parks and cultural spaces in Asia. SDL, HKDL, and TDL offer higher construction standards, Western aesthetics, and consumption patterns. Examples include Western-style restrooms, dining rooms, and architecture. By bringing these high standards, Asian Disney parks can potentially improve the competitiveness of local Asian theme parks.

Also significant are the regional competitors that offer entertainment alternatives to Disney's Asian parks. These Asian theme parks that compete with Asian Disneylands bring a distinct quality not found in American theme parks: they offer comparable Asian-themed consumer goods like merchandise and food. In short, they highlight Asian culture.

This chapter has contributed to Asian transnational comparisons. All three Disney Asian parks have different developmental histories, and this affected their reception by their Asian competitors. The results link to previous research by Andrew Lainsbury (2000), *Once Upon American Dream: The Story of Euro Disneyland*, Aviad Raz (1999), *Riding the Black Ship: Japan and Tokyo Disneyland*, Ni-Chen Sung (2021), *The Glocalization of Shanghai Disneyland*, and Kimburley Choi (2010), *Remade in Hong Kong: How Hong Kong People Use Hong Kong Disneyland*.

Laymen, students, and academics can be helped by reading this chapter to learn how other Asian Disneylands developed and how their local competitors reacted. Competitors to Asian Disney parks react differently to Disney's arrival in their countries. In the case of TDL, its competitors see Disneyland as complementary to their cultural norms, such as *Kawaii* culture. TDL is also 100 percent owned by OCL, a Japanese company, and is very profitable. HKDL's competitors offer a different story. Its main rival is OP, which offers something different from HKDL, which is jointly owned by the Walt Disney Company and HK International Theme Parks Limited. OP is seen as a hometown hero local entity, and the arrival of HKDL triggered OP's massive multi-million dollar redevelopment. OP complements HKDL, although some local people prefer it to HKDL because it is closer to their Cantonese cultural heritage. SDL is the newest Disney park and the third in Asia. It is jointly owned by the Walt Disney Company and Shanghai Shendi Group. SDL is enjoying surprising success, which has spurred local competition from mainland Chinese theme parks, particularly Wang and his Wanda Group.

Further research on labor, space, and consumption is needed to examine the effect of Asian Disney parks on competition from local Asian theme parks and cultural heritage sites. A robust country-to-country comparison with American and foreign Disneyland theme park competitors would be a rich space for further research. Disneyland in Asia never came to a barren land but was put into an ecosystem of many different visitors, regional theme park competitors, and cities. The significance of looking at other Disneyland competitors, labor forces, and communities is important to Disney studies.

Notes

1 Jenny Banh, *Fantasies of Hong Kong Disneyland: Attempted Indigenization of Space, Labor and Consumption* (New Brunswick: Rutgers University Press, 2025).
2 Fact Sheet Shanghai Disneyland Resort, 2024, https://disneyconnect.com/app/uploads/sites/4/2022/05/fact_sheet_shanghai_disney_resort_2022_Q2.pdf.
3 Aviad Raz, *Riding the Black Ship: Japan and Tokyo Disneyland* (Cambridge: Harvard University Press, 1999).
4 Disney Marcio, "1955 Disneyland Opening Day [Complete ABC Broadcast]," July 15, 1955, posted July 17, 2011 by the Disney Company, YouTube, 12:44, https://www.youtube.com/watch?v=JuzrZET-3Ew.
5 ReviewTyme, "The Disney Park Walt Never Wanted—Tokyo Disneyland History," posted March 21, 2021, by ReviewTyme, YouTube, https://www.youtube.com/watch?v=9i97JCqo_os&ab_channel=ReviewTyme.
6 Raz, *Riding the Black Ship*, 23.
7 Ibid.
8 Ibid.
9 Anne Allison, *Millennial Monsters: Japanese Toys and the Global Imagination* (Berkeley: University of California Press, 2006).
10 Yukio Toyoda, "Recontextualizing Disney: Tokyo Disney Resort as a Kingdom of Dreams and Magic," *Social Science Japan Journal* 17, no. 2 (2014): 207–26, http://www.jstor.org/stable/43920444.
11 Ibid., 207.

12 A kimono is a traditional Japanese-style dress and national dress from the eighth to twelfth century that is still worn today in festivals.

13 It is interesting to note that this individual payment for specific rides was in alignment with the original pricing structure of the California Disneyland when it originally opened.

14 Dong Wang, *China's Unequal Treaties: Narrating National History* (Lanham: Lexington Books, 2005).

15 John Carroll, *A Concise History of Hong Kong* (Lanham: Rowman and Littlefield, 2007).

16 Jenny Banh, "Workers' View on Indigenization of Theme Park: A Case Study in Hong Kong," *International Journal of Business Anthropology* 9, no. 1 (2019), https://doi.org/10.33423/ijba.v9i1.2225.

17 Nikki Sun, "City Wants a New Deal: Hong Kong Disney Sends Billions of Dollars Back to US Parent Company while Reporting Losses," *South China Morning Post*, February 28, 2017, https://www.scmp.com/news/hong-kong/economy/article/2074453/government-urged-renegotiate-unfair-treaty-over-hong-kong.

18 Banh, *Fantasies of Hong Kong Disneyland*.

19 Kirsten Day, "Fengshui as a Narrative of Localization: Case Studies of Contemporary Architecture in Hong Kong and Shanghai" (PhD diss., Swinburne University of Technology, 2015).

20 Banh, "Workers' View on Indigenization of Theme Park."

21 James Watson, *Golden Arches East: Mcdonald's in East Asia* (Stanford: Stanford University Press, 1998).

22 Tom Mehrmann and Michael Switow, *Taming the Mouse: How a Small Hong Kong Theme Park Came to Dominate Disney* (Switow Media, 2018).

23 Matt Glasby, "How Disney Got Kicked Out of China over Martin Scorsese's Kundun, a 1997 Movie that Ripped a Hole in US-China Relations," *South China Morning Post*, July 7, 2023, https://www.scmp.com/lifestyle/entertainment/article/3226599/how-disney-got-kicked-out-china-over-martin-scorseses-kundun-1997-movie-ripped-hole-us-china.

24 Ibid.

25 Ibid.

26 Ni-Chen Sung, *The Glocalization of Shanghai Disneyland* (London and New York: Routledge, 2023).

27 While outside the scope of this chapter, Disney's relationship to Asian culture in film is also significant. Disney has been accused of cultural appropriation in films such as *Mulan*. For more, see Jenny Banh, "#MakeMulanRight: Retracing the Genealogy of Mulan from Ancient Chinese Tale to Disney Classic," in *Recasting the Disney Princess: The Coming of Age of the Empowered Children's Heroine in the Wake of Social Movements*, ed. Shearon Roberts (Lanham: Lexington, 2020); Jenny Banh, "Moana: Daughter of the Chief and Polynesian (in)Visibility," in *Recasting the Disney Princess: The Coming of Age of the Empowered Children's Heroine in the Wake of Social Movements*, ed. Shearon Roberts (Lanham: Lexington, 2020).

28 Scott Cendrowski, "China's Richest Man Picks a Fight with Disneyland," *Fortune*, May 24, 2016, https://fortune.com/2016/05/24/chinas-richest-man-just-picked-a-fight-with-disneyland/.

29 Ibid.

Section III

Nostalgia and Innovation

Section Introduction

Nostalgia and Innovation

Jill Peterfeso

If innovation is something Disney wears proudly on its sleeve, nostalgia is the blood pumping through its veins. These concepts seem contradictory: "innovation" suggests change and newness and forward movement, while "nostalgia" captures an emotional attachment to the past. Yet Disney weaves these together so closely that both are key facets of Disney's impact and identity.

One particular Walt Disney World (WDW) attraction exemplifies this dialectic relationship between nostalgia and innovation: The Carousel of Progress. A revolving theater attraction with animatronics and detailed sets that resides in Tomorrowland, the Carousel of Progress was designed by Walt Disney himself for the 1964–5 New York World's Fair. The show depicts an American family from the turn of the twentieth century to some unspecified time in the twenty-first century. In each of four scenes, the family experiences and enjoys—and father John explains—the latest inventions that change the family's lives: an icebox, air conditioning, a dishwasher, a television set. "During each era, learn how the technological marvels of the day made life more comfortable—and paved the way for unimaginable innovations," Disney writes of this attraction. The theater's design is a marvel as well: "Presented inside a revolving theater, the show includes an innovative audience seating area that moves around a stationary central stage for each act." This "Classic Walt Disney Attraction" ties back to Walt himself, and alongside the show's original Sherman brothers' song, "There's a Great Big Beautiful Tomorrow," the show is "a tribute to nostalgia."[1] The Carousel of Progress synthesizes innovation and nostalgia.

My Disney course for first-year college students is subtitled Imagination and Innovation. Every fall semester when I teach this class, students and I discuss the seemingly endless ways Walt Disney himself was an innovator who surrounded himself with inventive minds. Students learn that Disney (both man and company) was a pioneer in the combination of animation with live-action; the creation of the first cartoon with a synchronized soundtrack; the development of an advanced multiplane camera; the release of the first full-length animated film; the early use of merchandising with Mickey Mouse; the building of the first theme park; and the invention of audio-animatronics. Students marvel that so much of the imaginative magic they have come to take for granted in Disney films, parks, and merchandise are in fact examples of groundbreaking business savvy and technological discovery.

As students and I explore innovation, we find ourselves drawn into the emotional and ineffable. We discuss Walt's biography, or the way the company "Disneyfies" its stories for an American milieu, or Imagineering's theme park designs, and students begin to recognize that Disney's innovative technologies are emotionally generative. The class starts to talk about innovation and *feeling* in the same breath. They observe that Disney's innovative magic is merely "cool new technology" until it pulls at the heart. Students' comments become personal. A student explains that her grandmother recently died and that she loved all things Disney, and now that she has passed away, Disney provides an anchor to treasured family memories. Another student recalls going to Disney World with their parents before their divorce and wearing matching family t-shirts. Students smile and talk about watching Disney Channel shows with their siblings, or visiting parks with cousins, or listening to Disney music while decorating for the holidays. Disney has somehow become intertwined with their lives and their memories. Disney's stories are *their* stories.

How do we describe that heart-warming aspect of Disney magic? I write one word on the board: nostalgia. "What is nostalgia?" I ask. Students respond in a flurry: Nostalgia is bittersweet. It's comfort. It's comfort*ing*. It's memories of the past that get better with the passage of time. It's a wish tinged with sadness. It's a sense of missing something you never quite had. It's longing. It's a feeling that can catch you unsuspecting and won't let go. It's hard to explain, but you know it when it hits you.

All of that nostalgia is good for business. As Len Testa quipped in a November 2024 episode of the *Disney Dish*, "Nostalgia sells!"[2] It keeps Disney customers and guests coming back for more of that emotional fix. In a 1978 *New West* magazine interview that is equal parts philosophy and psychology, Disney artist and Imagineer John Hench explained Disneyland's affective appeal. He drew upon concepts like order, harmony, and making peace with death to describe how Disney storytelling—particularly in the parks' themed environments—delivers such emotional heft. For nostalgia, he turned to Main Street, U.S.A.:

> Main Street, of course, has the Victorian feeling, which is probably one of the great optimistic periods of the world where we thought progress was great and we all knew where we were going. This form reflects that prosperity, that enthusiasm. Walt wanted to reassure people. There's some nostalgia involved, of course, but nostalgia for what? There was never a Main Street like this one. But it reminds you of some things about *yourself* that you've probably forgotten about.[3]

In Hench's telling, nostalgia turns on memory, and Disney provides reassurance amid a process of forgetting. Moreover, nostalgia can be manufactured. And the feelings it generates are real, even if the referent never was.

Innovation, too, is good for Disney's bottom line. The Walt Disney Company heralds its "magical legacy of innovation" on a Disney Experiences website. In addition to the innovations that I listed above, this article mentions rotoscoping (an animation technique whereby animators trace over live-action film footage to create more realistic hand-drawn images); Disneyland's monorail system (an efficient elevated train and one of the first such systems running daily in the Western Hemisphere); and Disney-Pixar films' use of computer-generated imagery (CGI). These innovations, readers are told, honor the founder's impulses:

> When The Walt Disney Company was Disney Brothers Cartoon Studio, animation technology was in its early years . . . Rather than wait for [new] technology to become available, Walt Disney, in his innovative style, ventured to build these capabilities in-house. The result was a great leap forward in filmmaking, ushering in new inventions that made full-length animated features possible.[4]

Disney's innovation is not just its past and present but has always been destined to be its future. Innovation makes for richer storytelling, and those stories pave the way for nostalgia. With Disney, these seemingly opposed concepts go hand-in-hand.

Many Disney scholars, fans, and observers will talk about nostalgia; others will list Disney's innovative contributions.[5] But in this volume, we pair innovation and nostalgia as an invitation to dialectical discovery.

Bonnie Rudner opens this section by inviting readers to explore some of Disney's Renaissance films using the inquiry-based learning model Rudner herself practices in the classroom. In "Only Correct: How Disney Revises, Rethinks and Re-edits Their Own Creations," Rudner introduces us to the concept of *corrections*. She outlines the changes Disney makes to its films' source material. She then takes us into new territory: how does Disney correct its films upon re-release, and how does Disney correct its familiar stories in the transition to live-action remakes? Audiences' nostalgia for the Disney classics is real; corrections (and innovations) do not, however, guarantee satisfying storytelling. Ultimately, Rudner's chapter offers us a theory of corrections that we can use now and into the future as Disney will undoubtedly continue to modify—and make money on—its beloved intellectual properties.

As both a Disney professor and practitioner of experiential learning, Christopher W. Tremblay has turned his affection for Walt Disney into an innovative learning adventure for his college students. Here, in a chapter titled "Teaching Walt: Place-Based Learning and SHAPE-ing Walt's Legacy," he brings readers along on Walt's Pilgrimage. From Walt Disney's birthplace in Chicago, Illinois, to his final resting place at Forest Lawn Cemetery in Glendale, California, Tremblay details the affective learning that occurs through place-based engagement with Walt Disney's biography. This chapter not only offers us a rich glimpse into Walt Disney's life but also introduces us to the author's SHAPE method. Standing for Storytelling, Historical Biography, Artifacts, Place, and Experiences, Tremblay's pedagogical design shows us how to study people through place.

Alex Hofmann's "Theme Park America" is next. Modeling the work he does for his students (who travel to Disneyland as part of their course), Hofmann's chapter complicates both Disneyland and historiography. He walks readers down Main Street, U.S.A., into Adventureland, and through Frontierland. Are these lands for family togetherness, consumptive entertainment, and easy fun? Or do these themed spaces tell deeper, more troubling American stories—about Cold War anxieties, discomfort with the legacy of slavery and the Civil Rights Movement, and settler colonialism? Hofmann challenges readers to hold in tension the Disney parks' pleasures with their potentially harmful narratives. Civic institutions like Disneyland in fact have much to reveal about the American cultural imagination: a nation's emotions have been built into Disney's themed environments. Ultimately, Hofmann's chapter reveals that in building parks, Americans are creating themselves. What, then, will we find if we look beneath the surfaces of nostalgia and innovation?

"World-building and Role-Playing Across Disney Production" by William S. Chavez rounds out this section. Chavez uses an amalgam of sources—including books, video games, and tabletop games—to explore Disney's innovative attempts to manufacture nostalgia and expand its cultural and transmedial reach. Chavez's theoretical approach here is rhizomatic, which allows him to analyze Disney not just as the top-down megacorporation it is but as an interconnected industry of creative content, material culture, and literary products, alive and growing outward via deeply rooted networks. What does it mean to "play" in a Disney-created immersive environment? Wherein lies agency, and when, where, and why is creativity stymied by Disney design? Chavez's multifaceted answers to these questions stem from media studies and religious studies, and readers are invited to rethink their own relationship to Disney consumption.

These four chapters show the emotional weight behind Disney's nostalgia and analyze Disney's ongoing identity as an innovating machine. Innovation can inspire awe; nostalgia can ground us in embodied memories. We—Disney's fans, students, and consumers—are at the heart of these stories. How, then, will we interpret the worlds Disney builds for us, whether in films, a founder's biography, themed park spaces, or immersive books and games?

Notes

1   "Walt Disney's Carousel of Progress," Disney World, https://disneyworld.disney.go.com /attractions/magic-kingdom/walt-disney-carousel-of-progress/ (accessed October 1, 2024).
2   Len Testa, "Muppet*Vision 3D's Curtain Call," November 24, 2024, in *The Disney Dish with Jim Hill*, produced by Jim Hill Media Podcast Network, podcast, 1:30:05, https:// podcasts.jimhillmedia.com/show/the-disney-dish-with-jim-hill/muppetvision-3ds -curtain-call-making-way-for-electric-mayhem-jollywood-nights-review/.
3   Charlie Haas, "Disneyland Is Good for You," *New West*, December 4, 1978, 13–19, 18.
4   "Disney & Technology: A History of Standard-Setting Innovation," Disney Experiences, published November 7, 2023, https://disneyconnect.com/disney -technology/. Some suggest that innovative entrepreneurs like Walt Disney build successful companies because the "psychology of innovation" aligns with successful business techniques, i.e., purpose, problem-solving, and being action-oriented. See Kristopher Jones, "The Psychology of Innovation: From Purpose to Gratitude," *Forbes*, April 6, 2016, https://www.forbes.com/sites/forbesagencycouncil/2016/04/06/the -psychology-of-innovation-from-purpose-to-gratitude/?sh=6a96d65c694a.

5   Two texts that I use in several of my Disney classes and that address nostalgia are
    Stephen M. Fjellman, *Vinyl Leaves: Walt Disney World and America* (Boulder:
    Westview Press, 1992) and Henry Giroux, *The Mouse that Roared: Disney and the End
    of Innocence* (New York: Rowman and Littlefield, 1999). Meanwhile, two biographies
    of Walt Disney that talk at length about his innovative contributions to his industries
    (even if not addressing "innovation" as a theme) are Bob Thomas, *Walt Disney: An
    American Original* (New York: Disney Editions, 1994) and Steven Watts, *The Magic
    Kingdom: Walt Disney and the American Way of Life* (Columbia: University of Missouri
    Press, 1997).

9

Only Correct

How Disney Revises, Rethinks, and Re-edits Their Own Creations[1]

Bonnie Rudner

Introduction: What Are Corrections?

The beginning of my Disney class presents a major challenge: I have to approach my students, who love the films intensely, with respect for what they already know. Then, I present them with new approaches for analyzing those films. I do not start with the Disney canon but with an early twenty-first-century American novel. Jonathan Franzen published *The Corrections* in 2001. It revolves around the troubles of an elderly Midwestern couple and their three adult children, tracing their lives from the mid-twentieth century to "one last Christmas" near the turn of the millennium. The main characters try to assess the mistakes, denials, and fictions they have been raised with—and they attempt to "make corrections."[2]

Franzen is, of course, talking about making psychological corrections in families. The novel does not go further than that idea. But there is a much broader use for the framework. Revision (literally meaning re-seeing) is based on the premise that we can improve. Tales can be modernized, and movies can be remade. Very often, the point of view of a new work is altered from the original.

An effective pedagogical approach to assessing corrections is inquiry-based learning, developed by Paula Mathieu, which starts by posing questions, problems, or scenarios.[3] The professor identifies questions, within a framework, in order to encourage students to develop their own theories based on the text. This is especially effective for college students who assume they already know the material.

Students who elect to take my course Disney and the Wonder Tale are usually completely unaware of Disney's source material. In their worlds, the only mermaid they have ever met is Ariel. They know of Maleficent as the uninvited fairy, Robin Williams as the Genie, and Pocahontas as a mature woman who falls in love with John Smith. They begin the semester with great confidence about their understanding of the films they love. The genius of the Disney writers is their unique ability to correct the early tales in order to present their worldview or to Disneyfy their movies. The term

"Disneyfy" was introduced by Richard Schickel in *The Disney Version: The Life, Times, Art and Commerce of Walt Disney*, first published in 1968. Disneyfication referred to the way in which the Disney Studios altered original stories in order to conform to their own vision. The term is now used in a multitude of ways, by scholars and non-scholars, to describe the cultural force of Disney.[4]

Any inquiry into Disney corrections must begin with the initial changes to the source material in order to create the enormously successful films *The Little Mermaid*, *Beauty and the Beast*, and *Aladdin*. The inquiry raises questions about theme, purpose, audience, and the use of magic. This will be followed by an examination of corrections to the films as they are released again. The final sections look closely at various versions of the Little Mermaid tales and the ways in which the Disney Studios has corrected the narratives for their own purposes.

Corrected Source Material

The animated film, *Beauty and the Beast*, is based on Madame LePrince de Beaumont's fairy tale (c.1757). The simple story centers around Beauty, a devoted daughter, who plans never to marry or to leave her father. When he offends the Beast by stealing a rose and is condemned to die, Beauty sweetly volunteers to take his place. Beast is a horribly ugly being who has been put under a spell by an enchantress. But he is a perfect, well-mannered, and generous host to Beauty. He knows he lacks "wit and intelligence," but because of his kindness, Beauty becomes accustomed to his ugliness, and she promises to be his friend, always.[5] The movement of the story concerns Beauty's maturation and willingness to leave home and marry Beast. Once she agrees to marry him, the spell breaks, thus revealing Beast's handsome former state. It is Beauty who first has to change in the original narrative to allow Beast's transformation.

Disney's animated *Beauty and the Beast* (1991) makes enormous changes in the narrative. Belle is an outcast in her village. She wants to leave her "poor provincial town" for a better life. She refuses Gaston, a boorish and unsuitable mate. She is a generous and loving daughter, protective of her father.

The Disney writers give Beast an anger management problem; his servants are terrified of his rage. He imprisons and threatens Belle, banging on her door for her to come down to dinner. When she refuses, he tells his servants, "If she doesn't eat with me, she doesn't eat at all!"[6] In Disney's film, it is Beast who must change in order to reverse the curse and free them all. Everyone in the enchanted castle is dependent on his transformation, which of course comes at the end. As Mrs. Potts says, "After all this time, he's finally learned to love."[7]

Sharon Downey, a communications scholar, suggests a reason for the corrections in the Disney version: "Worthy but misdirected boys, fathers or potential husbands must undergo a transformation in order to earn the love and respect of a female. This transformation leads to a transcendent resolution only when the male surrenders control, accepts the female's inalienable right to freedom, and validates her independent identity."[8] The transformation is not Belle's. Her mission is to help Beast transform, thus freeing all of his endearing servants and choosing to marry him. The Disney corrections completely alter the narrative of the original tale.

Disney also corrects the original "Aladdin and the Magic Lamp" in order to fit their model of a male able and worthy of change. In the story from the *Arabian Nights*, as translated by nineteenth-century adventurer and translator Richard Francis Burton, Aladdin is a selfish, lazy, and willful boy who causes his father's death and abuses his mother: "A long time ago in a city of China, there lived a poor tailor with his only son, Aladdin. Now this boy had been obstinate and lazy ever since the day he was born. . . . His father became so sick due to his son's vicious personality and indolence that he died."[9] This Aladdin is no "diamond in the rough."[10] Nor is he an orphan. He causes his father's death and abuses his mother. Aladdin does reform in the original story and becomes a beloved Sultan, but it takes him a long time, and he is hardly admirable along the way.

When the Walt Disney Studios decided to animate the story, they changed much of the plot. Aladdin becomes a street rat with a heart of gold, who shares his bread with hungry children and rescues a child from a horseman in the street. His mother and father are no longer in the story. Yes, he has to learn to "bee" himself (instructs the Genie in bee form) and to transform to be worthy of Jasmine. But of course, he does, liberating Agrabah and offering to sacrifice marriage to Jasmine for the Genie's freedom. These corrections to the original tales are brilliantly executed for the Disneyfication of the plot and for the theme that Disney's films thrive upon: true love conquers all.

Although history records Pocahontas as being somewhere between eleven and twelve years old, our animated hero is presented as a fully mature woman.[11] There was never a love affair between Smith and Pocahontas (she married John Rolfe), but their romance suits Disney's purposes. This change is less a correction than a complete revision, but it supports Disney's creation of a happy love story. *Pocahontas* raises other serious issues, which we will return to later in this chapter.

Corrections from "The Vault"

A second phase of Disney corrections involves altering existing versions of the films. The invention of home entertainment provided Disney with a rare opportunity to re-edit as well as to profit from the nostalgia of the old versions while adding innovative new elements. As they marketed the release of movies from the Vault, they advertised by including scenes that had been deleted from the original versions of the films, changed some lyrics, and added extra scenes as an incentive for their audience to purchase the videos or DVDs.

These changes are not as predictable as the earlier corrections, which were primarily changed to conform to Disney's formulaic themes. A few changes were in direct response to criticism leveled at them. *Aladdin* originally began with a song, "Arabian Nights" (original lyrics italicized):

Where they cut off your ear /Where it's flat and immense
If they don't like your face /And the heat is intense
It's barbaric, but hey, it's home.[12]

In spite of concerns from the Arab American League, Disney refused to change the original lyrics. It was only after an editorial in *The New York Times* argued "It's Racist, But hey it's Disney!" that Disney agreed to revise the song.[13] The corrections aimed to remove the stereotypical depictions and offensive language. Disney did not, however, replace "it's barbaric, but hey it's home," leaving their critics dissatisfied.

Another attempt at addressing the charge of cultural insensitivity centered around *Pocahontas*. Pocahontas and John Smith do not have a love duet in the original film. Critics accused the studio of cowardice because theirs is an interracial love story. In later editions, the love song "If I Never Knew You" was added to the scene in the tent and to their final farewell.[14] Unfortunately, most students groan throughout this song. This is an example of choosing a correction to address criticism over aesthetic concerns.

In the film *Aladdin*, the creators did not originally plan to "Eighty-six the Mother" for the animated film.[15] In a deleted scene, added to the DVD, Alan Menken discusses the late Howard Ashman's attachment to both the character of the mother and a song he wrote as an apology to her: "Proud of Your Boy." Both the song and the mother were cut from the final version—to Ashman's disappointment—to move the plot forward and bring on the Genie sooner. Interestingly, the Broadway production of *Aladdin*, in 2014, corrects the omission. Ashman's song is included at least three times over the course of the musical.

The Walt Disney Studio has been attempting to navigate the conflict between cultural insensitivity and aesthetics as they remake animated versions of their wildly popular films into live-action productions. But do the corrections actually address the initial problems with the films? Do they ruin our nostalgia for the originals? Or does the innovation create another whole range of problems? An inquiry into both Disney's animated *The Little Mermaid* and the live-action version explores these questions. The framework of corrections enables students to evaluate the new versions.

Hans Christian Andersen's *Little Mermaid*

Disney's *The Little Mermaid* is based on Hans Christian Andersen's story, written in 1837, about love and sacrifice. In Andersen's story, the heroine makes a bargain in which she loses her tongue forever to obtain human shape and life on earth. Her transformation brings her horrible pain and, although her sisters bring her a sword, she refuses to kill the prince in order to return to them. Instead, she throws herself, her heart breaking, into the "deathly cold sea foam" and dissolves into air.[16]

Jack Zipes has done extensive critical work on the history of "The Little Mermaid," revealing the way Andersen's tale draws upon both Andersen's biography and literature's

Romantic era.[17] Zipes's main focus is Andersen's preoccupation with social status and how the little mermaid's fantastic projection of a "better life" is representative of Andersen's own contradictory urges: to be accepted in Danish high society as well as to expose the shallowness of it. Andersen's adaptation and correction of earlier mermaid tales reflect these concerns.

The hierarchy in his "The Little Mermaid" is very significant. It is clear from the story's beginning that humans are the superior species: they have an automatic right to an immortal soul; mermaids, on the other hand, do not. "The Little Mermaid" questions this arrangement, as does the reader:

> "Why have not we an immortal soul?" asked the little mermaid mournfully; "I would give gladly all the hundreds of years that I have to live, to be a human being only for one day, and to have the hope of knowing the happiness of that glorious world above the stars."
>
> "You must not think of that," said the old woman; "we feel ourselves to be much happier and much better off than human beings."
>
> "So I shall die," said the little mermaid, "and as the foam of the sea I shall be driven about never again to hear the music of the waves, or to see the pretty flowers nor the red sun. Is there anything I can do to win an immortal soul?"[18]

The little mermaid is told by her grandmother (the old woman) that her future is predetermined: mermaids do not possess immortal souls.

But, everything about the mermaid world seems lovely: the sisters are supportive and the grandmother is loving. Even the Sea Witch warns the mermaid against making the trade: "But think again," said the witch, "for when once your shape has become like a human being, you can no more be a mermaid. You will never return through the water to your sisters, or to your father's palace again."[19]

Andersen's mermaid is a strange and thoughtful child, and she is very interested in the upper world. After she saves the prince, she becomes more silent and dissatisfied. She will not be dissuaded from leaving. The reader is never fully convinced by her obsession and sacrifice. The prince remains oblivious to the reality that the mermaid saved him: "As the days passed, she loved the prince more fondly, and he loved her as he would love a little child, but it never came into his head to make her his wife."[20]

And yet, the prince has an automatic right to an immortal soul, while the little mermaid is fated to be turned into sea foam. This contradiction seems to be based more on Andersen's personal obsessions than on the logical working out of the narrative. Andersen aspires, as Zipes shows, to belong to upper society, and yet he judges those members harshly enough to suggest that the prince be killed for his ignorance about the little mermaid's sacrifice.

At the last minute, Andersen gives the little mermaid an escape hatch: she can work for 300 years to earn an immortal soul.[21] Of course, the reader is happy about this correction to the original dichotomy (humans vs. merfolk) and grateful for a third option (daughter of the air). But again, the hierarchy does not feel justified, as the prince has no such stringent requirement placed on him for immortality.

Very few people feel nostalgia for Andersen's original, tragic tale in which the little mermaid painfully loses her song, her home, her family, and her life, only to watch as the prince marries another woman. The longings of the story are powerful: the seaweed is always greener. The mermaid's separation, pain, and sacrifice would all be worth it if the prince chose her. But he never knows who gave up her life for him. As I see time and time again with my students, the story ends in frustration and disappointment for the reader.

Andersen's tale was a perfect narrative for an innovative Disney upgrade. His patient, self-effacing little mermaid becomes Disney's Ariel, a modern, feisty, redheaded, rebellious teenager. And of course, in the Disney version, Ariel gets her prince.

The Little Mermaid (1989)

In 1989, Disney created their own version of a mermaid story, the animated *The Little Mermaid*. According to Laura Sells "Where Do Mermaids Stand?" this film represented Disney's first commercial success since Walt Disney's death in 1966 and "the first in a spate of new animated features that reaffirmed Disney's position as one of the largest producers of acceptable role models for young girls."[22] This is often referred to as the beginning of the Disney "Renaissance films": a period from 1989 to 1999, during which Walt Disney Feature Animation returned to producing critically and commercially successful animated films.

The Disneyfication of Andersen's story required many corrections. The easiest and most obvious one concerns the ending: true love conquers all, and the mermaid, Ariel, marries her prince, Eric. But the corrections are much more extensive than simply giving them a happily ever after. The entire structure of the film, as well as the new characters, creates a very different mermaid tale.

Andersen's tale begins under the sea, showing its beauty. Disney's begins with humans on the ship: this establishes their centrality and the film's hierarchy. It is not based on the importance of an immortal soul. It is, as Patrick Murphy (cited in Sells) convincingly argues in his ecofeminist criticism, a first world/third world relationship between the humans and the sea world. In the first scene, the mermaid is invisible to the humans on the ship. Sells argues that Ariel sees the land world as the place of "cultural vitality," whereas the sea creatures merely sing, dance, or hunt for treasures all day long.[23] In the event that they are discovered by humans, they are exploited as food: "guess who's gon be on de plate?"[24]

Ariel's actions reflect this hierarchy. She risks danger to explore the human ship, and she values any trinkets that she finds from the world of humans. She is dissatisfied with her life and wants more, even before she sets eyes on Eric and has the famous Disney look of love.

Sells discusses this in her examination of the song "Part of Your World," referred to, by Ashman and Menken, as Ariel's "I Want" song. The imagery reflects an "up there/down here" dimension.[25] In the song's final moments, the camera looks down on Ariel as she looks up to the sun. Everything she likes about the human world (dancing, books, art) are things she aspires to do: she is upwardly mobile, in a way that is very different from Andersen's "The Little Mermaid." Ariel has a collection of objects. As she says, "I don't see how a world that makes such wonderful things could be bad."[26]

Ariel wants to be in the world of human beings, which the film validates. The audience may believe that Sebastian's underwater world is appealing, but Ariel does not agree. She leaves in the middle of his show-stopping song, "Under the Sea." Of course, her deal with Ursula is for Eric, but her upward mobility is apparent before she even sees his face. The lyrics change from "Part of that world" to "Part of your world." Ariel's desire to move up (out of this provincial town, as Belle will sing a few years later in 1991's *Beauty and the Beast*) is already established as soon as we meet her. The theme of true love comes after she sees Eric and his dog, Max, on the boat.

The film gives the audience many reasons to support Ariel's quest. She is presented as a typically rebellious and curious teenager, fighting against an authoritarian and oppressive father who destroyed her possessions. She has no mother or grandmother, and her sisters are presented as mostly uninspiring. Merpeople, in general, are unattractive or unfortunate souls: "This one wanting to be thinner, that one wants to get the girl."[27] Aside from the beauty of Sebastian's calypso number, which does not feature any merpeople, Ariel does not value life under the sea.

Andersen's little mermaid, even according to the Sea Witch, makes the wrong choice by trading her voice for human legs. Disney corrects this by having Ursula entrap Ariel for her own ends. As such, the viewer does not really blame Ariel. All sympathy lies with her goal of getting Eric to bestow upon her the kiss of true love in three days. And even officious and stodgy Sebastian becomes complicit in her goal. "Alright, alright. I'll try to help you find that prince."[28] He, as do we, succumbs to her charm and innocence.

After Ariel trades her voice to Ursula, she is entirely helpless and is carried to the shore by Sebastian and Flounder. Ariel can no longer swim. Without their help, she would drown, new legs and all. She is washed up on shore, naked and completely vulnerable. She is a newborn human, unable to talk or walk. Her legs wobble and she falls into Eric's arms. She does not know how to eat human food: her first dinner is an adorable disaster as she combs her hair with the fork (dinglehopper) and blows into the pipe (snarfblatt). We have been told that Ariel is sixteen, but she seems younger than a teenager. And her naivete is endearing, both to Eric and to the viewer. Her behavior on the carriage ride and her innocence in the "Kiss the Girl" scene add to her vulnerability. Ursula's constant intervention creates total sympathy for Ariel's helplessness in the face of evil, magical manipulation. The film steadily moves toward having Eric fall in love with the lovely and deserving Ariel.

At the end of the movie, in only eighty-three minutes running time, the Disney corrections are complete: Triton has agreed to sacrifice himself in order to save his daughter. Eric realizes his love for Ariel and rows off to help save her, telling Grimsby, "I'm not gonna lose her again." Ursula, the evil, power hungry, vengeful witch is impaled by the mast of Eric's ship. Triton grants Ariel her freedom and legs and lets her go to Eric. And, of course, true love conquers all.

The Disney Studios were rewarded for these changes: the budget for the film in 1989 was $40,000,000. The original box office receipts were $235,000,000, a sixfold return.[29]

There were many criticisms leveled at the film: Ariel's lack of agency; Sebastian's Jamaican accent and teeth, criticized as racial stereotypes; Ursula's exaggerated female power grab; Ursula's lyrics about what men and women want in relationships ("Men up there don't like a lot of blabber / They think a girl who gossips is a bore . . . / and don't underestimate the importance of body language").[30] And, although those words are spoken by the villain, she is proven right: Ariel wins Eric's love before she regains her voice.

But there was no doubt that the film was beloved, charming, and effective. The music is fantastic, and, even for today's audiences, the film creates its own magical spell. The issue for anyone studying Disney is the way in which the corrections both add to the original story and create new problems.

The Little Mermaid (2023)

On May 26, 2023, the live-action *The Little Mermaid* was released. It had a budget of $240,200,000. The film earned $569,600,000 at the box office.[31] The return on the investment was a little over two times the outlay. It obviously drew on the audience's nostalgic affection for the 1989 film. It also attempted, in two hours and twenty-one minutes, to address the many criticisms of the animated film. The critical response was mixed. The inquiry for students concerns the corrections: What are they? Do they work? Does the new film cast its own magical spell?

The opening of the film begins with one huge correction in the form of an addition: the animated version made no reference to the tragedy that is Andersen's tale. The live-action version, however, begins with a quote from Andersen's *The Little Mermaid*: "But a mermaid has no tears. Therefore she suffers so much more."[32]

This quote fills the screen and introduces the theme of pain and suffering. The first characters presented are the human sailors. But we meet a different Eric: this Eric is an adventurer who is not under pressure to find a bride. And he is given a backstory: his parents died, and he was adopted by the present king and queen. His father disapproved of exploration. Eric is dissatisfied with his duties and wants freedom and escape. He will be the perfect mate for the adventurous mermaid whom he meets. In fact, Eric is given his own "I want" song, "Wild Uncharted Waters."[33]

Triton introduces his mermaid daughters, who come from all corners of the globe for a political forum. Ariel misses this conference, not—as in the 1989 version—a musical concert. As Triton berates her, we get another backstory: Ariel's mother was killed by humans. We also meet Ursula, who has her own backstory: she is Triton's sister, and he has banished her from the kingdom. She vows vengeance. Within minutes of the film, we are given three family histories: Eric is rebelling against his father; Triton hates humans for killing his wife; and Ursula despises her brother Triton for her banishment.

The added narratives feel ponderous and unnecessary. We do not need to be presented with so much background information. Villains can be bad and power hungry without historical reasons. It takes almost half an hour for Ariel to catch sight of and rescue Eric. The tone of the film is somber. Eric is dissatisfied, and Ariel is breaking rules, all before the ship explodes.

In the animated *Little Mermaid*, Ariel catches sight of Eric and says, "He's very handsome, isn't he?" Misunderstanding, Scuttle sees Max (Eric's dog) and says, "I don't know, he looks kind of hairy and slobbery to me."[34] There is a sweetness connected to the encounter that is absent from the live action.

Halle Bailey's mermaid's desire to be part of the human world, exploited by Ursula, is also corrected. Disney has altered the lyrics to eliminate the worst of Ursula's opinions about women and their need for, or lack thereof, a voice. But in the process, the idea of Ursula as an undersea Faust, making devilish deals with many merpeople, is changed as well. At the end of the animated film, when a defeated Ursula loses the trident, many merpeople are raised from limbo and given new lives. In the live-action film, the happy ever after is only about Ariel and Eric and their future adventures.

Bailey's Ariel is referred to in the film as "little," "young" and "child" by Triton. But unlike the animated Ariel, she does not seem vulnerable. This may have been necessary in order to present a live-action character who seems old enough to leave home, but it changes the audience's view of her independence and ability. Bailey's mermaid joins Sebastian in singing "Under the Sea," and she seems to enjoy the song more than the animated Ariel, who sneaks out as soon as she can.

After her transformation, Bailey's Ariel is capable of swimming to land on her own. Although she is caught in the fisherman's net and covered up, she seems well aware of her needs. She decides to wear sandals rather than uncomfortable shoes. And this mermaid seems too sophisticated to use the little trident to comb her hair. The writers may have kept this in the script because it is endearing in the original, but it is awkward in the live-action film. Another huge correction is the choice to give Bailey's mute mermaid a singing monologue. This emphasizes her fantastic voice, but it also exposes her complete understanding of her situation. Rather than use facial expressions to communicate with the audience, she sings to them. Ariel also finds a way to share her name with Eric, as opposed to having Sebastian help her in the animated version. This mermaid has agency and can take care of herself.

Any inquiry must center around the impact of these corrections. What elements have been added? What do they bring to the composition? Do they justify adding an extra hour to the film? Certainly, political considerations were involved in the casting of the actors: Bailey is a woman of color, as is Eric's mom. The mermaid sisters represent ethnicities from all over the world. What is the purpose of this casting? The setting is clearly meant to be somewhere in the Caribbean in the nineteenth century. Yet there is no allusion to the issue of the slave ships that were almost certainly present at that time. The casting seems to be color blind.

In a *New York Times* article, Kabir Chibber suggests that this type of casting represents a defiantly ahistorical setting: the Magical Multiracial Past. Every race exists, cheerfully and seemingly as equals, in the same place at the same time. But Chibber argues that "one can never fully envision the Magical Multiracial Past without having to mentally take apart the entire scaffolding of world history." He admits that the impulse behind such corrections comes from a good place: "wanting to include everyone in our storytelling, so we simply suspend disbelief; we imagine that everyone who is currently a part of our Anglophone culture has been there, a valued and equal participant, all along."[35]

Disney recreated (corrected? falsified?) history long before the introduction of their live-action films and Broadway productions. In the feature *The Making of Pocahontas*, Roy Disney, then vice chairman of the Board of the Walt Disney Company, claimed that "Pocahontas was a story that appealed . . . because it was basically a story about people getting along together . . . which is particularly applicable to lots of places in the world today."[36]

But *Pocahontas* creates a false equivalence: the settlers and the natives were hardly "two households alike in dignity."[37] The story of the colonization of the Americas is not about resolving a family feud and "getting along."[38] The lyrics in the *Pocahontas* song "Savages" may seem to reflect mutual distrust. But a closer reading of the lyrics reveals that the colonists use language that is much more extreme and racist in their depictions of the Natives, and in fact, predicts their future genocide:

Their skin's a hellish red
They're only good when dead
They're vermin, as I said.

The Natives, on the other hand, sing:

This is what we feared
The paleface is a demon
The only thing they feel at all is greed.[39]

As Disney repackages and resells some of their most popular stories in live-action and Broadway productions, they are correcting perceived problems from earlier versions. Certainly, the physical casting, as opposed to animated images, creates more obvious controversies, such as the furor over casting the amazingly talented Halle Bailey as Ariel, who was originally animated as a childlike redhead.

At the end of the live-action film, Ariel and Eric are engaged and sail off on adventures. Triton approves of his daughter's choice, and Ariel sheds real tears; apparently, based on the quote from Andersen's introduction, she no longer suffers. Both characters have full agency to decide on their futures. The two worlds seem to have reconciled. And everyone lives happily ever after.

Conclusion: Future Corrections

The real questions for all viewers are aesthetic: Do the corrections enhance our appreciation of the story? There is a joy in watching 1989's *The Little Mermaid*, even with its many problems, that is missing from the live-action version, in spite of Bailey's best efforts.

The French Chef, for example, and his song "Les Poissons," may be a silly and insensitive interlude in the animated film, but Sebastian's final struggle with him at the wedding, ending in his triumphant taunt on the cake, is memorably sweet.[40] My students love it.

Disney's future holds many adaptations and revisions, in live-action films, on Broadway, and in theme park productions. The reasons for these changes will vary. An analysis of the attempted corrections can give us a practical framework for understanding and evaluating new works. We have great nostalgia for the classic versions; the question going forward is whether or not the innovations will result in new and magical masterpieces.

Notes

1   This title is a play on "Only connect," as used and discussed in Mary E. Virnoche and Gary T. Marx, "'Only Connect'-E. M. Forster in an Age of Electronic Communication: Computer-Mediated Association and Community Networks," *Sociological Enquiry* 67, no. 1 (1997): #, https://doi.org/10.1111/j.1475-682X.1997 .tb00431.x.
2   Jonathan Franzen, *The Corrections* (New York: Farrar, Straus and Giroux, 2001).
3   Paula Mathieu, "A Guiding Question, Primary Research, and a Dash of Rhetorical Awareness," in *First-Year Composition: From Theory to Practice*, ed. Deborah Teague and Ron Lunsford (Anderson: ParlorPress, 2014), 114.
4   Richard Schickel, *The Disney Version: The Life, Times, Art, and Commerce of Walt Disney* (New York: Simon and Schuster, 1985), 225.
5   Madame Leprince de Beaumont, "Beauty and the Beast," in *The Twelve Dancing Princesses and Other Fairy Tales*, ed. Alfred David and Mary Elizabeth Meek. A Midland Book (Bloomington: Indiana University Press, 1974), 164.
6   *Beauty and the Beast*, directed by Gary Trousdale and Kirk Wise (1991; Burbank: Walt Disney Pictures), Disney+.
7   Ibid.
8   Sharon D. Downey, "Feminine Empowerment in Disney's *Beauty and the Beast*," *Women's Studies in Communication* 19, no. 2 (July 1996): 209, https://doi.org/10.1080 /07491409.1996.11089812.
9   Richard Francis Burton and Jack Zipes, eds., "Aladdin and the Magic Lamp," in *Arabian Nights: The Marvels and Wonders of the Thousand and One Nights*, Vol. One (New York: Signet Classic, 1991), 136.
10 *Aladdin*, directed by Ron Clements and John Musker (1992; Burbank: Walt Disney Pictures), Disney+.
11 *Pocahontas*, directed by Mike Gabriel and Eric Goldberg (1995; Burbank: Walt Disney Pictures), Disney+.
12 Clements and Musker, *Aladdin*.
13 "Opinion | It's Racist, But Hey, It's Disney," *The New York Times*, July 14, 1993, www .nytimes.com/1993/07/14/opinion/it-s-racist-but-hey-it-s-disney.html.
14 Gabriel and Goldberg, *Pocahontas*.
15 Linda Hass, "'Eighty-Six the Mother': Murder, Matricide, and Good Mothers," in *From Mouse to Mermaid: The Politics of Film, Gender, and Culture*, ed. Elizabeth Bell, Lynda Haas, and Laura Sells (Bloomington: Indiana University Press, 1995), 193.

16   Hans Christian Andersen, "The Little Mermaid," in *The Twelve Dancing Princesses and Other Fairy Tales*, ed. Alfred David and Mary Elizabeth Meek. A Midland Book (Bloomington: Indiana University Press, 1974), 273.

17   Jack Zipes, "Breaking the Disney Spell," in *From Mouse to Mermaid: The Politics of Film, Gender, and Culture*, ed. Elizabeth Bell, Haas Lynda, and Laura Sells (Bloomington: Indiana University Press, 1995), 21–42.

18   Andersen, "The Little Mermaid," 262.

19   Ibid., 265.

20   Ibid., 268.

21   Ibid., 274.

22   Laura Sells, "'Where Do Mermaids Stand?:' Voice and Body in The Little Mermaid," in *From Mouse to Mermaid: The Politics of Film, Gender, and Culture*, ed. Elizabeth Bell, Lynda Haas, and Laura Sells (Bloomington: Indiana University Press, 1995), 176.

23   Ibid., 178.

24   *The Little Mermaid*, directed by Ron Clements and John Musker (1989; Burbank: Walt Disney Pictures), Disney+.

25   Sells, "'Where Do Mermaids Stand?,'" 178.

26   Clements and Musker, *The Little Mermaid*.

27   Ibid.

28   Ibid.

29   "The Little Mermaid (1989)," IMDb, www.imdb.com/title/tt0097757/ (accessed April 27, 2024).

30   Clements and Musker, *The Little Mermaid*.

31   "*The Little Mermaid* (2023 film)," Wikipedia, en.wikipedia.org/wiki/The_Little_Me rmaid_(2023_film) (accessed April 27, 2024).

32   *The Little Mermaid*, directed by Rob Marshall (2023; Burbank: Walt Disney Pictures), Disney+.

33   Ibid.

34   Clements and Musker, *The Little Mermaid*.

35   Kabir Chibber, "Hollywood's New Fantasy: A Magical, Colorblind Past," *The New York Times*, March 31, 2024, www.nytimes.com/2024/03/31/magazine/hollywood -movies-race-diversity.html.

36   Leonardo Greco, "Interview Roy Disney & Glenn Keane 1995 *Pocahontas* Premiere," YouTube, November 18, 2020, video, 9:10, www.youtube.com/watch?v =2eXcF0HhdfA.

37   William Shakespeare, *The Tragedy of Romeo and Juliet*, ed. Louis B. Wright and Virginia A. Lamar, The Folger Library General Reader's Shakespeare (New York: Washington Square Press, Simon & Schuster Inc, 1959), 1.

38   *Mickey Mouse Monopoly: Disney, Childhood & Corporate Power*, directed by Miguel Picker and Chyng Sun (Media Education Foundation, 2002).

39   Gabriel and Goldberg, *Pocahontas*.

40   Clements and Musker, *The Little Mermaid*.

10

Teaching Walt

Place-Based Learning—SHAPE-ing Walt's Legacy

Christopher W. Tremblay

Imagine being in the room where Walt Disney was born. It was a humble beginning at 1249 Tripp Avenue in Chicago, Illinois. This is where my college students first encounter Walter Elias Disney on Day 1, Stop 1, of the undergraduate college course, Walt's Pilgrimage. This is a sacred moment as it showcases the unassuming start of a future American innovator. It is an educational kernel of information as most people do not realize that Walt was born in the Midwest, and not in a hospital. He was born on the second floor of a home that his mother, Flora, designed (revolutionary for a woman at that time in history), and his father, Elias, built in 1893.

Visiting birthplaces of famous people like Walt Disney offers a multifaceted experience, combining historical, cultural, educational, and inspirational elements. We can connect with the past, gain a deeper understanding of notable figures, and appreciate their significant contributions to society. This experience is nostalgic as it harkens back to Walt's childhood and the "good old days" of the early 1900s.

In a way, Walt is a mystery to be solved—to learn about his varied interests, aspirations, and origins of his inspiration and to dive deep into how his mind worked, how he enacted his dreams, and how his perseverance set the foundation for the Walt Disney Company's success today.

Most of us recognize that Walt Disney is an icon, a legend, and yet an enigma. Three distinct characteristics about Walt make him an enigma worth exploring: (1) his dual professional role as both micromanager and delegator, (2) his secretive projects and personal life, and (3) his contradictory reputation. Briefly, Walt was extremely involved in the details of his animated work and theme park designs, yet his "Nine Old Men" were trusted to execute his vision. On the secrecy level, Walt purchased land for Walt Disney World in Florida under multiple "dummy corporations" to avoid a price hike associated with his name and he was also extremely private about his personal life, adding a layer of mystery around him. Finally, he has a mixed reputation for being kind, but also tough and overbearing. This all represents the complexity of Walt.

This college course originated as a part of the Study in the States program for the Lee Honors College at Western Michigan University in 2014 and was first taught in the summer of 2015. It is the only known college course that studies the life of Walt Disney. Framed by a place-based learning approach, the course facilitates students' observing, researching, listening, and engaging with the spaces and places that are a part of Walt Disney's history and evolution.[1] The intention is to learn lessons from his life that we can apply to our own lives today.

This course explores the remarkable life, career, and enduring impact of Walt Disney—the visionary animator, filmmaker, entrepreneur, and cultural icon who transformed the entertainment industry. Through an in-depth examination of Walt's personal experiences, creative innovations, business strategies, and lasting influence, we gain a comprehensive understanding of how one individual's relentless pursuit of his passions shaped modern media, theme park design, and the nature of storytelling.

I teach this course because I have been intrigued by Walt's impact on American culture for most of my life. My focused research began as an undergraduate honors student when I studied the impact of the 1955 opening of Disneyland on American culture in my American Pop Culture honors course, where I described Disneyland as the "perfect museum for popular culture."[2] More importantly, I want others to learn about and understand Walt's life and how he was able to accomplish what he did in his 65-year lifelong pursuit of creativity, innovation, and perseverance—amid personal and professional challenges. In creating this course, I drew upon my time as a former Walt Disney World College Program cast member, my in-depth multi-year research, and my desire to create moments that replicate Walt's efforts of "plussing."[3]

The goal is to introduce students to the person behind the massive Disney brand, offer access to intimate knowledge of an individual whose life trajectory forever changed American culture, and create a deeper historical understanding of that impact—one geographic location at a time. Teaching this course for eight years to more than fifty undergraduate students allows me to demonstrate that we can not only learn about Walt's life and his impact, but that his story can also inspire any of us to pursue our dreams and passions. In a sense, this course is my version of Walt's dreams.

The Walt Disney Birthplace in Chicago is just one of nearly forty places in Walt's life that shaped his history, thoughts, approaches, and aspirations. After you visit the home where Walt was born, you realize that seeing the environment where an individual grew up can provide a better understanding of the historical and cultural context of their early life, which influenced their later work and achievements.

Brief Biography about Walt Disney

A short introduction about Walt Disney is necessary to offer some context. This is not easy to do since Walt, like every human being, is complex and multi-faceted as well as imperfect, despite his lifetime of achievements.

Walt Disney, born on December 5, 1901, in Chicago, Illinois, was an American entrepreneur, animator, film producer, and pioneer of the entertainment industry.

With a passion for storytelling ignited during his childhood in Marceline, Missouri, Disney pursued his artistic talents, eventually founding the Walt Disney Company as the Disney Brothers Cartoon Studio with his brother, Roy, on October 16, 1923 (hence why the Disney Fan Club is called "D23," in case you didn't already know that!).[4]

Disney's career began modestly, creating animated shorts featuring the iconic character Mickey Mouse (with major contributions from Ub Iwerks), which propelled him to international fame with the release of *Steamboat Willie* in 1928, the first synchronized sound cartoon. His visionary leadership and innovative techniques revolutionized animation, leading to groundbreaking achievements such as the first full-length animated feature film, *Snow White and the Seven Dwarfs* in 1937. Beyond animation, Walt expanded his empire to encompass theme parks, television productions, and live-action films. When Disneyland opened in 1955 in Anaheim, California, it became a symbol of his imaginative spirit and commitment to creating immersive entertainment experiences. Throughout his impressive career, Walt earned numerous accolades, including multiple Academy Awards. His enduring legacy continues to inspire generations worldwide, cementing his status as a cultural icon and visionary pioneer in the realm of entertainment. Beyond that impressive set of achievements, Walt was not a perfect person, despite the idyllic personification. Critics point to instances of antisemitism, labor disputes (based on the 1941 strike), and accusations of racial insensitivity in some of his early works.[5] Disney's testimony before the House Un-American Activities Committee in 1947 during the Red Scare era also raised concerns about his potential involvement in anti-communist activities.[6] Additionally, his authoritarian leadership style and quest for perfectionism reportedly created a stressful work environment. Walt experienced life stressors like a nervous breakdown and was a chronic chain smoker, reminding us that successful individuals also have faults and challenges—that they are also real people just like us.[7]

Throughout Walt's life, he enjoyed living a life that was a juxtaposition of nostalgia and innovation, another unique attribute about him. His nod to nostalgia can be seen in the re-creation of his version of Marceline's downtown as Main Street, U.S.A. in his theme parks, while his passion for innovation is observed with Tomorrowland and his urban planning vision for his Experimental Prototype Community of Tomorrow (EPCOT).

The SHAPE Method

In establishing this college course, I framed the design of the course around the SHAPE Method, which I coined. SHAPE stands for Storytelling, Historical Biography, Artifacts, Place, and Experiences.

My college course strives to unpack the enigmatic Walt Disney using the SHAPE methodology because it is comprehensive, represents a creative approach to learning, and can appeal to a variety of learning styles.

Figure 10.1 The SHAPE Method. Christopher W. Tremblay.

Storytelling

The best way to learn about Walt Disney is to hear stories from those who knew him. Since Walt died in 1966, as each year passes, there are fewer and fewer people on earth who are still alive to talk about him. Walt himself was a master storyteller, starting from his early days of animation and film making.[8] In Kansas City, he told stories of local happenings in his Newman Laugh-O-gram features.[9] His storytelling included cartoons, animated features, live-action films, and eventually a theme park called Disneyland. Sharing history involves storytelling. Students learn stories about Walt from reading the countless biographies, watching documentaries about him (the PBS version is the most thorough), viewing his early film clips (more on that later), and reading about him in museums.

Storytelling is a powerful tool in learning as it enriches the educational experience by making learning more dynamic, relatable, and impactful. It leverages the human propensity for narrative and applies it in a way that enhances academic understanding and personal growth.

I believe storytelling is impactful because of these four primary dimensions:

- Active Listening: To learn from a story, you must be an intentional listener, focused on the details that offer context to what is being described.
- Enhanced Memory Retention: Stories can make information more memorable by embedding facts within engaging narratives.

- Understanding of Complex Concepts: Complex people and ideas can be difficult to grasp. Storytelling can provide concrete examples and contextualize these concepts, making them easier to understand.
- Historical and Cultural Awareness: Stories often reflect the cultures and times in which they were created. This can provide valuable insights into different societal norms, historical events, and diverse perspectives (this ties into "H: Historical Biography," which comes next).

Finally, storytelling is not just limited to a single discipline. It can be used to teach nearly any subject. Storytelling is universal.

Historical Biography

All my life, I have been fascinated by biographies and documentaries. They are my favorite genre from which to learn about history and the people who constructed that history. A historical biography places a person's life story in the context of history at that time. Telling the story of Walt is one that is directly connected to the evolution of pop culture, filmmaking, and historical events.

What makes this course unique is that it is a chronological journey of Walt's life from birth to death. We are fortunate that his birthplace of Chicago is only a two-and-a-half-hour drive west from Kalamazoo, Michigan, which makes for a convenient start. To be able to travel his life in order adds another authentic dimension to the travels. We literally are walking in his footsteps.

Biographies provide insight into the lives of remarkable individuals, offering lessons and inspiration from their successes, failures, and experiences.[10] By studying the lives of others, we gain valuable perspectives on overcoming obstacles, achieving goals, and navigating challenges. Biographies offer a rich tapestry of human stories that can educate and inspire by offering insights into the complexities of the human condition and the diversity of human achievements. If you have read any of the various biographies on the life of Walt, you know his life was full of complexity and accomplishments.

Historical biographical research and education are critical skill sets based on these three aspects:

- Personal Connection: Biographies tell stories of real people, making historical events and times relatable and engaging. We develop emotional connections with these individuals, which may increase interest and investment in learning about the historical context surrounding their lives.
- Complexity of the Human Experience: As mentioned earlier, Walt is a complex individual. Biographies showcase the complexity of human behavior and motivations, making history feel less abstract. They can reveal how individual actions can influence larger social, political, and cultural movements (like we see with Walt's influence on American popular culture).

- Inspiration and Role Models: Learning about the challenges, successes, and failures of historical figures can be inspiring. We can find motivation in their perseverance and learn from their mistakes as well as their achievements.

Learning history is enhanced by the integration of artifacts.

Artifacts

The collection and dissemination of artifacts give the course an anthropological aspect and an archival take on Walt's life. To be able to see things like Walt's certificate of baptism, some of his 900+ awards, and his first business contract gives credibility to him and his life. Artifacts provide tangible connections to historical events, cultures, and people, making abstract concepts more concrete and relatable. The use of artifacts contributes to the "hands-on" learning approach of place-based learning. Finally, artifacts facilitate historical inquiry for students. For example, the $40 in play money and the recreated first-class train ticket I give students in Kansas City prompt conversations about how poor he was in 1923 and how he arrived in California. Overall, artifacts help students learn about Walt and his world.

Learning through artifacts offers a connection to the past and a diverse range of benefits. Engaging in hands-on, experiential learning helps bring history and culture to life. In any educational context, we can use artifacts to enhance curricula and encourage students to think like archaeologists and historians. Artifacts also add multidimensionality to the educational process. Specifically, artifacts support learning in these three ways:

- Tactile Learning: Observing and physically handling artifacts adds a tactile dimension to learning that is sometimes missing in traditional classroom settings. Kinesthetic learners value this aspect of learning.
- Enhanced Engagement: Artifacts can spark curiosity and interest in a way that textbooks may not. They can capture our attention with a direct and unique sensory experience.
- Critical Thinking and Inquiry: Investigating artifacts stimulates new questions, facilitates hypotheses about the object's use and significance, and prompts future research to uncover additional answers—which supports critical thinking and inquiry skills.

When united, artifacts and storytelling create a powerful learning connection because each artifact usually comes with its own story—the story of its creation, use, and journey over time—situated within a specific place.

Place

The course relies on place-based learning as its foundation.[11] Place-based learning is an educational approach that utilizes the local community and environment as a starting point to teach concepts across various subjects, such as history and social studies. The idea is to connect learning with the local context, making it relevant and engaging for students by focusing on local heritage, cultures, landscapes, opportunities, and experiences. Walt's Pilgrimage uses nearly forty different places to educate students about the various aspects of Walt's life.

The places along our route have been carefully curated to showcase where Walt lived, worked, and played. It includes locations of success (Disneyland) and failure (Laugh-o-Gram Films). Place is paramount to envisioning Walt's personal and professional life. When students step into Walt's apartment in Disneyland and look out the sacred window, they can be transported back to 1954 when Walt would look out, observing how a former orange grove in Anaheim was being transformed into his first theme park.[12] Place offers context for how Walt's mind worked. For example, we visit Griffith Park to see the place where Walt originated the concept of Disneyland on weekends when he took his daughters to ride the merry-go-round.[13] Place is also critical for examining how Walt re-shaped 100 acres of an orange grove into a park that transports visitors to different places (e.g., Fantasyland). Place-based learning encourages students to develop place consciousness, which involves an awareness and appreciation of the unique characteristics and significance of specific places.[14] This promotes a deeper connection to that environment and a sense of responsibility toward its preservation. So much of Walt's life has been preserved (his boyhood home/farm, his Carolwood barn, and his birthplace, for example) and some of it is in the process of being preserved (like the McConahay Building in Kansas City).[15]

Place-based education is an approach to learning that takes advantage of geography to create authentic, meaningful, and engaging personalized learning. Place-based learning, when enacted, creates these overall benefits:

- Confidence in Navigation: Because place-based learning involves travel, we can gain confidence in navigating to new destinations.
- Sense of Space: When we go to specific sites, we are often in the places where historical events take place. This lends itself well to multi-sensory engagement in which we can touch, hear, and smell the surroundings of the space.
- High Engagement: Place-based education typically drives higher levels of engagement, specifically being more attentive and motivated about the educational content.

Incorporating external locations into a curriculum makes abstract concepts concrete and stimulates the desire to learn more deeply. Place-based education can be an effective tool for connecting students to their own "place" and enhancing their learning experiences.

Experiences

Experiential learning is also paramount to gaining critical knowledge. If Walt were to describe his own pilgrimage, he would likely say it allows learning to go from the page to the stage. And that stage is every place where he dreamed his dreams, spent time with his family, and let his imagination run wild. Immersive experiences to acquire knowledge, develop skills, and gain insights help make sense of subject matter. We are simulating and/or reliving Walt's life, trying to imagine how, at the age of twenty, he became president of his own company in Kansas City, and, at the age of sixty-five, created his Experimental Prototype Community of Tomorrow (EPCOT).[16] Experiences allow all participants to put their own lives into context compared to Walt at that age, perhaps even coming to relate to Walt's humble beginnings. Experiential learning also prioritizes engagement in the learning process. For example, learning to play one of Walt's hobbies, lawn bowling, at Roxbury Memorial Park with the Beverly Hills Lawn Bowling Club, enables you to see how Walt experienced enjoyment in his life.

Experiences create a dynamic learning environment that produces these primary benefits:

- Active Learning: Experience-based learning is active rather than passive. It requires students to engage, participate, and often physically interact with the subject matter, which can lead to a deeper understanding.
- Sparking Enthusiasm: Experiences can spark interest and enthusiasm for the subject matter, leading to increased motivation and active engagement in the learning process.
- Reflection and Metacognition: Experiential learning often includes reflective components, requiring students to think critically about their learning processes (metacognition), which can lead to improved self-awareness and insight.

SHAPE integrates all the elements to provide a comprehensive educational experience, and it is an ideal acronym to discuss Walt Disney. In 1957, Diane Disney Miller (daughter of Walt), in the first published biography book about Walt, stated, "He [Walt] told me all he can of the influences that shaped him."[17]

Why a "Pilgrimage"?

A pilgrimage is a journey undertaken by individuals of religious or spiritual significance to a sacred place or shrine.[18] It is often motivated by a desire for spiritual growth, enlightenment, or to fulfill religious obligations. Pilgrimages can vary greatly in duration, distance, and purpose, but they typically involve rituals along the way.[19] The experience of pilgrimage can be deeply personal and transformative. The use of "pilgrimage" connected to Disney is not a new concept. In 1980, in a piece titled, "Walt Disney World: Bounded Ritual Space and the Playful Pilgrimage Center," Alexander Moore argues in the essay that the Florida theme park has all of the ingredients similar to a religious pilgrimage location—full of unique spaces, passages—acting as a playful shrine."[20] Years later, Cher Krause Knight wrote about "Disney World as Pilgrimage Center" in her 2014 book entitled *Power and Paradise in Walt Disney's World* (of course I love how she references Walt as "person" in the title).[21] In her chapter, Knight describes how Walt created "ceremonial spaces" and "ritual practices" similar to long-standing religious pilgrimages described above. Knight describes the strong emotions associated with visiting a Disney theme park, even stating the importance of Walt's impact: "Walt's legacy has an omnipotent presence in our culture," describing how much "heart" he put into his work.

"Walt Disney" as his own pilgrimage follows this same framework as I take students to ceremonial spaces (sometimes private, sometimes public) in Walt's life and participate in rituals that enable students to further connect to Walt as a person, beyond the brand they know. For example, we visit places of significance in Walt's life like his very formative years in Marceline about which Walt stated, "More things of importance happened to me in Marceline than have happened since—or are likely to in the future."[22] The idyllic rural surroundings and community spirit of Marceline left a lasting impression on Walt, influencing many of his later creations, including the concept of Main Street, U.S.A. in Disneyland. Marceline served as a source of inspiration and nostalgia for Disney throughout his life, shaping his creative vision and storytelling ethos. To this day, there is a spark in my students' eyes after spending a day in Marceline—it really is that magical.

Diving into Walt's Pilgrimage: Mineral King

With that context and understanding, it is time to travel through a mini-pilgrimage in the life of Walt Disney. This will be just a taste of what the course includes. In what follows, I use one site, Mineral King, to showcase the SHAPE Method in action.

Imagine driving two hours to go twenty-five miles to 7,580 feet up a mountain. A not-so-well-known (but growing in interest) connection to Walt Disney is Mineral King, which is now a part of Sequoia National Park. Mineral King is a glacial valley within the Sierra Nevada mountains in Eastern California. Its name derives from its exploration as a mining site in the 1870s. We travel to Mineral King on a single-lane, dirt road to learn about Walt's fascination with this place. He first visited here in the early 1960s, excited by its potential as a ski resort. Visiting Mineral King is to learn about opportunity, conservation, and conflict.[23]

What Was Mineral King?

Walt's Mineral King project was an ambitious plan to develop a large, all-season ski resort in the Mineral King valley of the Sierra Nevada mountains in California. Envisaged in the 1960s, the resort aimed to include up to fourteen ski runs, lodges, restaurants, and entertainment facilities that reflected Walt's reputation for family-oriented destinations and themed environments. The project would have capitalized on the area's natural beauty and high elevation, offering year-round recreational opportunities. Despite Disney's intentions to create a unique mountain resort that extended beyond his company's successful theme parks, the project spurred substantial environmental opposition due to concerns over ecological impact and the potential commercialization of the wilderness area. The controversy played a role in broader movements for environmental protection, resulting in the abandonment of the resort plans following Walt's death and eventually leading to Mineral King's annexation into Sequoia National Park in 1978 through the National Parks and Recreation Act, thereby protecting it from large-scale development.[24]

From a nostalgic perspective, Mineral King was a nod to the European alpine ski villages, and on the innovation side, it represented new frontiers and a demonstration of how a ski resort could be used throughout the entire year.

Because of the growing interest in skiing and ski facilities, the US Forest Service issued a prospectus to invite proposals for a future ski resort in Mineral King.[25] The Forest Service received six proposals, including one submitted by Walt on behalf of Walt Disney Productions. Walt had many goals for this ski resort development:

- Family-Friendly Destination: In line with the Disney brand and Disneyland, the Mineral King resort was intended to provide entertainment and activities for families and visitors of all ages.
- Conservation and Preservation: Walt aimed to develop the resort with environmental conservation in mind, taking measures to preserve the natural beauty and minimize the ecological impact on the valley. Walt had a lifelong passion for nature.

Figure 10.2 Students on Walt's Pilgrimage, July 11, 2015, at Mineral King Valley in California. Christopher W. Tremblay.

- Unique Experiences: The concept included features that would set Mineral King apart from other resorts of the time, such as a five-mile-long cable car system to transport guests from the parking areas to the village.
- High-Quality Amenities: Plans for the resort included top-notch accommodations, dining options, and facilities that matched the Disney standard for quality and service.

Let's explore how The SHAPE Method enables us to immerse ourselves in learning about Mineral King.

S: Storytelling

Teaching students about Mineral King is also a chance to inform them about Walt's personal interest in skiing and his connection to the 1960 Winter Olympics. In the 1930s, Walt's doctor recommended that he take up the sport of skiing to reduce stress.[26] We learn stories about Willy Schaeffler and Bob Hicks, both of whom were involved with the Mineral King project. Walt first met Willy during the 1960 Winter Olympics, and he encouraged Walt to follow his interest in skiing while helping Walt scout a potential location.[27] Hicks served as the Mineral King project manager for Walt Disney Productions.[28] The final part of the story involves Walt's passing in 1966, the role of the Sierra Club fighting against the project, and the annexation of Mineral King into the US National Park Service, using some of the artifacts mentioned below.

H: Historical Biography

In telling the history of Mineral King, we learn about the details of the ski resort that Walt planned, one component of which was going to be called Sky Crown. The name "Sky Crown" was coined to evoke images of majestic mountain peaks and a regal, commanding presence within the natural beauty of the high Sierra. It was meant to suggest a resort element at the pinnacle of mountain vacation destinations—literally a "crown in the sky." Some people are also surprised to learn that possibly the Country Bear Jamboree was originally created for Mineral King.[29] That attraction ended up in the Disney theme parks instead.

A: Artifacts

Mineral King is rich in artifacts that allow us to learn about Walt and his development. Here, I will highlight just a few of them.

The five-page 1965 press release announcing Walt's bid is an important artifact. It recounts how Walt hand-delivered his proposal in person in Porterville, California, on

August 31. This news release concluded with a direct quotation from Walt: "I sincerely believe that the proper development of Mineral King will make Tulare County one of the finest outdoor recreational centers in America," a reflection of Walt's commitment to quality and excellence.[30] There is even a photograph of Walt exiting the airplane in Porterville. Walt's personal delivery of his application demonstrated how important this project was to him.

The April 20, 1966, Economic Impact of Mineral King Development is a fourteen-page report that demonstrates Walt's business sense as he commissioned the Economics Research Associates in Los Angeles to produce this report. This report educates all of us on how major this development was at the time. According to the ERA report, this project's benefits included "$57 million of new investment, 2,500 new jobs, $100 million in payrolls and $200 million in retail sales" through 1976.[31]

Public Law 95-625 of 1978 is a concluding artifact of this project. Known as the National Parks and Recreation Act of 1978, this document reminds us that not all dreams come true.[32] Section 314 of this act added Mineral King Valley to Sequoia National Park and ended the thirteen-year controversy over the proposed ski resort development in the area. This is a great introduction for students to learn about legislation and public laws, especially those related to land conservation.

One of the most intriguing artifacts is a map of the property that Disney still owns and pays taxes on annually. During my research in 2022, I confirmed that Walt Disney Productions still owns three parcels totaling 28.75 acres in Mineral King, and in 2021, they paid $3,291.66 in taxes on that land.[33]

P: Place

In terms of place, there are three important locations within the Mineral King stop: (1) standing on Disney property (using the aforementioned map), (2) visiting the "Honeymoon Cabin/Point Cabin" where there are historical documents about the Sky Crown ski resort project, and (3) visiting the Mineral King Room at the Three Rivers Historical Museum. As mentioned above, anyone going to Mineral King can stand on Disney property that is within the national park. It is a way of taking in a 360-degree view and imagining what Walt saw when he stood there as he envisioned a ski resort. The Honeymoon Cabin is a way to introduce anyone to the concept of the National Register of Historic Places, which supports the preservation of important places for their significance in American history, architecture, and/or culture. The cabin is also a place that tells the story of Walt Disney's visits and vision for Mineral King. The Mineral King Room is dedicated to telling the history of Mineral King and "The Disney Dream."[34] Here we can review newspaper clippings (artifacts) written about the proposed development. Besides physical spaces, there are digital places that allow us to learn the Mineral King story. The Mineral King Preservation Society's website maintains a robust collection of photographs and documents about Walt.

E: Experiences

The experiences of Mineral King include the long drive on a winding road, an outdoor hike, and visiting the local museum. The long van ride serves as a metaphor for the lengthy process of this development from its inception to its eventual demise. The students and I take a hike through Mineral King in the same way that Walt roamed the untouched land, admiring the tall mountains, the blue sky, the green trees, and the wildlife. It is a way to connect with Walt's love of nature.

As you can see, the SHAPE Method allows Mineral King to come alive by understanding the project's origins, components, complexities, and eventual demise. From a pedagogical standpoint, one major learning outcome of visiting Mineral King includes being able to articulate the challenges and conflicts that arise when entertainment and development interests intersect with environmental and conservation priorities. Students gain perspective on how such conflicts have historical precedents and continue to shape land use and development policies today. It is also an example of a post-death failure of Walt Disney, since this dream did not come to fruition.

There are a variety of lessons we learn about/from Walt and the Mineral King initiative:

- Entrepreneurial Vision: Students learn about Walt's broader vision beyond animation and theme parks. The Mineral King project reflects his innovative spirit and willingness to venture into new industries, such as an alpine ski resort, showcasing his entrepreneurial mindset.
- Environmental Controversies and Corporate Responsibility: The Mineral King project illustrates Walt's complex relationship with environmental conservation and the emerging environmental movement of the 1960s and 1970s. Students learn about the scrutiny and backlash corporations face when development plans are perceived to threaten natural landscapes.
- Influence on Land Use and National Park Policies: The project offers a case study in how private development proposals impact public land management decisions and policies, highlighting Disney's influence and the eventual federal response that pushed Mineral King into Sequoia National Park, preserving it forever.

Monumental Walt

At the intersection of museum studies and memory studies are monuments. According to James D. Nunez, "Monuments and memorials provide a visual representation of ideals, achievements, and heroes that existed at a point in time."[35] As of 2024, there are now ten monuments, statues, or busts of Walt Disney throughout the world. Eight of them are in Disney theme parks. The first such physical monument honoring Walt was in 1986—his bust at the Television Academy Hall of Fame.[36] This statue honored Walt's "lifetime of dedicated service to the cause of wholesome family entertainment, for his vision and stamina in bringing to fruition many revolutionary concepts in live film and programming, for allowing us to enter the wonderful world he inhabited, making us feel young again."[37]

When I take my students to see Walt's bust in the Hall of Fame Garden on the Television Academy campus in North Hollywood, California, they not only see that his peers recognized his entertainment career, but they also see him featured with more than 100 other fellow entertainers. This reminds them of his impact, his place in the world of entertainment, and the shoulders he stood on.

It was not until 1993 that the Walt Disney Company honored Walt with his own statue, the Partners Statue, which features Walt and Mickey Mouse. It has become one of the most photographed places in Disneyland. It was installed in front of Sleeping Beauty Castle at Disneyland on Mickey Mouse's birthday.[38] The Partners Statue reminds us of the importance of Mickey Mouse to Walt Disney's success. The fifth Partners Statue was most recently installed in 2002 at the Walt Disney Studios Park at Disneyland Paris.

Then, likely as part of commemorating its 100th anniversary, the Walt Disney Company installed two additional Walt monuments: "Walt the Dreamer" at EPCOT's Dreamer's Point (unveiled on Walt's birthdate—very fitting), featuring a smiling and sitting Walt Disney, and the Dream Makers Statue at Hong Kong Disneyland, featuring Walt Disney sitting on a park bench with Mickey Mouse, a nod to the time when Walt took his daughters to Griffith Park in Los Angeles to ride the merry-go-round.[39] These eight statues of Walt remind all Disney park visitors that these creations and theme parks would not exist without the dreams and visions of one person, Walt Disney.

Young describes monuments as "essentially celebratory markers of triumphs and heroic individuals."[40] All of these Walt monuments celebrate his triumphs in the entertainment industry and his heroic rise to fame and impact. It is a bit surprising that there are only six unique statues of Walt in the world, considering that half of them are the same statue, just in different locations (and all Disney theme parks).[41]

Conclusion

Imagine yourself standing at the unassuming grave of Walt Disney at Forest Lawn Cemetery in Glendale, California, after visiting dozens of places that were pivotal and transformative in his life. Imagine listening to Walt's favorite song, "Feed the Birds," from *Mary Poppins* as you reflect on his life, your pilgrimage through his life, and now how you think about the Disney brand and his creations that changed American culture forever. Imagine leaving a flower at Walt's grave as a way of thanking him for all that you learned about him, the Disney movies that impacted your childhood, the Disney theme parks that give you so much joy, and how you are forever changed because of one single person. As you can imagine, the emotions are high and there are usually tears. It is both a challenging ending and a powerful reflection on how we can all make our dreams come true. I imagine Walt would be humbled, tickled, and impressed that there was a college course based on his own life.

In traveling through Walt's life, we can reminisce about the days gone by in a nostalgic fashion while also learning about the innovations that Walt brought to life (such as the multiplane camera and audio-animatronics). The SHAPE Method can be used to study any historical figure or event. In fact, I have often considered creating a pilgrimage for another childhood hero, Dr. Seuss. For several years, I had students create their own pilgrimages based on a historical or current figure, and it was fascinating to learn what they deemed important about someone else's life based on the historical sites and stops along the way. Students have created pilgrimages on their own heroes such as Lin-Manuel Miranda, Martin Luther King, Jr., Abraham Lincoln, Michelangelo, Marie Curie, Steve Jobs, P. T. Barnum, and Steven Spielberg.

From that original 1249 Tripp Avenue to the cemetery at 1712 South Glendale Avenue, we can travel Walt Disney's life to recreate a version of the life he led. Just like walking in Walt's footsteps is a pilgrimage, every step we take creates our own pilgrimage. One can only wonder—who one day will embark on a biographical pilgrimage of your life? Just imagine.

Notes

1   Miri Yemini, Laura Engel, and Adi Ben Simon. "Place-Based Education—A Systematic Review of Literature," *Educational Review* (2023): 1–21. http://doi.org/10.1080/00131911.2023.2177260.

2   Christopher Tremblay, "Disneyland: The Capstone of a Time, Place and Person," December 7, 1992.

3   Sonika Suman and Matthew Kuofie, "Future Opportunities in Imagineering Management," in *Handbook of Research on Future Opportunities for Technology Management Education*, ed. Basheer Ahmed Khan, Matthew H. Kuofie, and Sonika Suman, 178–200 (Hershey: Information Science Reference, 2021).

4   Christopher Tremblay, *Walt's Pilgrimage* (Seattle: Kindle Direct Publishing, 2017).

5   Lynn Elber, "Walt Disney Experts Rebut Dogged anti-Semitic Allegations | AP News," *AP News*, August 3, 2015, https://apnews.com/movies-general-news-arts-and-entertainment-4716906a97fc4952b297151aaafd9131; Jake S. Friedman, *The Disney Revolt: The Great Labor War in Animation's Golden Age* (Chicago: Chicago Review Press, 2022); Jessica L. Laemle, "Trapped in the Mouse House: How Disney Has Portrayed Racism and Sexism in Its Princess Films" (Student Publications, 2018), 692. https://cupola.gettysburg.edu/student_scholarship/692.

6   Critical Past, "Walt Disney Studios Owner Walt Disney Testifies against Communism at Hearings of . . . HD Stock Footage," July 4, 2014, https://www.youtube.com/watch?v=8rujLwY1C8k.

7   Neal Gabler, *Walt Disney: The Triumph of the American Imagination* (New York: Alfred A. Knopf, 2006).

8   American Experience, PBS, "Walt Disney the Storyteller," https://www.pbs.org/wgbh/americanexperience/features/walt-disney-storyteller/.

9   Timothy S. Susanin, *Walt Before Mickey: Disney's Early Years, 1919–1928* (Jackson: University Press of Mississippi, 2011).

10 Albert Jay Nock, "The Purpose of Biography," *The Atlantic*, March 1940, https://www
.theatlantic.com/magazine/archive/1940/03/the-purpose-of-biography/654280/.

11 Yemini, Engel, and Simon, "Place-Based Education—A Systematic Review of
Literature."

12 Sophie Jo, "A Second Home: Walt Disney's Fire Station Apartment," June 20, 2020,
https://www.waltdisney.org/blog/second-home-walt-disneys-fire-station-apartment.

13 Todd James Pierce, "Walt Disney and the Griffith Park Zoo," Disney History
Institute—Celebrating and Preserving Walt Disney's Creative Legacy, June 19, 2017,
https://www.disneyhistoryinstitute.com/2014/06/walt-disney-and-griffith-park-zoo
.html.

14 Yilmaz M. Akkaya and U. Karakuş. "The Impact of Place Based Education Approach
on Student Achievement in Social Studies," *Review of International Geographical
Education Online* (RIGEO) 8, no. 3 (2018): 500–516, http://www.rigeo.org/vol8no3/
Number3winter/RIGEO-V8-N3-5.pdf

15 Walt Disney Hometown Museum (WDHM), "Disney—Walt Disney Hometown
Museum," n.d., https://www.waltdisneymuseum.org/disney; "Walt's Barn," Walt
Disney's Barn, February 3, 2022, https://www.carolwood.org/walts-barn/; The Walt
Disney Birthplace, "Home—the Walt Disney Birthplace," May 1, 2023, https://www
.thewaltdisneybirthplace.org/.

16 "EPCOT," D23. https://d23.com/a-to-z/epcot/ (accessed June 29, 2024).

17 Diane Disney Miller, *The Story of Walt Disney: A Fabulous Rags-to-Riches Saga* (New
York: Dell Publishing Co., Inc., 1956), 5–6.

18 National Trust, "What Is a Pilgrimage? | History," https://www.nationaltrust.org.uk/
discover/history/what-is-a-pilgrimage (accessed June 29, 2024).

19 Robert Stoddard, "Defining and Classifying Pilgrimages," 1997. DigitalCommons@
University of Nebraska—Lincoln, https://digitalcommons.unl.edu/geographyfacpub
/2/.

20 Alexander Moore, "Walt Disney World: Bounded Ritual Space and the Playful
Pilgrimage Center," *Anthropological Quarterly* 53, no. 4(1980): 207.

21 Cher Krause Knight, *Power and Paradise in Walt Disney's World* (Gainesville:
University Press of Florida, 2014), 24–6.

22 Robin Seaton Jefferson, "Inside Walt Disney's Life in Marceline," March 2020, https://
missourilife.com/inside-walt-disneys-life-in-marceline/.

23 "Mineral King, Sequoia National Park | Sierra Nevada Geotourism," https://sierran
evadageotourism.org/entries/mineral-king-sequoia-national-park/be437c91-da70
-4954-8c34-d342410e7459 (accessed June 29, 2024).

24 Greg Glasgow and Kathryn Mayer, *Disneyland on the Mountain: Walt, the
Environmentalists, and the Ski Resort That Never Was* (Lanham: Rowman &
Littlefield, 2023).

25 Nathan Masters, "Disney's Lost Plans to Build a Ski Resort in Sequoia National Park,"
PBS SoCal, https://www.pbssocal.org/shows/lost-la/disneys-lost-plans-to-build-a-ski
-resort-in-sequoia-national-park (accessed April 14, 2023).

26 "Walt Disney Skiing? A Less Known Love of Walt's | the Walt Disney Family
Museum," *Walt Disney Family Museum Blog*, https://www.waltdisney.org/blog/disney
-skiing (accessed June 29, 2024).

27 Jim Korkis, "The Story of Mineral King," *Mouseplanet*, June 12, 2019, https://
mouseplanet.com/the-story-of-mineral-king/7014/#google_vignette.

28 Robert B. Hicks, "Mineral King Preservation Society," n.d., https://mineralking.org/biographies/hicks-robert-b/ (accessed June 29, 2024).

29 Glasgow and Mayer, *Disneyland on the Mountain.*

30 Walt Disney Productions, "Walt Disney Submits Application for Mineral King Recreation Development," August 31, 1965, 5.

31 Economics Research Associates, "Economic Impact of Mineral King Development. Los Angeles, California," April 20, 1966, 11–13.

32 National Parks and Recreation Act of 1978. Pub. L. No. 95–625, 92 STAT. 3467 (1978).

33 County of Tulare, California. Map of Tax Code Area 146–002. Assessor's Maps, Book 70, page 10. (n.d.); Wise, Steve. Email message to author, August 29, 2022.

34 Mineral King Room, "Mineral King Preservation Society," https://mineralking.org/mineral-king-room/.

35 James D. Nunez, "Teaching Historical Skills Using Monuments, Markers, and Online Museums" (PhD diss., University of Alabama at Birmingham, 2021).

36 Tremblay, *Walt's Pilgrimage.*

37 Television Academy, "Walt Disney Hall of Fame Induction 1986," n.d., https://www.emmys.com/video/walt-disney-hall-fame-induction-1986.

38 D23, "Partners—D23," March 5, 2018, https://d23.com/a-to-z/partners/.

39 Will Baggett, "World Celebration Gardens, 'Walt the Dreamer' Statue Debut Dec. 5 at EPCOT," *Disney Parks Blog*, https://disneyparksblog.com/disney-experiences/world-celebration-gardens-walt-the-dreamer-statue-debut-dec-5-at-epcot/ (accessed November 23, 2023); "Hong Kong Disneyland Resort Celebrates 100 Years of Disney With Unveiling of 'Dream Makers' Statue—Hong Kong Disneyland," https://news.hongkongdisneyland.com/en/press/2023-10-15/ (accessed October 15, 2023).

40 James E. Young, *The Texture of Memory* (New Haven: Yale University Press, 1994), 3.

41 A complete list of these monuments is online: waltspilgrimage.com/monuments.

11

Theme Park America

Alex Hofmann

Jean Baudrillard, Patrick Wolfe, Edward Said, Michel Foucault: these storied names can make the eyes of even the most resolute undergraduates glaze over. Delve into the intricacies of their concepts of simulation/simulacrum and hyperreality, settler colonialism, orientalism, and heterotopias, and students go catatonic—that is, unless you frame them in Disneyland.

I teach a college course titled Theme Park America, which examines the history of themed spaces in the United States from the colonial era to the present, considering the evolution, functions, and ethics of that quintessential American desire to visit the past as a form of leisure. Since the nation's founding, these places have been sites where an anxious people have grappled with their fluctuating identities, inventing versions of the past that suited the contemporary needs of people who have never been fully comfortable with the full implications and promises of technological, social, and ideological "progress."[1] We trace the evolution of the form and function of proto-themed spaces from pleasure gardens to world's fairs, amusement parks, roadside attractions, and living history museums. The course concludes with an in-depth examination of how Disneyland blended these predecessors together to become the world's first theme park.

In part, this is personal for me. For nearly three years after college, I endured a number of nineteen-hour shifts working in Disney's Animal Kingdom merchandising and then Magic Kingdom Guest Relations by wondering what made these places tick and why people kept returning to them. I then turned this into a career, becoming a cultural historian, where thinking about the serious meaning underlying the seemingly unserious and bizarre elements of life, often dismissed by other fields, is my whole professional raison d'être.

Since opening in 1955, Disneyland has captured the fascination and imaginary of Americans.[2] Within its first four years of operation, fifteen million guests visited, amounting to nearly one in ten of every American.[3] Such immediate blockbuster success suggests deeper significance than an affinity for kinetics and Mickey Mouse. As the world's first theme park, Disneyland was distinct for its overarching, unifying, immersive narrative told through individual themed lands. According to Walt Disney in his own dedication of the park, this story was "the ideals, the dreams, and the hard facts that have created America."[4]

It was his narrative, but guests were and are welcome to experience it in their preferred way. To this day, guests choose how to interact with the overarching narrative by shuffling the order of the lands and attractions they visit. But the historical selection has already been made for them. To this day, the Walt Disney Company conceptualizes their Magic Kingdom parks as "Our Big Theater." The only non-negotiable is that everyone starts and ends their day by traveling through the two tunnels on either side of the railroad station that hides the park behind it, which Disney says, builds anticipation and symbolizes a curtain rising and falling on the "show" of the park.[5] From here, the guests become actors, the lands radiating off the central "hub" become genres, and the day becomes a choose-your-own adventure for how you want to experience the narrative laid out before you, linked together by affect, function, and history.

It has now been seventy years since Disneyland opened its gates, and yet history is inertial. For this reason, I focus on Disneyland at its inception, reading it in its purest form for what it can tell us about contemporary Americans' beliefs, desires, and fears. Over subsequent decades, Disneyland's layout, lands, and attractions would change radically. However, new generations of guests would have to contend with these animating forces when grafting new meanings onto the changing landscape of the park—forces that long outlived the built environment.

Every narrative has a point of view. Make no mistake: Disneyland's America as authored by Walt Disney was largely white and male. It was this telling of America that in 1955 seemed besieged from without and within. An ever-heightening Cold War meant containment abroad proceeded lockstep with containment at home; both spurred and exploited atomic fears. Communism, "urban blight," and the automobile were the ideological tools of white fright leveled at racial unrest beyond the American South, while *Brown v. Board* kicked off the classical Civil Rights Movement. The suburb became a bunker offering physical and psychological protection against Communist and Black Americans, yet it also quickly became a prison of solitude. What popular culture and memory fondly recalls as one of the most idyllic times in US history was in reality the start of a great white American unraveling felt to this day.

Disneyland encoded all of this into its built environment. Though some of the most blatant and repugnant features have been removed, they remain legible even as they seed new interpretations of our past today. As a cultural historian, I will walk you through the parts of Disneyland that (mis)represent the past: Main Street, U.S.A., Adventureland, Frontierland—and back again.

Yet, it won't be simple. Traversing these lands requires us to negotiate several temporalities at once. And yet this is one pedagogical power of Disneyland: it offers an opportunity to explore history as it is lived across multiple temporalities. For all its triteness, Disneyland bucks the narrative simplicity that is often found (for good reason) in our historical narratives for effective argumentation.[6]

But we can have both—and Disneyland demonstrates how. Michel Foucault believed that Westerners had come to have a fundamentally different relationship with time in the twentieth century. Nineteenth-century faith in linear time bent toward progress had given way to a new "epoch of simultaneity" where a single space could counterintuitively contain several places Foucault called "heterotopias." Heterotopias, in part, were distinguished by their capacity to juxtapose otherwise incompatible places and timescales.[7] Historian Scott Magelssen specifically applied this concept to living history museums when referring to them as heterochronistic spaces (places where there are breaks in normal experiences of time) due to interpretive splits among individual and institutional levels. The result was to elevate a singular historical interpretation—what historians call historiography—that, in turn, comes to seem immutable to guests who literally walk the narrative in an interactable space.[8] Similarly, in Disneyland we have the opportunity to examine how memory interacts with a naturalized historiography in the built environment to create multiple temporalities guests occupy at the same time from today's vantage point: the one(s) Disneyland's lands represent; the one Americans occupied at Disneyland's opening at the height of the Cold War, generating specific meanings and functions; and the present.

Main Street, U.S.A., Adventureland, and Frontierland paint the tryptic of white America's vaunted self-figuring: small-town values, rugged adventure, and frontier individualism. Today, they can be read to reveal the connections among consumption, enslavement, settler colonialism, and imperialism. Through the interweaving stories these lands tell across interlocking temporalities, Disneyland renders complex, cutting-edge historical thought and theory comprehensible and the functioning of the historical discipline legible. The park provides a lens for history as both past and practice.

Capitalizing Main Street

Main Street, U.S.A. had an important role to fill: it was a portal between two worlds, cloaking visitors in Walt Disney's particular, limited iteration of American civics as they entered and left the parks. Depending on interpretation, Main Street, U.S.A. could either represent a town produced by the frontier experience and sustained by colonial extraction or one setting out to conquer the frontier and make the world in its image. Whichever the view, it relied on an unbroken chain of consumerist memory for Cold War Americans that couched mass consumption in 1890s small-town aesthetics and ethos. Main Street, U.S.A.'s purported time period shifted frequently in Disneyland's promotional materials before and after opening, ranging somewhere between the 1890s and 1910s. Wherever one landed, it was a period of transition. "America was growing fast," Walt Disney described. "Towns and villages were turning into cities. Soon the gaslight will be replaced by electricity. But that was still in the future. At this time little main street was still the most important spot in the nation, combining the color of frontier days with the oncoming excitement of the new twentieth century."[9] It was this transition that would speak to Cold War Americans.

The Main Street, U.S.A. of 1955 was not the Main Street, U.S.A. of today. Walt Disney lined the road with retailers that would make the town seem real. Original tenants included Bank of America, Eastman Kodak, Wurlitzer Piano, Gibson Greeting Cards, Swift's Market House, Puffin Bake Shop, and even the Hollywood-Maxwell Brassiere

Company. Significantly, there were also what we would now call "third spaces" (areas of community) such as a bandstand, penny arcade, and town square.

This was not the Main Street of reality for turn-of-the-century America. Purported models for Main Street, U.S.A. included Fort Collins, Colorado; Bay City, Michigan; and, of course, memories of Walt's brief childhood hometown of Marceline, Missouri.[10] Missing are the vagabonds, panhandlers, saloons, pool halls, telegraph wires, telephone poles, unpaved roads, and dirt that made up just a small part of the more unaesthetic elements of turn-of-the-century small-town life.

The absence of these realities was just one part of crafting a reassuring and nostalgic form of memory of small-town life at the turn of the century. It went down to the very architecture. As art historian Karal Ann Marling wrote, Disneyland built an "architecture of reassurance" that planned everything down to guest affect by drawing on Hollywood tricks like forced perspective to make people feel bigger and the surroundings more orderly to instill a sense of inner peace.[11]

Why did Cold War Americans need to be reassured? This idyllic, walkable main street was vanishing as a new set of commercial values undermined the very type of local commerce depicted here. Or so it seemed. For, although Main Street, U.S.A. had a number of different vendors, the facade only created the illusion of these being separate buildings; in reality, they were all connected in one nearly unbroken structure on either side of the street. In effect, this meant that Walt Disney beat architect Victor Gruen to the debut of the first shopping mall by a year.[12] It was no coincidence that other corporations like Walmart would take a similar approach within a decade, weaning shoppers off of the walkable Main Streets they helped destroy through what historian Bethany Moreton called "theme parks of landlocked small-town life, reservations for an imagined homogenous yesterday that only the technologies of tomorrow could render."[13] Like Disneyland, Walmart saw the increasing malaise of suburbia and shopping centers created by the postwar reorientation of good citizenship around consumption.[14] In response, they cloaked crass materialism in small-town nostalgia, rendering it a safe—if not admirable—part of America's character.

Adventureland: From Congo to Frontier

Notably, Main Street, U.S.A. is a jumping-off point for the West. In one reading of the land, it is the feminine domestic counterpart to white men pushing the nation's boundary toward the Pacific.[15] By 1850, "manifest destiny" had become a full-throated rallying cry fused permanently to ideas about race.[16] The term may not have been on the lips of every American, but it was in their hearts and minds—and the careless ways they viewed the continent and their natural claims to it. Long before Cold War Americans saw it as their duty to spread this capitalistic consumption overseas as a bulwark against communism, nineteenth-century Americans headed west to seize indigenous land for personal enrichment. And a principal means of achieving this was through enslaved people who provided the labor, credit, and collateral necessary both to settle the West and build modern capitalism.[17]

Disney's Adventureland illustrates this well. Especially at park opening, the land was a hodgepodge of exoticized areas of beastly animals and beastlier men. According to Bob Cummings' script at the 1955 dedication of Disneyland, one officially endorsed reading of this place was as "an African trading post, the spearhead of civilization in those primitive lands."[18] Trading in what, exactly, remains unstated, yet the land is also undated, floating somewhere above history.

One possibility was that Disney was nodding to the international slave trade. Admittedly, this might sound outlandish, especially in light of the Walt Disney Company generally and the Adventureland specifically as we know them today. Yet, when Disneyland opened in 1955, the only people depicted in the land were not any characters from Disney films but rather "primitive" African Natives who formed warring tribes along the Jungle Cruise. Moreover, it is telling that in blending the transition between Adventureland and Frontierland, guests in early years of the park would walk through a narrow passage around a rotunda with a thatched roof labeled "Aunt Jemima's Kitchen."

Following to the front of the building, guests were now in front of a plantation home in the New Orleans Street section of Frontierland. With the architectural shift, guests traveled from Africa to the American South. The implicit narrative completed is of the "civilizing" role of enslavement that proslavery ideologues and most white historians of the 1950s alike espoused: Africans were cannibals, uncultured; enslaved peoples were subservient, civilized.

Figure 11.1 Aunt Jemima's kitchen. From the davelandweb.com collection.

This had profound importance amid the classical Civil Rights Movement taking hold at the same time Disneyland was opening. Aunt Jemima was one example of a broader stereotypical mammy trope created to make racist beliefs about the benefits of enslavement and the inferiority of Black Americans seem true during the Jim Crow Era. In this case, that enslaved women were desexualized obese caretakers who were happy to be enslaved, well taken care of, and a bonded part of the family. Since the 1920s, Aunt Jemima sold the idea that white women could reap the benefits of enslavement without the enslaved by purchasing the timesaving pancake mix.[19] Aunt Jemima appears briefly in the *Dateline Disneyland* opening special as a minstrel performance of this mammy caricature. It is the popularization of these stock figures that helped prop up the very segregationist laws, customs, and beliefs that the Civil Rights Movement was trying to dismantle in law and in practice; in Disneyland, white Americans did not have to relinquish anything.

Frontierland: Settler Colonialism

The frontier has always been a mindset—conjured, fantasized, always out of reach. Both a temporality and an imagined space, it was and is an asymptote of white desire. Few captured this sentiment as effectively as Walt Disney.

Frontierland is a manifestation of historian Frederick Jackson Turner's 1893 "The Significance of the Frontier in American History" in the built environment. Catastrophizing the fallout from the alleged death of the frontier in the 1890 census, Turner announced to a gathering of the American Historical Association, "The frontier is the line of most rapid and effective Americanization. The wilderness masters the colonist."[20] Pushing west gave Americans their character and America its history: reborn as white self-reliant individualist men and reinvigorated as a civilization, democracy, and nation.[21] Turner's thesis was bunk, predicated on patently false ideas about frontier self-reliance, an independence ironically propped up by an unprecedentedly strong federal government, and racist beliefs in white Americans' innate cultural superiority over indigenous peoples, but it drove scholarship for decades and still powers the popular imagination.[22]

But Turner only put to paper what had long been prevalent in popular culture. Two decades prior, John Gast painted the now iconic *American Progress*, which offered a similarly romantic depiction of the settling of the West. The painting depicts an allegorical woman standing in for America quite literally carrying progress westward, stringing telegraph lines behind her as she leads farmers, settlers, and railroads to land indigenous peoples simply flee without conflict. As historian Adam Arenson wrote, this painting reflected a will to reorient the nation's axis from North-South to East-West after the Civil War for the sake of reconciliation.[23] Indeed, white Southerners looked to the West as a place free from supposed Republican tyranny on one end and sectional weariness on the other through a return to nature.[24] Although considered a masterpiece today, *American Progress* had far less auspicious origins: a promotional tourism guide for a Western railroad.[25]

How fitting, then, that Frontierland became a four-dimensional rendering of *American Progress*. Walt Disney's dedication read, "It is here that we experience the story of our country's past—the color, romance and drama of frontier America as it developed from wilderness trails to roads, riverboats, railroads, and civilization . . . a tribute to the faith, courage, and ingenuity of our hearty pioneers who blazed the trails and made this progress possible."[26]

Walking deeper into Frontierland from New Orleans Street underscores how enslavement and settler colonialism—long held as separate in scholarship—were actually two counterparts of a broader white supremacist project. Scholars have increasingly understood the Civil War as not only an evolving war for emancipation but also a war over the fate of labor in the West and therefore—regardless of outcome—a war for settler colonialism.[27] As historian Stephanie Smallwood put it, "We can understand territorial conquest and chattel slavery as twin tools of settler colonial dominion across the hemispheric Americas, where nothing conferred personhood more securely than property in seized land and enslaved humans."[28] It was historian Patrick Wolfe who first coined "settler colonialism" in the Australian context yet quickly found use for it in the American one as well. Most simply, he defined it as a systematic invasion of indigenous peoples that "destroys to replace" in order to expand territorial holdings.[29] The concept has two key dimensions: first, settlers have a "logic of elimination" that drives people off the land but does not necessarily eradicate them, often reintegrating them into society in ways that often reify settler society instead.

Throughout US history, this took rough and overlapping stages of assimilation, violence, and removal. Between 1795 and 1890, there were at least 1,642 armed conflicts and 400 treaties between indigenous and US military forces.[30] Removal and containment efforts escalated after the Civil War, first with Indian War Campaigns but especially after the Dawes Act in 1887. In an attempt to dissolve reservations, this broke all tribal treaties in favor of individual land allotments to compliant indigenous peoples, stripping tribes of three-fifths of their remaining land, defaulting the rest to the federal government, and confining noncompliant indigenous peoples to ever smaller reservations.[31]

This first element of settler colonialism—its violent removal of indigenous populations—is rarely acknowledged within Disneyland today, though it was certainly hinted at in the park's early years, first and foremost through the figure of Davey Crockett. Walt Disney did for Davey Crockett what Coca-Cola did for Santa Claus. To fund Disneyland, Walt Disney sold an eight-month-long TV series to ABC that would double as an advertisement for his coming park. Each week's episode revolved around one of the park's lands, providing plans and construction updates. As a way to fill airtime and generate buzz, Walt added in additional original programming. In the premiere episode of the series, ninety million Americans—over half the population, which would be more than would tune in for the future moon landing—watched Walt explain what Disneyland would be.[32]

They also met actor Fess Parker in character as Davey Crockett as he sang "The Ballad of Davey Crockett" for the very first time. The first verse established Crockett as the bear-wrestling "King of the Wild Frontier" at age three. In the second, Crockett recounts how he "Fought single-handed through the Injun War/Til the Creeks was whipped and the peace was in store./While he was handlin' this risky chore,/Made himself a legend forever more." All the while, a still frame shows a cartoon Crockett, dagger reared, with his hand around the throat of an indigenous man who had an ax raised over Crockett's head, home and hearth in the background.[33] Overnight, Crockett became a household name: his anthem landed at number one in the charts, and licensed (and unlicensed) merchandise sold $300 million.[34]

On Disneyland's opening day, Fess Parker made an appearance in Frontierland as Davey Crockett. When radio and television personality Art Linkletter asked why he was late, Crockett responded he took a shortcut, which ran them into "redskins . . . just itchin' to lift our scalps." He then sang an homage to "Betsy," his gun that got them out.[35] It was the start of a common conditioning exacted by Crockett and Frontierland writ large: indigenous people were to be seen as violent at worst and the butt of the joke at best.[36]

It is essential to note that because this "logic of elimination" need not end in genocide but rather thrives off the very reintegration of indigenous peoples into settler society, settler colonialism takes on a second quality even more evident in Disneyland.

As Wolfe wrote, settler colonialism is "a structure not an event"—that is, an ongoing process that continues to the present, made and remade to this day and through pop culture spaces like Frontierland.[37] Hugging the Western bank of the Rivers of America between 1955 and 1971, Indian Village illustrates how settler colonialism functioned as structure.

Before Disneyland opened, Walt specified that Indian Village was supposed to represent a reservation.[38] Partnering with the local Drum and Feather Club, it featured sixteen different tribes.[39] The message was clear. Outside the village, indigenous peoples were dangerous. When shown wandering in the frontier town, children pointed their guns at them: "Careful, Davey," the narrator of one promotional film said, "those are *real* Indians."[40] Inside the reservation depicted in Indian Village, on the other hand, indigenous peoples were perceived as civilized and good, performing ceremonial dances for guests and showing off teepees. Here, the same narrator told the children looking at indigenous ceremonial dress with patterns like bullseyes, "This isn't a moving target, kids, so put those six-shooters back in their holsters."[41] This has an even more biting irony when considering that it was the Ghost Dance that would lead to the Wounded Knee Massacre in 1890 that would effectively end indigenous armed resistance to the United States.[42]

While this looks like progress—and in some ways is—it still backs the settler colonial project by playing into white expectations about the "authentic" indigenous person through what historian Katrina Phillips calls "salvage tourism."[43] It plays off the "vanishing Indian" trope, which exploits indigenous cultures under the ruse of saving them from being lost forever.[44] This was the same myth used to justify and naturalize the decimation and containment of indigenous populations in reservations just like the one Indian Village was supposed to represent. Through Indian Village, we understand settler colonialism as a structure that necessitates an obsession with indigeneity as an ongoing sign of its own vitality.

From the vantage point of settler colonialism, these different "phases" of attitudes toward indigenous policy that were originally evident at Disneyland are ultimately a distinction without a difference. Whether indigenous peoples are subjected to violence or narratives of vanishment, they are condemned to the same logic of elimination.[45] It is telling that at the very same time Americans were first visiting Frontierland in 1955, state governments were in the process of separating 100,000 indigenous children from their parents without cause in custody cases and placing them with white families.[46]

This "conquered" frontier had particular salience for Cold War Americans. They could not only imagine themselves as a kind of suburban pioneers abroad but also relish the simplistic, mythical, sentimental moralism of the West that Frontierland fed them. As an analog for the United States and the USSR, respectively, guests could imagine themselves stepping into stories of sheriffs and outlaws, cowboys and Indians, civilized and uncivilized.

Adventureland Revisited: Old Methods for New Frontiers

On dedication day, time ran short, so Adventureland barely got a mention in *Dateline Disneyland*. However, one of the hosts, radio and television personality Bob Cummings, quickly noted, "And we are now at the beginning of a true-life adventure into a still unconquered and untamed region of our own world."[47] It seemed almost unthinkable to Americans at the time that a place like this could still exist—where man and nature had yet to diverge in that false Western dichotomy. Returning to Adventureland from Frontierland, the area takes on new meaning and temporal contexts. "Civilization" has justified heinous acts, and that is no less true here, where Adventureland collapses nonwhite continents into a singular exotic aesthetic.

This is most apparent in the land's rampant use of tiki culture. "Tiki" was a Māori creator god transformed into an aesthetic in American hands.[48] Tiki culture started after the Second World War with sailors returning from the Pacific. It got a second wind with Hawaiian statehood, seeding a proliferation of restaurants, bars, literature, TV shows, and music that depicted a loose blend of Polynesian aesthetics.[49] Adventureland rode this same wave, including shops like "Tiki's Tropical Imports" and "General Lee's Bamboo Alley." Most important, though, was Adventureland's use of music. Its music was ominous, featuring tribal beating of drums that was supposed to simulate exotic cultures in ways that predate the genre's accepted founder, Martin Denny's *Exotica* album to come two years later.[50] The result of tiki culture and its attendant tribal, exotic music was to feed Adventureland's creation of the "other."[51]

This was just one way Adventureland became a means of constructing and reifying white identity through the often invisible yet frequently invoked other. As scholar of American Culture and Music Amy Kuʻuleialoha Stillman wrote, "othering" results from colonizers projecting uninformed ideas about what authenticity is upon local peoples.[52] This is especially clear with the attraction now called the Jungle Cruise. The Jungle Cruise is a boat ride originally described as embarking from a "Tahitian setting and an international dock" to take "an excursion trip through nature's secret world."[53]

To this day, the Walt Disney Company maintains that this voyage takes you through an impossible hodgepodge of geographies as you sail down the Amazon, Congo, Nile, and Mekong Rivers—entirely unconnected bodies of water except for the fact that they run through nonwhite areas.[54]

The result was a place where death lurked behind every plant, every stream, every Native. In stark contrast to the jocular nature of the attraction today, the original script for the Jungle Cruise played up the dangers of this area. "The air grows thick with menace and mystery," the guide said. "You notice that tingling in your scalp? You feel that danger is lurking behind every log? Well, it is. These fellows know some wonderful tricks with a head!" With that cue, the boat passed by a group of Black Natives. Further down, the guide repeated, "This is a village of souvenir hunters, and the trophy here once belonged to a passenger who tried to make a shortcut through the jungle," gesturing to a skull on top of a pike. Meanwhile, another Native was referred to as a "cannibal chieftain."[55]

All of this is a clear contributor to and functioning of what activist and literary critic Edward Said called orientalism. Orientalism is the pervasive colonial logic that naturalizes not only the concept of but also the seemingly innate differences between East and West and their various peoples by boiling diverse populations down into a simple binary that serves as a tool of domination over the Near and Far East.[56] Although Said's foundational text traces primarily the relationship between England, France, and then post-Second-World-War America and the Near (i.e., Middle) East, Said later expanded his concept to Africa, India, and the Far East—the very areas jumbled together along the Jungle Cruise. Here, Said described how the same process of "othering" served Western domination by falling back on stories and symbols that looked to conquer Natives through emphasis on mysticism, savagery, and a need for uplift.[57] The image and the word preceded the truth: this was the functioning of Adventureland for 1950s Americans as it depicted adventures into Africa, the "Orient," and Latin America at the time the world was de-colonizing.

It also leads to something bigger today: a current historical interpretation that settler colonialism in the American West informed imperialist methods overseas. Americans tend not to recognize indigenous relations as a matter of foreign affairs.[58] First, as legal scholar Maggie Blackhawk wrote, Americans mentally divorce the constitution from colonization due to the Janus-faced nature of the US state that stands to benefit morally from arguing that the constitution is for internal affairs and that the empire is external to it.[59] Second, as historian Stefan Aune suggested, the geographical distance between the American Great Plains and the Philippines may sever the temporal continuity that tethered them together.[60]

With Frontierland and Adventureland mere paces apart, Disneyland bridges space and time, physically (though unwittingly) depicting a new interpretation of the actual connections between empire building in North America and on faraway continents. Despite a tendency to view the Spanish American War as a rupture in US history, with the nation turning to colonial ventures for the first time, it would turn out that there was nothing new in spirit about 1898.

In the war's wake, the United States fought ruthlessly to quell guerrilla activity in the Philippines that aimed to sink the re-election of imperialist President McKinley by destabilizing the region enough to tank the occupation's popularity at home. McKinley countered by intentionally tapping military leaders and veterans from postbellum Indian Wars and the Wounded Knee Massacre to wage total war against civilians and guerrillas alike by utilizing the same tactics they learned on the frontier: surprise attacks, roving units, civilian containment, and destabilization. Meanwhile, the press and politicians back home linked the experience of conquering indigenous people at home to suppressing Filipinos abroad.[61] Afterward, the colonial officials put in charge of the Philippines, Puerto Rico, and Cuba all cut their teeth in the Indian Wars.[62] Traversing Frontierland to Adventureland brings into focus this story of settler colonialism seeding an imperial empire.

Conclusion

One of Walt Disney's favorite adages was that Disneyland would never be completed.[63] This serves as a fitting analog for the historical discipline. That Disneyland could hold radically different interpretations in 1955 and the present with relatively similar raw data is a striking demonstration of how history works: the "facts" remain more or less the same, but the interpretations change in light of the questions we ask as historians.

Disneyland is also a window into the animating forces of the history of our nation, including capitalism, enslavement, settler colonialism, and imperialism. I ask students to consider how we might understand themed spaces as a lens for US history. What masquerades as a college course about the development and expansion of themed spaces has always somewhat deceptively been about how people imagined their worlds, with all the discriminatory baggage that entailed. It was a history of technology, and what it meant to the people who seemed to be both driving and being driven by it—and the affective and mental frameworks we could read into and out of these inventions. A history of how Americans came to conceptualize their nation and processed and experienced its changes. A history of how people remember and forget for various ends. Finally, a history of fear, and how people work that out through civic institutions like Disneyland that depict historical memory, fantasy, and visions of the future.

Much of this is bleak. History is not supposed to make you feel good. Yet it begs the question: considering this dark history, what ethical responsibility do we have when it comes to themed spaces? At this point, panning Disney is jejune—a relic of the high/ low culture wars that passed long ago.[64] At the same time, hagiography is no more revelatory.

As I tell my students, the purpose of examining all this is not to make them feel guilty for enjoying a visit to a theme park or to deter them from going in the future. I love and hate theme parks. They are fun, yet they are harmful. They forge powerful images of America and Americana, and yet they are something more: backdrops for personal memories that have nothing to do with representations of the past. The point, then, is to remain aware and curious about the built environment around them, and how it registers the distance between fact and fantasy, form and function, narrative and reality.

Why the Magic Matters

We look because we must. We look because Jean Baudrillard was right: Disneyland is not America; America is Disneyland. There is no reality at the core of the myths we tell ourselves. And so many Americans go to Disneyland to see them confirmed as true by seeing them manifested in the built environment.[65] Thinking with Foucault, Disneyland is one example of a heterotopia, the function of which is to show how the space of everyday life is an illusion itself.[66] Self-awareness is the first step in breaking the chain. As an artistic postcolonial activist group called New Red Order put it in a recruiting video shown at *The World's UnFair*, a reappropriation of world's fairs around decolonization, "We can't know where we're going unless we know where we've been. And we won't know where we've been unless we look to the past for the future. Because the future is starting to feel a lot like the present, and we all know you'd do anything to escape that."[67]

Notes

1   See, for instance, Naomi Stubbs, "Pleasure Gardens of America: Anxieties of National Identity," in *The Pleasure Garden, from Vauxhall to Coney Island*, ed. Jonathan Conlin (Philadelphia: University of Pennsylvania Press, 2012), 127–49. These particular forms collapsed urban and rural space and past and present time, so that wilderness and city life alike were rendered safe in the mind of colonial and early Americans. See Stubbs, "Pleasure Gardens of America," 13541.

2   I mean to invoke the concept of "social imaginary," which refers to the totality of how people imagine their worlds and their position within it, which may differ drastically from reality—and from others. See, for instance, Charles Taylor, *Modern Social Imaginaries* (Durham: Duke University Press, 2004), 23.

3   *Walt Disney Presents*, Season 5, Episode 27, "Kodak Presents Disneyland '59," aired June 15, 1959, on ABC, https://archive.org/details/disney-anthology-television-series /1958-1961+-+Walt+Disney+Presents/Walt+Disney+Presents+-+S05E27+-+Kodak +Presents+Disneyland+'59+(June+15%2C+1959).mp4.

4   *Disneyland*, Season 1, Episode 22, "Dateline Disneyland," aired July 17, 1955, on ABC, https://archive.org/details/disney-anthology-television-series/1954-1958 +Disneyland/Disneyland+-+S01E22+-+Dateline+Disneyland+(July+17%2C+1955). mp4.

5   *Disney's Keys to the Kingdom Tour* Training Guide, February 2014, in possession of the author, 3.

6   Disneyland is the focus of this study because of its importance as the first theme park. When the Magic Kingdom opened in Orlando in 1971, it expanded upon Disneyland, repeating many of the same general themes but with different details that would need to be explored further. This park was meant to replicate its predecessor's established success so that it could generate revenue for Walt Disney's true desire: to construct the unprecedented model city of EPCOT. Because the Floridian version of Disneyland is more or less a copy, I believe it to be less indicative of 1970s Americans' beliefs than 1950s.

7   Michel Foucault and Jay Miskowiec, "Of Other Spaces," *Diacritics* 16, no. 1 (Spring 1986): 22, 25–6.

8   Scott Magelssen, "Stepping Back in Time: The Construction of Different Temporal Spaces at Living History Museums in the United States," *The Theatre Annual* 57 (2004): 44–5.

9   *Disneyland*, Season 1, Episode 1, "The Disneyland Story," Aired October 27, 1954, on ABC, https://archive.org/details/disney-anthology-television -series/1954-1958+Disneyland/Disneyland+-+S01E01+-+The+Disneyland +Story+(October+27%2C+1954).mp4.

10 Richard Snow, *Disney's Land: Walt Disney and the Invention of the Amusement Park That Changed the World* (New York: Scribner, 2019), 61–2.

11 Karal Ann Marling, "Imagineering the Disney Theme Parks," in *Designing Disney's Theme Parks: The Architecture of Reassurance*, ed. Karal Ann Marling (New York: Flammarion, 1997), 79–86.

12 Ibid., 29.

13 Bethany Moreton, *To Serve God and Wal-Mart: The Making of Christian Free Enterprise* (Cambridge, MA: Harvard University Press, 2009), 41.

14 For more on this, see Lizabeth Cohen, *A Consumer's Republic: The Politics of Mass Consumption in Postwar America* (New York: Vintage Books, 2004), 257–9.

15 Deborah Philips, "Consuming the West: Main Street, U.S.A." *Space and Culture* 5, no. 1 (February 2002): 34.

16 Reginald Horsman, *Race and Manifest Destiny: The Origins of American Racial Anglo-Saxonism* (Cambridge, MA: Harvard University Press, 1986), 1–6.

17 See, for instance, Edward E. Baptist, *The Half Has Never Been Told: Slavery and the Making of American Capitalism* (New York: Basic Books, 2016); Walter Johnson, *River of Dark Dreams: Slavery and Empire in the Cotton Kingdom* (Cambridge, MA: Harvard University Press, 2017).

18 "Dateline Disneyland."

19 M. M. Manring, *Slave in a Box: The Strange Career of Aunt Jemima* (Charlottesville: University of Virginia Press, 1998), 127 and 140.

20 Frederick Jackson Turner, "The Significance of the Frontier in American History," *Annual Report of the American Historical Association for the Year 1893* (Washington: Government Printing Office, 1894), 201.

21 Ibid., 199, 221–2, and 225.

22 For an overview of the deathgrip the frontier has on the American imagination, see Richard White and Patricia Nelson Limerick, *The Frontier in American Culture*, ed. James R. Grossman (Oakland: University of California Press, 1994). See also Heather Cox Richardson, *West from Appomattox: The Reconstruction of America after the Civil War* (New Haven: Yale University Press, 2007), 273–4 and 304.

23 Adam Arenson, "John Gast's *American Progress*: Using Manifest Destiny to Forget the Civil War and Reconstruction," in *Empire and Liberty: The Civil War and the West*, ed. Virginia Scharff, 122–39 (Los Angeles: University of California Press, 2015), 123–5.

24 Richardson, *West from Appomattox*, 116–17.

25 Arenson, "John Gast's *American Progress*," 129–34.

26 "Dateline Disneyland."

27 See, for instance, Walter L. Hixson, *American Settler Colonialism: A History* (New York: Palgrave Macmillan, 2013), 106; John Mack Faragher, "And the Lonely Voice of Youth Cries 'What Is Truth': Western History and the National Narrative," *Western Historical Quarterly* 48, no. 1 (Spring 2017): 9–10.

28   Stephanie E. Smallwood, "Reflections on Settler Colonialism, the Hemispheric Americas, and Chattel Slavery," *The William and Mary Quarterly* 76, no. 3 (July 2019): 413.

29   Patrick Wolfe, "Settler Colonialism and the Elimination of the Native," *Journal of Genocide Research* 8, no. 4 (December 2006): 388 and 395.

30   Elspeth Martini, "Toward a 'New Indian History' of Foreign Relations: U.S.-American Indian Diplomacy from Greenville to Wounded Knee, 1795–1890," in *A Companion to U.S. Foreign Relations: Colonial Era to the Present, vol. 1*, ed. Christopher R. W. Dietrich, 113–41 (Devon: John Wiley & Sons, 2020), 114.

31   Hixson, *American Settler Colonialism*, 142; Martini, "Toward a 'New Indian History' of Foreign Relations," 115; Mikal Brotnov Eckstrom and Margaret D. Jacobs, "Teaching American History as Settler Colonialism," in *Why You Can't Teach United States History Without American Indians*, ed. Susan Sleeper-Smith, Juliana Barr, Jean M. O'Brien, Nancy Shoemaker, and Scott Manning Stevens (Chapel Hill: University of North Carolina Press, 2015), 259.

32   Snow, *Disney's Land*, 257.

33   "The Disneyland Story."

34   Snow, *Disney's Land*, 163–4.

35   "Dateline Disneyland"

36   Ibid.; *Disneyland*, Season 1, Episode 8, "Davey Crockett Indian Fighter," Aired December 15, 1954, on ABC, https://archive.org/details/disney-anthology-television -series/1954-1958+Disneyland/Disneyland+-+S01E08+-+Davy+Crockett+Indian +Fighter+(December+15%2C+1954).mp4.

37   Wolfe, "Settler Colonialism and the Elimination of the Native," 388–90 ānd 402.

38   *Disneyland*, Season 1, Episode 16, "A Progress Report and Nature's Half Acre," Aired February 9, 1955," on ABC, https://www.youtube.com/watch?v=b4xM3Z_ZkDs.

39   "Kodak Presents Disneyland '59."

40   *Disneyland*, Season 4, Episode 23, "An Adventure in the Magic Kingdom," aired April 9, 1958, on ABC, https://archive.org/details/disney-anthology-television-series /1954-1958+Disneyland/Disneyland+-+S04E23+-+An+Adventure+in+the+Magic +Kingdom+(April+9%2C+1958).mp4.

41   Ibid.

42   Martini, "Toward a 'New Indian History' of Foreign Relations," 113–14.

43   Katrina M. Phillips, *Staging Indigeneity: Salvage Tourism and the Performance of Native American History* (Chapel Hill: University of North Carolina Press, 2021), 11.

44   Ibid., 7. Of course, this is not to fault indigenous peoples who took advantage and even benefited from a bad system economically and culturally. For an example of this, see Abigail Markwyn, "'I Would Like to Have This Tribe Represented': Native Performance and Craft at Chicago's 1933 Century of Progress Exposition," *American Indian Quarterly* (July 2020): 329–61.

45   J. Kēhaulani Kauanui and Patrick Wolfe, "Settler Colonialism Then and Now," *Politica & Societa* 2 (2012): 241–2.

46   Maggie Blackhawk, "The Constitution of American Colonialism," *Harvard Law Review* 137, no. 1 (November 2023): 13–16.

47   "Dateline Disneyland."

48   Scott A. Lukas, "The Cultures of Tiki," in *A Reader in Themed and Immersive Spaces*, ed. Scott A. Lukas, 61–73 (Pittsburgh: ETC Press, 2016), 61.

49 Ibid., 62–3.

50 Walt Disney with the Disneyland Concert Orchestra, "Adventureland," on *Walt Disney Takes You to Disneyland*, Disneyland—WDL 4004, 1956, Vinyl, LP, Album, Mono.

51 Francesco Adinolfi, *Mondo Exotica: Sounds, Visions, Obsessions of the Cocktail Generation* (Durham: Duke University Press, 2008), viii.

52 Amy Ku'uleialoha Stillman, "Beyond the Coloniality of Authenticity," *American Quarterly* 73, no. 1 (March 2021): 164.

53 "A Progress Report and Nature's Half Acre."

54 *Disney's Keys to the Kingdom Tour* Training Guide, 10.

55 *Disneyland*, Season 2, Episode 21, "A Trip Through Adventureland" Aired February 29, 1956, on ABC, https://archive.org/details/disney-anthology-television-series/1954-1958+Disneyland/Disneyland+-+S02E21+-+A+Trip+Through+Adventureland+-+Water+Birds+(February+29%2C+1956).mp4.

56 Edward Said, Orientalism (New York: Vintage Books, 1979), 1–3.

57 Edward W. Said, *Culture and Imperialism* (New York: Vintage Books, 1994), xi.

58 For an overview of the problem in scholarship, see Brian Delay, "Indian Polities, Empire, and the History of American Foreign Relations," *Diplomatic History* 39, no. 5 (2015): 927–42.

59 Blackhawk, "The Constitution of American Colonialism," 10.

60 Stefan Aune, "Indian Fighters in the Philippines: Imperial Culture and Military Violence in the Philippine-American War," *Pacific Historical Review* 90, no. 4 (2021): 421.

61 Bonnie M. Miller, *From Liberation to Conquest: The Visual and Popular Cultures of the Spanish-American War of 1898* (Boston: University of Massachusetts Press, 2011), 191–3; Aune, "Indian Fighters in the Philippines," 420, 429–30, and 434–5.

62 Katharine Bjork, *Prairie Imperialists: The Indian Country Origins of American Empire* (Philadelphia: University of Pennsylvania Press, 2019), 4–15.

63 In one iteration, Walt's daughter Diane reported him saying, "The park will never be finished. . . . It's something I can keeping improving every year." See Disney Disney Miller, "Small Boy's Dream Come True," *Saturday Evening Post*, January 5, 1957, 81.

64 Lawrence W. Levine, *Highbrow/Lowbrow: The Emergence of Cultural Hierarchy in America* (Cambridge: Harvard University Press, 1990).

65 Jean Baudrillard, *America* (New York: Verso, 1996), 114.

66 Foucault and Miskowiec, "Of Other Spaces," 27.

67 New Red Order, *Never Settle: Calling In*, 2020, https://vimeo.com/447606235.

12

World-Building and Role-Playing across Disney Production

William S. Chavez

"Imagine Key" | $399 | Macrofiction

In July 2023, I walked into a Barnes & Noble bookstore in Daytona, Florida, and saw a promotional setup for what fanfiction writers call the "alternate universe" subgenre. "Once upon a DIFFERENT time . . ." the promotional poster read. Upon this display were books and games from the Walt Disney Company, official invitations to explore further "secondary worlds" within the Disney multiverse, as previous-era fantasylands become static, fixed, and unchanging. Entries in the popular *Villains* book series (debut, 2009) were featured, reshaping backstories of fan-favorite baddies, interweaving connections across tales, and introducing new reprobates that contribute to the downfall of canonical villains. *Twisted Tale* books (debut, 2015) were included, each proposing a hypothetical scenario akin to how Marvel Entertainment would later expand its cinematic universe through the *What if . . . ?* animated series (2021). The promotional table, lastly, included copies of *Pure of Heart* (2023), the literary supplement to the *Disney Mirrorverse* (2022) mobile combat game, following the adventures of a reimagined, battle-tested Snow White and others amid a fractured multiverse, and the popular *Villainous* (debut, 2018) tabletop game where players compete as and against canonical Disney villains in unique objectives specific to the occupation of realms. As famed *Batman* writer Dennis O'Neil observes of the modern comic book, popular culture—"a strange amalgam of fiction, instant mythology, and imaginary history"—derives its value not from singularity but multitude: "a series of heroic tales that, although complete in themselves, are serially related and are part of a much larger fictional construct."[1] Disney produces such a "macrofiction" but, as I argue, one largely without strict narrative cohesion, engaging the intertextual and self-referential nature of mass media production.

Disney's cultural power extends beyond screen media, park attractions, merchandise, and literature. As media change, so too does Disney's synergy—that is, combined actions or operations working together to achieve a total outcome greater than the sum of independent parts. Consider *Epic Mickey: Rebrushed* (2024), remaster of a game popular over a decade prior on the Nintendo Wii, announced as playable on PC and other contemporary platforms in 2024. Gamer Kurt Indovina calls this re-release a "full-circle moment for the game's original narrative," its mission to rescue the past from cultural oblivion.[2] In the game, Mickey Mouse accidentally damages a sanctuary world created by Yen Sid from *Fantasia* (1940), jeopardizing the safety of Disney characters forgotten by the public such as Oswald the Lucky Rabbit, Horace Horsecollar, and Clarabelle Cow. Mickey inadvertently mixes paint with thinner to create the chaotic "Blot" monster, whom Mickey must now defeat to save said members of a forgotten, "bizarro Disneyland, dour and gray in tone."

As digital media scholar Lisa Dusenberry observes in her analysis of the original game, *Epic Mickey* (2010) applies a "dystopic twist" onto a world previously registered as "safe [and] familiar" for initiated Disney fans, the same world rendered foreign yet blatantly incomplete for those uninitiated.[3] All players are incentivized "to repair/redeem the game world to match the ideal Disneyland" and "rewarded for acting on or building nostalgic connections" to the company's historic characters and park attractions. With the passage of time and the game's remastered release, the content of *Epic Mickey* achieves its own second-order degree of nostalgia. As Indovina argues, the remastered game "stops [it] from being forgotten and abandoned" due to its now-obsolete game console.[4]

Both versions of the game reveal the corporate strategies of producing and marketing Disney content. Dusenberry observes that *Epic Mickey* uses a vast multimedia canvas of storytelling "to build and exploit players' competencies with [Disney] film, television, games, and merchandise," as a means to immerse players within the company's "manufactured nostalgia" and facilitate further participation within adjacent consumer markets.[5] Reflective of the company's perpetual anxiety concerning its cultural legacy and profit margins, Disney battles time itself. The company is a victim of its own success, at times unable to reproduce the magic it once wielded.

Yet the story of this chapter concerns more than the re-release of legacy content. Though dynamics of nostalgia are involved, I analyze recent trends in Disney's continued experimentation with commodity creation: a story of nostalgia *and* innovation. I argue that Disney expands consumer immersion within its mythology and fantasy through an assortment of elective gaming possibilities and the simulation of active role-playing. Optional entries into an alternate secondary world are a testament to Disney's corporate strategy: produce, acquire, gatekeep, market. Although consumers are invited to participate and "play" in Disney's carefully curated world of entertainment, contrary to their marketing, the "freedom" and "agency" of play remain largely restricted and predetermined. For this chapter, I demonstrate such limitations of play primarily through an examination of Disney parks and gaming experiences.

"Enchant Key" | $649 | Methodology

This chapter prompts readers to study Disney's mass production of myth and culture, as well as the stakes and implications of its eclecticism and assemblage of entertainment. The Forest Friends Unit of the Jubilation! parade at Tokyo Disneyland (2008–13), for example, reveals, first, the complex ideology that Disney sells to its audience and, second, my capacity as a consumer to disrupt it. As the parade featured familiar characters organized into themed, motorized floats, the Forest Friends Unit showcased Pocahontas and raccoon Meeko as costumed cast members positioned beneath a large animistic tree and stream of vegetation, the latter of which is an animatronic simulacrum of the Spring Sprite from *Fantasia 2000* (1999). Additional cast members include the Br'er Critters from *Song of the South* (1946) and stuffed animals from *The Many Adventures of Winnie the Pooh* (1977). Pooh Bear, perhaps the most popular character on the float, brings with him associations of innocence and purity, a toy brought to life through the "magic" of Christopher Robin's childhood imagination. The float preserves one of the company's leading sentiments: creation is constant, positive, and limitless.

How else can I decode and understand this hodgepodge assemblage of Disney-constructed media? Applying the interpretive strategy of anthropologist George Bey III, this float presents an "alternate positive reality," "sanitized and simplified" in design.[6] The cast member portraying Pocahontas remains the only explicit human on this float. Her inclusion in the forest (and notably not the Princess Garden Unit, though she is an official Disney princess) perpetuates the "ecological Indian stereotype" that romanticizes indigenous peoples as environmentally incompatible with modern industrialization.[7] The cartoony forest dwellers alongside Pocahontas solidify a tone of cheerfulness and positivity. The Br'er Critters reflect a "Zip-a-Dee-Doo-Dah" day wherein such self-manifested happiness improves the conditions of southern plantation life—especially as a Black man post-abolition and a seven-year-old boy forced to visit his grandparents, as depicted in *Song of the South*. Within this Forest Friends Unit, I see the plight of Native Americans and African Americans overcome with smiles and systematic erasure. Racial and colonial hostilities are suspended from view within a simulated world of friendly animals and supernaturally benevolent forces, a world made politically safe for children, parents, and international audiences to consume.

I introduce this example of an ideologically loaded, discontinued, non-American park attraction to demonstrate the premise and theoretical basis of the current chapter. The Disney industry is not as centralized as one expects, nor is it devoid of ideological messages. To study this industry, we approach Disney production as a complex assortment of media—both physical and digital—that operates without strict linearity, full symmetry, and singular continuity. Let us refer to *transmedia* as the cross-media promotion of interrelated narratives and/or secondary worlds of fiction made available for consumption and purchase. The various floats of the Jubilation! parade present multimedia examples of interconnections drawn between Disney's animated canon: motorized vehicles carrying mostly animated characters and sets reconfigured into costumed cast members and animatronics, exclusive to Disney parks. As media scholar Dan Hassler-Forest observes, content creators release such intertextual and self-referential products within a "more participatory culture of media convergence"[8]— that is, "hybrid networks," convergent in their storage and distribution of "spreadable" media, increasing the likelihood that consumers elect to participate given the wide array of products made to entice them. Disney, thus, communicates with its audience via market saturation and the increasing multimedia convergence of products available on said market. The Jubilation! parade, as with other transmedia analyzed in this chapter, conveys messages that are on brand and in theme with the values of the company but are also available for unofficial deconstructions and interpretations by consumers and scholars.

To further embrace the Forest Friends Unit as metaphor, readers may be tempted to view Disney's industrial production as a sacred tree centralized in its roots, with variously decorated branches leading to new heights or peripheries. There is a basis for approaching Disney in such fashion. The company's booming financial periods trace to the global success of animated features released during the "Disney Renaissance" (1989–99) and "Revival" (2008–19). Such animated media functions as the chief identity of Disney's modern American mythology. Many of their theme park attractions, merchandise, and studio acquisitions creatively stem from this musical, whimsical, and dramatic tradition of storytelling or are otherwise made to loosely conform to said creative signatures. Yet I believe it is a mistake to confuse centralized history and tradition with increasingly decentralized modes of production and marketing.

To demonstrate this popular misconception of Disney's top-down centrality, this chapter investigates the literature, material culture, and games that stem from the company's presumptive nucleus: Walt Disney Animation Studios (WDAS). I investigate the ideological features of the Disney brand, as established in parks and merchandise, which the company extends and reconfigures into gaming. I employ a theoretical approach to Disney production that we shall call *rhizomatic*, named in reference to the interconnected, underground stem of laterally growing plants coined by French philosophers Gilles Deleuze and Félix Guattari and later adapted by video game theorist Colin Cremin in his normative approach to game design.

Deleuze and Guattari bifurcate the intellectual frameworks that structure our bodies of knowledge, presenting a contrast between *arborescent*—arbor as in tree— and *rhizomatic* constructions. Arborescent systems prescribe hierarchy, statuses of privilege, linearity, and genealogy. "[U]nlike trees or their roots," the authors write, "the rhizome connects any point to any other point [in its structure], and its traits are not necessarily linked to traits of the same nature."[9] The rhizome functions like a map "that is always detachable, connectable, reversible, modifiable, and has multiple entryways and exits and its own lines of flight." As institutions construct bodies of knowledge and scholarship as rigid territories wherein derivative branches function akin to their roots, Deleuze and Guattari implore their readers to adopt rhizomatic systems of thought, just as I do in my teaching and research, to resist and contest traditional confinements wherever possible. "Always follow the rhizome by rupture; lengthen, prolong, and relay the line of flight; make it vary, until you have produced the most abstract and tortuous of lines of *n* dimensions and broken directions," the philosophers write.[10]

Cremin teaches that games should inherently foster what he dubs as "rhizome-play": the "deterritorialization and reterritorialization" of videogame space.[11] Games structured like trees are predictable, restricted in scope and capability due to predetermined story progression and/or limited in-game objectives. "[Trees] are strong enough to support daddy's tree house for his son to dwell in and in which [the latter's] affects are boxed," Cremin writes.[12] Games structured like rhizomes, meanwhile, are "open" systems which "oppose rigidity." Every video game, according to this philosophy, should allow space for players to resist and/or manipulate the game design, to play in—and outside the preconceived parameters of its creator—just as scholars, cultural critics, and consumers play interpretative "games" with Disney's ideological content.

"The common image of a rhizome," Cremin writes, "is the root of networks of plants such as [weeds or] potatoes that spread along the surface of the soil and sprout saplings at various points."[13] In my own scholarship and teaching, I approach the Disney industry as a rhizomatic cross-media production of content that, indeed, "sprouts" at various points. "Rhizome-play," while provided to Disney producers of content, is not always encouraged for consumers. As Karen Wohlwend, scholar of children's literacy and education, notes of Disney princess doll play: "[A child] can be Cinderella all day long, sleeping in pink princess sheets, eating from lavender Tupperware with Cinderella decals, and dressing head to toe in licensed apparel, from plastic jewel encrusted tiara to fuzzy slipper-socks."[14] Detailed costume outfits or masks, meanwhile, may not be worn in Disney parks by guests older than age fourteen.[15] This chapter, thus, demonstrates how Disney seeks to territorialize and delimit the creative space of its consumers.

This chapter also draws attention to the ways in which scholarly publications are traditionally organized, not as rhizomes but as arborescent systems: my section titles are named after the key-themed Disneyland Resort package deals that signal a hierarchy of increasing value and/or meaning.[16] Inspired by Deleuze and Guattari and the structure of their text *A Thousand Plateaus: Capitalism and Schizophrenia* (1980), the sections of this chapter "may be read independently of one another, except the conclusion, which should be read at the end."[17] I include the real prices of the resort packages in the section headings to simulate (and mock) the arborescent systems of capitalism and academia. I mark the concluding section as "free" in further subversion. "A rhizome has no beginning or end; it is always in the middle, between things, interbeing," Deleuze and Guattari write. I approach Disney industry as the same and structure this chapter in its form for readers to notice.

"Believe Key" | $949 | Rules of Design

How may we assess the level of choice available to Disney consumers, the variety of actions as prescribed by the creative institution? The dialogue from the Wintertime Enchantment (debut, 2007) light show at Disneyland reveals the degree to which park attendees are coached or simulated into passive role-playing "believers." Music plays and park attendees gather in gaze as the lighting ceremony illuminates Sleeping Beauty Castle with icicle and snow projections. The recorded exchange between adult and child simulates the religious "call and response" style of interaction between Christian pastors and their congregants.

Child: Oh, I wish, I wish it would snow.

Adult: Well, anything is possible. But for your wishes to come true, you have to believe. Do you believe?

Child: Oh, yes. I believe with all of my heart.

To be clear, snowfall is not withheld until the park attendees participate. Disney parks predetermine the belief recital of said attendees via this staged recording.

At other times, the Disney path for participation is signaled through allegory, as in the cruise line stage show *Disney's Believe* (debut, 2011). "Joined by a host of Characters," the website promotes, "[the Genie from *Aladdin* (1992)] takes [workaholic father] Dr. Greenaway on a magical ride into the world of Disney stories. Along the way, the doctor makes a personal discovery—magic isn't fantasy, but a remarkable reality that has touched both him and his daughter." Within this "spellbinding musical," the Genie (performed by a cast member) jokes that being trapped in his magic lamp is akin to the three-to-five-day cruise experience parents wish to escape. The stage show politely communicates a message to stressed fathers that the trip will go much smoother if they "just believe."

How then do games differ from park and cruise experiences in the agency provided to consumers? The *Villainous* tabletop game, for instance, structures gameplay around the player's choice of villain, realm exploration, and individual objectives made available through puzzle-solving mechanics. Optimal gameplay exists for each character, as marketed by the creators: "Discover your character's . . . winning strategy [and] thwart your opponent's schemes," reads the back of the boxset. As reviewers note online: "[Y]ou are essentially playing a solo game until interaction is forced to stop another [player from] winning."[18] *Villainous*, thus, allows players to traverse game space in tracings of the predetermined roots and branches of the arborescent game design. Players of official games like these do not manipulate, create, or rupture Disney content, but rather interact with its rules of design. The core set of the *Disney Sorcerer's Arena: Epic Alliances* (debut, 2020) tabletop game markets this principle best: "Strategize and create exciting combinations of actions using special character abilities for endless replayability." Like chess, players of these games traverse numerous computational positions ultimately bound within the delimited set of possibilities of decision tree complexity.

The waves of Disney-themed digital and material games, post 2000, imply hitherto unparalleled degrees of freedom and agency in the manipulation of Disney content. However, in most instances, this remains a phenomenon in marketing rather than gameplay. The toys-to-life adventure game *Disney Infinity* (2013–16), whereby players synchronize collectible figurines with gameplay software, remains the exemplum of such marketing: "Their worlds. Your imagination. No rules," reads the back of the game case. While the game's narrative campaigns were limited in-depth and playable characters, this series from Avalanche Software grew in popularity due to the imagined gaming possibilities born from "toy box"/sandbox gameplay—for example, Mulan surfing the skies with Jim Hawkins's Solar Board from *Treasure Planet* (2002), Jasmine atop Aladdin's Magic Carpet, and Merida from *Brave* (2012) sporting Buzz Lightyear's

Jetpack from *Toy Story* (1995). Players could build their own worlds and minigames in unprecedented capacities of control whenever operating the level editor and arena builder.

In his review, gamer Myles McNutt writes that the shortcomings of *Disney Infinity* lie in the "[designers' choice] to place key Toy Box content behind its 'playwall.'"[19] His critique continues:

> *Disney Infinity* represents a clear shift in Disney's approach to licensing their valuable intellectual property, but it comes with as many limitations as possibilities. While Disney is promising an epic scale, and has still yet to fully tap into the incredibly valuable "golden age" animated properties of the 1990s, their efforts with *Disney Infinity* prioritize the business of licensed gaming without necessarily being able to offer gamers the scale they've promised without substantial investment.

Reviewers on Metacritic similarly criticize Disney's "precisely coordinated marketing strategy" that forces players to "buy-it-all-to-collect-it-all."[20]

Others criticize the training-wheels structure of *Infinity* gameplay and its "limited" world creation tools.[21] "Avalanche Software," one reviewer notes, "has created a game that doesn't just let you play in the Disney sandbox, but gives you the bucket and trowel to build your own castle in it."[22] Based on one's gaming experience and philosophy toward game design, such structure may not be welcomed by older players and cultural gamers. As Andrew Reiner writes for the now defunct Game Informer site:

> If Minecraft is the Lego of video games, Disney Infinity is the [child-friendly] Duplo. Houses, castles, and most of the components are pre-built. The colour and texture of many of these objects can be altered, but that granular level of sculpting them to exact specifications is not available. Creativity is tied to how these pieces are used in the context of playing with them.[23]

Reiterating the tagline of *Epic Alliances*, players may "strategize and create exciting combinations" of Disney's prescribed content but not much more. As another reviewer on Metacritic adds, "the game doesn't quite nail those moments of carefree child's play found in every real-world toy box, but it gets closer than any other game we've played."[24] Ironically, at times, players exercise more freedom outside of Disney games than within them.

"Dream Key" | $1,399 | Gaming Possibilities

Conflict in the typical Disney universe is controlled and formulaic. "The villain acts and the hero reacts," former animators Ollie Johnston and Frank Thomas write in their retrospective book on Disney villain design, published in 1993.[25] Defeated villains are allowed to resurface across media as foes cosmically tethered in combat against Disney heroes. The Disneyland attraction Fantasmic! (debut,

1992), for instance, presents a pyrotechnic voyage through Sorcerer Apprentice Mickey's imagined battle against villainy. "Good clashes with evil in a nighttime spectacular," reads the soundtrack CD cover, with promotional artwork including the fire-breathing Maleficent dragon from *Sleeping Beauty* (1959) and Chernabog from *Fantasia* (1940).

Mythically, Disney stages elaborate recreations and continuations of such conflict in ways that are crucial to the elective worldbuilding expansions of their parks, merchandise, and games. At D23 2024, Disney's biennial fan event and expo, Josh D'Amaro, chairman of Disney Experiences, revealed plans for a "Villains Land" section of the Magic Kingdom.[26] As D'Amaro stated to Disney consumers: "This land will be home to the villains that you know [and] loathe, which means 'happily ever after' . . . may feel like just a distant dream." Hitherto, villain cast members were primarily relegated to the Villains Mix and Mingle nighttime show (2005–14) of Mickey's Not-So-Scary Halloween Party (debut, 1995) and accompanying parade (debut, 1999). Disney's production of villain merchandise and inclusion of characters in parks and games has steadily gained momentum since the 1990s, culminating in the Disney villains brand receiving a trademark in 2018—a process representative of how the company acts to repackage its legacy content.

Disney first marketed a limited-edition *Villains Chess Set* (1997) capitalizing on the success of their Renaissance, with variants such as the *Disney Chess Set* (2004) and *Heroes & Villains Chess Set* (2004). Such games were distinct only in the characters chosen to represent each game piece. *Disney's Villains' Revenge* (1999), released at the close of the same era, was an interactive "point-and-click" game on PC whereby the player assists Jiminy Cricket from *Pinocchio* (1940) in stopping the villains from altering the storybook happy endings of Disney tales. The game offers multiple decision tree trajectories, with some choices—for example, striking an unarmed Captain Hook from *Peter Pan* (1953) or poisoning the Evil Queen from *Snow White and the Seven Dwarfs* (1937)—clearly marked as morally reprehensible, which the Blue Fairy instructs players against. Other villain-themed materials include memorabilia produced for the Disney Disneyana Convention in 1997, pin sets such as *Disney Villains Fearly Departed* (2000), and the action role-playing video game *Kingdom Hearts* (2002) developed by Square Enix.

As influenced by its parent Japanese franchise *Final Fantasy*, the gameplay of *Kingdom Hearts* involves a battle party led by Sora, a series-exclusive young boy in search of adventure, assisted by AI-piloted Donald Duck and Goofy with alterable move settings. While other heroes occasionally assist Sora in battle, most of the "over 100 Disney characters" with which to "team up [against] evil," as the back of the game case markets, appear as cameos in non-gameplay cinematics—an illusion of in-game interaction. *Kingdom Hearts* includes the most original cast, storyline, and worldbuilding content relative to games that followed it, with much of the combat waged against mindless goons in the form of knights, monsters, and machines. Although a new final boss, exclusive to *Kingdom Hearts*, is later revealed as manipulating the game's conflict, players traverse multiple worlds in battle against familiar Disney villains. Players level up their party and advance the story through fights with Cerberus from *Hercules* (1997), the sand guardian of the Cave of Wonders in *Aladdin* (1992), Maleficent in her dragon form, the Chernabog on Bald Mountain, and others.

Some players take issue with the degree to which these game worlds are interactable. YouTuber "NotAbsolutelySure," in his retrospective review, critiques the fighting mechanics of the game's more bait-and-switch type of battles.[27]

> So class, what do we think [this] final fight's main mechanic is? Did you guess that you don't actually fight the giant transformed evil genie version of Jafar at all? That you don't hit him at all? No, no. You slap the bird carrying his lamp that just flies away the whole fight. [. . .] Yet again [as with other fights], it's visually stunning but mechanically so weak [of an experience].

Cultural gamers strive for more agency in, interaction with, and control of their game environments. This includes having heroes and villains available for manipulation by players.

Consumers became divided over the place of Disney content in later *Kingdom Hearts* games as well. "I honestly feel Disney should no longer play a part in this franchise due to the untapped potential that Square Enix's own roster of characters can do to add to this ridicoulous [*sic*] world that was built," one player writes in his blog.[28] "If put to work in an intentional and clever way, Disney can enrich the story in ways that original characters simply cannot. It's called Disney Magic for a reason," another player writes in contrast.[29] The main criticism stems from the *meaningful* way in which Disney properties are incorporated into gameplay and story progression, as the following forum post details.

> The problem with Kingdom Hearts is the lack of proper character interactions in and out of Disney worlds. The Disney worlds in KH1 had way more weight outside of their world. Certain characters in the worlds were well aware of what was going on outside the worlds, interacted with other Disney characters from other worlds, and even participated in outer worldly conflicts.[30]

Indeed, the "magic" of Disney is, in part, its interconnections to larger worlds. To silo familiar characters in separate arenas and adventures works against the hybrid networks of Disney content, its convergent distribution of media, and the gaming possibilities that cultural gamers seek.

What then are the implications of Disney providing consumers opportunities to *fail* in gameplay—beyond obvious "pay-to-play" profit motives? Though the game remains bound to combinations of prearranged actions and fixed optimal strategies to discover, the now-retired Sorcerers of the Magic Kingdom (2012–21) was distinct as a transmedial park attraction in that it allowed villains to win (at least until the next battle). The game combined collectible cards with theme park portal stations whereby players summon dozens of Disney characters to resist a Hades rebellion. "Learn magic spells to fight the forces of evil!" park posters read. Guests would travel to stations all around the Magic Kingdom, triggering augmented game animatics and battling lower villains before reaching the final bosses of Hades and the Chernabog.

For comparison, there is no alternative whereby evil emerges victorious during the Fantasmic! night show, just as, barring technical complications, the simulated snow will fall during the Wintertime Enchantment show independent of audience participation. As an interactive park attraction, Sorcerers of the Magic Kingdom, to apply analytics from Hassler-Forest, "takes place across media" with cards and portal stations, "involves audience participation" with skill and strategy, and, at least partially, "defers narrative closure."[31] Whether or not the bosses are defeated, Disney consumers know that there is no true end to such reiterative mythic combat. Villains seemingly allow for initiations of conflict and expansions.

If Disney industry transcends the bounds of narrative finitude or continuity, this credo allows space for villains to also temporarily "win." *Disney Heroes: Battle Mode*, a "beat 'em up" mobile game, involves a virus that infects Digital City, creating dark goons and virus-copies of classic characters. In this game, as in *Epic Alliances* and *Mirrorverse*, consumers have agency to mix and match heroes and villains in their team constructions. Villains are provided in the roster for role-playing variance, just as virus or multiversal variant heroes alter the ideological landscape of Disney content: at times, villains need to defeat heroes. Just as the *Villainous* tabletop game is distinct in its alternate-perspective gameplay, a parallel to the alternate-perspective live-action films *Maleficent* (2014) and *Cruella* (2021), players controlling villains to defeat heroes marks a trend in Disney's re-evaluation and repackaging of their legacy content. Villains, however extended or reimagined, provide consistent utility for Disney's worldbuilding aspirations.

"Magic Key" | Free | Variance

Disney, as a content creator and gatekeeper, provides calculated means by which consumers can interact with and engage their intellectual properties. Though their games are presented as the next step in active role-playing in the Disney universe, this chapter reminds us how belief and practice are coached, restrained, and predetermined by governing institutions. Folk relationships—that is, removed from official "church" sanction—persist nevertheless, especially amplified by the democratization of digital creation platforms and game-modifying skills, e-commerce companies such as Etsy that sell crafts and homemade creations, and the increasing number of popular culture characters entering the public domain following the completion of their copyright duration. The Walt Disney Company profits from storage—for example, Disneyland, the Disney Vault, Disney+. It segregates the sacred behind walls of magic, belief, and childhood innocence, with passage safeguarded through purchase systems and exchange of leisure time.

We must not forget, however, that such multiversal expansion remains, as religious studies scholar William Arnal writes of Disney park experiences, "personal and choice-oriented," "never dictated" by institutionality.[32] Though conservative viewers may detest that Mulan is bisexual in *Once Upon a Time* (2011–18) or that Ariel is played by a Black actress in the live-action *The Little Mermaid* (2023), let the reader recognize that neither instance is definitive. There are multiple Mulans, Ariels, and so forth available to purchase and consume. This is the Disney way. Such outrage reveals a fundamental misunderstanding of Disney's content, approaching it as singular and without variance.

Disney produces and reproduces its cultural capital: the transmedial and intermedial connections that occur between material culture, literature, motion pictures, and now games.

It "operate[s] within a rich new media ecology," to borrow a phrase from game studies scholars Laurie Taylor and Zach Whalen.[33] The result is a bizarre Disney-themed *heterotopia*—a space unlike any other though still fractally representative of the world outside it—full of action and adventure, where eclecticism, character design, and worldbuilding possibility matter more than narrative continuity. For this reason, consuming so much Disney can feel kaleidoscopic.

The company experiments with multiple cross-media platforms and creative synergy to reify, combine, and/or expand single-media constructions of an imaginary world—at once increasing the likelihood of content consumption through surplus creation. For many consumers, Disney popular culture inserts magic, charm, and optimism back into a hyper-capitalist world. Those already indoctrinated by Disney may likewise search for means to reignite their sense of wonder and mischievous curiosity through the company's latest products. Disney's stories are all too familiar now. Games, alternate universe literature, and other media give a necessary infusion of dynamism and innovation in the company's attempts to retain mass market appeal.

Notes

1 Dennis O'Neil, "Afterword," in *Batman: Knightfall*, ed. Dennis O'Neil (New York: Bantam Books, 1994), 347.

2 Kurt Indovina, "Disney Epic Mickey Rebrushed Is a Full-Circle Moment for the Game's Original Narrative," *GameSpot*, April 9, 2024, https://www.gamespot.com /articles/disney-epic-mickey-rebrushed-is-a-full-circle-moment-for-the-games -original-narrative/1100-6522520/.

3 Lisa K. Dusenberry, "Epic Nostalgia: Narrative Play and Transmedia Storytelling in *Disney Epic Mickey*," in *Game On, Hollywood! Essays on the Intersection of Video Games and Cinema*, ed. Gretchen Papazian and Joseph Michael Sommers (Jefferson: McFarland, 2013), 186.

4 Indovina, "Disney Epic Mickey Rebrushed Is a Full-Circle Moment."

5 Dusenberry, "Epic Nostalgia," 183, 196n.3.

6 George J. Bey, III, "On the Count of Three: Magic, New Knowledge, and Learning at Walt Disney World," in *Disney, Culture, and Curriculum*, ed. Jennifer A. Sandlin and Julie C. Garlen (New York: Routledge, 2016), 183, 188.

7 Cf. Dina Gilio-Whitaker, "The Problem with the Ecological Indian Stereotype," *PBS SoCal*, February 7, 2017, https://www.pbssocal.org/shows/tending-the-wild/the -problem-with-the-ecological-indian-stereotype.

8 Dan Hassler-Forest, *Science Fiction, Fantasy, and Politics: Transmedia World-Building Beyond Capitalism* (London: Rowman and Littlefield, 2016), ix, 14.

9   Gilles Deleuze and Félix Guattari, *A Thousand Plateaus: Capitalism and Schizophrenia*, trans. Brian Massumi (Minneapolis: University of Minnesota Press, 2005), 21.

10 Ibid., 11.

11 Colin Cremin, *Exploring Videogames with Deleuze and Guattari: Towards an Affective Theory of Form* (New York: Routledge, 2016), 64. One of Cremin's axioms of gameplay prescribes that proper "videogame play is rhizome-play, the capacity of player to compose with forces whose intensities enable discovery of new possibilities through which lines of flight can be taken: to disentangle the design through a process of deterritorialization" (24).

12 Ibid., 61, 16.

13 Ibid., 61. This "subterranean stem is absolutely different from roots and radicles," Deleuze and Guattari (*A Thousand Plateaus*, 6) command.

14 Karen E. Wohlwend, "Damsels in Discourse: Girls Consuming and Producing Identity Texts through Disney Princess Play," *Reading Research Quarterly* 44, no. 1 (2009): 57–8.

15 Hannah Sampson, "Disney Parks Ban Costumes for Adults. These Fans Have a Way Around It," *Washington Post*, April 21, 2023, https://www.washingtonpost.com/travel/2023/04/21/disneybounding-meaning-ideas/.

16 Michael Ramirez, "Disneyland Resort Introduces Magic Key Program, a New Guest-Centric Offering with Choice, Flexibility and Value," *Disney Parks Blog*, August 3, 2021, https://disneyparks.disney.go.com/blog/2021/08/disneyland-resort-introduces-magic-key-program-a-new-guest-centric-offering-with-choice-flexibility-and-value/.

17 Deleuze and Guattari, *A Thousand Plateaus*, xx, 25.

18 See the comment from @Da_Nuwt on the following game review: @hutter1450, "A Villainous Review of Villainous," *Board Game Geek*, June 21, 2024, https://boardgamegeek.com/thread/3264596/a-villainous-review-of-villainous.

19 Myles McNutt, "Disney Infinity: Behind the P(l)aywall [Part Three]," *Antenna*, August 29, 2013, https://blog.commarts.wisc.edu/2013/08/29/disney-infinity-behind-the-playwall-part-three/.

20 See reviews from "Hardcore Gamer" and "COGconnected," respectively. "Disney Infinity: Xbox 360 Critic Reviews," *Metacritic*, September 13, 2013, https://www.metacritic.com/game/disney-infinity/critic-reviews/?platform=xbox-360 (accessed May 5, 2024).

21 Ibid., see review from "Levelup."

22 Ibid., see review from "Game Revolution."

23 Dan Pearson, "Critical Consensus: Disney Infinity, Where Merchandising Dreams Come True," *GamesIndustry.biz*, August 19, 2013, https://www.gamesindustry.biz/critical-consensus-disney-infinity.

24 See review from "Polygon," "Disney Infinity: Xbox 360 Critic Reviews."

25 Ollie Johnston and Frank Thomas, *The Disney Villain* (Westport: Hyperion, 1993), 15.

26 Dewayne Bevil, "Disney World Expansion Plan Includes Villains Land," *Orlando Sentinel*, August 11, 2024, https://www.orlandosentinel.com/2024/08/11/disney-world-villains-land-magic-kingdom-d23-monsters-inc-parade/.

27 "A Complete Kingdom Hearts (2002) Retrospective," *NotAbsolutelySure*, YouTube, June 3, 2024, https://youtu.be/hH9BiFC0C5s?t=3642.

28 Michael Baginski, "Kingdom Hearts Doesn't Need Disney Anymore and 3 Is Proof of This," *Medium*, February 11, 2019, https://medium.com/@bagmanman/kingdom -hearts-doesnt-need-disney-anymore-and-3-is-proof-of-this-fdd529242049.

29 Brett Williams, "Kingdom Hearts Has a Disney Problem," *Middle of Nowhere Gaming*, June 3, 2017, https://middleofnowheregaming.com/2017/06/03/kingdom -hearts-has-a-disney-problem/.

30 See the forum post from "Kirabook" on "Where Kingdom Hearts Is Failing," *KHInsider*, June 19, 2021, https://www.khinsider.com/forums/index.php?threads/ where-kingdom-hearts-is-failing.227918/.

31 Hassler-Forest, *Science Fiction, Fantasy, and Politics*, 5.

32 William Arnal, "The Segregation of Social Desire: 'Religion' and Disney World," *Journal of the American Academy of Religion* 69, no. 1 (2001): 4–5.

33 Laurie N. Taylor and Zach Whalen, "Playing the Past: An Introduction," in *Playing the Past: History and Nostalgia in Video Games*, ed. Zach Whalen and Laurie N. Taylor (Nashville: Vanderbilt University Press, 2008), 9.

Section IV

Leisure and Labor

Section Introduction

Leisure and Labor

Alexis T. Franzese

American-born artist Melissa Pinney's photograph *Washroom, Disney World, Florida* (1998, printed 2003) depicts five women in a Walt Disney World bathroom changing diapers and responding to the outstretched or preoccupied hands of children that need their care.[1] The labor in this picture is palpable, yet these mothers and their children are by all accounts engaged in leisure—they are vacationing at Disney, after all. These mothers, despite their scurrying and the almost frenzied nature of the scene, are engaging in the labor needed in order to find the happiness and leisure Disney promises.

This volume closes with three chapters that address the dialectical pairing of leisure and labor, which captures the way that Disney recruits and maintains its consumers as its cast and demands their efforts in the pursuit of happiness. Travelers happily don their uniforms, use company language, and work grueling hours as part of their vacation experience. Disney film viewers often endure cognitive dissonance and struggle to reconcile discrepancies to a degree that may be unexpected in films marketed toward children.[2] Corporate employees take pride in not being just employees but for some imagineers or cast members. The tension between leisure and labor may be, to my thinking, where Disney is acting the most implicitly and with its efforts most deeply embedded. Disney itself does not name the labor it expects of its media viewers or park guests. Disney seems designed to convince its consumers, and especially parkgoers, that it is offering an inclusive approach where someone else is concerned with your personal experience and the reduction of your labor.[3] And yet work we do, amid our leisure. Disney may offer a break from work, but Disney vacations involve work.

Disney, at its roots, is deeply tied to the American leisure explosion and the distinctly American view that happiness should be pursued and is within reach.[4] This explosion and view preceded Disney's theme parks. When Walt Disney and Ub Iwerks started sketching out the first Oswald the Rabbit short in 1927, their goal was to entertain. Movies were a relatively recent invention and attendance at movies was soaring at the time that Oswald launched. The country had survived the demands of the First World War, and with new technologies came both increased leisure time and a desire to be entertained. Walt Disney's efforts occurred at a critical moment that was truly pregnant with possibility. His unveiling of parks in the mid-1950s was at an equally ideal moment, taking advantage of American post-Second World War optimism and the growth of the highway system. With the introduction of household appliances that decreased time demands paired with shifts away from more agricultural lifestyles, the lore is that people had more time on their hands and time to focus on enjoying themselves. Ever upholding an American way, if not *the* American way, Disney emerged as a key player in the pursuit of happiness, and that happiness pursuit was tied with leisure.[5] Walt Disney was dissatisfied with the unsavory atmosphere that was known to be occurring at places like Coney Island, which, despite their early success as family destinations, were neglected and falling into disrepair by the mid-1950s.[6] Wishing to share time with his own children in a family setting, Walt Disney set out to create the ultimate leisure destination. Beginning with Disneyland, the Disney parks were introduced at a pivotal time in America's leisure revolution.[7] Then, as now, Disney acted as a recreational opportunity through which working and middle-class families can have a break from the everyday.

Leisure can be considered as time, as activity, or as a state of mind.[8] Leisure as time entails a break from paid or unpaid work, and leisure as activity is defined as activities completed during free time that are not work oriented or involve life maintenance.[9] Disney engagement is indeed perceived by those pursuing it as a break from work (time), and something distinct from life maintenance (activity). And yet, Disney vacations involve work and many maintenance tasks, just completed under different conditions. Most relevant, though, when considering Disney is the approach to leisure as a state of mind. As a state of mind, leisure is about freedom, intrinsic motivation, and positive affect.[10] Disney manufactures each of these for its guests: it gives guests a sense of freedom by offering an array of options on how to spend their time; it allows guests to plan those activities and experiences that they are motivated to pursue and gives them a sense of competence when they can effectively do so; and it creates positive affect by facilitating experiences designed to bring happiness. But guests must play their part, and that comes with labor costs. As consumers of Disney products and experiences, and like the frenzied mothers in that Walt Disney World washroom, guests collude with Disney in pursuit of the constructed myth of happiness.

Across definitions, leisure commonly refers to time spent with no need for outcome or any tangible product. A sociological perspective emerged in the late 1960s that viewed leisure as a social construct, rather than simply the absence of work or labor.[11] Much like health is not merely the absence of illness, leisure is not just the time away from work. Rather, leisure is an experience that is shaped by socioeconomic and cultural backgrounds and that is intrinsically connected to how individuals construct and perform identity. The relationship between leisure and capitalism is relevant to understanding Disney. Leisure in a capitalistic society is marked by entertainment and tourism that have been commodified and can be consumed.[12] Prior to capitalism, leisure had been related to engagement and fulfillment.[13] Disney, at present, appears to be operating at the intersection of pre-capitalist and capitalist ideas of leisure, as it does seem to offer its consumers a sense of identity and belonging (as can be seen in the first section of this book, Magic and Strategy), yet is undoubtedly a commodified experience.

Labor, similarly, has specific meaning within the American capitalist context. American cultural understandings of labor are informed by Marxian views of labor power as the capacity to do work (in contrast to labor as the physical act of working). While the labor of guests at Disney is not exchanged for money (which is part of the traditional Marxian idea of labor), it is the entrance fee for continuing to be able to uphold the myths of happiness Disney offers and to access the Disney guest experience. Disney guests are paying for the opportunity to labor at the parks as they work together with Disney to pursue and attain happiness. Leaning on Marx's *Das Kapital*, in which commodity value is measured by the number of labor hours to produce that commodity, the exorbitant cost of a Disney vacation alone reveals the social value of gaining access to Disney.[14] Parkgoers will save their money for months or years, giving Disney an exceptionally high commodity value. Then, once one has paid the fee for entry, there is additional labor to be done in pursuit of a happy experience. The work that guests and consumers do through planning their travel, theme park participation, and film merchandising is just part of the labor involved with Disney. While we of course expect cast members and employees who work for Disney to labor, the tension here is that Disney convinces those of us who are slated for leisure that we should labor, and those who are there for labor (cast members, employees, producers) that their work has components of leisure.

When I first proposed my Disney course in 2014, I was concerned that my colleagues and potential students would see the course as merely a leisurely vacation experience. This concern was grounded in the fact that Disney so effectively convinces those who visit its parks and engage with its films (through its use of strategy disguised as magic) that Disney is unequivocally an experience of leisure. Through simulated places and experiences that feel authentic, and through simultaneously activating deep feelings of sentimentality and nostalgia while also upholding innovation, Disney ensures that many users may be unaware of how much they labor for their leisure.[15] Part of my delight in teaching my course Happiest Place? The Science of Happiness at Disney for the first time in January 2016 was witnessing how quickly students discovered the amount of work or labor that goes into a Disney travel experience once in the parks.[16] Of course, my students, like those in Jeffrey Barnes's chapter in this volume, gain so much in the edutainment model Disney offers. Students in my course do the labor of reconciling what they thought they knew about Disney with what they discover during the course, and they complete extensive (often ethnographic) research projects. By the end of the course, they see their own labor differently, as well as the labor of cast members, filmmakers, imagineers, and even parents. Together we explore the myths we hold about happiness and the labor we and others are willing to perform in pursuit of that happiness.

Perusing the parks, we can see many examples of where and how Disney facilitates leisure and labor concurrently. Take, for example, the effort in designing or purchasing "costumes" (customized clothing, Mouse ears, etc.) to wear in the parks.[17] Once at the parks, guests are glued to their phones as they use the My Disney Experience app, busily planning activities, ordering food, and reviewing images available for purchase through Memory Maker. None of this is passive enjoyment; it demands time, energy, and decision-making.[18] Moreover, Disney parks will, occasionally (although increasingly rare), give guests line length markers as a means to track the amount of time spent in line, and in doing so, explicitly assign guests the (work) role of data collector. For many, this labor and leisure may afford a sense of mastery, which perhaps contributes to why Disney parks have so many repeat customers.

Marx's ideas of the self-alienation that can occur in labor may be relevant here. Guests are expected to play along with the emotional milieu of the setting.[19] There are soft sanctions for those who refuse, penalties that may include not feeling a sense of belonging or even receiving judgmental looks or comments from others. Some at Disney seem distraught or guilty for not feeling "happy enough." It could also be said that by internalizing Disney narratives, we then labor for Disney as we transmit the narratives to others.

At the parks, but to a greater degree within films, those narratives are strained by controversial social issues. As Bonnie Rudner describes (Chapter 9), Disney uses an iterative process of revising its own works for consumer palatability and for alignment with current social views and perspectives. These corrections are often necessary because of the leisure created by straightforward plots and characters that reflect black-and-white notions of good and bad, desirable and undesirable, right and wrong.[20] Yet, concurrent with the leisure to come from simplified portrayals arises criticism of Disney films for performing ideas of "wokeness." I propose reading this as an example of the leisure-labor tension: many Disney consumers have become frustrated by the labor that comes with having to release long-held ways of thinking and understand complexity, and now they must do the work of accommodating more expansive views and ideologies.[21] Meanwhile, the labor for members of historically marginalized groups may come in the form of feelings of guilt for indulging in the viewing and support of Disney products that display themes of cultural appropriation and colonialism. Such a sentiment is conveyed by Lucy Buck (Chapter 7) in his reflections on viewing Disney films; his Disney-related leisure becomes emotion work within his ethnic identity.

Finally, within Disney's corporate setting, leisure and labor coexist and are upheld. The terminology of "imagineering" can be seen as an effort to make labor into a playful—and not solely a work-filled—enterprise. In the parks specifically, the language for referring to laborers or workers as "cast members" who are making magic versus workers performing labor demands consideration.[22] Disney is trying to convince its workforce and its consumers that their labor is leisure and that they should "whistle while they work," as the Seven Dwarfs did in Disney's first animated film. For those who consume Disney as well as those who create it for others, the myth of Disney powerfully shapes experience and may be the underlying factor that allows for Disney's blurring of leisure and labor.

The three chapters in this section address labor and leisure at Disney in very different ways, yet each reflects the mythos of happiness that is the lifeblood of Disney. To open, Jacob Hayward and I (Alexis Franzese) offer a deep dive into the demands of leisure and labor at Disney in the chapter "Making 'Happy' Happen: What Disney

Teaches Us about the Hidden Costs and Labor of Leisure." Here, Jacob and I explore the sociological concept of emotion work within the park setting. Although the labor is unpaid, most parents participate willingly in Disney's labor demands, and this chapter highlights the gendered, psychological, and sociological elements of that (often invisible) effort. Readers will find themselves pondering the degree to which they themselves may be unknowingly (or quite knowingly) performing Disney's labor.

The next chapter is authored by Jeffrey A. Barnes, whose own professional labors center around his love and knowledge of Disney. As a keynote speaker and author who presents Disney-informed lessons on leadership and success, Barnes's chapter brings readers into "The Happiest Classroom on Earth: Edutainment as Experiential Learning and Emotional Intelligence" to demonstrate the implicit learning opportunities that are present in the Disney setting. The idea of "edutainment" (a term employed by several authors in our text) captures the idea that individuals are both educated and entertained by Disney. Barnes's chapter addresses how we become students of Disney. For Barnes, education is a source of labor that can (and should!) be levied by the leisure and happiness that a Disney classroom can offer. As Barnes describes, the edutainment at Disney happens with a dizzying amount of fantasy and engagement that gives us a sense of leisure.

Disney strives to package its products and experiences as leisurely for all, despite the labor that is inherent in that experience. Yet the degree of labor does differ from guest to guest. As our final chapter shows, leisure and labor are experienced differently by Disney guests with disabilities. "Wheelchairs, Magic Carpets, and a Community of Tomorrow: Constructing Disabled Utopia in the Disney Parks" comes from a family of authors: Mason J. Shrader, Benjamin Shrader, and Carol Mason Shrader. Mason's anthropological expertise, combined with Benjamin's background in disability advocacy and Carol's deeply informed perspective as a mother of two children with cerebral palsy, offers a uniquely situated evaluation of Disney's constructed leisure. In a chapter that weaves personal testimonies with academic analyses, this chapter reveals Disney through the eyes—and bodies—of some guests who require accommodations. Is leisure at Disney accessible to all? This chapter shines a distinctive spotlight on what labor Disney is willing to do, and what labor it expects of its park guests.

These chapters independently and uniquely address the ways in which leisure and labor are intertwined within the Disney experience and synergistically contribute to the allure of Disney. Considered together, these chapters help us to see that Disney is not a day in the office, but neither is it a lounge chair on a beach. Disney offers leisure experiences yet also requires that its guests engage in effortful practices and experiences. How has Disney been a place of leisure for you, and what visible and invisible labor have you performed for yourself and others or in pursuit of experiencing Disney magic? And, most importantly, how might our longing for happiness contribute to the labor we do in pursuit of leisure?

Notes

1 Melissa Pinney, *Washroom, Disney World, Florida* (1998, printed 2003), Chromogenic print, Art Institute Chicago, https://www.artic.edu/artworks/182733/washroom-disney-world-florida.
2 Leon Festinger, *A Theory of Cognitive Dissonance* (Stanford: Stanford University Press, 1957).
3 While Disney consumers undertake work in exchange for a desire for leisure, it may be argued that Disney corporate takes efforts to similarly convince its employees and laborers that they are not in fact laboring, despite the fact that they are exchanging their efforts for pay/tangible reward. This happens in explicit and implicit ways and is addressed further later in this Introduction. Expectations of Disney cast members and employees are described within many memoirs written by (former) Disney cast members, many of which are self-published, as well as within books published by former Disney corporate leaders. As a cast member example, consider Chris Mitchell's text *Cast Member Confidential* (New York: Citadel Press, 2009), and as a corporate leadership example, consider Homer Brightman's text *Life in the Mouse House: A Memoir of a Disney Story Artist* (Edited by Didier Ghez and Bob McLain. Filmography and comicography by Alberto Becattini. New York: Theme Park Press, 2024).
4 For consideration of travel as leisure activity, see John Urry, *The Tourist Gaze: Leisure and Travel in Contemporary Societies* (London; Newbury Park: Sage Publications, 1990). The pursuit of happiness as an American construct is well-documented. Here, I am invoking the twentieth-century emphasis that happiness can be acquired through consumption of products and experiences.
5 Several chapters in this book address the factors that contributed to the development of the parks, namely Bemis (Chapter 5), Tremblay (Chapter 10), and Hoffman (Chapter 11).
6 For discussion, see Raymond Weinstein, "Disneyland and Coney Island: Reflections on the Evolution of the Modern Amusement Park," *Journal of Popular Culture* 26, no. 1 (1992): 131–64.
7 As ambitious as his hopes for Disneyland were, Walt Disney had even greater aspirations for Walt Disney World, centered around the creation of a place that was not just a setting of leisure for those visiting for short stays, but a more experiential immersion into a world of leisure in which the world outside of the setting could be temporarily forgotten.
8 Amy Hurd and Denise Anderson. Park and Recreation Professional's Handbook (Ebook, 2011), https://us.humankinetics.com/blogs/excerpt/definitions-of-leisure-play-and-recreation.
9 Ibid.
10 Ibid.
11 In 1967, Justin Voss, writing for the *Journal of Economic Issues*, felt it necessary to redefine leisure. Please see Justin Voss, "The Definition of Leisure," *Journal of Economic Issues* 1, no. 1–2 (1967): 91–106. https://doi.org/10.1080/00213624.1967.11502742.
12 Ibid.

13   Ibid.

14   Karl Marx, *Das Kapital: A Critique of Political Economy* (Washington, DC: Eagle, [1867] 1996).

15   Kaskowtiz's chapter in this volume (Chapter 4) offers a unique perspective on the motivation for this leisure, inviting readers to recognize what problems a Disney trip "resolves."

16   Relatedly, it's interesting to observe the U-shaped curve that students seem to experience after about a week in the park. The initial excitement and joy slowly shift as students acclimate to the environment and see its demands. Enthusiasm typically returns as students recognize the experience is nearing its end.

17   Disney bounding (invoking Disney characters through clothing and accessories), customized shirts and gear, and park-specific accessories are all commonly viewed in Disney parks.

18   Guests can be observed relying on their Magic Bands that allow for tracking consumer behavior and functioning. Earlier systems like Genie+, FastPass, and their precursors required a similar degree of labor of their users. These examples of the gamification of labor, and specifically the purchasing experience, are a great example of how Disney has made something that may be considered aversive or undesirable (spending money) more tolerable if not enjoyable for some. Disney's efforts at gamification are addressed by Chavez (Chapter 12) of this volume.

19   See Hayward and Franzese (Chapter 13) in this section of this volume, for discussion of emotion work at Disney.

20   Although it may be beyond the scope of this Introduction, interested readers may find it fruitful to ponder the additional burden of being an "active" vs. a "passive" consumer of film, particularly Disney films. As my coauthor of Chapter 13 notes via personal communication, with Disney's emphasis on songs, emotionality, and fantasy imagery, viewers are expected to consume the films and then accept certain ideas in a particular way. The dissonance viewers who more actively engage may experience results from depictions that often suggest a world that truly only exists in fantasy, and in some cases, identity depictions that contribute to the continued marginalization of certain groups. And yet, for many, the myths can feel so compelling or appealing.

21   This process is undoubtedly complicated by the sentiment of nostalgia, which heavily permeates Disney culture and is addressed in the third part of this book, "Nostalgia and Innovation."

22   Sociologist Robert Merton in *Social Theory and Social Structure* (New York: The Free Press, 1949) introduced the idea of manifest and latent functions. Manifest functions are the stated, on the surface, easily understood functions of something. Latent functions, on the other hand, are those more embedded and implicit functions of a system or institution. While historical review indicates that the manifest function of this approach to cast members was to bring the movies to life in theme parks, it could be argued that the reframing of the work experience in this way is a latent function of that section.

13

Making "Happy" Happen

What Disney Teaches Us about the Hidden Costs and Labor of Leisure

Jacob Hayward and Alexis T. Franzese

Since their inception, Disney parks throughout the world have been overwhelmingly marketed toward families and promoted as essential vacation destinations. Commercials, branding, and testimonials used to promote the parks feature parents presenting the parks to their children and enjoying a magical experience with them. Parents often undertake great effort to maintain their child's happiness, especially while accompanying their children through Disney parks. And yet, the actual experiences of parents seeking to make family happiness happen within "the Happiest Place on Earth" and "the Most Magical Place on Earth" are varied and not always as euphoric as Disney marketing would suggest. For this reason, parents' real experiences provide valuable insight into many of the psychological and sociological phenomena that underpin human experiences of emotion and family bonding. By looking at how and why parents may behave differently at Disney theme parks than they do at home or at more traditional family leisure destinations such as beaches or playgrounds, this chapter helps readers understand the labor, gender inequity, and costs lurking behind the idea of a perfect family vacation.

While the financial costs and logistical difficulties of bringing one's family to a Disney park are easy to observe and quantify, the mental strain and emotional effort involved are far less easy to calculate. Research into the sociology of emotions has revealed that the emotional costs of making others happy can be quite burdensome—and are not equally distributed among parents and caregivers. In this chapter, we apply sociological concepts to parental experiences in Disney parks. We start with an overview of vocabulary and theory behind emotion management and its relevance to parenting and leisure. We then discuss how Disney embraces gendered expectations of emotion management and thereby exhibits growing influence on family leisure. Finally, we demonstrate how Disney parks present an exemplary venue to observe parental emotion management. We conclude by discussing the potential implications of such study.

Our work on this topic is the outgrowth of Jacob's participation as an undergraduate sociology major in the course Happiest Place? The Science of Happiness at Disney in 2019, which Alexis taught. Jacob's enthusiasm within the course was clear, and after completing the course, their conversations continued and blossomed into mentored research which extended beyond Jacob's graduation. Their work together continued during Jacob's pursuit of his JD and through his subsequent work as an attorney.

Emotion Work and Family Leisure

Sociologist Erving Goffman brought life to the term "impression management" in 1959 to describe the ways an individual attempts to impact the way others perceive them in a social setting.[1] Scholars of impression management examine an individual's behavior within social interactions and relationships in order to gauge the authenticity and motivations of their actions.[2] The act of engaging in impression management is often quite effortful, conscious or otherwise, as one tries to mask one's authentic feelings and resist impulsive behavior; one frequent form of this is *emotion management*.[3] Emotion management refers to the process of controlling one's emotional affect and displays, while the broader term "impression management" refers to the manipulation of not only emotion but also appearance, language, movement, and any other perceivable behavior.[4]

Sometimes emotion management can involve cognitive effort, termed *deep acting*, to change the emotions one naturally experiences in a situation to more desirable feelings.[5] For example, a person experiencing fear about a new situation may mentally downplay potential risks and exaggerate potential rewards until their fear has turned to excitement. Emotion management without any effort to change how one actually feels is referred to as *surface acting*, where one purposefully expresses emotions they are not genuinely experiencing.[6] Sometimes, people can automatically recognize the need for a specific emotional response in a given situation and mentally adjust their psychological state without any actual cognitive or physical effort.[7] Many people may experience such automatic emotion management when they instantly feel excitement upon entering the Magic Kingdom for the first time, even if they are not genuinely excited about being at the park. Regardless of the approach (automatic or effortful), emotion management remains an important social process through which people seek to elicit emotional responses from others that conform to societal expectations. It is a process regularly activated within us all through social interaction, which has a tremendous effect on ourselves and those with whom we engage, yet most people go through life without the vocabulary or motivation to critically evaluate this fascinating area of everyday life. For example, Disney villains like Scar easily shift their emotional output based on the situation, seemingly effortlessly, to manipulate others and navigate in communities opposed to their agenda.

While emotion management is a regular feature of human interaction, it remained largely under-researched even as societal demands for emotion management increased. In the early 1980s, sociologist Arlie Russell Hochschild pioneered the application of emotion management to people's daily lives, distinguishing between emotion management expected by employers and other authoritative figures, which she calls *emotional labor*, and emotion management one chooses to engage in due to norms and other widespread societal pressures, which she calls *emotion work*. A workplace can implicitly set expectations for emotional labor by promoting a rigid emotion culture, encouraging employees to collectively manage their own emotions as well as those of consumers.[8] Disney parks and resorts are such workplaces, with emotional labor being an integral part of the job for guest-facing cast members, who are expected not only to have a consistent smile on their face but to go above and beyond in creating magic moments for guests.[9] Scientific interest in emotional labor arose alongside mid-twentieth-century economic changes in the United States, such as the widespread addition of women to the workforce, the labor market shift from manufacturing jobs to service-based jobs, and the rise of a middle-class market for industries such as tourism, travel, and leisure. Emotional labor emerged as a regular expectation for workers in many fields so that businesses could capitalize upon these recent changes by selling consumers a positive experience rather than merely a product.[10]

In recent years, scholars have started to focus their research on emotion work because it applies to an even larger population than does emotional labor.[11] And yet, there is still limited research into the effect emotion culture has on consumers of leisure activities. These consumers may be engaging in their own emotion work to collaborate with employees to collectively work toward a goal of promoting positive emotions and suppressing negative ones.[12]

Just as a spoonful of sugar helps the medicine go down, so too does a bit of sociological perspective help us process our experiences in the working world and find an element of fun in all the jobs that must be done. To help categorize those jobs, scholars have created a robust vocabulary to explain differences in various types of work within a social system.[13] Terms like "blue-collar work" and "white-collar work" are certainly familiar, but this dichotomy does not capture occupations that require a high degree of emotional labor or demand conformity with established emotional norms. Terms such as "care work" and "pink-collar work" have been applied to such occupations, but outside of the realm of paid labor, fewer distinctions have been made about the reasons why people might engage in emotion management.[14] While there may be internalized motivations based on personality or ideology, the primary motivation behind emotion work is a desire to conform with the demands of one's social environment.[15]

Some places or events present unique environments with strong institutionalized *feeling rules*. Feeling rules are standards and norms regarding what emotional affect is appropriate and expected within a given context; these serve as important social indicators, with character judgments being formed based on others' conformity or deviance from these rules.[16] Feeling rules create an *emotion culture*, a structure of norms and beliefs about the validity, value, and acceptance of emotions within an institution; scholars label those who behave in a manner that appears to reject an institution's emotion culture as *emotional deviants*.[17]

Emotional deviance can have serious social consequences. Imagine the likely judgments aimed at a widow who laughs and grins throughout her spouse's funeral, thereby flaunting the solemn emotional culture of the room. It is easy to imagine that those who observe her appearing to express joy—in violation of feeling rules about what grief should look like—may ostracize or openly criticize her. The idea of emotional deviance underlies much of the plot of Pixar Animation Studios' film *Inside Out*, in which the anthropomorphized emotions of Joy and Sadness get lost, leading young Riley to react with inappropriate feelings of anger and disgust during a pleasant conversation with her parents, spurring them to discipline her for being moody. People have even introduced names for emotional deviants into the popular lexicon, referring to others as, for example, a "Negative Nelly" when they fail to adapt to a positive emotional culture. Such depictions of emotional deviance are common enough that they have been satirized in popular media, with Saturday Night Live creating a "Debbie Downer" character and, in one memorable skit, ridiculing her melancholic, unenthused attitude on a visit to none other than Disney World. Note that emotional deviance can come not only through someone displaying a different emotion from that which is socially prescribed and culturally accepted, but can also occur when someone does not perform emotion to the degree expected—like SNL's Debbie who is not appropriately happy at Disney.[18]

Enter *enchanted work*, a sociological term that seems ready-made for Disney analyses.[19] Enchanted work is emotion work that promotes meaningful relationships and fosters creativity and communal participation.[20] Hochschild argues that the greatest distinction between emotion work and enchanted work is that emotion work causes some degree of distress, while enchanted work brings one joy and satisfaction.[21] Enchanted work can, unfortunately, be reduced to emotion work when the individual performing it becomes so alienated from their task that they no longer feel any personal satisfaction from its completion.[22] The concept of enchanted work has relevance within the domain of parenting—a laborious act certainly, but one that hopefully is imbued with some satisfaction. The elements of parenting that involve personal interaction with one's child, especially in leisure settings, should, according to Hochschild, be enchanted work.[23] It is less clear whether parents actually find the work of managing the emotions of oneself and their child at Disney to truly be enchanted, and it is to this question that we now turn.

Theme parks are governed by strong feeling rules. Some parks, such as Disneyland and Walt Disney World, openly flaunt their rigid emotion culture through marketing campaigns and taglines that stress the positive emotions deemed valid within the park.[24] Cast members are trained and expected to only model positive emotions, with their jobs requiring the suppression of any frustration, sorrow, or exhaustion they may experience while interacting with guests.[25] By equating the park with a supreme level of happiness, the taglines and cast member performances invalidate other emotions one might realistically experience in a hot, crowded theme park, thereby making any negative emotions deviant.[26] Additionally, the high financial costs associated with a family visit to Disneyland or Walt Disney World also exert pressure on visitors to achieve the maximum amount of happiness for their money.[27] Parents at Disney parks will often struggle to make sure they, and the children in their care, comply with the park's well-publicized emotion culture.

Engagement in emotion work is not restricted to any identities or personality types, and people of various backgrounds and with a diverse array of personalities visit theme parks like Disney. Society exerts pressure on its members to act in accordance with unspoken feeling rules, especially when interacting with others with whom one shares a close personal bond, such as a romantic partner or family member. Engaging with close acquaintances in this manner fosters a sense of self-sacrifice, which at best can provide a feeling of purpose and contribute to one's life satisfaction and overall happiness, and at worst can normalize uneven labor expectations and foster feelings of exploitation or resentment.[28] Psychological and sociological researchers have observed that people will even engage in activities which detract from their immediate joy or satisfaction in order to promote the wellbeing of others and maintain positive relationships.[29] This is exemplified by parents engaging in burdensome, labor-intensive tasks for the fun of their child and masking their own disinterest or frustration to ensure their child experiences the positive emotions normalized by the feeling rules.[30] Next time you are in line for your favorite Disney attraction after a long day, take a look around: there is likely at least one tired, sweaty parent mentally preparing themselves to be tossed about in a teacup or a minecart when they long for nothing more than the padded seats and air conditioning of the Hall of Presidents. You may not be able to spot them right away, however, because they are hiding their discontent so as to reinforce for their child the mythology that negative emotions are invalid within the Disney parks.

The role of parent is undoubtedly labor intensive, often accompanied by stress and conflict with other roles such as employee, friend, or spouse.[31] Parents are among the most consequential agents of socialization for children due to both the intimacy of their bond and the frequency of their interactions.[32] While emotion management is a tool of parenting, the extent to which parents use emotion work and their motivations for doing so range widely.[33]

Feeling rules permeate the act of parenting. Society places an expectation of unconditional love between parent and child and dictates that, despite the stresses of parenting, children will primarily be a source of happiness for parents.[34] Stigma surrounds parents who are not seen as prioritizing their children above all else or who do not outwardly express parental love and contentment.[35] One way that parents display their conformity with these feeling rules is through emotion work when interacting with their children. Like the hot, tired parent feigning happiness for their child's sake at a Disney park, parents reassure children even when they themselves are scared, summon or perform excitement at a child's unimpressive action, or mask their anger or frustration at their child's reckless or harmful actions. Parents regularly suppress negative emotions and amplify positive ones for their children's comfort, often at the expense of their own mental and emotional health.[36]

Parents' ability to successfully navigate the task of altering their children's feelings through emotion work is impacted both by the context in which they are performing emotion work and by the parent's own *emotional capital*.[37] Emotional capital refers to one's "emotion-based knowledge, emotion management skills, and feeling capacities."[38] Through the lifelong process of socialization, people develop emotional capital in the same way social and cultural capital is accumulated: by observing others and engaging in new experiences. Differences in individuals' emotional capital are explained by different levels of exposure to demands for emotion management, prior experience with emotional regulation strategies, and differing expectations of *emotionality* based on age and gender.[39] Emotionality refers to the degree of expressiveness with which an individual demonstrates their emotions, with low emotionality equated with stoicism and high emotionality manifesting in melodramatic and volatile displays.[40] Due to societal stereotypes of women as more overtly emotional than men, combined with the unequal division of care work within American society, women are socialized to accumulate more emotional capital than men.[41]

Leisure activities in particular lend themselves to parental emotion work. Here, parents assume the burden of ensuring their child's entertainment by masking their own negative emotions and often by participating in or reinforcing imaginary play scenarios built around *fantasy imagery*.[42] Fantasy imagery refers to the creation of a multisensory mental image drawn from the imagination rather than from past experiences.[43] It is through fantasy imagery that a child is able to imagine themself as an astronaut without ever having actually ventured into outer space. When children invite parents to participate in play and engage with fantasy imagery, they are often asking parents to manufacture emotional responses to nonexistent situations—and to engage in emotion work.

Family leisure activities often involve high levels of planning and preparation that can cause great deals of stress, but parents' commitment to providing enjoyable experiences for their children prompts them to practice emotion work during leisure activities.[44] Some environments, such as theme parks, provide fantasy imagery that makes extrinsically oriented emotion work more accessible to so-called "unimaginative" parents who do not possess the large amount of emotional capital needed to effortlessly immerse their children in fantasy. Part of the appeal of a Disney park, resort, or cruise is the assurance that there will be familiar characters and settings presented through the theming, as well as cast members ready to amplify positive emotions, which parents can rely upon to make up for deficiencies in their emotional capital. While for some a family trip to a Disney park may be enchanted work, other parents feeling burdened by societal expectations of emotion management enjoy Disney as a means of outsourcing the emotion work involved in family leisure.

Inequities in Emotion Work at Disney and Beyond

That people engage in emotion work during leisure activities has implications ranging from mental health and stress to alienation from self. Emotion work and emotional labor, especially deep acting, can prove challenging and mentally taxing. When performed regularly, emotion management can alienate people from their emotions, making it difficult to experience genuine positive feelings.[45] The regular suppression of negative emotions and amplification of positive emotions can also lead to feelings of inauthenticity which in turn contribute to low self-esteem and chronic stress.[46] There may be real emotional costs, then, to taking a family vacation to a Disney park—and such costs may not be equally distributed by gender.

Emotion work in Disney parks and other leisure settings is not immune from gendered entanglement. Patriarchal norms have, both historically and at present, built up an emotion culture in which women are simultaneously expected to be more open and expressive than men and to exercise greater regulation of their emotional displays when fulfilling roles such as caregivers, romantic partners, and service workers. The emotion culture of any given space or event, then, varies by gender.[47] It is important to note here the distinction between the socially assigned, traditionally binary status of gender and one's self-defined gender identity. The ways in which transgender and gender-nonconforming individuals are socialized by, and respond to, gendered emotion culture is an important area of study beyond the scope of this chapter. The gendered distinctions discussed here refer to the different feeling rules between those society labels and treats as female and those labeled and treated as male. For this reason, jobs that require higher levels of emotional labor—so-called "pink-collar" work— have typically been within female-dominated fields, such as nursing and teaching. Many social institutions, including marriage, the family, media, and medicine, have responded aggressively to emotional deviance from women, often while praising men for otherwise identical emotional conduct.

Not surprisingly, even in Disney films, these role-specific feeling rules are regularly projected onto characters: mother figures such as Cinderella's Fairy Godmother or Bambi's mother are expected to be nurturing caregivers and dutiful stewards of children's experiences in the world, while fathers such as King Triton or Pocahontas's father are allowed to be more distant and focused on the "tough love" necessary to protect their children from the world and to protect their own values and traditions from being eroded by their willful daughters. It is no coincidence that some of the most iconic villains of Disney films—*Snow White's* Evil Queen, *Cinderella's* Lady Tremaine, and *Tangled's* Mother Gothel—are mother figures who have subverted the traditional feelings associated with motherhood to instead flaunt feelings of envy, resentment, or disinterest toward those in their care. Similarly, fathers in Disney films who fail to model the sternness and emotional rigidity associated with the emotion culture underlying traditional masculinity—most notably, Jasmine's father the Sultan from *Aladdin* and Belle's father Maurice in *Beauty and the Beast*—are depicted as weak, foolish, and incompetent.

Stating that there are differing emotional expectations for men and women may seem about as groundbreaking as saying that the sun rises in the east, but this is nonetheless a consequential baseline for emotion work within leisure settings. Like other areas of family life, mothers often put a majority of effort into family leisure, yet this often goes unrecognized and underappreciated.[48] As family leisure comes to more closely resemble a Disney model, with an emphasis on shared engagement with fantasy imagery and greater expectations of parental emotion work, the unequal division of labor in parenting might risk worsening gender disparities within parenting and leisure.[49]

Beyond these gender issues, as the Disney parks model of family leisure becomes more widespread, pressure on parents increases: they are expected not only to participate in leisure activities with their child but also to engage in the requisite emotion work to maximize their child's happiness during such activities. We should presume that parents' susceptibility to this pressure will vary based on societal factors, such as gender and cultural differences in how the role of "parent" is defined, and individual factors, such as a parent's personality, ability, and mental health. Further examination will be necessary to confirm if this is the case, and Disney parks present an optimal laboratory for future research.

Emotion Work at Disney

Disney is the quintessential model of family leisure. The rise of Disney and other theme parks has spurred changes in the norms of modern leisure and consumption far outside their own gates. In 1999, social scientist Alan Bryman used the term "Disneyization" to describe the changes taking root in many industries including travel, sports, dining, and especially leisure. Bryman saw that these sectors of society were increasingly relying upon four central components popularized by the Disney theme parks' business model: theming, hybrid consumption, merchandising, and emotional labor.[50] Disney has helped make these components commonplace, pushing past the leisure sphere and now occupying areas ranging from housing complexes to universities to dining, rendering almost any form of consumption a hedonic experience as consumers vie not only for goods or services but for the enjoyable *experience* of procuring such a good or service.[51] For parents and children in these Disneyized spheres, the emotional labor component reinforces an emotion culture that calls upon parents to manage their emotions and their children's, and the theming component presents fantasy imagery which aids in that task by giving parents tangible cues to engage in their own emotion work. For example, the theme of Fantasyland encourages parents to buy their children tiaras, dresses, or wands; tell them they can be a princess or a wizard; and present them the large castle and the medieval-themed buildings as evidence.

Disney utilizes parental emotion work as a valuable tool to alter children's affect. One of the primary appeals of Disney parks and other Disneyized leisure spaces is the deep level of theming that allows children to easily immerse themselves in fantasy. Disneyized leisure spheres encourage parents to use emotion work to reinforce feeling rules and to make theming and fantasy imagery more appealing to child consumers. Disney markets meals with character meet-and-greets and autograph books to parents rather than directly to young children since kids lack purchasing power. Marketing of these opportunities recruits parents to not only finance their children's meeting with characters, but also to hype up the experience for their children by acting as if they have procured a real opportunity to meet with a famous individual, rather than just a costumed actor. Often, parents must facilitate such character meetings because they are better equipped than cast members to address their childrens' doubts and hesitations about interacting with a stranger. By using parents as unpaid collaborators, the Disney form of hedonic consumption can reduce labor costs and double Disney's consumer base—for each child paying admission, there is a parent also paying *and* promoting the child's enjoyment, thereby building Disney's reputation and ensuring repeat business.

Observation of parents and children interacting with costumed characters within the Walt Disney World Resort, conducted as part of the aforementioned Science of Happiness at Disney course, showed that parents often do engage in emotion work and fantasy imagery construction with their children by vouching for the characters' authenticity.[52] Even among the stifling crowds and hot Florida sun, put-upon parents smile in amazement and tell their excited but shy daughter that a *real* princess wants to take a picture with them, and they show her how to curtsy when meeting Cinderella. Of course, parents understand that "Cinderella" is a young woman playing a character for a paycheck—but that's an unspoken secret that Disney recruits parents to keep from their children. While many parents accept this invitation, some reject the request by allowing their children to experience the parks without prompting or emotion work. Then there are parents who actively engage in emotional deviance by rejecting the pressure to model happiness or excitement, like the one mother we observed openly telling her awe-struck children that the castle is not actually that impressive because most of it is fake, and that *real* castles are not as colorful.[53]

Observing parents' emotion work at a place like Disney allows researchers to uncover those factors that parents evaluate, consciously or unconsciously, when engaging with children at Disney. Researchers can also seek to determine the actual effect that parents' emotion work has on children's experience of fantasy imagery. Psychologists, for instance, can seek to uncover the extent to which personality type influences either a child's receptiveness to fantasy imagery or a parent's propensity for emotion work. Economists and marketing researchers can determine how emotion culture influences a parent's decisions as consumers of family leisure opportunities. Historians, anthropologists, and even political scientists could all contribute by examining the ways in which people across time, place, and culture have used fantasy imagery to shape collective identity. Perhaps most importantly, this scholarly effort could someday help parents gain insight into ways to connect with their children and promote happiness without emotionally overburdening themselves.

For better or worse, parents deploy many strategies and approaches to embrace or reject the emotional burden of Disney. Emotion work can be taxing and lead to feelings of burnout, frustration, and alienation.[54] Parents must learn ways to adapt when entering new emotion cultures with their children so as to maximize leisure and family cohesion while minimizing emotional strain. Some parents will sacrifice their own positive affect and authenticity through near-constant surface acting, to ensure that their children—and any outside observers—do not perceive them as emotionally deviant. Other parents employ more deep acting to combat naturally arising negative emotions, often by committing more fully to engaging with the fantasy imagery of the constructed environment.

Conclusion

Since the 1983 publication of *The Managed Heart*, sociologists and psychologists have devoted a great deal of time and resources to the study of emotion management and feeling rules in hopes of better understanding the causes and effects of inauthentic emotional displays.[55] It is unlikely that our highly commercialized society will ever fully move away from valuing emotion work in parenting. Disney parks, and the other themed leisure destinations they have spawned, are not going anywhere. Being "the Happiest Place on Earth," Disneyland and its fellow Disney parks have been studied as hubs for emotional regulation activity, providing important insight into theme parks and their effects on human behavior and happiness.[56]

Looking beyond the park setting, consideration of emotion work within the Disney setting can and has also been considered in relation to Disney films. For example, who is depicted as engaging in emotion work in Disney films? Beyond Disney films, how is emotion work at play in Disney corporate settings? What emotion work is involved in being an "imagineer" or holding other roles within Disney?

Extending research on Disney parks' emotion culture to parental behavior provides a larger picture of the social influence of theme parks and the way that people respond to the artificial, hedonistic environment presented by this modern form of leisure. By using Disney parks as a case study in emotion work, we can unlock new understandings of how parents engage with children in such environments and how families can seek to make their leisure experiences enchanted. While Disney is a beloved source of leisure activity for tens of millions of guests who visit the parks each year, it is also a place of labor—not only for its cast members and employees but also for its guests, particularly parents.

Notes

1   Erving Goffman, *The Presentation of Self in Everyday Life* (New York: Anchor Books, 1959).

2   Arlie Russell Hochschild, *The Managed Heart: The Commercialization of Human Feeling* (Berkeley: University of California Press, 1983).

3   Ibid.

4   Ibid.

5   Ibid., 38.

6   Ibid., 37.

7   Dieter Zapf, "Emotion Work and Psychological Well-Being: A Review of the Literature and Some Conceptual Considerations," *Human Resources Management Review* 12, no. 2 (June 2002): 237–68.

8   Jordan McKenzie et al., "Emotion Management and Solidarity in the Workplace: A Call for a New Research Agenda," *Sociological Review* 67, no. 3 (May 2019): 672–88; John Van Maanen and Gideon Kunda, "'Real Feelings': Emotional Expression and Organizational Culture," *Research in Organizational Behavior* 11 (1989): 43–103; Maurice Yolles and Gerhard Finke, "Collective Emotion Regulation

in an Organisation—A Plural Agency with Cognition and Affect," *Journal of Organizational Change Management* 28, no. 5 (August 2015): 832–71.

9   Anne Reyers and Jonathan Matusitz, "Emotional Regulation at Walt Disney World: An Impression Management View," *Journal of Workplace Behavioral Health* 27, no. 3 (July 2012): 139–59.

10 Hochschild, *The Managed Heart*, 137.

11 Laura Little, Don Kluemper, Debra L. Nelson, and Janaki Gooty, "Development and Validation of the Interpersonal Emotion Management Scale," *Journal of Occupational and Organizational Psychology* 85, no. 2 (June 2012): 407–20; Karen Niven, Peter Totterdell, Christopher B. Stride, and David Holman, "Emotion Regulation of Others and Self (EROS): The Development and Validation of a New Individual Difference Measure," *Current Psychology* 30, no. 1 (September 2011): 53–73; Ronnie J. Steinberg and Deborah M. Figart, "Emotional Labor since The Managed Heart," *Annals of the American Academy of Political and Social Science* 561 (January 1999): 8–26.

12 Elizabeth Hirschman and Morris Holbrook, "The Experiential Aspects of Consumption. Fantasies, Feelings, and Fun," *Journal of Consumer Research* 9 (March 1982): 132–40.

13 Amy S. Wharton, "The Sociology of Emotional Labor," *Annual Review of Sociology* 35 (2009): 147–65.

14 Ibid.

15 Hochschild, *The Managed Heart*, 56.

16 Ibid.

17 Peggy A. Thoits, "Emotional Deviance: Research Agendas," in SUNY series in the sociology of emotions. *Research Agendas in the Sociology of Emotions*, ed. T. D. Kemper (State University of New York Press, 1990), 180–203.

18 Ibid.

19 Nada Endrissat, Gazi Islam, and Claus Noppeney, "Enchanting Work: New Spirits of Service Work in an Organic Supermarket," *Organization Studies* 36, no. 11 (November 2015): 1555–76.

20 Ibid.

21 Julie Beck, "The Concept Creep of 'Emotional Labor,'" *The Atlantic* (November 26, 2018).

22 Ibid.

23 Ibid.

24 Reyers and Matusitz, "Emotional Regulation at Walt Disney World," 139.

25 Ibid.

26 Nick Johns and Szilvia Gyimothy, "Mythologies of a Theme Park: An Icon of Modern Family Life," *Journal of Vacation Marketing* 8, no. 4 (September 2002): 320–31.

27 Nick Stanley, "Out of This World: Theme Parks' Contribution to a Redefined Aesthetics and Educational Practice," *International Journal of Art & Design Education* 21, no. 1 (February 2002): 24–35.

28 Ed Diener and Robert Biswas-Diener, "Psychological Wealth: The Balanced Portfolio," in *Happiness: Unlocking the Mysteries of Psychological Wealth* (Malden, MA: Blackwell Publishing, 2008), 3–12; Majorie L. DeVault, "Comfort and Struggle: Emotion Work in Family Life," *Annals of the American Academy of Political and Social Science* 561 (January 1999): 52–63.

29 Roy F. Baumeister and Mark R. Leary, "The Need to Belong: Desire for Interpersonal Attachments as a Fundamental Human Motivation," *Psychological Bulletin* 117, no. 3 (1995): 497–529; Christopher K. Hsee and Reid Hastie, "Decision and Experience: Why Don't We Choose What Makes Us Happy?" *Trends in Cognitive Sciences* 10, no. 1 (February 2006): 31–7; David G. Myers, "Close Relationships and Quality of Life," in *Well-Being: The Foundations of Hedonic Psychology*, ed. E. Diener, D. Kahneman, and N. Schwarz (New York: Russell Sage Foundation, 2003), 374–91.

30 DeVault, "Comfort and Struggle," 52–63.

31 Jessica L. Collett and Ellen Childs, "Meaningful Performances: Considering the Contributions of the Dramaturgical Approach to Studying Family," *Sociology Compass* 3, no. 4 (July 2009): 689–706; Jessica L. Collett, "What Kind of Mother Am I? Impression Management and the Social Construction of Motherhood," *Symbolic Interaction* 28, no. 3 (December 2011): 327–47; Susan M. Shaw, "Family Leisure and Changing Ideologies of Parenthood," *Sociology Compass* 2, no. 2 (March 2008): 688–703.

32 Niven et al., "Emotion Regulation of Others and Self (EROS)," 53; Craig T. Palmer and Kathryn Coe, "Parenting, Courtship, Disneyland and the Human Brain," *International Journal of Tourism Anthropology* 1, no. 1 (November 2010): 1–14.

33 DeVault, "Comfort and Struggle," 52.

34 Shaw, "Family Leisure and Changing Ideologies of Parenthood," 688–9.

35 Ibid.

36 Bonnie M. Le and Emily A. Impett, "The Costs of Suppressing Negative Emotions and Amplifying Positive Emotions during Parental Caregiving," *Personality and Social Psychology Bulletin* 42, no. 3 (February 2016): 323–36.

37 Diane Reay, "A Useful Extension of Bourdieu's Conceptual Framework?: Emotional Capital as a Way to Understand Mothers' Involvement in their Children's Education," *The Sociological Review* 48, no. 4 (2000): 568–85.

38 Marci D. Cottingham, "Theorizing Emotional Capital," *Theory and Society* 45 (October 2016): 451–70.

39 Reay, "A Useful Extension of Bourdieu's Conceptual Framework?" 568.

40 Agneta H. Fischer, "Sex Differences in Emotionality: Fact or Stereotype?" *Feminism & Psychology* 3, no. 3 (October 1993): 303–18.

41 Cottingham, "Theorizing Emotional Capital," 454; Fischer, "Sex Differences in Emotionality," 303; Reay, "A Useful Extension of Bourdieu's Conceptual Framework?" 568.

42 Shaw, "Family Leisure and Changing Ideologies of Parenthood," 688–9; Stanley, "Out of this World," 24.

43 Hirschman and Holbrook, "The Experiential Aspects of Consumption," 132.

44 Shaw, "Family Leisure and Changing Ideologies of Parenthood," 688–9.

45 Hochschild, *The Managed Heart*, 185.

46 Le and Impett, "The Costs of Suppressing Negative Emotions and Amplifying Positive Emotions during Parental Caregiving," 327.

47 It is important to note here the distinction between the socially assigned, traditionally binary status of gender and one's self-defined gender identity. The ways in which transgender and gender-nonconforming individuals are socialized by, and respond to, gendered emotion culture is an important area of study beyond the scope of this chapter. The gendered distinctions discussed here refer to the different

feeling rules between those society labels and treats as female and those labeled and treated as male.

48   Shaw, "Family Leisure and Changing Ideologies of Parenthood," 688–9.

49   Loes Meeussen and Collette Van Laar, "Feeling Pressure to be a Perfect Mother Relates to Parental Burnout and Career Ambitions," *Frontiers in Psychology* 9 (2018).

50   The interested reader may be curious about the distinctions between Disneyization, introduced by Bryman (1999), and the idea of Disneyfying, which was described by Richard Schnickel in his 1968 text "The Disney Version." It should be noted that Bryman specifically rejected the "Disneyfication" terminology in favor of "Disneyization," in part due to a view of Schnickel's conceptualization as overly negative and focused on marketing, while his idea was broader in scope. Our review of Schnickel suggests that Schnickel does not address the role of emotion culture within his "Disneyfication" concept. That exclusion is unsurprising given that Schnickel was writing prior to landmark studies by Hochschild in the early 1980s and Thoits in the early 1990s. Emotional labor is a core component of Bryman's (1999) concept of Disneyization. (Prior to Schnikel's 1968 text, Lawrence Lipton is credited with using the term "Disneyfication" in *The Holy Barbarians* (New York: Julian Messner) as a broader commentary and critique of mainstream culture.

51   Alan Bryman, "The Disneyization of Society," *Sociological Review* 47, no. 1 (February 1999): 25–47; Elizabeth Hirschman and Morris Holbrook, "Hedonic Consumption: Emerging Concepts, Methods and Propositions," *Journal of Marketing* 46, no. 3 (July 1982): 92–101.

52   Alexis T. Franzese and Jacob Hayward, "Smile, or Else, Please: Emotion Work, Enchanted Work, and Parent Behaviors at Theme Parks," Poster presented at the annual meeting of the International Society for Research on Emotion, Los Angeles, CA, July 2022.

53   Ibid.

54   The research literature on the psychological effects of emotion work is vast. A few relevant and key publications include the following: Zapf, "Emotion Work and Psychological Well-Being," 237; Meeussen and Van Laar, "Feeling Pressure to be a Perfect Mother Relates to Parental Burnout and Career Ambitions"; Rebecca J. Erickson and Amy S. Wharton, "Inauthenticity and Depression: Assessing the Consequences of Interactive Service Work," *Work and Occupations* 24, no. 2 (May 1997): 188–213.

55   Steinberg and Figart, "Emotional Labor since The Managed Heart," 561.

56   Reyers and Matusitz, "Emotional Regulation at Walt Disney World," 140.

14

Disneyland

The Happiest Classroom on Earth

Jeffrey A. Barnes

Sitting on a Park Bench

Imagine strolling through the bustling pathways of Disneyland, surrounded by the joyful cacophony of laughter and music, the air filled with the sweet scent of popcorn and churros. You've whisked past the thrilling drops of Space Mountain and the swashbuckling adventures of Pirates of the Caribbean. Perhaps you've even braved the snowy slopes of the Matterhorn Bobsleds. Each of these attractions offers a pulse of excitement, a dash of danger, a world of wonder—all elements that make Disneyland a place of endless possibilities.

Yet, amid these celebrated spectacles lies my favorite attraction, profoundly simple yet deeply significant. It isn't heralded by flashing lights or marked on any map. It's a modest park bench, tucked away inside the grandeur of the Main Street Opera House, now the stage for Great Moments with Mr. Lincoln.

This is no ordinary bench. It is where Walt Disney, one random afternoon at Griffith Park in downtown Los Angeles in the 1940s, sat and watched the world go by, children laughing and parents smiling, and dreamt of a place where such simple joys could be everyday magic. Here, Walt envisioned a realm where education and entertainment intertwine seamlessly—where learning is an adventure, and imagination is the curriculum. Walt called this "edutainment," which is the art and science of blending education with entertainment. This approach aligns with educational theorist David Kolb's notion that "learning is the process whereby knowledge is created through the transformation of experience."[1] This bench, weathered and unassuming, stands as a testament to the power of a single idea—a vision that blossomed into the world-renowned Disneyland, transforming entertainment and education on a global scale. It represents the essence of what it means to be an educator: to inspire, to dream, and to create spaces where minds can explore and spirits can soar.

As we delve into the narrative of Disneyland, often hailed as "The Happiest Place on Earth," we uncover its dual identity as a vibrant educational landscape. Here, every corner teaches a lesson, every ride tells a story, and every character embodies a dream.

Walt Disney's legacy is a reminder that the most profound learning often comes not from textbooks, but from experiences that stir the heart and stimulate the mind. A call back to the words of acclaimed poet Dr. Maya Angelou, "People will forget what you said, people will forget what you did, but people will never forget how you made them feel."[2]

Join me as we explore how Disneyland serves not just as an amusement park but as a dynamic classroom. Here, the power of imagination fuels the pursuit of knowledge, and every visit is a journey into the heart of education itself.

My Mickey Mouse Idea

As this realization deepened during my early years in Southern California, a transformative idea began to take shape, almost as if inspired by the magical essence of Disneyland itself. In 2011, when I joined California Baptist University as the dean of student success and professor of humanities, I was thrilled to be just a short drive away from Disneyland, the park that first introduced and has mastered the art of blending entertainment with experiential learning. It was during these visits, surrounded by the park's vibrant storytelling and immersive experiences, that a novel concept struck me.

What if the principles that make Disneyland such a captivating place could be harnessed to enhance educational outcomes? Many of the students I worked with possessed the potential to excel—they simply lacked engagement and/or exposure to traditional academic models. Recalling my own experiences at the park—where every corner promises discovery and every attraction teaches a lesson—I wondered, could a classroom capture this same magic? Could the history of such a place offer more than just facts, instead providing a blueprint for success that resonates with students across various disciplines?

Fueled by the spirit of innovation that Walt Disney himself championed, I envisioned a course that would go beyond textbooks and lectures. This course would use Disneyland not just as a case study but as a living example of creativity, persistence, and dreams turned into reality—a place where learning is more than just acquiring information; it is about engaging deeply with experiences. According to education philosopher John Dewey, "We do not learn from experience . . . we learn from reflecting on experience."[3] This principle was central to the course design, encouraging students not only to participate in the immersive environments of Disneyland but also to reflect critically on those experiences to deepen their understanding and apply these lessons to their own personal and academic growth.

With this foundation in mind, I sought to redefine academic engagement by incorporating Disneyland as more than just a setting for experiential learning but as a blueprint for innovative thinking and problem-solving. As organizational psychologist Adam Grant notes, "A hallmark of wisdom is knowing when it's time to abandon some of your most treasured tools."[4] Inspired by this, I was determined to break away from traditional academic models that often leave students disengaged. In Southern California, where diverse cultures converge and In-N-Out Burgers are a unifying delight, Disneyland stood out as a universal symbol of creativity and joy—a place my students already cherished and could readily connect with. By tapping into this shared cultural touchstone, the course became not just an academic endeavor but a meaningful exploration of how passion, creativity, and persistence can turn dreams into reality.

This prospective course, titled The History of Disneyland, would not merely cover the chronological events leading up to the creation of the park but would delve into the methodologies that made Disney's vision a reality. It would challenge students to see beyond the facade of the theme park and understand the depth of thought, leadership, and sheer perseverance that Walt Disney embodied. Walt once said, "All of our dreams can come true if we have the courage to pursue them."[5] Inspired by his legacy, I decided to champion this seemingly "Mickey Mouse idea" into a robust academic syllabus. Despite initial apprehensions—fearing the risk of proposing such an unconventional idea in a traditional academic setting—I was compelled by the potential of what this could mean for educational engagement. I believed that every student, from every academic discipline and all walks of life, would benefit from knowing Walt's story and the stories told in the park. Disney has mass appeal, and I wanted this course to be equally appealing.

As I prepared to pitch this course to my supervisor, who would be responsible for its approval and success, I remembered Walt's initial presentation of Disneyland: a place for happiness, knowledge, and shared experiences not just for families but also for teachers and pupils. His vision was clear—a place for active learning and discovery, echoing the principles I wished to instill in my classroom. Thus, armed with a vision and driven by the transformative power of education, I set forth to create what I hoped would become the Happiest Classroom on Earth. The journey, however, was not without its degrees of difficulty, rooted deeply in the very essence of the educational philosophy of edutainment I sought to embrace—a philosophy pioneered by none other than Walt Disney himself.

Degrees of Difficulty: Thinking Outside the Box of Academia

In the halls of academia and beyond, the mention of Walt Disney often evokes a spectrum of responses, particularly when discussing his qualifications as an educator. Skeptics point to his brief formal education—his academic journey halted prematurely when he was only a freshman in high school. "Where were his credentials? Where was Disney's diploma?" they ask. The truth is, Walt possessed neither. Due to his family's financial struggles, which many students can identify with, Walt never progressed further than the ninth grade.

Yet, despite this, Walt Disney's contributions to education and learning exceed those of many formally educated individuals (as do his numerous honorary degrees and doctorates). In 1918, he left school to serve in the First World War, where he drove ambulances for the Red Cross in France. This unconventional path led him not back to the classroom but onto a trajectory that would surprisingly redefine the educational landscape. Walt understood something profound about learning: it doesn't end with the ringing of a school bell. Lifelong learning was his pursuit, echoing the lives of his heroes like Abraham Lincoln, Thomas Edison, and Charlie Chaplin—all largely self-taught figures who changed the course of history. As described in Pat Williams and James Denney's *How to Be Like Walt*, Disney was a voracious learner, drawing lessons not from textbooks but from life itself, embodying the true spirit of an autodidact. The Walt Disney Family Museum highlights this: "Walt pieced together an education through his own life experiences, using the world as his classroom."

Moreover, Walt recognized his limitations and never pretended to know all. He valued practical knowledge over formal education, famously remarking to his studio nurse, Hazel George, about trading all his honorary degrees for real-life experience, wisdom, and a real degree. His humility in acknowledging what he didn't know opened the door for continuous growth and learning.

His fear? Not failure, but boredom—his own and that of his audience. Walt's drive to keep audiences engaged led him to pioneer technologies and storytelling methods that transformed entertainment into a rich, educational experience. Disneyland itself is a testament to this philosophy: a place where joy and learning are intertwined, where every attraction holds a lesson. "I would rather entertain and hope that people learned something than educate people and hope they were entertained,"[6] Walt famously said. This approach underpins the educational value of Disneyland, which goes beyond mere amusement to stimulate curiosity and inspire a deeper connection to the material presented.

As we delve into the innovative educational strategies inspired by Walt Disney, we recognize that his approach offers a robust framework for reinvigorating contemporary education. His philosophy underscores that learning extends beyond mere information transfer—it's about igniting a spark that encourages his guests to think creatively and pursue their dreams with vigor.

This concept extends beyond Disneyland itself, shaping broader societal trends. As sociologist Alan Bryman describes, "The principles of the Disney theme parks are coming to dominate more and more sectors of American society as well as the rest of the world."[7] This process, termed "Disneyization," reflects how various sectors adopt Disney-like practices of theming and hybrid consumption, influencing how we learn, shop, and engage with the world around us.

Why Disneyland? Transforming Education through Inspiration

Inspired by Walt Disney's own educational journey, which defied traditional paths yet had profound impacts, I designed my course, The History of Disneyland, to challenge students to think differently about success, engagement, and learning. The journey to launch a course on the history of Disneyland, which I envisioned as more than just an academic endeavor, also mirrored the visionary zeal of Walt Disney himself.

After years of meticulous planning, curriculum development, and collaboration with various experts, I taught the first iteration of the course in 2014. This wasn't just about teaching history; it was about bringing the magic of Disneyland into the classroom, making learning a dynamic and immersive experience. It also turned Disneyland itself into a classroom twice a week during the semester.

Imagine stepping into a classroom where every lecture is an adventure, every assignment a discovery, and every guest speaker a window into a world of creativity and dreams. This is what students experience in courses that blend history with storytelling, just as Disneyland blends fantasy with reality.

Walt Disney created Disneyland out of a desire to build something magical, a place where dreams could come alive. Just as Disneyland has continued to inspire millions of visitors from around the globe, educational experiences inspired by such creativity can ignite the imaginations of students. For educators, it's about crafting learning experiences that resonate deeply, encouraging students to explore, question, and transform the world around them.

The impact of such educational initiatives extends far beyond the classroom. For instance, integrating the principles learned from Disneyland's success into courses across various disciplines—from leadership studies to history and beyond—provides a model of how passion and perseverance can lead to extraordinary outcomes. As educational theorist Michael Fullan insightfully puts it, "Change really isn't as hard as we thought if we capture people's interest and give them enjoyable, worthwhile experiences."[8] This principle was vividly demonstrated in the overwhelmingly positive feedback I received from students who found that learning in an environment inspired by Disneyland made the educational process not only engaging but transformative. The course provided them with the opportunity to connect deeply with the material and see immediate, real-world applications.

For example, students who had failed their first classes were encouraged to learn that Walt Disney himself failed with his first studio, Laugh-O-Gram Studio in Kansas City, at the ripe old age of twenty-one. These teachings not only enhance academic engagement but also prepare students to be innovators in their fields. In fact, one of my students finally finished his first screenplay during our semester together, while another secured an internship with local actor Dean Norris, aka Hank Schrader from *Breaking Bad*.

Every year, as part of their PhD program in leadership, students from my school participate in a unique residency that includes a tour of Disneyland, exemplifying experiential learning at its finest. This approach not only deepens their understanding of leadership concepts but also inspires them to apply these lessons in real-world contexts.

Your Journey of Discovery: Learning on a Virtual Stroll around Disneyland

I now invite you to join me on a virtual stroll through Disneyland. Together, we'll explore the park not just as visitors but as learners and leaders, drawing insights from every corner of this magical realm. Whoever you are, and wherever you might be reading this book, I want to invite you to use your imagination as I invite you to join me on a virtual stroll through Disneyland. In the spirit of Albert Einstein, who is often credited with saying, "knowledge is limited. Imagination is everything and a preview of life's coming attractions," let's explore this iconic park not just as guests, but as learners and leaders. Let's discover seven leadership lessons learned in the Happiest Classroom on Earth.

Like every guest's day at Disneyland, our visit begins with a stroll down Main Street, U.S.A. This picturesque street transports us to America at the crossroads of the nineteenth and twentieth centuries, an era of transition and technological evolution. Gas lamps illuminate the paths, while electric lights twinkle overhead, highlighting the charm of horse-drawn buggies alongside the clang of the streetcar. Main Street may not offer thrill rides, but its charm leaves a lasting impression and offers our first leadership lesson.

We turn right into the opulent lobby of the Main Street Opera House, where history whispers through the walls. Here, you'll find what you may recall is my favorite attraction: the famed bench from Griffith Park in downtown Los Angeles. Its green paint is weathered and chipped, telling stories of a time when Walt Disney sat here on Saturday afternoons, watching his daughters ride the merry-go-round. It was on this very bench that he first imagined Disneyland—a place where "parents and children can have fun together."[9]

This brings us to our first lesson: the Power of Vision. Vision is the lifeblood of life and leadership. Leaders are responsible for taking their teams, companies, and ideas to the next level. Anything less is simply maintaining the status quo. Walt Disney was always curious, always opening new doors, always moving things forward.

Maintenance is for managers.

In his book *Disney and His Worlds*, British sociologist Alan Bryman describes Walt as a "serial visionary . . . someone who had big dreams about new ways of doing many things, whether it was making animated cartoons, designing amusement parks, or creating new approaches to urban living."[10] Everyone, especially leaders, needs their own park bench—a place to sit, think, and dream. A place where you, like Walt, can envision your own "Great Big Beautiful Tomorrow."[11] Encourage everyone around you to do the same. Why? Because leaders develop their teams by allowing them to dream. Business and leadership consultants Bill Capodagli and Lynn Jackson, who are often credited with translating Disney practices into winning strategies for any business, say that "Dreaming was the wellspring of Disney's creativity."

Our next stop and lesson await at the end of Main Street, U.S.A. While Main Street serves as an excellent introduction to our Disneyland adventure, the best stories and attractions lie deeper within the park. The iconic Sleeping Beauty Castle beckons us forward, urging us to continue our exploration and embrace the journey ahead. John Hench, one of Walt's esteemed Imagineers, once said, "A castle is fantasy in any language."[12] It's a fantasy to think that anyone can truly lead based solely on position, title, power, or authority. You know you're a leader when people choose to follow you. Leaders give followers a compelling reason to keep exploring, to keep moving forward.

Our second lesson is the Importance of Influence. Leaders inspire others to live a bigger and better story. Influence attracts the best of the best, who will want to follow you. Together, you can create magic and accomplish anything! Walt Disney exemplified the concept of a charismatic leader, as originally defined by German sociologist and philosopher Max Weber. Weber explained, "By virtue of both the extraordinary qualities that followers attribute to the leader and the latter's mission, the charismatic leader is regarded by his or her followers with a mixture of reverence, unflinching dedication, and awe."[13] Disneyland's design is an extraordinary example of charismatic leadership. Charismatic leaders must have followers who willingly choose to follow them.

As you stand in front of Sleeping Beauty Castle, you find yourself in the central plaza, a crossroads of Disneyland and the heart of our third leadership lesson: the Strength of Empowerment. From this vibrant hub, the park's distinct lands fan out like spokes on a wheel, each offering its unique adventures and enchantments. Walt Disney, with his filmmaker's eye, meticulously crafted how visitors enter and leave Disneyland, guiding them through the nostalgic Main Street, U.S.A. But once you arrive at the central plaza, the story changes. Here, Walt entrusts you, the guest, with the power to choose your own adventure. Will you veer left into the lush, mysterious jungles of Adventureland or head into the rugged, untamed wilderness of Frontierland? Perhaps you'll be drawn straight ahead into the whimsical, storybook realms of Fantasyland. Alternatively, you might be tempted to turn right, toward the futuristic promise of Tomorrowland. The choice is entirely yours, for Walt believed in empowering his guests to create their own narratives, crafting a personal journey through the magic of Disneyland.

But Walt's trust extended far beyond his guests. He believed passionately in the people who brought the park to life every day: his team of "cast members." To Walt, they were not merely employees but performers in an elaborate show, each playing a crucial role in ensuring every guest's experience was unforgettable. Whether a janitor sweeping the streets, a baker crafting sweet delights, or a ride operator managing an attraction, every cast member was empowered to take responsibility for the happiness of the visitors they interacted with. This approach, which we now recognize in academic circles as "empowering leadership," emphasizes the importance of autonomy and self-management within teams. It encourages leaders to build confidence in their employees and foster their ability to make independent decisions. Empowering leadership creates an environment of trust, where team members feel encouraged to take on leadership roles themselves, driving the organization forward with their initiative and creativity.

Disneyland stands as a testament to the effectiveness of empowering leadership. Walt Disney's trust in his cast members allowed them to make real-time decisions that enhanced the guest experience, solidifying Disney's reputation for exceptional customer service. This legacy was built on Walt's belief that in the mind of the guest, every employee represented the company. "As well as I can, I'm untying the apron strings—until they scream for help," Walt would say, demonstrating his commitment to letting his team members exercise their judgment and creativity. To achieve similar success, gather the right people and train them well. Empower them to make magic, encourage them to create happiness, and trust them to amaze your guests, customers, and clients. If you don't trust your team to make decisions, then you need to make better decisions in choosing the right people. Empowerment isn't just a strategy; it's the foundation of building an exceptional organization that thrives on innovation and excellence.

Due to the abbreviated nature of today's tour, we only have time to visit one of the Magic Kingdom's themed lands. Let's head north, across the drawbridge, through the enchanting Sleeping Beauty Castle, and into the heart of the park: Fantasyland. This whimsical realm embodies Walt's vision of a place where "parents and children can have fun together." It also presents us with our fourth leadership lesson: the Acceptance of Accountability. Walt Disney aspired to be remembered as a master storyteller, and Fantasyland is the canvas upon which he painted his most imaginative tales. When the park first opened, the premier attractions were the original "dark rides" that are fortunately still found in Fantasyland today: Snow White's Adventures, Peter Pan's Flight, and Mr. Toad's Wild Ride. Each ride was crafted to evoke a specific emotion, immersing guests in a narrative journey. In Snow White, guests feel the thrill of fear and danger as they navigate a dark forest filled with lurking threats. Peter Pan takes riders soaring over moonlit London and into a world of awe and wonder. Meanwhile, Mr. Toad invites adventurers on a wild and comedic escapade through the English countryside.

On opening day, visitors were captivated by these stories and enchanted by these attractions. Yet, they were also baffled. Why? Because Walt had intentionally omitted the heroes and lead characters from these rides. He wanted the audience to be active participants rather than passive observers. There was no Snow White because *you* are Snow White. There was no Peter Pan because *you* get to be Peter Pan. *You* are Mr. Toad! For thirty years, guests visited Guest Services at Disneyland's City Hall with puzzled expressions, remarking and complaining, "I just rode Snow White; did you know she's not there?" Finally, in 1983, Fantasyland was "fixed" by incorporating the heroes and lead characters into these narratives.

Here is my challenge to you: Stop looking for a hero! As a leader, you must embrace the fourth lesson and accept accountability. You are the hero. No one else is coming. Identify what needs to be done and take action. Leaders are not only responsible for their actions but also for the culture they create. The best leaders foster a culture of empowerment and accountability. Research indicates that when leaders are accountable, they set a standard for the entire organization, promoting transparency and trust.[14] This environment encourages employees to take initiative, make decisions, and contribute more effectively to organizational goals. At Disneyland, Walt Disney exemplified this by cultivating a culture where every employee, or cast member,[15] is empowered and accountable for delivering a magical guest experience.

Throughout our tour, I hope you've been observant of a subtle yet profound detail unique to Disney—the name badges worn by every cast member. These badges, seemingly simple, carry only a first name and a hometown, eschewing formal titles and ranks. This small feature illuminates Walt Disney's distinctive approach to leadership. Walt Disney championed a culture of accessibility and familiarity, rejecting formalities that could distance him from his team. He insisted on being addressed simply as "Walt," a practice that embodied his empowering ethos. This was epitomized during an encounter recounted by Renie Bardeau, Disneyland's official photographer. While sharing coffee on Main Street, a nervous waitress approached to take their order, referring to him as "Mr. Disney." Walt's response was telling: "Young lady, there are only two misters in Disneyland, Mr. Lincoln and Mr. Toad. You can call me Walt."[16] This exchange highlights not only his approachable nature but also his intent to foster an environment where everyone stood on equal footing.

Walt Disney's leadership extended beyond personal interactions. He was a visionary who transformed his bold ideas into reality without waiting for external validation or instructions. His innovations began with synchronized sound in cartoons, as seen in *Steamboat Willie* (1928), and continued with the revolutionary *Snow White and the Seven Dwarfs* (1937), the first full-length animated feature film. His visionary spirit didn't stop at film: he reimagined the amusement park experience with Disneyland, ensuring it was a place where families could together create joyful memories. Even in his final days, he was planning EPCOT and "The Florida Project," envisioning a new type of community. His philosophy was clear: do not wait for permission to act. Leadership involves seeing what needs to be done and doing it. This ethos was evident in how he maintained the standards at Disneyland, often personally picking up litter to keep the park pristine. He believed in leading by example, setting a standard that every team member, regardless of their role, was expected to uphold.

As you consider your own life and leadership path, remember Walt's example. Leadership isn't about titles or waiting for directions: it's about our fifth lesson: Taking Initiative and Embodying the Change You Want to See. At Disneyland, this meant creating an environment where every cast member felt empowered to contribute to (what I call) "The Cleanest Place on Earth." Emulate Walt: start with small acts, like picking up trash, to demonstrate your commitment to your values and mission. By leading through example, you not only guide but also inspire your team to embody the principles of responsibility and proactive action, essential for any successful leader.

On my tours through Disneyland, a highlight is always a stop at Coke Corner at the very end of the west side of Main Street and right before Jolly Holiday. This spot might seem like just another charming corner of the park, but it holds a whimsical secret that embodies Disney's magic: the red-and-white lightbulb affectionately known as "Walt's Lightbulb." As we gaze upward, you'll notice a captivating array of alternating red and white lightbulbs. This pattern, however, faced a quirky challenge due to the asymmetrical architecture of the building—a mismatch that could disrupt the perfect alternation. Legend has it that this tiny imperfection was a thorn in Walt Disney's side. His solution? One quiet evening, Walt himself climbed a ladder with a paintbrush in hand and transformed the final, mismatched bulb into a half-red, half-white spectacle, thereby preserving the harmony of his beloved pattern.

This lightbulb isn't just a piece of decor; it's a testament to Walt's meticulous attention to detail and his insistence on maintaining the visual integrity of Disneyland's design. This story leads us to our sixth leadership lesson: Pay Attention to the Details. Was Walt Disney a genius? Undoubtedly. A visionary? Without question. Obsessive? Sure, some might say that. But Walt's commitment to the smallest details underscores a profound leadership principle: if you aren't fully invested in the vision and details of your projects, how can you expect others to be? Walt's hands-on approach wasn't just about aesthetics; it was about setting a standard of excellence that permeates every corner of Disneyland.

Each bulb on Main Street, each paint stroke on that infamous lightbulb, speaks to a larger ethos that Walt Disney instilled within his park: a relentless pursuit of perfection and a commitment to creating an immersive experience that delights every guest. As leaders, when we echo Walt's dedication to detail, we not only honor his legacy but also elevate our own endeavors to new heights of success and influence.

Next, as we prepare to exit Disneyland and make our way back down the nostalgic avenue of Main Street, U.S.A., let's pause for one final leadership lesson, a lesson etched into the architecture itself. Keep gazing upward at the second- and third-floor windows above the quaint shops and bustling restaurants. Here, each window serves as a tribute, adorned with the names of individuals, such as the aforementioned Renie Bardeau and John Hench, who played pivotal roles in the creation and life of Disneyland. These aren't just decorations; they're Walt's way of giving credit where it's due, a form of opening and closing credits that weave together the many stories that make Disneyland a reality. Consider these tribute windows as more than just names etched in glass. They are acknowledgments of hard work and dreams realized, a reminder that no grand vision is achieved alone. Walt Disney once said, "You can design, create, and build the most wonderful place in the world, but it takes people to make the dream a reality." This speaks to the core of our seventh and final leadership lesson: The Power of Consistent Encouragement and Recognition.

Ask yourself, who are the members of your team, that is, family, friends, colleagues, communities. When was the last time you truly acknowledged their contributions? It's not just about saying thank you; it's about making them feel seen and appreciated, ensuring they understand their vital role in the success of the collective endeavor. Your team needs to feel that their efforts are not just noticed but valued. This principle of acknowledgment isn't just a lesson; it's a call to action. Consistent encouragement fosters a strong, cohesive team. Remember, like Walt Disney, you have the potential to make a significant impact. Embrace the belief that it is possible to bring a touch of Disneyland's magic into everyday leadership. The real world might indeed be fraught with challenges, more mundane than magical, but the principles of visionary leadership can transform everyday hurdles into opportunities for growth and inspiration.

Drawing inspiration from Walt Disney's leadership, consider how you can bring a touch of Disneyland's magic into your everyday approach. The real world may not always seem magical, but the principles of visionary leadership can transform everyday challenges into opportunities for growth. Walt envisioned the park as a "live, breathing thing"[17]—a community vibrant with energy and driven by imagination. Its legacy, its personality, endures because it continues to inspire and engage all who visit. If you listen closely, the stories and history of Disneyland offer endless lessons on how to lead with vision, creativity, and, most importantly, a deep respect for the people who turn dreams into reality. So open your heart to the Wisdom of Walt and discover how his style of leadership can illuminate your path. And remember, you don't need Mickey

Mouse ears to see the magic—it's all around you, in the people you lead, the lives you influence, as well as the communities and classrooms you build.

Life Lessons from the Happiest Classroom on Earth

As you can see, Disneyland, "The Happiest Place on Earth," transcends its role as a theme park to serve as a dynamic classroom that redefines learning. This unique educational setting not only entertains but also deeply engages students of all ages, proving that fun and education are not mutually exclusive but rather complementary.

- Universal Appeal of Experiential Learning: Students have found that learning about Disneyland's history isn't just about acquiring facts but experiencing the story. This approach demonstrates how experiential learning can evoke strong emotional connections, making the educational process both memorable and impactful. Those who have participated in courses or tours focused on Disneyland often express a common sentiment: they wish such engaging educational experiences were more prevalent during their schooling.
- The Power of Engagement: Engagement is key in education, and Disneyland provides a perfect backdrop to explore this concept. Participants in educational programs set in Disneyland report a high level of engagement, not just with the material but with the environment itself. This heightened engagement facilitates a deeper connection to the learning objectives and fosters a dynamic educational experience that participants describe as unlike any other.
- Encouraging Words: Educators and leaders are reminded of the importance of acknowledgment and encouragement. Recognizing someone's effort and contribution can significantly boost their morale and performance. Just as Walt Disney created tribute windows to honor those who helped build his vision, educators and business leaders are encouraged to acknowledge the efforts of their teams regularly. Students are encouraged to take this lesson to heart by writing a note of thanks to a parent, expressing gratitude to faculty and mentors who have guided them, and offering support to their peers as they navigate their shared academic journey.
- A Call to Action: Consider how you can apply these principles in your own professional and personal development contexts. Whether you are an educator designing a course, a leader guiding a team, or someone curious about innovative educational practices, there is much to learn from the Disneyland model. It challenges us to make every learning opportunity engaging and impactful, to recognize and credit contributions, and to ensure that fun and seriousness are not seen as opposites, but as partners in successful education.

Student feedback from my own Disneyland course often reflects a profound appreciation for the innovative teaching methods that integrate history, art, physics, and engineering into a cohesive learning journey. For instance, multiple students have commented that the History of Disneyland isn't just the best history course they have ever taken but also the best course they've ever experienced in their entire academic journey. In another example, one student wrote that "I do not feel that I have learned AND RETAINED as much information as I did from this class." Student evaluations of my course reveal that participants were more interested, highly engaged, and able to see immediate real-world applications from the course content. The overwhelming positive response, from students, educators, and even a Board of Trustee member, highlights how such educational experiences can inspire and motivate learners to see their subjects in new lights.

Reflecting on my experiences as both an educator and a student, it is clear that Disneyland offers an unrivaled educational experience. During a memorable field trip, the profound impact of this unique learning environment became clear when a father—one of the family members invited to join the students on our Disneyland day—shared how the opportunity to explore Disneyland with his daughter made for their best day ever, highlighting the deep emotional resonance and transformative potential of learning in such a dynamic setting.

This narrative not only enriches the academic discourse around educational innovation but also invites readers to consider how they might create similarly impactful learning experiences in their own contexts, using Disneyland's model as a beacon of inspiration and engagement.

Walt's Legacy and Our Potential

In 1956, a year after Disneyland opened its gates, Walt returned to Marceline with his wife, Lilly, and his brother, Roy, along with Roy's wife, Edna. The small town of 3,172 people celebrated their hometown hero on July 4 by dedicating the new Walt Disney Municipal Park and Swimming Pool. During this visit, Walt revisited the two-story, red-bricked school he once attended. Amid a flurry of camera flashes, he squeezed into a small first-grade desk, showcasing the initials "WD" he had carved into the wood—a youthful act of rebellion that marked his early distaste for convention. This was more than a return; it was a reaffirmation of his roots and his journey.

Despite never receiving formal degrees, Walt Disney's education from the school of life led him to educate and entertain the world, leaving a legacy that extends far beyond any traditional academic accolades. His work transformed entertainment, creating a lasting impact on global culture and education. Walt Disney taught us that one need not be confined by traditional paths to make a significant impact. We are reminded that our actions, big and small, can ripple through generations.

As we reflect on Walt's journey, we must ask ourselves: What legacy do we aspire to leave? How can we bridge our past experiences with our hopes for the future? How do we want to be remembered?

So, as you step forward from this reading, think about the marks you leave on the lives you touch and the environments you inhabit. Consider how you can infuse your work, whatever it may be, with the magic of creativity and the joy of discovery. Walt Disney turned a dream into a destination that continues to inspire millions. With vision and dedication, what could you achieve that might similarly inspire others?

Each of us has the potential to be an edutainer—someone who educates and entertains, who inspires and informs. Make your mark by being an edutainer, by merging creativity with purpose, and by transforming everyday experiences into extraordinary memories. Let's make every day a little more like a day at Disneyland, filled with wonder, learning, and laughter.

Notes

1   David A. Kolb, *Experiential Learning: Experience as the Source of Learning and Development* (Englewood Cliffs: Prentice Hall, 1984), 38.
2   Maya Angelou, "People Will Forget What You Said, People Will Forget What You Did, But People Will Never Forget How You Made Them Feel," Chicago Bar Foundation, https://chicagobarfoundation.org/bobservations/people-remember -made-feel/ (accessed September 4, 2024).
3   John Dewey, *Experience and Education* (New York: Simon and Schuster, 1938), 25.
4   Adam Grant, *Think Again: The Power of Knowing What You Don't Know* (New York: Viking, 2021), 197.
5   Dave Smith, *The Quotable Walt Disney* (New York: Disney Editions, 2001), 18.
6   Ibid., 36.
7   Alan Bryman, *The Disneyization of Society* (London: Sage, 2004), 1.
8   Michael Fullan, *Stratosphere: Integrating Technology, Pedagogy, and Change Knowledge* (Toronto: Pearson Canada, 2012), 34.
9   Walt Disney, interview by Fletcher Markle, *Telescope*, Canadian Broadcasting Corporation, November 16, 1963.
10 Alan Bryman, *Disney and His Worlds* (London: Routledge, 1995), 2.
11 "Great Big Beautiful Tomorrow" is the song from Walt Disney's Carousel of Progress. It premiered at the 1964–5 World's Fair, opened at Disneyland in 1967, and then moved to Walt Disney World in 1975.
12 John Hench, *Designing Disney: Imagineering and the Art of the Show* (New York: Disney Editions, 2003).
13 Max Weber, *The Theory of Social and Economic Organization*, trans. A. M. Henderson and Talcott Parsons (New York: Free Press, 1947), 358.
14 Culture Partners, "The Importance of Accountability in Leadership: A Key to Organizational Success," *Culture Partners*, https://culturepartners.com/insights/ the-importance-of-accountability-in-leadership-a-key-to-organizational-success/ (accessed September 4, 2024).
15 Ibid.
16 Renie Bardeau, interview by Jim Korkis, "Renie Bardeau: The Man Who Shot Walt Disney," *MousePlanet*, https://mouseplanet.com/13086/Renie_Bardeau_The_Man _Who_Shot_Walt_Disney (accessed September 4, 2024).
17 The Walt Disney Family Museum, "Walt's Own Words: 'Plussing' Disneyland," *The Walt Disney Family Museum Blog*, https://www.waltdisney.org/blog/walts-own-words -plussing-disneyland (accessed September 4, 2024).

15

Wheelchairs, Magic Carpets, and a Community of Tomorrow

Constructing Disabled Utopia in the Disney Parks

Mason J. Shrader, Carol Mason Shrader, Benjamin Shrader

To explore disability together with Disney in a volume such as this may seem odd to those unfamiliar with the formal discipline of critical disability studies. After all, when the average American hears the term "disability," they more than likely will not think of a sociocultural phenomenon but rather of a purely physiological phenomenon. Critical disability scholars, however, argue that people's experience of disability is irreducible to merely physiological variance within individual bodies, and instead claim that the social and cultural interpretation surrounding that physiological variance must be considered to fully grasp disability. Broadly, this chapter draws from this articulation of disability and shows how a narrative of one family's experience within the Disney theme parks can be used as a case study to explore issues of the sociocultural construction of disability. More specifically, we argue that by setting the standard for accessibility throughout the parks and properties, Disney has created a space of community for families with disabilities that momentarily alleviates much of the sociocultural stigma faced by those families in the wider world, thus approximating something akin to what disability liberation activists identify as utopia.

Before we begin to expound upon that argument, however, we introduce the methodological and formal conceits of this chapter. To use Disney as an avenue to explore disability is not a novel concept, as there has been increasing scholarship in recent years that analyzes various Disney media such as films and television shows through the lens of disability studies.[1] While such media analysis has illustrated excellently some of the analytic potential which lies in the intersection of these two subjects, the discourses and representations of disability presented in media are only one aspect of the sociocultural construction of disability. There is more to be said than simply how sociocultural constructions of disability are produced and enforced, and it is crucial to consider how these constructions shape and structure the lives of the people they impact most. We have opted to discuss specifically the Disney theme parks because not only are they understudied in the scholarship surrounding Disney and disability, but the parks allow us to discuss disability from an experiential perspective that is lacking in the more traditional media analyses.

Disability studies have long recognized the importance of lived experience in the production of alternative academic knowledge, with much work drawing upon first-person narratives of disabled people and their families in order to showcase how disability is lived out through everyday lives, as a way to restore grounding a discussion too often abstracted. Drawing from first-person academic narratives such as the anthropological tradition of autoethnography—a cultural study in which the author themselves is self-reflexively a subject of analysis—these narratives serve as academic memoirs.[2] Memoirs allow for the exploration of subjects that could not otherwise be explored through more traditional methods and thus are uniquely suited to explore embodied experiences of disability.

As such, this chapter uses the academic memoir format to illustrate its larger argument about the Disney parks, through the first-hand lived experience of its authors, while also employing a more traditional academic format drawing from disability and anthropological theory to analyze the larger sociocultural constructs at play in those experiences. We have chosen to write this chapter from the collective perspective of our family—as two disabled brothers and one non-disabled mother—in order to illustrate how the social realities of disability are felt in different ways by people with different relationships to disability. Too often, non-disabled parents of disabled people have spoken over and on behalf of their children, limiting the ability to make disabled people's own perspectives heard. Here we offer a corrective by presenting the narrativized perspective of a disabled person alongside and in conversation with the narrativized perspective of a non-disabled mother. Thus, though the entirety of the chapter reflects the collective views and experiences of the three authors, the memoir section is written together by Benjamin—a disability rights activist trained in dramatic writing who has cerebral palsy (CP)—and Carol—a disability policy director trained in journalism. Their sections are presented in italicized text with headings to designate each authorial voice. The remaining sections are written by Mason—an anthropological archaeologist with CP who studies disability.

Memoir Narrative

Carol

Our trip to Walt Disney World was coming to a close when four-year-old Benjamin looked at us and declared that "Disney really is where dreams come true," confirming exactly what his dad and I had been feeling since the first day of the vacation.

The triplets—Benjamin, Mason, and Claire—were born three months prematurely. One year after receiving an official diagnosis of CP for Benjamin and Mason, Benjamin had his first orthopedic surgery. In the recovery room as he woke from anesthesia with two big leg casts, his dad, Wade, asked him what he needed and this sweet three-year-old replied, "To go to Walt Disney World."

Honestly, we weren't surprised by his answer. Wade and I honeymooned in Walt Disney World. Six years later, when Wade finished medical school, we wanted to celebrate as a family and so even though the triplets were barely two years old, we drove to Florida. We knew they didn't remember much about that trip, but it was enough to ensure the videos they watched on repeat were Disney movies, Disney Sing-Alongs, and Disney cartoons—most of which opened with picture-perfect ads for Walt Disney World.

So, over the next nine months while their parents scrimped and saved for a magical birthday trip, Benjamin and Mason worked in physical therapy multiple times a week learning how to use a reverse walker and cuff crutches (we called them "power sticks") respectively in order to "walk to Mickey Mouse."

Our first morning at Walt Disney World, we had breakfast at Cinderella's Royal Table. Claire, the triplet without CP, could not wait to meet her favorite princess! We were all surprised and thrilled to meet Belle, Mary Poppins, and Aladdin. The movie Aladdin *was Benjamin's current favorite, and he had already told us he wanted an Aladdin's lamp as a souvenir. Wade and I were concerned about finding souvenirs from a nine-year-old movie, but we didn't want to upset him. When Aladdin sat down on the floor of the restaurant with Benjamin in his lap, Benjamin told him he loved him and how much he wanted a lamp. Aladdin left our table only to return a few minutes later to assure Benjamin that at some point in the trip a magic lamp would appear.*

I was already teary-eyed. How did this young man know to sit and hold my son, who could not stand up on his own, who had been in a highchair but desperately wanted to be closer to his hero? The trip could have ended right there. We would have been hooked on Disney forever. Our hearts would have felt the balm of someone seeing and caring for our child. It would have been enough. But the trip didn't end there.

Cinderella had torn her dress that morning and did not actually appear for our breakfast. We were given a pass to return later in the day for photos with her. As we entered the castle that afternoon, the line was long to see her. A few families motioned us—a mom, dad, little girl in her Cinderella-best, one boy in a little walker, and one with power sticks—to cut the line in front of them. Wade and I shook our heads—we were grateful but were just fine waiting in line. Just a few years into this road as a family with disabilities, Wade and I were still learning to navigate. We thought blending in was the answer. We worked for just that and so standing in line like all the other preschoolers was just fine . . . right until Cinderella's Fairy Godmother spotted us and waved her magic wand at the crowd. Everyone in the crowd turned to look at us and, without a word, every single family moved to the side and waved us forward. I can hardly type the words for crying all these years later. The gesture spoke to me at the very deepest of levels as it demonstrated a goodness in humankind—at least on Disney property—in seeing my children and showing them care. It was in that moment that I realized blending in was not only impossible, but it would rob others of seeing, knowing, and yes, showing kindness to my children. As a family, we had yet to experience all the hard things that must be faced. But we had also not had the opportunity to recognize the beauty. A little Disney magic changed that.

We returned late that evening to find our hotel room filled with Aladdin toys: a lamp with a Genie for Benjamin, stuffed Genies for Mason and Claire, notepads, and a myriad of other items. We were greeted in the parade later that week by friends of Aladdin who recognized the triplets as Aladdin's special friends and wanted to speak to them. And we were given a private meet-and-greet with this now-hero of the entire family in his parade costume!

Our last morning, we checked in at Chef Mickey's Restaurant for our final breakfast. The host told me that our wish would come true. I remember smiling at the clever way they said they had our reservation. But then, the manager came to our table to ask permission to film our "wish." Unbeknownst to us, the boys' physical therapists had contacted Walt Disney World to alert them to the work Benjamin and Mason had been doing in therapy. They were prepared for us.

Goofy was sent to block traffic so no other children could get to Mickey Mouse. A film crew, a photographer, and Wade and I stood watching as all three of our children were told they could walk to Mickey. And then we watched Benjamin, Mason, and Claire walk to Mickey again because no one was expecting the boys—and their sister—to RUN to their favorite mouse. By the time we returned to our room, a printed book of photos and a video of what four-year-old Benjamin called "our dreams coming true" were waiting for us.

Subsequent trips provided additional magic—accompanying Aladdin on his newly opened Magic Carpet Ride, meeting Tarzan and the stars of the "Tarzan Rocks!" stage show behind the scenes, being interviewed for an internal video for Walt Disney Imagineering. But we didn't look for or seek out any of those special experiences, and in many ways, the experiences that were the most magical had less to do with the efforts of official Disney cast members and more to do with the experience of Disney.

Benjamin

Even before I was old enough to put it into words, seeing people who were also in wheelchairs or who walked with walkers was an earth-shattering moment. Mason was the only other disabled person I had ever spent time with until at Disney I sat in accessible viewing sections waiting for parades, shows, or alternative ride entrances and exits. The idea that there was a whole community of people like me was something I had no frame of reference for prior to Disney. It filled me with immense curiosity. There were people using wheelchairs who had jobs and families of their own? It was a complete shifting of my paradigm. But these experiences went beyond just seeing other disabled people. We made friends.

In order to secure the most ideal viewing for the nighttime show Fantasmic! *we always arrive as soon as the rope drops for entry, leaving us to wait in the accessible section of the amphitheater for at least an hour or sometimes two. It is in this waiting that I meet people often older and further in their disability journey. As conversations were struck and friendships formed—some we correspond with still—I was given a glimpse into a future for myself. The vast majority of my ways of connecting with the larger disabled community these days is through social media, because it is so difficult to guarantee any physical space will be accessible for us all. Disney guaranteed us that space, and because of it, I found disabled community in real-life, face-to-face interactions. The magic of finding solidarity and being overwhelmed with the amount of possibility and optimism therein was and is in many ways a greater, more lasting act of magic than any character or show.*

In most other areas of my life, what I can't do vastly outweighs what I can. But at the Disney parks, this equation is completely reversed. The late Judith Heumann, a fierce advocate for disability rights, once said that "disability only becomes a tragedy when society fails to provide the things we need to lead our lives."³ While no experience of this scale is perfect, the Disney parks are a place where the gap between the ambition and reality of that quote is much smaller.

Carol

My hesitancy to join a support group was mainly driven by the fact that finding time available for one, in the midst of raising triplets, was more than impossible. So, I was not prepared for the solidarity I would find waiting in the accessible viewing locations with other families. Initially, it was just a nod—a nod packed with understanding—to another mother standing behind her son's wheelchair. And then the longer we waited, small conversations would ensue: sharing tips for keeping our children cool in the intense Florida heat, sharing rainy day strategies, discussing the wheelchair entrance at our various locations. The families with adult children had a tremendous impact on us. We found comfort in their older children still enjoying the parks, yes, but really felt so fortunate to have a glimpse into adulthood and how we might expect future trips—and perhaps life—to look.

Long before I had heard this quote by Ms. Heumann that Benjamin shared above, I recognized the value in seeing all my children included, able to participate, and being told YES instead of "we're sorry" or even "Oh, we never thought about all these stairs." I recognized the lightness we felt in the Disney parks was less about the thrill of the rides and very much connected to the lack of obstacles allowing Benjamin and Mason to participate, to be included, to just have fun. The fun was accessible. The magic was in the design. The thrill was in the inclusion.

As a family, we often had to watch from the sidelines while other families climbed in backyard playhouses, hiked nature parks, and biked through the neighborhood. We drove by little league fields without a way to participate. We had scout troops refuse admission because of our disabilities. We were excluded from birthday parties with rock walls, bounce houses, and trampoline parks. We dealt with playground equipment that wasn't accessible, recess activities that were not inclusive, and even had one school where the door to get back inside was not automated—so not possible for a young boy with CP to open. But at the Disney parks, access is a priority. The road had seemingly been paved with us in mind.

Perhaps not literally paved for us. There are certainly instances of lawsuits surrounding accessibility in the parks. But in a world where access and entry can be a struggle in the most surprising of places—churches, schools, medical offices—the ease with which Benjamin and Mason navigate Walt Disney World is a balm to our exhausted souls.

Benjamin

I will never forget how excited I was when I saw the accessible vehicle for Toy Story Mania. Not only could I stay in my wheelchair for the ride, but the accessible car has a button to make participating in the games easy for me. I felt as if Disney had designed it specifically with me in mind. The same goes for the accessible vehicles in rides like Ariel's Undersea Adventure, Remy's Ratatouille Adventure, and it's a small world.

Even on certain rides that require me to transfer from my chair, such as Disneyland's Space Mountain, the loading space accommodates me by sliding over and out of the main track, so that my family can take their time loading (and unloading) me for the ride. When we are ready, our car slides back onto the main line. The cast members make it fun as well. I often enjoy my own back and forth with the skippers of the Jungle Cruise since I am the first to load the accessible boat and the last to leave. They often have jokes prepared specifically about the long process of lowering/raising me and my wheelchair from the dock down into the boat. It makes what would otherwise be a tedious process part of the ride experience. These touches may not seem like much, but to a family who is often told no, they are profound.

Carol

To be perfectly honest, typing our stories about the magic leaves me equal parts teary-eyed and exhausted. Because even as finding access is a balm to our souls, ensuring our children can experience that magic is extremely labor-intensive. In the early days before the boys were using wheelchairs to navigate the parks, we pushed them in a double stroller. The designated stroller parking areas for each ride meant we were unloading the boys and carrying them. One particular day, the stroller park for the Pirates of the Caribbean ride was overflowing, and I had passed exhaustion hours prior. I tried to just leave the stroller closer to the entrance, only to be severely reprimanded by a cast member. I reacted in what can only be described as a crying, angry plea for him to help us. He did not. I still don't choose to ride Pirates in Walt Disney World more than twenty years later.

Loading the buses between resorts also proved taxing in those days. Buses required the stroller to be folded, so it required one of us to hold two boys while the other one folded and carried the stroller, all while keeping up with the triplet sister.

And as they grew, most of the rides did not have an accessible vehicle where Benjamin can drive his chair and still experience the thrill. Rather, we have to lift him, secure him, and then wedge him between us when possible, so that he can remain upright. Or, in the case of one of his favorite rides, Big Thunder Mountain, hold him from losing a shoe at best, to jostling off the seat at worst, as we are slung from side to side on the run-away mine train in the wildest ride in the wilderness.

Benjamin

As much as I love to experience the quality of artistry on display at various attractions, there are times when that desire clashes with the very real limitations of my body. Certain rides require both my parents to work collaboratively to lift me, and the result can often lead to uncomfortable—painful even—positioning. This reality has led me to create a kind of "economy of risk" where I assess the level of risk for discomfort in a given ride with my love for the artistic merits of the ride. Therefore, some rides that I historically loved—such as Disneyland's Matterhorn Bobsleds—simply do not meet the proper ratio within my economy of risk. It saddens me greatly to not be able to ride some childhood favorites, but it is necessary to recognize my body and its limits.

Carol

By the time the triplets were in first grade, I had learned the necessity of fighting for my boys. I had fought with school administrators who told me my boys would burden their school staff. I had fought with teachers for the accommodations they required to succeed in school. And I had fought with the leaders of the PTO because they refused to support efforts to build an accessible playground.

Our time in the Disney parks was a stark contrast. Not only were we assured of access to the resorts and the restaurants, but there were always cast members standing by to ensure the boys could experience attractions in the same manner as their sister. And sometimes, something magical occurred: seeing our Aladdin, for instance, a year after he had given Benjamin his magic lamp. Aladdin's eyes lit up as he recognized the triplets immediately. He scooped Benjamin up for a hug and then told us he had to fly to Agrabah the next day but would love to spend time with us before then. He asked if we could meet him at his brand-new Magic Carpet Ride attraction.

Loading the carpet with Aladdin, I was overwhelmed with the thought that, yes, there would be times in the lives of our boys where they had to sit on the sidelines and watch. But not here. Not at Disney. And sometimes, their CP would open doors to literal magic.

Theoretical Analysis

Let us begin this analysis where Carol ended her narrative: with a discussion of magic. A great deal has been written in Disney studies about how the Disney parks facilitate what the Walt Disney Company calls magic. Many scholars have discussed how the secluded environment and immersive-themed architecture of the parks function as a religious pilgrimage site, and others have written about how the discursive themes exposed by Disney park attractions serve to teach guests to believe in magic.[4] Such experiences of Disney magic have been functionally explained as contributing to the role of the parks as a simulacrum of reality: an idyllic alternative world into which guests can escape the quotidian mundanities of the real world. It has largely been through this escapist framing that scholars have referred to the parks as utopic.[5] While this is certainly true in many respects, the magic showcased in Benjamin and

Carol's narrative is something far more particular: the experiences generated at the Disney parks allowed our family to briefly inhabit a utopia specifically in reference to disability.

To understand how the parks can function as a disabled utopia, it is necessary to define what will constitute "disabled" and "utopic" in the context of this chapter, beginning with the latter. As alluded to in the introduction, disability studies scholars locate disability within the varied interplay of two factors: the physiological conditions of people's bodies—sometimes called impairment—with the social stigmas, stereotypes, and interpretations of that impairment in a given sociocultural context. To the critical disability studies scholar, then, CP is not disabling merely because it impairs muscular function: it is disabling because it exists in a social context which does not adequately care for and accommodate that impairment. There is some debate among disability theorists regarding the relationship between impairment and disability, with some arguing that the locus of disablement is placed entirely in the social world with nothing inherently disabling about any physiological impairment, while others argue that impairment must be considered disabling alongside these social factors.[6] Regardless of where one positions oneself in this theoretical debate, the field agrees that disability is, to some degree, socially conditioned and constructed.

From here, we can begin to understand the utopic. Disability liberation activists draw on a social understanding of disability to form their political goals, arguing that since so much of disability is socially constructed, it is also socially mutable. They therefore organize around a goal of abolishing the social conditions of disability, thus working toward constructing a utopia for people with disabilities.[7] We argue that it is this notion of utopia which the Disney parks approximate, as the parks become spaces where our disabilities do not hold the same negative social meanings that they so often do in the wider world. Here, we speak in terms of approximation for two reasons: first, because, as we will note in the conclusion of this chapter, Disney's utopia is politically limited definitionally through its existence within a multibillion-dollar corporation. Second—as Benjamin and Carol note—the utopia of the parks is a qualified one. For all the ways in which the parks are liberatory for us, they are still quite difficult to navigate, with miles of walking and rides requiring a risk/benefit analysis. This underscores our fundamental departure from the escapist utopias of leisure which have been previously discussed in scholarship. Our family goes to the parks not because it is a relaxing place of escape where the concerns of our impairment evaporate. Rather, we go because it is the closest approximation available to us of a world which consciously accommodates and cares for us. This approximation is the magic of the parks. This magic is achieved, we argue, primarily through performative labor and designed material spaces of inclusion.

Performative Labor, Care, and Spaces of Cultural Reproduction

Foundational Disney scholar Alan Bryman noted that one of the main ways Disney theme parks generate a sense of magic is through fastidiously trained cast members engaging in a form of labor wherein every employee, from character actors to food service workers to custodial staff, adopts a specific affective persona like a theatrical performance.[8] Once again, these performances—at their most basic level—can be read as adding to the immersive properties of the theme parks by giving guests a sense of heightened reality, generating the feeling of magic. When the host of Chef Mickey's came to our table and announced that we would be able to walk to Mickey, he could have stated it simply, but instead he assumed the specific heightened language of Disney magic: "your wish has been granted." Yet, in the specific context of disability presented above, the labor done by these cast members achieved far more than simply contributing to theatrical immersion: it provided care.

The Jungle Cruise skippers joking with Benjamin while helping him load the ride vehicle or Aladdin immediately knowing to sit and hold him were just as much part of the performative labor as the elevated language of wishes being granted. Moreover, these were significant to Benjamin and Carol because it is exceedingly rare for non-disabled people to recognize the needs of disabled people and so quickly move to meet those needs. Every disabled person knows what it feels like to have to fight for basic accommodation because we are forced to do it in so many settings. As Benjamin and Carol both noted, we fight for learning accommodations in the classroom, fight for access to healthcare in hospitals, and fight for the basic ability to enter the places we live and work every day. At its most basic level, this is a type of ableism which functions through a denial of what biological and medical anthropologists often discuss as social networks of care. While healthcare is popularly understood as solely within formal and institutionalized medicine, the anthropological understanding of care recognizes that formalized healthcare is not the only factor which enables a healthy and thriving life.[9] From upbringing in kinship structures to labor at every point on the supply chain, we are all enabled to live through the interdependent assistance, work, and accommodation of others around us. While this social interdependency is a simple fact of living which all humans experience, not all of us are granted equal levels of care. The lack of accommodation from society at large—as Benjamin and Carol spoke about—speaks to the very specific denial of care which disabled people so often experience. This is all due to the fact that the status quo of neoliberal capitalist societies is an able-bodied one.

Paradoxically, it is exactly these ableist notions which make the performative labor at Disney so magical by contrast. Where basic accommodation was a fight in the outside world, in Disney World, Aladdin knew immediately how to interact with Benjamin. Where the extra time and energy needed to help Benjamin load a vehicle may be seen as a chore to cab and bus drivers in so many cities—if accessible transportation is even available at all—to the Jungle Cruise skippers, loading someone on their readily available accessible vehicle was just another opportunity to make a guest laugh. The performance of the cast members is still part of the general theatrical affect being conveyed in the parks, but it also becomes an act of care, whereby cast members recognize a need and willingly meet it. The performative labor is care and care is the magic.

This magic extends to the very design of the parks as well. Much has been written about the meticulously constructed landscape of the parks and the various ways Disney intentionally uses space and what its Imagineers term "environmental storytelling" to convey its themes and immerse guests in an affective mood.[10] Benjamin and Carol's narrative invites us to go further with this notion and see how the park's spaces are intentionally constructed not only to be immersive and affective, but also accessible. The guaranteed designated seating areas for shows, the ability for Benjamin to ride attractions without transferring from his wheelchair, even the simple assurance of access to all the resorts and restaurants all serve as testament to the fact that even beyond the performance of the cast members, the parks' physical space serves as a form of accommodation and care. In the parks, our needs are met simply because the space we are inhabiting is accessible.

The significance of these accessible spaces extends even beyond care. For instance, Benjamin and Carol note that part of the magic of early Disney experiences involved meeting other families with disabilities. Engaging with others like our family—in various stages of life—taught our family what to expect of our lives and the ways to navigate it from people who already had experience. This kind of teaching is a form of what social scientists broadly refer to as cultural reproduction. Originating from sociologist Pierre Bourdieu's articulation of the subject, cultural reproduction is the passing down of shared knowledge, norms, and values from one generation to the next.[11] Archaeologists frequently discuss the ways in which physically constructed spaces can aid in cultural reproduction, with regularly cited examples being how large open spaces found in churches, temples, and mosques provide space where collective behavior can be observed and replicated.[12] Similarly, the accessible queues and seating sections of the Disney parks became for Benjamin and Carol culturally reproductive spaces in which they were taught shared knowledge from the larger disabled subculture. As Benjamin notes, the physicality of the space is in stark contrast to the online space in which he usually engages with that subculture, and is yet another way in which the Disney parks seem utopic in contrast to wider society.

Compulsory Able-Bodiedness and the Disability as Good-Difference

Thus far, we have illustrated how the significance of the Disney parks as a disabled utopia lies in their juxtaposition with a largely inaccessible world. It should be noted, however, that this Disney magic does not provide just an escape from ableism but also transforms perceptions of disability itself, as seen in Carol's narrative. She notes that during their first trip, she felt the need to "blend in." Scholars of crip theory—the intersection between disability theory and queer theory—note that this need to be perceived as normal is a widespread phenomenon in neoliberal society. Crip theorist Robert McRuer identifies the structural force behind this need as "compulsory able-bodiedness": much like how the mores of heteronormativity impose upon people the assumption that cisgendered heterosexuality is the "norm" and every other gender and sexual identity is a "deviation," so too does compulsory able-bodiedness impose an able-bodied norm.[13] Carol wanted to blend in to be perceived as less different, more normal, and thus more able-bodied because of the pressure compulsory able-bodiedness puts on disabled people and their families. Yet, with a wave of her magic wand, the Fairy Godmother not only took away that pressure but also transformed Carol's entire perception of disability.

Philosopher of disability Elizabeth Barnes categorizes notions of disability into three broad responses to difference, with "bad-difference" being the notion that disability is a difference that makes a person lesser, "mere-difference" being the notion that disability is but one of many value-neutral variations in humanity, and "good-difference" being the notion that disability is a difference that actually makes a person better, akin to a superpower. Barnes calls this third notion of disability the "Magneto view of disability," after the mutant revolutionary in Marvel Comics who considers mutants superior to humans.[14] While disability studies scholars may be skeptical of someone actually adhering to the Magneto model, Carol's narrative showcases how transformative the Disney parks were to her perception of disability. When Carol says she "realized blending in was not only impossible, but it would rob others of seeing, knowing, and yes, showing kindness to my children," she was experiencing my and Benjamin's disability as "good-difference," asserting that our disability actually produced a kind of net positive in the world. Here she was able to feel free from compulsory able-bodiedness and see disability not as something to be diminished by blending in but openly embraced. To Carol, the performative labor of the Fairy Godmother became a moral exemplar for the rest of the people in line, catalyzed by our disabilities. We thus—in Carol's eyes—became participants in the production of the magic for everyone else watching.

The Spectacle of Disability, Handicapitalism, and the Limitations of Disney's Utopia

While we have thus far spoken of the park's liberatory potential as something monolithically achieved by "Disney," we would like to close by acknowledging the contradictions inherent in the production of this utopic approximation. Like all capitalistic entities, the Walt Disney Company as a corporation has fundamentally different motivations than the laborers who produce for the corporation. This contradiction is perhaps most apparent in an episode of the Disney+ show *Behind The Attraction*—a show produced by Disney to show how their theme park attractions were built—which discusses the various themed transportation systems within the theme parks. While discussing California Adventure's trolley car themed after the turn-of-the-century Pacific Electric Railway trolleys, Imagineer and trolley designer Ray Spencer tells the viewer:

The ADA requirements to get a wheelchair in was a huge engineering challenge. One night, I was at California Adventure, and there's a ten-year-old boy in a wheelchair. And you could tell he'd been in the wheelchair for his entire life. He knew everything about the Pacific Electric railroad. And he was so excited and enthusiastic. And they put the conductor's cap on him. He blew the whistle. He was ringing the bell. The windows were open in the front. His mom was out in front, taking pictures with tears streaming down her face. And I was crying. Because I thought that's why, as Imagineers, we do the stuff that we do. It's for our guests and for people to be supported and loved through their experience. That probably was the most meaningful, important day of my life in Imagineering.[15]

Here, Spencer echoes with seemingly genuine conviction much of our overall argument by saying that Imagineers, as laborers who design the parks, do so because they want people to "be supported and loved." Undoubtedly, many of the cast members who helped and cared for our family in the narrative felt similarly, and through their genuine compassion and labor made our experience magical. Yet, when this quote is viewed in its context as part of official promotional material for the parks, one begins to see the different impetus within the corporation. Through this segment, the company consciously showcases their attention to access as a deeply meaningful magical moment for both the guest and the magic makers. Disney is thus turning disability into a spectacle through what activists call "inspiration porn," wherein the audience is moved to inspiration because a disabled person is able to achieve or access something in spite of their disability.[16] Fundamentally, these stories use the disabled person as a one-dimensional prop to achieve the desired affect within the audience. By placing such a scene in a product which essentially functions as an advertisement for the parks, Disney is utilizing a representation of disability as a feel-good moment to reinforce the design of the parks as thoughtful, caring, and meaningful in the mind of its audience. This same logic can be applied to many of the stories shared in the narrative above. While the Fairy Godmother parting the crowd for us to see Cinderella gave Carol the language to overcome her own struggle with compulsory able-bodiedness, it also—regardless of the intent of the cast member—functionally turned our disabilities into spectacles by which the company showcased its supposed values of kindness and benevolence to the rest of its guests. These values undoubtedly gave ideological reassurance to those guests that Disney was a worthwhile company to continue to purchase and consume from. Because as utopic as the parks may seem, their fundamental distinction from the utopia of disabled liberation is the corporate motivating factor of profit, which subsumes any more altruistic motive the parks' laborers may have. These utopic attributes, for the Walt Disney Company, function to simply make their parks more appealing to a specific demographic of consumers, in what the Marxist disability theorist Marta Russel refers to as "handicapitalism."[17] Russel notes that companies may seem to progress toward greater disabled inclusion but definitionally are limited because profit is the ultimate motivation of that progress, not liberation.

The limitations of Disney's handicapitalistic utopia can be seen in the parks' recent rising prices. As Disney continues to raise prices which outpace inflation, they in turn are pricing out much of the disabled demographic. CP, due to its correlation with traumatic births, is also correlated with lower socioeconomic levels; thus, a large portion of families with CP are becoming less likely to be able to afford access to the

Disney parks as the prices go up.[18] The disabled utopia of the parks then—as magical as it can be—is sequestered behind an increasingly large paywall, which specifically excludes disabled people themselves.

Carol

A neighbor once commented on the frequency with which we vacation in a Disney park, noting that his family could not financially afford the luxury. I gently reminded him that his family paid for four children to play a myriad of sports, as well as paid for a multitude of lessons, uniforms, and gear. He paid for participation his way, while we found participation, inclusion, and experience in the one place we could be certain to find it: Walt Disney World.

Benjamin

The very first thing Walt Disney said on the opening day of Disneyland in 1955 was, "To all who come to this happy place, welcome." As corny as it may sound, that line has always stuck with me because of how rare it is. How often do we see a place that is truly welcoming to all? Whenever I find myself in a building without automatic doors, or at a street corner without a ramp on its sidewalk, I'm reminded that people have built this world without thinking of "all" and without valuing the experiences of "all." It is very meaningful to me that Disney chose to begin with that word. Whether he intended it or not, it speaks to something I find profoundly needed and depressingly lacking in much of society. A sort of radical kindness and boundless compassion, which, when we act on it, becomes its own form of magic.

As one can see, our family has celebrated and continues to celebrate the alleviation the Disney parks offer, but we also recognize the severe limitations of that alleviation. The Marxist political philosopher of utopia, Ernst Bloch, spoke of seeking the utopic in the quotidian relations of everyday life, prompting us to look for the radicality Benjamin spoke of in the potentialities all around us.[19] Perhaps then, we should ask ourselves why we are content to build utopic communities in fantasy lands rather than taking the lessons of this magical access and making it available to everyone always.

Notes

1   For examples of media analysis, see Johnson Cheu, *Diversity in Disney Films: Critical Essays on Race, Ethnicity, Gender, Sexuality and Disability* (Jefferson: McFarland, 2013) and Jeanne Holcomb and Kenzie Latham-Mintus, "Disney and Disability: Media Representations of Disability in Disney and Pixar Animated Films," *Disability Studies Quarterly* 42, no. 1 (2022): 1–21..

2 See Rosemarie Garland-Thomson, "Shape Structures Story: Fresh and Feisty Stories about Disability," *Narrative* 15, no. 1 (2007): 113–23, for this format's relevance to disability studies. For examples, see Anjali J. Forber-Pratt, "'You're Going to Do What?' Challenges of Autoethnography in the Academy," *Qualitative Inquiry* 21, no. 9 (November 1, 2015): 821–35 and Debby Sneed and Mason J. Shrader, "Digging While Impaired: Promoting the Accessibility of Archaeology as a Discipline," in *Archaeological Ethics in Practice*, ed. Sarah Lepinski and Sarah Kielt Costello, Annual of ASOR Series (Alexandria: American Society of Overseas Research, 2024), 51–67.

3 Joseph Shapiro, "Activist Judy Heumann Led a Reimagining of What It Means to Be Disabled," *NPR*, March 4, 2023, sec. Obituaries, https://www.npr.org/2023/03/04/1161169017/disability-activist-judy-heumann-dead-75.

4 For the Disney parks as religious site, see Alexander Moore, "Walt Disney World: Bounded Ritual Space and the Playful Pilgrimage Center," *Anthropological Quarterly* 53, no. 4 (1980), 207–218 and William Arnal, "The Segregation of Social Desire: 'Religion' and Disney World," *Journal of the American Academy of Religion* 69, no. 1 (2001): 1–19.

5 For a discussion of utopia, Baudrillard's simulacra, and Jameson's analysis of post-modernism vis-a-vis the Disney parks, see Stephen M. Fjellman, *Vinyl Leaves: Walt Disney World and America* (New York: Routledge, 2018).

6 The former position is typically characterized as the "social model of disability." For an overview of this position, see Elizabeth Barnes, *The Minority Body: A Theory of Disability*, First edition, Studies in Feminist Philosophy (Oxford: Oxford University Press, 2016). The latter position has a wide array of articulations, but perhaps the most influential is the "interactionalist model of disability" in Tom Shakespeare, *Disability Rights and Wrongs Revisited* (Routledge, 2014).

7 Paul Abberley, "Work, Utopia and Impairment," in *Disability and Society: Emerging Issues and Insights*, ed. Len Barton, Longman Sociology Series (New York: Routledge, 2014), 61–82; Arianna Introna, "Pandemic Lived Experience, Crip Utopias, and Dismodernist Revolutions: For a More-Than-Social Model of Disability," *Social Inclusion* 11, no. 1 (2022): 1-10; and Charles Masquelier, *Intersectional Socialism: A Utopia for Radical Interdependence* (Bristol: Bristol University Press, 2023).

8 Alan Bryman, *The Disneyization of Society*, Reprint (London: SAGE Publications, 2008), 103–30.

9 See Lorna Tilley, *Theory and Practice in the Bioarchaeology of Care, Theory and Practice in the Bioarchaeology of Care* (London: Springer International Publishing, 2015) for an overview of the anthropological approach to care.

10 For how the Disney parks construct narratives through environmental storytelling, see Henry Jenkins, "Narrative Spaces," in *Space Time Play: Computer Games, Architecture and Urbanism, the Next Level*, ed. Friedrich von Borries, Steffen P. Walz, and Matthias Böttger (Basel: Birkhäuser, 2007), 56–60.

11 Pierre Bourdieu, "Cultural Reproduction and Social Reproduction," in *Knowledge, Education, and Cultural Change* ed, Richard Brown (London: Routledge, 1973), 71–112.

12 See Ruth M. Van Dyke and Susan E. Alcock, "Archaeologies of Memory: An Introduction," in *Archaeologies of Memory*, eds. Ruth M. Van Dyke and Susan E. Alcock (Malden: Blackwell, 2003), 1–13 for an overview of space and cultural reproduction.

13   Robert McRuer, *Crip Theory: Cultural Signs of Queerness and Disability*, Cultural Front (New York: New York University Press, 2006).

14   Barnes, *The Minority Body*, 69.

15   Season 1, Episode 9.

16   For a discussion of inspiration porn, see Beth Haller and Jeffery Preston, "Confirming Normalcy: 'Inspiration Porn' and the Construction of the Disabled Subject?" in *Disability and Social Media,* eds. Katie Ellis and Mike Kent (New York: Routledge, 2016), 41–56.

17   Marta Russell, *Capitalism and Disability: Selected Writings by Marta Russel*, ed. Keith Rosenthal (Chicago: Haymarket Books, 2019).

18   For epidemiological analysis of CP, see Maureen S. Durkin et al., "The Role of Socio-Economic Status and Perinatal Factors in Racial Disparities in the Risk of Cerebral Palsy," *Developmental Medicine and Child Neurology* 57, no. 9 (2015): 834–843.

19   Ernst Bloch, *Atheism in Christianity: The Religion of the Exodus and the Kingdom,* trans. J. T. Swann (New York: Verso, 2009); for an overview of Bloch's thought, see Jonathan Greenaway, *A Primer on Utopian Philosophy: An Introduction to the Work of Ernst Bloch* (London: Zero Books, 2024).

Takeaways

We want readers to experience Disney magic as learners. The following takeaways from our expert educators and contributors help you turn Disney into your own "laboratory for learning."

Takeaways and Tips for the General Reader

- Active participation rather than passive viewership is a strategy not just for Disney parks but for life (Cher Krause Knight).
- Disney spaces teach us more about ourselves in the present than they do about the past. How we choose to remember is representative of who we are (Bethanee Bemis).
- Watch the four-hour PBS documentary on the life of Walt Disney. It's called *American Experience: Walt Disney*. Then watch the History Channel's *How Disney Built America* series (Christopher Tremblay).
- Disney stories give us references for our reactions to real life: Simba's loss of his father and guilt about it; Elsa's fear of her hidden powers; Moana's desire to leave her safe home. These are stages all of us have gone through or that lie ahead. They reflect essential human experience (Bonnie Rudner).
- Pay attention to how queues are organized and moved. When you are standing in line to enter an attraction, note all the ways that Disney keeps your mind off the fact that you are waiting. These include shows and bands as well as interactive components to the queue. Don't rush through the line! Half the experience is the build-up to the attraction itself (Gary Kaskowitz).
- In 2023, as part of the Disney100 Years of Wonder celebration at Disneyland, a photo of a statue of Mickey Mouse was posted with the widely circulated but incorrect Walt Disney quote that the company he had founded had "all started *with* a mouse." The actual statement was, "I hope that we never lose sight of one thing . . . that it was all started *by* a mouse." For Disney, the mouse was the bearer of creative knowledge that is at the heart of the company. Many of you, who have visited Disney's Adventureland, rode on the Jungle Cruise attraction, or toured Disney's Animal Kingdom theme park might have wondered about their origins. Think about all the animals and plants that inhabit Disney's theme parks, films, and television shows. How did Disney's love of animals and nature shape your entire Disney experience? And why are so few of us aware that Walt Disney was a vocal animal lover and a wildlife conservationist? How does this image of Disney conflict with the ones that you have? And why? (Sarah Nilsen)
- Disney is fun, but it's also a space of unconscious learning. The first image your mind conjures of the American frontier is very likely to be based on something you either experienced at a Disney Park or saw in a Disney film (Bethanee Bemis).

- It is important to take the seemingly frivolous things like theme parks seriously, for the inane is where people process, make meaning of, and register seismic historical shifts through their everyday lived experience. Additionally, the parks demonstrate how the historical discipline is one of refinement of questions and interpretations (Alex Hofmann).
- Fairy tales are our earliest references for poetic justice, true love, and the way we wish the world worked. We use expressions like "Cinderella" stories for sports teams, dark horse candidates, and any number of real-life experiences (Bonnie Rudner).
- Remember that Walt Disney World employees (called cast members) are part of the show! Be sure to interact with as many cast members as you can (on attractions, at the food centers and gift shops, or just walking around). Pay special attention to their name tags. You will see their first name and then a hometown. This is designed to build familiarity and bonding. If you see a college name instead of a hometown, then this cast member is a college student on an internship at Walt Disney World. Be sure to talk to them and ask them about their experiences! (Gary Kaskowitz)
- Reflect on your favorite aspects of the Walt Disney Company and ask the following questions: (1) What is this trying to teach me? (2) What are the hidden lessons in my Disney favorites? (3) If I were a student of the magical curriculum associated with the Disney products I consume, what would I be learning? (Gabriel Huddleston, Blake Lentz, Nicole Weinberg)
- Ask cast members what they like about the job, how long they've been working there, what all they do during a typical shift, and if they have any favorite stories of interacting with guests. You will develop a greater appreciation of the Disney experience knowing the work and emotion that the many hardworking cast members put into curating your experience (Jacob Hayward & Alexis Franzese).
- In the parks, slow down a little and take some time to engage with the exhibits about the history of Disney. Consider the social, cultural, historical, and political context in which Disney evolved (films and parks). While the attractions are engaging, Disney is a total immersive experience. Regarding the films, if there is a film that really resonates with you, learn the story's background—think through how the story was Disneyfied (Alexis Franzese).
- I've created an in-park assignment called QUESTT to help students get the most out of Disney parks' rides and attractions. Anyone can try it! Pay attention to the QUESTT elements: Queue (how is the line constructed and designed, and how does the wait build anticipation?); Users (who are the people who have chosen this attraction, and how are they behaving?); Emotion (what does the ride make you feel and how?); Story (what's the ride's story, who are the characters, and how are you made a participant in the plot?); Theming (what are the design elements, from sight to sound to smell to texture to flooring to physical space?); and how are you Transported on ride vehicles and Transformed (or changed, or impacted) as part of your ride experience? There's lots to discover if you know how to notice Disney's efforts to make magic (Jill Peterfeso).

Takeaways and Tips for Educators

- Many students who sign up for Disney classes do so because they have wholly positive views about Disney, and it is exciting to watch them expand their knowledge and perspective as they learn more about Disney. This provides educators with the opportunity to observe how students react to having their views of Disney expanded. Festinger's (1957) theory of cognitive dissonance describes the discomfort of trying to accommodate competing and contradictory ideas (and new information). This is educationally valuable as it provides students a way to engage with complexity and nuance and minimize black-and-white thinking (Alexis Franzese).
- Engaging in a compare and contrast of what students might think of the past as seen at Disney versus reality is a great way to get them to think about how history is remembered and often smoothed over in time (Bethanee Bemis).
- Walt Disney touches so many academic disciplines—look for ways to connect Walt Disney to your academic discipline for life lessons for your students. And when you can, incorporate field trips into learning! (Christopher Tremblay)
- Leslie Silko, in her novel *Ceremony*, says about stories: "they aren't just entertainment. Don't be fooled . . . they are all we have to fight off illness and death"[1] Educators must understand Disney adaptations as both historical records and as reactions and guides to changing ethos (Bonnie Rudner).
- Much of the academic writing on Disney tends to be critical and negative. Relying heavily on media literacy and presentism, the over hundred-year history of the Walt Disney Company is often framed by contemporary understandings of the issues of race, class, and gender. Much of this analysis lacks a historical dimension that reveals how Disney is embedded within specific cultural, social, and political contexts. Because of this, you might be surprised to learn that Disney's films are overwhelmingly pro-social and encourage working together as a group for the betterment of all. You might want to ask your students why so few people are aware of Disney's biospheric values and his significant involvement in the development of the modern environmental movement (Sarah Nilsen).
- Educators must understand Disney Parks as time capsules of the eras in which they were created, not of the time periods they refer to, if hoping for students to engage in cultural critique. This is true for Main Street, U.S.A., but also true for other Disney lands. Early Future World at EPCOT was filled with attractions sponsored by large corporations that showcased how the America of the 1980s was holding up capitalism as inherently good and future-building. Today, post-transformation, EPCOT incorporates sections that showcase community and environment as important ideals, reflecting America's concerns over forty years later (Bethanee Bemis).
- Walt Disney World can be thought of as a living laboratory for many of our disciplines. Each park has its own unique flavor that can be incorporated into various topics. The Magic Kingdom is all about story. EPCOT is about technology

and partnerships. Animal Kingdom is about conservation and Hollywood Studios is about immersive entertainment. Use these foci to help build your course! (Gary Kaskowitz)

- By virtue of students' familiarity and physicality, Disneyland renders complex historical topics and theory comprehensible (Alex Hofmann).
- One engaging way to explore the multiple curricula of Disney is to assign students the task of planning a Disney vacation with two different sets of resources. One group would only use resources officially offered by the Walt Disney Company, while the other could rely on any non-official sources. Afterward, groups can compare their planning processes and itineraries to identify similarities, differences, and difficulties. The ultimate goal is to work toward a magical curriculum that combines elements from both vacation plans (Gabriel Huddleston, Blake Lentz, Nicole Weinberg).
- Be sure to take your students on the behind-the-scenes tours and training sessions when learning about Walt Disney World. There is nothing like walking through the utilidors to get a real sense of the logic and history behind the parks (Gary Kaskowitz).
- Courses on Disney are often cross-curricular, allowing students to approach the subject using the critical lens and skills they pick up from their preferred discipline—embrace this! Fight the urge to overemphasize your own area of scholarship and use the course as an opportunity to learn from your students about the fields they enjoy (Jacob Hayward & Alexis Franzese).
- Disney theme parks are amazing places to engage ethnographic skills and practice participant observation. The parks offer a safe environment; other guests are generally personable and willing to connect; and time waiting in line or resting on benches can become chances to conduct informal interviews and deep observation. So, pick a theme (colors, costumes, queuing areas) or provide a task (talk to at least five people about their Disney t-shirts; ask three people where they got something they're eating or drinking; strike up a conversation with a cast member) and invite students to collect data and stories (Jill Peterfeso).
- Immersion and engagement always win—at theme parks and in your classrooms (Cher Krause Knight).

Favorite Disney Gems

- Recreating and assembling Walt's resume for my students, which later became a book (titled Walt's Resume: Walt Disney's Jobs Through the Years) for middle school students as they think about their future careers. It includes Walt's jobs but also his education, extracurriculars, and some honors he received (Christopher Tremblay).
- I love watching *Enchanted* (2007), a perfect Disney movie which manages to be both a fabulous film and a "meta" critique of itself. Having animals, normally considered "vermin" in NYC, in the "Happy Working Song" is brilliant, funny and disgusting (Bonnie Rudner).

- For a deeper dive into FastPass (a precursor to Genie+), watch "Disney's FastPass: A Complicated History" from the Peabody Nominated *YouTube* series Defunctland (Gabriel Huddleston, Blake Lentz, Nicole Weinberg).
- To become introduced to Walt Disney as a wildlife conservationist, the first thing to do is watch the public service announcements that he produced for the National Wildlife Federation that are currently streaming on YouTube. Next, view a True-Life Adventure nature documentary streaming on Disney+ to better understand Disney's biospheric values. I would recommend *Perri* (1957) since it stars an animal we often ignore—the squirrel. Finally, to get a clear understanding of Disney's view of animals, I would recommend reading something Walt Disney himself wrote, "What I've Learned About Animals" (*American Magazine* 155 [1953]: 106–109) (Sarah Nilsen).
- Watching *Dateline Disneyland*, the television special in which Walt introduced Disneyland to the world, gives great insight into what Walt wanted guests to get from the parks—and also a good view of just how much has changed in them over time (Bethanee Bemis).
- Technically, the Beatles broke up in Walt Disney World. In his room at the Polynesian Resort, John Lennon became the last member to sign the legal documents to formally dissolve the group on December 29, 1974 (Alex Hofmann).
- When you walk down Main Street, U.S.A. toward Cinderella Castle, you will see the names of stores and proprietors on the windows. These are laid out as rolling credits of everyone who helped make Walt Disney World a reality, just like in the movies of the time! The last shop you will see is the Old Time Ice Cream Parlor with Walter Disney's name as the proprietor. As the "director" of the parks, it is only fitting that his name is last in the credits. Also, his name was put on an ice cream shop because that was Walt's favorite dessert. And his favorite flavor? Vanilla! Because you could add anything and make it whatever you want (Gary Kaskowitz).
- "The Disney Dish" is a podcast that touches on both the official and hidden curricula of Walt Disney theme parks in almost every episode. Moreover, they present their own magical curriculum as they critically consider both in terms of the history and future of the theme parks (Gabriel Huddleston, Blake Lentz, Nicole Weinberg).
- There is an article (1945) written by Walt Disney called "Mickey as Professor"—it's a blast to read about Walt Disney's vision of how his products could be used for educational purposes. (Walt Disney, "Mickey as professor," *The Public Opinion Quarterly* 9 no. 2 (1945): 119–125) (Alexis Franzese).

Note

1 Leslie Marmon Silko, *Ceremony* (New York: Penguin, 1977), 2.

Contributors

Jenny Banh is an associate professor of Asian American studies and anthropology at Fresno State. She received her BA from UCLA, her MA from Claremont Graduate University, and her PhD from the University of California, Riverside. She edited *Anthropology of Los Angeles* and *American Chinese Restaurants*. Her most recent book is *Fantasies of Hong Kong Disneyland*.

Jeffrey A. Barnes, "Dr. Disneyland," is a best-selling author and Disney expert. Known for *The Wisdom of Walt* books, he inspires with lessons on leadership and success. A History Channel contributor and former educator, Jeff now writes and speaks full-time, sharing Walt Disney's legacy of resilience, creativity, and innovation.

Bethanee Bemis is a public historian specializing in public memory of the national narrative. She is the author of *Disney Theme Parks and America's National Narratives: Mirror, Mirror for Us All* and curator of the Smithsonian exhibition *Mirror, Mirror: Disney Parks and American Stories*.

Lucy Buck is an urban Native from Pomona, California, and a recent undergraduate of Northern Arizona University in university studies, specializing in music education policy. He uses his knowledge to bridge connections in order to advance education for Native youth and generations to follow.

William S. Chavez is an assistant professor of religious studies at Stetson University. He studies American religion, folklore, and popular culture. William began his research on Disney animated features in 2017, expanding to Disney transmedia and merchandise thereafter. He has since taught courses on religion and Disney in California and Florida.

Lucy D'Agostino McGowan is an assistant professor in the Department of Statistical Sciences at Wake Forest University. Her research focuses on analytic design, statistical communication, causal inference, and data science pedagogy. She integrates Disney data into her undergraduate and graduate statistics courses and in a textbook for her causal inference class.

Alexis T. Franzese is a professor and chair of the Department of Sociology and Anthropology at Elon University. Her research reflects expertise in both sociology and psychology, and she is passionate about the study of authenticity and identity in travel and tourism. She approaches Disney as a strategic domain for exploring these interests and has taught her travel-embedded course on happiness at Disney since 2016.

Jacob Hayward currently works as a trial attorney in Boston, Massachusetts. After being inspired by his participation in a research class on-site at Walt Disney World as a sociology student at Elon University, he has continued to study and write about the ways people utilize emotion within Disney parks.

Alex Hofmann was once a Magic Kingdom Guest Relations Cast Member and is now a Johnson Instructor of History at the University of Chicago. He is a cultural historian of the American South who teaches a course called Theme Park America on the contingent and contested meanings of themed spaces throughout history.

Gabriel Huddleston is an associate professor in curriculum studies, department chair of Counseling, Societal Change, and Inquiry, and the director of the Center for Public Education and Community Engagement at Texas Christian University (TCU). His research interests include popular culture, spatial theory, new materialism, and postcolonial studies.

Gary Kaskowitz is a professor of marketing at Moravian University, specializing in marketing strategy with an emphasis on branding and marketing analytics. Gary has worked closely with Walt Disney World (WDW) cast members and has developed and led over ten undergraduate and graduate courses and trips to WDW.

Cher Krause Knight is a professor of art history at Emerson College and a specialist in public art. Among her books are *Power and Paradise in Walt Disney's World* (hardcover 2014/paperback 2019) and *Memorials Now* (coauthored with Harriet F. Senie, 2025).

Blake Lentz is a doctoral student in the curriculum studies PhD program at Texas Christian University. She holds an MEd in secondary education from the University of North Texas and a BFA in theater from TCU. She has yet to receive a visit from her fairy godmother but remains hopeful.

Sarah Nilsen is an associate professor in film and television studies at the University of Vermont. A noted Disney historian, she has appeared on ABC, Disney+, the History Channel, NPR, and PBS. Sarah writes and publishes about, and teaches courses in, Disney history, critical animal studies, and critical race theory and the media. Her current book project is *The Lurking Camera: Walt Disney's True-Life Adventures*.

Jill Peterfeso is the Eli Franklin Craven and Minnie Phipps Craven Associate Professor of Religious Studies at Guilford College. She is the author of *Womenpriest: Tradition and Transgression in the Contemporary Roman Catholic Church*. She has taught a range of Disney classes since 2015.

Bonnie Rudner, a Jersey girl, graduated from Douglass College, Rutgers University, and has been teaching at Boston College since the early 1980s. Her Survey of Children's

Literature eventually became Disney and the Wondertale, which involves a close reading of the original sources, followed by analysis of the Disney films.

Benjamin Shrader is a disabled self-advocate, writer, and public speaker. He is a member of the Delaware State Council for Persons with Disabilities. He is also a lifelong fan of the Disney parks and the singular inclusion they provide to all who come through their gates.

Carol Mason Shrader and her husband have been Disney fans since honeymooning at Walt Disney World in 1991. Carol is the mother of triplets—two with cerebral palsy—as well as a teenage daughter. She is a writer, speaker, and disability advocate, sharing her family's story around the world.

Mason J. Shrader is a PhD student in archaeology at Brown University. He has an MA in anthropology and an MA in classics from Texas Tech University. He first began to study Disney during his undergrad at Millsaps College, when he took a life-changing course on the Anthropology of Disney.

Len Testa is a computer scientist who studies theme park operations. Len runs the theme park trip-planning website TouringPlans.com. He's the coauthor of the Unofficial Guides to Disney's theme parks and cruise line and co-hosts the popular Disney Dish podcast.

Christopher W. Tremblay, creator of the Walt's Pilgrimage course and author of "Disney for Credit," published in *College & University Journal*, holds a Doctor of Education and has three decades of higher education leadership. He has authored over ten books on the life of Walt Disney. Learn more at waltspilgrimage.com.

Nicole Weinberg is a doctoral student in the curriculum studies PhD program at Texas Christian University. She holds an MA in education, health promotion, and international development from University College London. Nicole's interest in Disney reflects her academic interest in how cultural phenomena shapes early childhood education.

Acknowledgments

We thank Alyssa Palazzo for her enthusiasm for this project from start to finish. We thank the team at Bloomsbury for bringing the book to print, especially Anna Eggers and Crystal Branson. We are grateful to the peer reviewers whose feedback helped us focus and encouraged us onward. And we are grateful to Len Testa for being a cheerleader for this volume and writing the Foreword.

We thank our contributors who have been such fun to work with. Getting this unique, interdisciplinary volume to speak with a shared voice was always going to be a welcome challenge, and our authors met the moment with aplomb. Thank you for bringing your unique voices and perspectives. You indulged our suggestions and edits and were willing for this book to be an interactive process as we worked together in thinking through your specific areas of Disney expertise and the stories you wanted to tell. We are thrilled about our contributors' diversity of backgrounds, perspectives, and experiences.

And of course, we thank one another for the unique contributions and ideas we each brought to the table (er, to the google docs) that allowed this volume to be the strong multidisciplinary work it has become.

As educators, we continue to see how Disney can teach and transform, and so we thank our students who have helped inspire this volume. Your excitement for learning to think critically about some of your favorite entertainments and your willingness to develop a new, richer relationship with Disney has been inspiring. You have simultaneously tolerated the dissonance of our classes unpacking treasured beliefs about Disney while continuing to be excited and enthusiastic about Disney.

Alexis wishes to thank Elon University for boldly saying "yes" a decade ago to a course about Disney, which then became the catalyst for her Disney scholarship; departmental and university colleagues and friends who provided encouragement, many sharing their own experiences working in the Disney College Program; students who sought mentoring on Disney-related scholarship; and colleagues Matthew Buckmaster and Brooke Buffington. Alexis's course has undoubtedly been enhanced by connecting with fellow Union College alum (and chairman of Walt Disney Studios from 2012 to 2020) Alan Horn, Len Testa of TouringPlans, and Alison Hart (an amazing travel companion). Elon University holds the Scholarship of Teaching and Learning (SoTL) as a significant academic contribution, and it is Alexis's hope that this volume offers Elon some return on investment.

Alexis's gratitude extends to her four children: Alexis's understanding of Disney has been enriched through seeing the parks and the films through your eyes and across the years. You've fully embraced Disney and fallen in love with it, yet also been willing to look around the corners into the shadows at the parks. This book will undoubtedly be a core memory of your childhood (thanks, *Inside Out*), and your encouragement meant so much. Thanks to family (Mom!) and long-term friends who have offered their support along the way (Laura, Terri, Kara, Heather, Carrie); Sarah, my gratitude for your support and editing prowess; and appreciation too for new friends made in this process (same bus, Bonnie!). Finally, special thanks to John who has spent countless hours hearing about this book and has provided support and encouragement every step of the way.

Jill wishes to thank Guilford College colleagues for supporting Disney research and courses; steadfast academic friends Elizabeth DeGaynor and Sarah Thuesen; wise mentors Kathryn Burns and Scott and Sarah Madry; Paulina Cossette and the academic editing crew; and invaluable guidance from Max Carter, Vernie Davis, and Nancy Riemer. Thanks to Disney travel friends Benjamin Wrench, Melody Davis, Clara Sandrin, Annie Coleman, Al and Dana Peterfeso, and the whole Hays family. Thank you to Sarah Hays for feedback, travels, and best-friendship.

Finally, thanks to friends, family, and neighbors, and in memory of both John Cronin and (feline) Hamilton. Love to furry boys Marshall and Phineas.

We are so glad to see this book come to fruition. We delight in imagining the value it will have for those teaching about Disney and students learning about Disney, as well as for those outside of academia who are curious about all things magical.

Index

www.ingramcontent.com/pod-product-compliance
Lightning Source LLC
Chambersburg PA
CBHW071842270326
41929CB00013B/2074